Massive Resistance

Massive Resistance

The White Response to the Civil Rights Movement

GEORGE LEWIS

First published in Great Britain in 2006 by
Hodder Education, part of Hachette Livre UK,
338 Euston Road, London NW1 3BH

www.hoddereducation.com

Distributed in the United States of America by
Oxford University Press Inc.
198 Madison Avenue, New York, NY10016

Hodder Headline's policy is to use papers that are natural, renewable and
recyclable products and made from wood grown in sustainable forests. The
logging and manufacturing processes are expected to conform to the
environmental regulations of the country of origin.

The advice and information in this book are believed to be true and accurate
at the date of going to press, but neither the authors nor the publisher can
accept any legal responsibility or liability for any errors or omissions.

British Library Cataloguing in Publication Data
A catalogue record for this book is available from the British Library

Library of Congress Cataloging-in-Publication Data
A catalog record for this book is available from the Library of Congress

9780 340 90022 2

2 3 4 5 6 7 8 9 10

Typeset in 10.5 on 12.5pt Apollo by Phoenix Photosetting, Chatham, Kent
Printed and bound in Great Britain by Antony Rowe Ltd

What do you think about this book? Or any other
Hodder Education title? Please send your comments to
the feedback section on www.hoddereducation.com.

CONTENTS

Contents

ACKNOWLEDGEMENTS

The collective historical understanding of the actions of segregationists in the massive resistance years, the motivating factors that drove certain southerners to resist racial change, and the intricate ideological strands that served to underpin the southern segregationist position have all altered dramatically in recent years. There are two over-riding reasons for those changes. The personal papers and manuscript collections of an increasing number of southern segregationists and state-sponsored segregationist agencies have been opened to researchers and historians, ensuring that a richly textured collection of sources is now available to document massive resistance in all its forms. Not altogether coincidentally, historians have returned to the study of segregationists in a bid to afford them the nuanced and subtle historical analyses that have long documented other aspects of southern history.

This book has benefited immensely from both of those recent trends. The indefatigable work of curators and librarians at manuscript collections across the United States has helped to guide me first to, and subsequently through, many of the relevant collections of segregationists from the massive resistance era. I would like to thank in particular the archivists of the following: the Library of Congress, Washington DC; the Mississippi Valley Collection, McWherter Library, University of Memphis, TN; the Southern Historical Collection, Wilson Library, University of North Carolina at Chapel Hill, NC; the Special Collections Library, Duke University, Durham, NC; the State of North Carolina Department of Cultural Resources, Division of Archives and History, Raleigh, NC; the Albert H. Small Special Collections Library, University of Virginia, Charlottesville, VA; the Virginia Historical Society, Richmond, VA; the Earl Gregg Swem Library, College of William and Mary, Williamsburg, VA; and the Archives and Research Services, Library of Virginia, Richmond, VA. I would also like to thank the inter-library loans staff here at the University of Leicester for dealing with my requests for materials from the outer margins of the historical record, and their colleagues who manage to oversee the University's microfilm holdings with a sunny disposition that belies the lack of windows that bedevil their basement workplace.

I have also been fortunate to enter into discussion, debate and dialogue with many of those scholars who have decided that moral opprobrium for a particular subject is insufficient reason to justify its continued neglect from the historical record. Those that deserve mention here include Karen S. Anderson, David Appleby, Ray Arsenault, Tony Badger, Dan T. Carter, Derek Catsam, David L. Chappell, Robert Cook, Joe Crespino, Jane Dailey, Charles Eagles, Adam Fairclough, Scott French, Allison Graham, M. J. Heale, James H. Hershman, Jr., John P. Jackson, Jr., Yasuhiro Katagiri, Richard H. King, John A. Kirk, Michael J. Klarman, Kevin M. Kruse, Peter J. Ling, Andrew M. Manis, Elizabeth Gillespie McRae, Steven J. Niven, J. Douglas Smith, Brian Ward, Clive Webb and Jeff Woods. The enthusiasm for this project from Michael Strang and then Tiara Misquitta at Hodder was palpable, as it was in the initial reports submitted by the publisher's four anonymous readers of my original proposal, and the sharp and insightful comments made by the two anonymous readers of the manuscript itself. If they are reading this, I hope that they recognize all of the changes that I have made at their suggestion, and that they understand that any errors that remain are purely my own.

There are two other categories of people who made the completion of this book possible. The first are those whose financial contributions and scholarship schemes allowed much of the research and writing to take place. The University of Leicester supported this project in its infancy by granting me a period of study leave, which was further extended by the very generous support of the Arts and Humanities Research Council, from whose Research Leave Scheme I benefited immeasurably. I would like to thank both of those institutions, as well as the patience and understanding of those colleagues and students whose own teaching and research plans were necessarily altered as a result of my absence. The British Academy also played an essential role by providing funds for trips to archives and conferences in many different locations across the United States. I would also like to mark my gratitude to those individuals who offered rather less prosaic but no less essential support and encouragement to me at various stages of this project: Sarah Graham, Virginia and Ginny Gunter, Andrew Johnstone, Claire Lindsay, Tim Lynch, Grant McLennan, Anshu Mondal, Mike Ruddock, Chris Szejnmann, Emily West and in particular Martin Halliwell, who somehow found the time to stop publishing his own books for long enough to offer generous and objective advice on this one. Finally, I would like to thank my family, whose number grew by two between the first and final drafts.

George Lewis
Leicester, June 2006

FOR MAGS

1

THE ORIGINS OF MASSIVE RESISTANCE

'MASSIVE RESISTANCE': MEANINGS AND METAPHORS

On 14 February 1956, Senator Harry Flood Byrd of Virginia travelled to the old Confederate capital of Richmond to address the state legislature. Once he had completed his duties there, he made the short journey to the city's Richmond Hotel where he was assailed by reporters wanting to know his thoughts and strategies on a number of pressing political issues. Of particular interest to them was the developing battle over the desegregation of schools in Byrd's home state. James Latimer, a veteran political reporter for the *Richmond Times-Dispatch*, quickly left his coverage of the Virginia General Assembly when news reached him that Byrd was holding an impromptu press conference in the hotel, but when he arrived in the lobby he found it so crowded with journalists jostling for an audience with Byrd that it proved difficult to hear what was said with any great clarity. Nevertheless, Latimer thought that he heard the senator declare that 'Passive resistance is the best course for us to take' in response to federal plans to force the desegregation of southern schools. His reporting of those comments duly appeared in the next day's *Times-Dispatch* and Byrd, who had close ties to a number of writers on the newspaper's staff, appeared content with the journalistic treatment that he had received and returned to Washington without further comment.[1] Just 12 days later, on 26 February, comments that Byrd made on the school question again made the headlines. This time there were two clear differences: unlike Latimer's earlier report, which had only made the front pages of newspapers in his home state, Byrd's latest comments also attracted the interest of the *New York Times* and were printed on its front page; more importantly, Byrd was now quoted as calling not for 'passive' but for 'massive' resistance. It was the first time that the phrase 'massive resistance' had appeared in print in the context of southern race relations. He was calling southern segregationists to arms.[2]

Byrd was speaking both in a personal capacity as a committed and lifelong proponent of racial segregation and in an official capacity as the most senior politician that Virginia's voters sent to Washington, DC. In a political context, his comments formed a direct response to the Supreme Court's *Brown* decision of 17 May 1954, which had declared the provision of separate schooling for white and non-white pupils unlawful. 'If we can organize the Southern States for massive resistance to this order', Byrd was quoted as saying of *Brown*, 'I think that in time the rest of the country will realize that racial integration is not going to be accepted in the South.' Byrd and the vast majority of his southern peers were, however, well aware that the full ramifications of *Brown* were likely to be wider than such a literal interpretation suggested. Having heard testimony from an array of witnesses including educational psychologists Kenneth B. Clark and Mamie Phipps Clark, the court had decided not only that genuine equality was a chimera in the South's segregated school system, but also that such segregation had a negative psychological effect on those pupils who were forcibly separated from whites. The lawyers of the National Association for the Advancement of Colored People (NAACP), who had brought the case before the court, had launched an unprecedented attack on southern segregation, and had forced the federal judiciary to alter the context within which the African American struggle for full constitutional rights was being played out. In that context, the resonance of Byrd's phrase was such that it has led to an often-held assumption that is parable-like in its simplicity. A clarion call was issued by one of the South's leading political figures, and it was so well timed and so effectively presented that the massed ranks of southern segregationists clamoured to answer it. For over a decade, they responded by fighting back against the might of federal forces that were intent upon altering the region's racial status quo.

For a number of reasons, however, that narrative is deceptive in its simplicity and inaccurate in its veracity. When he read of Byrd's second pronouncement, Latimer was puzzled by so swift a change from 'passive' to 'massive' resistance and re-examined his notes. He was aware that southern segregationists had mulled over a number of possible strategies that they hoped would allow the region to cling on to its segregated way of life in spite of the Justices' decision in *Brown*, and that 'passive resistance' had been used fairly frequently by other southern opinion makers. The Charleston *News and Courier*'s William D. Workman, Jr. was probably the best-known proponent of passive resistance as a means of combating federal desegregation mandates, but Latimer was not familiar with the use of 'massive resistance' in the same context. 'Passive resistance' was a far more muted phrase, which to Workman at least suggested 'non-compliance rather than open defiance'.[3] It seemed as though Byrd was now signalling a force of resistance that was far more intemperate than anything that had preceded it. Indeed, that simple change of a single letter had such a transformative effect that Latimer later wondered whether he had in fact misheard Byrd in the Richmond Hotel's noisy lobby, and that the change from 'passive' to 'massive' resistance was the result of his misreporting the senator, rather than a tactical rethink by Virginia's dominant political figure. As Latimer knew full well, however, Byrd had a number of close contacts on the *Times-Dispatch*, any number of whom could have been contacted to correct the mistake. It was, he later surmised, far more likely that in the days between the two newspaper articles either Byrd himself or a close adviser had seen the benefits of a change of approach, and had countenanced a subtle change in the senator's language. 'Massive resistance' not only offered a more menacing alternative to Martin Luther King, Jr.'s 'passive' resistance, but also played upon Secretary of State John Foster Dulles' advocacy of 'massive retaliation' against a Soviet strike in the Cold War.[4]

Latimer may have mused over the etymological path that had taken Byrd to 'massive resistance', but few other contemporary commentators showed much initial interest. Byrd had submerged the phrase in complex arguments surrounding the rights of individual states to 'interpose' their own authority before that of the Supreme Court. As the further details of the *Times-Dispatch* and *New York Times* stories made clear, Byrd had also called for all southern states to 'stand together in declaring the court's opinion [in *Brown*] unconstitutional'. In what amounted to a campaign for 'interposition', Byrd urged the individual states of the South to refuse to implement federal decrees on desegregation by declaring the primacy of their own sovereign authority on racial matters. Such a stance, he erroneously believed, offered the South a 'perfectly legal means of appeal' from *Brown*.[5] Of the few columnists who did venture early opinions on the subject, one in the *New York Times* noted that, 'while Mr Byrd did not cast it in that light, his call for Southern unity on the school issue apparently was akin to the "passive resistance" urged by some proponents of racial integration'.[6] Perhaps more surprisingly, another sought to place Byrd – the epitome of established southern white privilege – in the pantheon of America's iconic non-conformists and rebels. As Raymond J. Crowley explained in the *Times-Dispatch*, 'massive resistance' appeared to signal a 'refusal to go along when the government is considered wrong'. That, concluded Crowley, was exactly what had driven Henry David Thoreau to undertake 'passive resistance' and to decide upon his course of civil disobedience some 110 years previously.[7] As time went on, Byrd's ill-judged interposition campaign was largely forgotten, and it was to the enigmatic and resonant 'massive resistance' that commentators and writers were inexorably drawn to return. However he had stumbled over the phrase, it soon became clear that Byrd had captured the *zeitgeist*.

Those commentators played an essential role in unleashing the full potential of the phrase 'massive resistance', for the attention that they paid to it not only elevated its position in the national consciousness, but equally importantly helped to separate it from its original close links to the abortive interposition campaign. In the half century that has followed Latimer's first

Times-Dispatch story, others have continued a process that has effectively broadened out the meaning of massive resistance to such an extent that it is now widely accepted as a term that describes white southern opposition to the *Brown* decision specifically, and to the federal government's drive to equalize race relations in the South more widely. Indeed, its use has become so divorced from Byrd's original intentions that scholars in particular have become content to use the phrase as historical shorthand, and 'massive resistance' has emerged as what might best be described as a generic term for white southern opposition to the struggle for civil rights in the post-Second World War South. By doing so, however, a number of those scholars have been guilty of collapsing what was an often complex historical phenomenon into a simple phrase. While the civil rights movement itself is often brilliantly represented as a fluid and fluent force in the historical record, the same cannot be said of its southern white opponents. Instead, if those segregationists – or 'massive resisters' – receive any historical analysis at all, it is most often to portray them in passing as monolithic, one-dimensional reactionaries possessing little guile and even less intelligence in their attempts to cling on to their segregated way of life. It is indicative of the lack of interest that scholars have shown in segregationists more broadly that, while many have pored over the origins of King's use of 'passive resistance', the origins of Byrd's use of 'massive resistance' have been virtually ignored.[8] As with segregationists themselves, those origins are more complex and shrouded with more ambiguities than is often recognized, and offer the first indication of the extent to which certain facets of the South's segregationist history have been misunderstood and misrepresented.

Once Byrd had used the term 'massive resistance' and, more importantly, once columnists and commentators had begun to dissect its possible meanings and implications, it entered the public consciousness. There was still a central problem, however, for while many contemporaries realized that it was a beguiling phrase and sought to incorporate it into their vocabulary, the lack of clear definition that had accompanied its first use in a domestic southern context left them bereft of its precise meaning. The immediate upshot of that confusion was that many of Byrd's contemporaries found themselves using 'massive resistance' in slightly different ways to refer to subtly different styles and measures of resistance. It was readily assumed that Byrd was giving voice to a collective refusal by segregationists to cede power to the region's blacks, but beyond that the immediate details were distinctly hazy.

In the longer term, that initial uncertainty has trickled through to published historical accounts of the period of southern resistance, for historians have also failed to agree upon what exactly massive resistance entailed, or what precisely was included within its margins. In the late 1950s, for example, some southerners used it only to refer to a particular session of the Virginia state legislature which was called – again by Byrd – in summer 1956 to pass a catalogue of laws designed to stave off desegregation in the state for as long as possible. That, certainly, was the view taken by the NAACP, one of the enduring enemies of the segregated South, and by implication one of the main targets of resistance forces. Three years after that 1956 session, for example, the NAACP's leading officers were still referring to massive resistance as nothing more than the specific 'programme' of laws passed within the confines of that one state legislature.[9] Burke Marshall, assistant attorney general and stalwart of the Civil Rights Division of the Justice Department, understood the phrase very differently. Speaking publicly in 1964, he referred to 'massive resistance in the sense of outright defiance of federal authority'.[10] While Marshall's definition offers the more accurate assessment of the obduracy and eventual range of southern segregationist reaction to threatened desegregation, it should also be noted that many of his contemporaries who were actively involved in the civil rights battles of the post-*Brown* era eschewed the phrase altogether in favour of looser terms such as 'southern resistance', 'pro segregation forces' and 'white supremacists'.

THE IMPACT OF HISTORIES

For all the interest surrounding the phrase, the process by which 'massive resistance' emerged fully fledged as shorthand for southern reaction to racial change was not completed until over 20 years after it had first been popularized by Byrd. It was not until historians began to look back on the phenomenon of southern resistance once it had begun to dissipate in the late 1960s that it became possible to establish its true patterns and the confines within which it had operated. Specifically, it was not until the publication of Numan V. Bartley's brilliant historical work, *The Rise of Massive Resistance: Race and Politics in the South during the 1950's* in 1969 that much of the confusion surrounding the meaning of Byrd's phrase began to be laid to rest. As was made clear by his title, Bartley had chosen to use 'massive resistance' to cover not just Virginia's special legislative session in 1956, but the entire resistance effort of the segregationist South, although his focus was drawn to the rise of the phenomenon and did not seek to trace its development far beyond the end of the decade. In that respect, he was echoing Marshall's understanding of the full breadth of segregationist reaction. The impact that Bartley's work has had on successive generations of civil rights historians has effectively cemented that interpretation into the historical record.[11]

For decades, Bartley's volume was a rarity, for it stood as one of the very few works that focused not on the civil rights movement itself, but instead on its white segregationist opponents.[12] In many respects, the decision of historians to limit their horizons to the black side of the southern freedom struggle is understandable. It was such a dynamic movement in and of itself, and was so multifaceted that it has taken successive waves of historiographical reinterpretation to uncover its true nature and nuances. Whereas initial accounts presented the African American freedom struggle as largely created, led and run by national figures such as Martin Luther King, Jr., and national organizations such as the Southern Christian Leadership Conference, subsequent attention has been drawn to community studies, from William Chafe's pioneering work on Greensboro to J. Mills Thornton's majestic analysis of local activity and municipal politics in three Alabama cities. Such work has conclusively proven that African Americans were more than able to agitate for their own rights, in their own communities, without a discernible national impetus.

Other studies have suggested the importance of seeing both national and local movements through the lens of an international Cold War prism, and still others have highlighted such issues as the movement's internal gender dynamics, and, for example, internal conflicts that emerged from within the ranks of African American protest organizations. Because the discipline and focus of those studies has intentionally been on African American activism, there has both figuratively and literally been less space in which to treat segregationist opposition with similar subtlety and complexity. At best, such studies leave us with a compressed view of white southern opposition to civil rights change; at worst, segregationists are rendered as no more than monolithic reactionaries, their actions condensed and flattened. It is a situation rife with irony, for one of the principal reasons that the civil rights movement has received such nuanced study is because it was such a dynamic and vigorous movement. Given the intricate network of barriers that southern segregationists were able to assemble as part of their attempts to halt its progress, it had to be.

There are, of course, other contributory factors to this marginalization of southern white resisters in the historical record. As David Chappell has noted, for too long scholars have been content simply to explain away segregationists' actions by labelling them 'racist'. The vast majority of them most certainly were, but that should not preclude historians from seeking to understand how that racism manifested itself, how those manifestations were transmitted, or what the effect of that transmission was. Charles Eagles, too, has argued that the scholarly concentration on the African American side of the struggle has been a product of the perceived 'nobility' of the quest for civil rights, and of the fact that a number of the early producers of civil rights histories had themselves been active players in the movement itself.[13] By contrast, histories written by supporters of southern resistance, let alone its active proponents, are a rarity indeed.[14] There are also a number of more mechanical, less ideological problems associated with the raw materials involved in the production of histories of southern segregationists. As attitudes towards race, especially in the South, have changed over time, so individuals are surely less likely to lay bare their past as massive resisters than they are to reveal their participation in the civil rights movement. It is a corresponding and attendant danger for researchers that the papers of leading players in the segregationist struggle may have been bleached of evidence of the worst excesses of white supremacy before being deposited in archives. Finally and more prosaically, the architects of white resistance were a generation older than the young, student-based activists who were at the forefront of the non-violent direct action movement. As a consequence, while survivors of the black freedom struggle have been able to provide those chronicling their efforts with richly textured oral testimonies and first-hand reminiscences, many of massive resistance's leading proponents died long before the re-ignition of historical interest in their particular version of events.

It has only been in recent years that scholars have decided to confront many of those problems and have returned to the subject of white resistance so that southern segregationists can be subjected to the same level of historical scrutiny that has long been afforded to advocates of civil rights. Bartley's pioneering work should certainly not be forgotten either by scholars or by students of southern resistance as those new historical works on segregationists emerge. Given the breath-taking diversity and sheer scale of resistance measures that became part of the segregationist South's defence of its traditionally segregated way of life, Bartley's broadening of 'massive resistance' into what amounts to a metaphor for the full range of southern strategies of defiance remains a useful and above all workable historical term. Even Byrd himself would surely have been taken aback in 1956 to learn of just how 'massive' southern resistance would, for a while at least, become. That said, there are a number of compelling reasons for overhauling Bartley's work, not least of which is the number of relevant archival collections that have been opened up to scholars in the decades since he completed his study.

The need to return to his analysis is also to an extent driven by the changing nature of historical enquiry since the 1960s. In much the same way that the first histories of the African American freedom struggle concentrated on prominent leaders, national organizations and 'top-down' elite forces, so Bartley viewed resistance as a process driven by 'neo-bourbon' politicians and political activists, who 'unfurled the banner of massive resistance' in defence of 'segregation and southern tradition'. For Bartley, those neo-bourbon leaders of 1950s southern resistance were still firmly situated both geographically and ideologically in the Black Belt, where the density of cotton production had underpinned the institution of slavery for centuries. They were the natural descendants of the powerful rural and county-town elites who had resisted the first Reconstruction after the Civil War, and who 'strove to crush the Second Reconstruction' just as eagerly almost a century later. Neo-bourbons were suspicious of progress and outsiders, especially where those outsiders were federal Yankees, and they harked back to the halcyon days of an agrarian lifestyle, King Cotton and strong southern influence in national affairs.[15] As new histories emerge, especially in the form of highly concentrated and focused case studies, it has become increasingly apparent that there were other, more complex dynamics at work. This was more than a top-down, elite-led phenomenon.[16]

THE CONCOMITANT CONVERSATIONS OF RESISTANCE

Concentrating on the confusion that surrounded the early development of the term 'massive resistance' is not solely important as a matter of historical accuracy, or even professional pedantry. Rather, chronicling the untidy origins of the phrase is an important step in bringing to light the fact that resistance itself was essentially a disorderly and far from uniform historical phenomenon. It is simply not accurate to claim of southern segregationists, as a recent and otherwise exemplary case study has done, that 'Even the name they chose for their cause, massive resistance, suggested that southern whites would be both unified and uniform in their response to court-ordered desegregation.'[17] Resistance, in stark contrast, was an unruly and protean beast, and the pro-civil rights forces who encountered southern resistance must at times have felt as though they were up against the multi-headed Hydra that had once faced Hercules. Its proponents developed a wide array of ploys, tactics, mechanisms and arguments in defence of the southern status quo. Such diversity reflected the fact that massive resistance was not an isolated historical event, for its supporters were as comfortable in drawing upon rich historical precedents as they were in constructing new defences of their position, and they were as likely to call upon long-entrenched historical traditions as they were to react to recent upheavals in either the regional or national political landscape. The devices that they chose to employ ranged from race-free appeals to the sanctity of states' rights to playing upon latent fears of miscegenation that were saturated in brutally racist rhetoric; legislative and legal rejoinders that varied from subtle and effective stalling tactics to poorly thought-through obstructions that reeked of short-term expediency; attempts to undermine southern segregationists' opponents as 'outsiders', which could be taken to mean either those outside the South or those outside the democratic, capitalist traditions of the United States; legislative committees and subcommittees that hid their racist agendas under the banner of 'state sovereignty' or 'security' issues; threats of economic and violent reprisal; and, of course, sporadic descents into mob rule that brought ephemeral threats of violence into the sharp focus of reality.

With resistance encompassing such a diverse array of ploys and strategies, it could only be expected that there were times during which the South's defence would be led by Bartley's neo-bourbon elites. Equally, though, there were times when grassroots segregationists shaped the agenda, and any analysis of resistance cannot be simply confined to the political manoeuvrings of those neo-bourbons. The immense variation within massive resistance was also in part a reflection of the variety of conditions that existed within the South. There were inevitably some starkly different people, with noticeably different attitudes, contributing to the southern cause. Perhaps the most fundamental result of that diversity was that, even under the single banner of massive resistance and within a shared belief in the need to continue racial segregation across the region, there were groups and individuals who were aiming to achieve subtly different ends by what were often markedly different means. Some segregationists, for example, believed that the South could only be victorious by finding ways of appealing to non-southerners for support in a bid to transform what was often seen as a purely sectional conflict into a national one. Others felt that massive resistance's most important goal was the imposition of absolute unanimity of cause and homogeneity of purpose among white southerners, and thus concentrated on shoring up morale within the South's borders and creating common lines of attack. While a number of the region's politicians chose to manipulate and prey upon racial tensions in an attempt to increase their political longevity, others, notably but not exclusively those with a national reputation to uphold, sought to temper the worst excesses of southern racism and strove to present a moderate façade in its place. Still others were adamant that the South should not give up an inch of its segregated systems on the whim of federal judges comfortably ensconced in Washington, DC. Even that was not a unanimous view, for there were other resisters who, while not exactly conciliatory, did see the efficacy of allowing slow paced token integration in the short term in the belief that it would stave off full-scale integration in the long term. Massive resistance, in other words, was more of an umbrella term than a clearly defined counter-revolutionary programme. There was no single spokesman for massive resistance, for it was possible to hear concomitant conversations of resistance within segregationist ranks.

Although the region's most committed segregationists would no doubt have vehemently disagreed, the lack of uniformity in both the strength and strategic outlook of that resistance was in no small part the product of a distinctly heterogeneous White South. As the native southern poet and novelist Robert Penn Warren wrote in 1957, having travelled through Kentucky, Tennessee, Arkansas, Mississippi and Louisiana in an attempt to fathom the region's response to the *Brown* decision, southern whites were so uncertain as to which way they should turn that there were not only 'divisions between man and man' but also 'lines of fracture' within individuals.[18] Hodding Carter III, son of the influential owner and editor of Greenville, Mississippi's *Delta Democrat-Times*, believed that the years leading up to *Brown* witnessed the emergence of a growing band of white southerners who were coming to terms with the fact that their children might have to live with desegregation, even if it did not occur in their own lifetime. Carter believed that such a change went hand in hand with a growing sense of tolerance for those 'who sought to eliminate the more blatant forms of discrimination' from southern life, but with the forceful caveat that change should only occur 'within the framework of segregation'.[19] It appeared as though certain elements of the segregationist South were moving towards the view that at least some change was necessary to the region's rigid demarcation of separate racial spheres, although they certainly would not have countenanced pressure from the federal government as the catalyst. Even Carter himself found it necessary to temper such an apparently optimistic outlook. Having noted the presence and influence of a number of progressive liberals in the region, he nevertheless felt obliged to caution his readers that the term 'southern liberal took in many who were far more Southern than liberal'.[20] Aubrey Williams, a southern educator, publisher and activist who had played a prominent role in the New Deal, was less equivocal still: 'In the South we have no liberals – only conservatives and radicals', he memorably noted.[21]

The existence of such different perspectives on the southern race problem, especially from white southerners themselves, had a number of important knock-on effects. First, it forced a number of the region's most committed segregationists to expend considerable time and energy in attempting to portray the White South as unified. Just as Supreme Court Chief Justice Earl Warren worked doggedly to ensure that the first *Brown* decision was presented to the public as the undisputed decree of a harmonious court, so the most hard-line proponents of southern resistance understood the importance of projecting a united front of segregationist ideology and opinion. As J. Mills Thornton's study of municipal politics has vividly exemplified, many local segregationists were clearly of the opinion that the muzzling of white dissent would bring swift victory to the segregationist cause.[22] Many resisters soon realized that the most effective way of ensuring that white unanimity at the grassroots community level was to establish a network of local segregationist organizations. When White Citizens' Councils emerged across the South in the months following the *Brown* decision, it was soon obvious that they were as committed to stamping out dissent among white southerners as they were dedicated to the intimidation of local black activists. As the investigative reporter Paul Anthony revealed in 1956, all 11 former Confederate states boasted Council organizations, and many were so committed to outward 'respectability' that they had already dropped the 'White' prefix from their titles.[23] They were also particularly keen to hand their many supporters what amounted to a ready-made definition of southern identity, in an attempt to bring a veneer of homogeneity to the many strands of the region's resistance effort. 'God wanted the white people to live alone. And He wanted colored people to live alone', reasoned one Council pamphlet in an attempt to find some common, unifying strands.

> The white men built America for you. White men built America so they could make the rules ... The white man has always been kind to the Negro. We do not believe that God wants us to live together. Negro people like to live by themselves. Negroes use their own bathrooms. They do not use white

people's bathrooms. The Negro has his own part of town to live in. This is called our Southern Way of Life.[24]

Despite such attempts to channel the broad spectrum of southern opinion into a single voice, ideological differences and vestiges of internal dissent continued to hamper its development throughout the resistance years. That was especially true of the region's business progressives, who grew weary of the economic ramifications of segregation which effectively halved the customer base of many southern businesses while simultaneously doubling the cost of providing resources as basic as separate black and white washrooms. Many also correctly believed that northern investors were increasingly loath to pour money into a region that was as racked with internal divisions as the South, and that a continual stream of demonstrations and counter-demonstrations compromised the stability of local economies.[25] Newspapermen and journalists compounded the problems posed by those businessmen, for a number of them offered a steady stream of dissent ranging from the careful and considered liberalism of established figures such as the *Atlanta Constitution*'s Ralph McGill and the *Arkansas Gazette*'s Harry Ashmore, to the more *ex tempore* and radical satire of the *Petal Paper*, produced by Mississippi's P. D. East.

While the edifice of the solid White South was continually compromised by certain businessmen and newspapermen, a number of dilemmas and contradictions that lay at the heart of southern segregationist ideology served to deepen those internal fissures. As Chappell has argued, the astute tactics of a new generation of civil rights activists in the 1950s increasingly exposed those latent contradictions. Segregation's apologists had long rationalized their refusal to afford full constitutional rights to the region's African Americans with the paternalistic argument that innate black inferiority left them insufficiently equipped to make full use of such rights. Increasingly those same segregationists were forced to recognize that the sanctity of their beloved all-white institutions was under unprecedented threat from the tactical acumen displayed by black civil rights protesters, who were clearly proving themselves to be capable of organizing a complex and far-reaching civil rights movement.[26]

Other, more subtle contradictions continued to emerge. One of segregationists' central fears concerning *Brown* was its focus on desegregating the region's schools. They feared that the inevitable result of such close social contact between impressionable young students from both races would be widespread inter-racial sexual relations. Since segregation rested upon the premise of the clear inferiority of African Americans, its apologists had to explain why in such circumstances southern white belles would allow their innate purity to be besmirched by their new black male peers. Since the days of slavery, the propaganda of southern white supremacy had attempted to offer an explanation for this conundrum by portraying black men as voracious sexual predators whose bestial strength and primal urges would overcome the most zealous defences southern womanhood could offer. That was a far more difficult task when newsreel footage and newspaper photographs revealed the majority of black protesters to be non-violent, disciplined Christians, faced with white opponents whose brutal violence was often seen to be urged on by white crowds contorted with rage and hatred.

The lack of homogeneity among southern whites contributed in turn to the unevenness of massive resistance. There were undoubtedly periods during which apologists for continued segregation were able to impose their will upon the South, but there were also times when – and places where – moderate southern voices were able to defy hard-line segregationist opinion, or at least temper its excesses. The existing historical discourse on massive resistance has tended to focus either on the dominant role played by south-ern political elites in the post-*Brown* South, or on what might be termed the grand 'set pieces' of resistance such as those played out at Little Rock, Ole Miss, throughout the Freedom Rides, and the Birmingham campaigns. It is increasingly clear that those traditional studies need to be amalgamated with views from the grassroots to allow the full textures and breadth of south-ern resistance to emerge. The actions of those elites must be viewed in conjunction with the actions and activities of local southern communities from their initial reactions to *Brown* onwards, which have been highlighted in a number of recent case studies. Those new histories have in turn highlighted the need to take into consideration the pivotal roles played by hitherto forgotten groups, such as pro-education pressure groups in general and the Parent Teacher Associations who consistently preferred the option of desegregated schools to closed schools in particular.

There are other vital indicators of segregationist mood and expressions of resisters' rationales that have long been overlooked by historians, notably the mixture of eloquence and ranting that characterized the myriad handbills, broadsheets and pamphlets that were distributed locally as part of resistance campaigns, and more formally the outcome of state referendums which saw over 2.3 million southerners casting votes between November 1952 and September 1956 on state constitutional questions directly relating to desegregation.[27] It is only then that a full picture of the diversity of the southern battle over continued segregation can emerge, for massive resis-tance was not a static phenomenon but a fluid movement that ebbed and flowed over time and place.

PATTERNS OF SEGREGATION, TRADITIONS OF SUPREMACY

One of the major problems that faced the architects of the South's resistance strategies was the wide number of impulses that drove southerners to show support for massive resistance, and the great variance that existed in the sacrifices those resisters were willing to make in order to cling on to a segregated society. There were certainly a great number of southerners who were ideologically disposed to white supremacy, and who could not conceive of a world in which non-whites were both their de jure and de facto equals. There were others, however, whose primary motive for resistance was not the will to cling to white supremacy per se, but to cling to a past with which they were familiar and comfortable. White supremacy was clearly a central pillar around which that past had been constructed, but there is neverthe-less a distinction that should be made between white supremacy as a primary and as a secondary motivating factor in resistance participation. The uncer-tainties created by the speed with which southern society was changing in the 1950s, including the emergence of a youth culture, associated notions of delinquency and teen rebellion, the fast pace of post-war modernization and the escalating tensions of the new Cold War unsettled a generation of south-erners who no longer recognized the landscape of the South as that in which they had been raised.[28] As a result, they yearned for a past in which they were more certain of their role and more assured of their position in society. There were also those who viewed post-*Brown* resistance as an essential stage in the protection of the traditions and prevailing social mores of a region that, by and large, had been wedded to systematic and institutionalized racial inequality for 300 years. It is in that context that massive resistance must be seen not as an isolated historical phenomenon, but one that drew from a long and rich tradition of white supremacy and racial segregation. When Byrd issued his call for widespread resistance in 1956, he was in effect urging his fellow white southerners to defend regional traditions and segre-gated systems that had been painstakingly constructed and defiantly imposed over generations.

As a number of historians have cogently argued, white supremacy in the post-Emancipation South was not merely the product of historical happen-stance, but was created, crafted and carefully managed. While acknowledg-ing that southern whites worked hard to impose segregated systems on the South, historians have nevertheless continued to argue over the date by which segregation was effectively imposed upon the former Confederate states, and the strength that it assumed once it was in place. Traditional views have tended to argue that after the turmoil of the Civil War and the uncertainties of Reconstruction, white southerners had completed the task of reimposing a rigidly stratified system of separation and inequality based solely upon race by the 1920s: the colour line, in other words, had been effectively and efficiently reasserted.[29] More recently, however, a new gener-ation of historians has demanded a re-evaluation of both the chronology of fixed segregation, and of the extent to which African Americans allowed themselves to become subordinated to whites within those segregated systems.

Much of that recent work has focused on the way in which white south-erners fought to ensure that race remained the defining characteristic around which southern society was organized. Glenda Gilmore, for example, has sought to force the date of racial segregation's rigid imposition backwards by arguing that Populists' attempts to build inter-racial alliances along class lines in the mid-1890s sparked a determined move to 'regulate whiteness in public and social relations'. For Gilmore, rigid white supremacy was primarily a product of southern elites who feared that class might subsume race as a defining indicator of southern life. Those elites therefore took active measures to reassert race as the dominant category in southern social relations. As part of that concerted campaign, Gilmore has argued, the region's elites sought to stigmatize inter-racial sexual relations between white women and black men. Working-class white women were therefore rescued from what had previously been a lowly societal position, and as a result were welcomed into the bosom of pure white womanhood regardless of their social standing. It was a 'coldly calculated effort to defame black men' and it added a gendered perspective to the white supremacy that was continually refined by southern whites.[30] Others have argued that it was not until much later that race was finally able to subsume class. In a pioneering study that examined the culture of segregation, for example, Grace Elizabeth Hale has argued that it was not until the 1930s that predominately middle-class southern whites were successful in crafting a common identity based around race rather than class. After a period of great contest, Hale argues, they succeeded in fashioning 'a common whiteness out of the racial absolutes of the color line'. What amounted to a culture of violence dominated and oppressed blacks in public displays of white unity, in which lynching once again became a central spectacle.[31]

Other historians have continued the process of uncovering the extent to which southern whites had to battle to assert and then maintain their supremacy in the region, either because of the particular demands of the state in which they lived, or because of the ongoing efforts of blacks to draw attention to the inherent absurdities and inequalities of segregation. In an astute study that draws attention to the different forces acting upon white supremacy in the states of the Border and Deep South (also known as the Upper and Lower South), J. Douglas Smith has argued persuasively that the imposition of white supremacy was a more fluid and complex affair than had previously been recognized. This is certainly true of Virginia, the 'Old Dominion' state, which Smith uses as a case study to demonstrate the extent to which African Americans were still fighting hard against the racial status quo well into the 1930s. Their task was made all the more difficult by the actions of local whites, who sought to mask their support for white supremacy with a veneer of genteel paternalism. As Smith has shown, population shifts, economic opportunities and growing urbanization at the start of the 1920s 'exposed the limitations and inherent contradictions of paternalism', and in doing so not only revealed the harsh realities of segregated life but also 'contributed to an erosion of managed race relations'.

Surprisingly, once the paternalistic system began to disintegrate it was not the state but private individuals and organizations who lobbied most vociferously – and most successfully – for state-sanctioned white supremacy. The most notable of those private groups were Richmond's Anglo-Saxon Clubs, whose members were at the forefront of a crusade to ensure that bills were passed that actively legislated for racial difference. By May 1924, there were legal standards for 'whiteness' in the Old Dominion, and the impetus for passing such a law clearly came from more than just the 'small but determined group of racial zealots' claimed by historian Richard B. Sherman. By 1926, under yet more pressure from private white supremacist organizations, the Virginia Assembly passed the Public Assemblages Act, mandating separation of races in all public places.[32]

As well as establishing de facto separation in social spheres, southern white supremacists also ensured that non-whites were denied access to the institutions that should, constitutionally, have afforded them some redress. Segregationists developed what V. O. Key, Jr. has termed 'a variety of ingenious contrivances' to ensure that blacks were unable to seek effective redress through the ballot box. Indeed, so effective was disfranchisement that Key talks of the 'decimation of the southern electorate'.[33] The franchise was tightly controlled via a lattice work of interconnecting and mutually reinforcing local ordinances and provisions originating in Mississippi, Louisiana and South Carolina, but soon taken up in one guise or another by all southern states. They included poll taxes, residency requirements, literacy tests, early registration dates, disqualification for petty crimes, the grandfather clause, and the creation of the 'all-white primary'.[34] That final provision was cruelly effective. By the dawn of the twentieth century, the Democratic Party was, to all intents and purposes, the South's sole functioning political party. Although the Fifteenth Amendment made it clear that citizens' voting rights should not be abridged 'on account of race, color, or previous condition of servitude', segregation's apologists were quick to remind their critics that the Amendment only guarded against such discrimination by individual states or by the United States. Southern white Democrats swiftly pointed out that their party was a private organization, and was thus able to sidestep the provisions of the Amendment. As a result, non-whites were excluded from voting in any of the processes to determine the nomination of Democratic runners until the Supreme Court ruled otherwise in 1944, effectively leaving blacks with no say in the formalized political processes of the South.

If blacks were minded to attempt legal redress in a bid to obtain their constitutional rights, the White South's privileged position was further insulated by rampant inequalities in the judicial system. It was not just, as Gilmore has suggested, that white supremacy had become so entrenched, and so gender conscious, that in any criminal case involving allegations of inter-racial rape the assumption was always of black male responsibility and guilt. As the

NAACP's Charles Hamilton Houston established in his defence of George Crawford in 1933, every lawyer working in the county in which Crawford's alleged offence was tried was white, along with all of the grand jurors who indicted him.[35] The lack of black lawyers was no idle coincidence, either. By denying African Americans entry into southern law schools, southern segregationists were, albeit circuitously, limiting the number of trained black attorneys available to plaintiffs.[36] Such constraints on blacks' collective ability to obtain justice in the South allowed whites to reinforce their supremacy with violence if need be, especially in the Deep South. Between 1880 and 1940, for example, not only were nearly 600 African Americans lynched in Mississippi, but there were also no instances of juries convicting whites for the crime.[37]

The pervasiveness of white supremacy ensured that it was entrenched in all aspects of southern life, not just in the political and judicial systems. Throughout the twentieth century, for example, there were obvious and often openly acknowledged differences in the state funding afforded to white and black schools. That funding gap was greatest in the years between the end of the Civil War and the 1920s, but even when it began to close at the start of the 1930s, the average expenditure of six southern states on African American schools remained under 30 per cent of that spent on whites. By the mid-1930s, the inequality of schools was also clearly demonstrated in physical terms: in Mississippi, 1,440 of the state's 3,753 black schools were situated not in purpose-built school houses, but in 'churches, lodges, old stores, or tenant houses'.[38] As late as 1948, the annual salary for a black teacher in Mississippi was $711, over 40 per cent lower than that received by whites.[39] Such clear discrepancies were not always justified in purely racial terms, although the preservation of racial inequalities always lay at their root. One doctor who had nearly half a century's experience of running a segregated practice explained in the wake of *Brown* that there were a number of corollary effects from the Supreme Court justices' decision to effectively end the South's 'separate but equal' system. Drawing upon traditional arguments that claimed less public money was spent on black institutions because blacks collectively paid less in tax, he spoke of

> the wonderful schools for white children we could have without the tax burden of negro education! Let us say to the negro: we will continue to educate you in the schools which we have prepared for you if you wish your children educated, but if you insist on sending your children to our white schools we will educate our own and you can educate yours.[40]

Given that the South has such long traditions of white supremacy, and that successive generations of southern whites spent significant time and energy ensuring that white supremacy remained entrenched, it is not a simple task to distinguish specific periods of resistance from the general history of the South's protection of its racially stratified way of life. In terms of massive resistance, a number of historians who have studied the phenomenon have cast around for a historical moment, movement or date with which to pinpoint its origins. It is a task that has become increasingly difficult, not least because of the number of recent histories that have argued convincingly that African American attempts to challenge, and, ultimately, overthrow white supremacy started in earnest in the late 1930s. Long before the *Brown* decision, and even some years before the Second World War, whites in the South were having to respond to attacks that, in the words of historian Adam Fairclough, 'constituted more than the prelude to the drama' of the post-*Brown* civil rights movement. In effect, the first act of the civil rights movement's 'two act play' was underway before *Brown*, and whites were drawn into resistance in order to protect the racial status quo.[41] The question that remains is whether that resistance was truly 'massive' in scale. For, rather than a simple reaction against local civil rights activity – however well organized that activity may have been – what made massive resistance stand out from the actions of those generations of southern whites who had sought to protect white supremacy in the region was its scope and scale. It was a movement of opposition not just against local civil rights protest, but against the concerted effort of federal forces to desegregate the South in conjunction with local protest movements.

For many, the convenience of situating massive resistance's origins in a sectional split that took place in the Democratic Party in 1948 has been hard to resist. Such a split had appeared increasingly inevitable since the end of the Second World War, when the national Democratic Party had begun to venture in political directions that alarmed many of the members of its southern wing. Those southern Democrats were alienated by a series of pronouncements from the White House which appeared to signal President Truman's intentions for the root and branch reform of southern racial practices, starting with the establishment of the President's Committee on Civil Rights (PCCR) in early December 1946. When Truman announced in his January 1948 State of the Union address that he intended to devote a speech to Congress on the specific issue of civil rights, that emerging southern distrust finalized. To further exacerbate southern fears, only two of the 15 members of the PCCR were southerners, Frank Porter Graham and Dorothy Rogers Tilly. Both of them were committed progressives, and their involvement with Truman's civil rights proposals saw them cast as pariahs by many in their native South. The fact that Graham wrote the dissenting opinion when Truman sought to end racist hiring practices in federal industries on a permanent basis was of little solace to those segregationist critics. Indeed, committed segregationists often chose to forget that Graham had opposed attempts to make the Fair Employment Practices Committee permanent, especially when he was up for election against a less liberal opponent.[42] It was largely in response to Truman's initiatives that concerned southern Democrats established a splinter group that better represented their interests, the official title of which was the States' Rights Democratic Party but which was soon widely known by the more colloquial 'Dixiecrats'. When the entire Mississippi delegation and 12 Alabama delegates staged a walkout from the National Democratic Party's nominating convention in Philadelphia in July 1948, it precipitated a third party presidential campaign by Democrats who were utterly disaffected with their political colleagues. Proceeding under the popular title of the 'Dixiecrat Revolt', its members and supporters attempted to derail Truman and restore the political hegemony of white supremacy in the South.[43]

Scholars should exercise some caution, however, when seeking to establish clear-cut links between the Dixiecrat Revolt and the start of massive resistance. For, just as the precise origins of that resistance are somewhat hazy and ill-defined, so too are the foundations of the southern bolt from the Democratic Party. Both phenomena had longer gestation periods than are often acknowledged, and both drew upon historical traditions and were the product of a long-standing, simmering discontent in the South. As Alexander Heard recalled in an interview in 1991, 'the Dixiecrat movement didn't come about just because somebody thought of it over a tea cup one day.' Likewise, William Munford Tuck, the former governor of Virginia who hailed from Halifax County, the only county in Virginia to vote for the Dixiecrats in 1948, remembered that the party's principles were ones 'which we had contended throughout the years'.[44] As with much segregationist history, the deficit in scholarly analysis of the Dixiecrat campaign has led to common misunderstandings and too narrow a view of both the campaign itself and its origins.[45] Recent close studies of the revolt reveal that, as Heard suggested, there were important factors that led to the development of what was, in effect, an independent southern campaign long before it finally emerged in 1948.[46]

That said, as Kari Frederickson's work has shown in particular, there are many clear parallels that can be drawn between the Dixiecrat Revolt and massive resistance, not least because elements of the revolt presaged much that became familiar in massive resistance. Those parallels, though, are often not the ones that have previously been identified. What emerges from Frederickson's study is a southern revolt that suffered – just as massive resistance would – from having broadly agreed aims, but highly contested methods for best achieving those aims. It was never clear, for example, even within the highest echelons of leadership, whether the States' Rights Democrats had officially broken away from the National Party and were therefore running as an independent third party, or whether they merely represented a dissatisfied southern faction of a national whole. Such misunderstandings arose because the Dixiecrats were bereft of clear and dynamic leadership, especially in the figure of presidential hopeful Fielding Wright of Mississippi, who loathed campaigning and who disagreed publicly with his own vice-presidential candidate, South Carolina's Strom Thurmond, over the States' Righters' relationship with the National Party.[47] In an early indication of the extent to which circumstances at the state level were central to segregationists' campaigns to protect racial privilege throughout the ensuing decades, the electoral success of the Dixiecrats was highly dependent upon local conditions. Although the Dixiecrats showed up well in those states of the Deep South that boasted a monolithic political structure with a dominant single party, there proved to be very little support for the defection elsewhere.[48] What is more, no state that supported the Dixiecrats in 1948 faced gubernatorial elections in that same year, which strongly suggests that support for the Dixiecrats was a luxury solely for those politicians certain of their immediate political futures. Louisianans and Georgians, for example, proved to be so absorbed in their own gubernatorial contests that they virtually ignored the Dixiecrats altogether, and there was certainly no enthusiasm from the governors' mansions for the defection.[49]

Of equal importance to an understanding of later resistance is the finding that the Dixiecrats, too, were not simply the top-down, elite-driven phenomenon that past histories have claimed for massive resistance.[50] In South Carolina, for instance, the home state of Dixiecrat vice-presidential hopeful Strom Thurmond, grassroots organization was so adept that it proved possible to entice 2,000 people to attend a protest meeting in support of the Dixiecrat stand in a single county, and two counties passed a number of resolutions condemning Truman's pro-civil rights programme. Rather than an elitist response to the National Democratic Party's attempts to sideline the power of the southern voting bloc, the Dixiecrat revolt was, as Frederickson has concluded, a response to 'mounting agitation for racial and economic democracy at the local level' and a clear exhibition of the fact that 'the increasingly self-conscious activities of the Black Belt/industrial elite were a direct response to grassroots challenges'.[51] Even with the apparent support of grassroots electors, however, the States' Rights Party could not muster sufficient votes to derail Truman's attack on civil rights. The insurgency was ultimately unsuccessful, and the Dixiecrats carried only South Carolina, Mississippi, Alabama and Louisiana. Crucially, those were the four states in which the Dixiecrats ran under the Democratic Party emblem. The South, it would seem, was not ready for a full-scale uprising; or, if it was, then that uprising would have to be better planned and more astutely managed than the Dixiecrats' had been. Nonetheless, the 1948 revolt had set a precedent. Some of the South's foremost political leaders had shown a willingness to rebel against their national political leaders when threatened with the forced reform of their established racial practices, and, although they did not always offer them sufficient support to succeed in their overall quest, certain sections of the southern electorate proved that they were openly willing to support such a rebellion.

The other significant precedent set by the Dixiecrats lay in the rhetorical and organizational foundation blocs that they carved out for their campaign, many of which formed the basis for future resistance efforts. Southern

Democrats who split from the National Party based their political challenge around their collective opposition to Truman and his advocacy of civil rights, but were also concerned to promote a strong states' rights stance and a return to small town '*laissez-faire*' economics.[52] They were, in other words, strongly opposed to the centralization of government powers in Washington, and many Dixiecrat supporters shared a belief that if federal power in the South could not be controlled, then it should at least be restricted. The 1948 campaign also provided valuable experience for a number of southerners who were later to become central figures in different areas of the massive resistance struggle. The Citizens' Councils movement, which became an essential part of grassroots resistance organizing post-*Brown*, was staffed by men who had performed prominent roles in the Dixiecrats' campaign, notably Alabama's Walter C. Givhan and John U. Barr, a Louisianan industrialist who briefly stood as the head of the Federation for Constitutional Government which sought to bring together resisters from 12 southern states. Tom P. Brady, an iconic figure who became central to massive resistance strategy, served in 1948 as chairman of the Dixiecrats' Speakers' Bureau.

THE SELECTIVE RHETORIC OF RESISTANCE

Such clear links in personnel obviously had knock-on effects in ideology, and historian Neil McMillen has commented that, although the Citizens' Councils did not strictly constitute a political movement, their ideology 'closely resembled the doctrines and beliefs of the States' Rights Democratic Party'.[53] While those that joined the Citizens' Councils were often energetic adherents of southern resistance, their membership did not necessarily represent all of those in favour of resisting federally mandated racial change in the region. There was variation in the extent to which white southerners sought to pursue resistance strategies, just as there was variation in the rationales that brought southern whites to a pro-resistance position. Different elements within the White South, in other words, clung to different versions of the myths of white supremacy, and by the mid-century segregationists were armed with a cornucopia of rationales, justifications and explanations for the continued dominance of whites in southern life. Many of massive resistance's proponents were sufficiently astute to recognize that fact, and as a result modified the level of racist and demagogic appeals that punctuated their rhetoric to suit the particularities of their intended audiences. At one extreme, segregationists played to the basest level of unreconstructed racism, giving vent to the belief that the integration of schools would induce their children

> at a tender and impressionable age, through close contact, heavy pressure and continuous propaganda to lose all racial pride and restraint, to ignore their parents and to sink in delinquency, degradation, filth, total sin and the

early destruction of the white race in the South through the pollution of their blood streams and total mongrelization.[54]

At the other extreme were the arguments of those southerners who knew that they were playing to a non-southern audience, and who, more often by design than by belief, blanched their arguments of the worst excesses of racism, and indeed on occasion managed to defend the southern caste system without reference to race. At mid-century, perhaps the clearest exposition of such arguments was provided not by a politician or any political movement, but by an attorney, John W. Davis.

Davis, who defended the South Carolinian case for continued segregation before the Supreme Court in the hearings leading up to the *Brown* decision, possessed the breadth of worldly, political and judicial experience that often — but by no means always — marked out those who brought a more object- ive, detached view to the problems of southern segregation. A committed foe of desegregation and upholder of southern mores, Davis had also served in national and international capacities, including as solicitor general of the United States and ambassador to Great Britain.[55] For supporters of segrega- tion, it was of paramount importance that Davis argued the southern position before the Supreme Court as effectively as possible. As Michael J. Klarman has recently argued in a revisionist history, the outcome of the *Brown* cases was far less certain than some scholars previously believed.[56] In the arguments that he put forward before the Court, Davis provided the clear- est contemporary example of the construction of a coherent case to justify the southern position not on the grounds of non-white inferiority, but on a particular interpretation of the founding documents of the United States. Davis and his team argued that the Tenth Amendment and the Bill of Rights gave state governments the right to operate public schools to their own specifications on the grounds that the right to operate those schools had never been granted to the federal government, and as a result remained within individual states' powers. In a bid to continue to base his defence within the lofty language of the Constitution, Davis looked to the Fourteenth Amendment's 'equal protection' clause and remained adamant that the framers of the Amendment never intended its provisions to cover public schools. When pushed by the justices, who suggested to him that social and economic circumstances might have changed between the Amendment's framing in 1867 and judicial argument in 1953, he replied sharply, 'changed conditions may effect policy, but changed conditions cannot broaden the terminology of the Constitution.' If there was going to be such a change, he was implying, the correct way to bring it about was via congressional law, not judicial fiat.[57]

As though not content to suggest that the founding documents of the nation were on the segregationists' side, Davis also intimated that the weight of legal precedent was soundly behind the South's position. If the legal principle of *stare decisis* was applied to the Fourteenth Amendment, he argued, 'controlling precedents preclude a construction which would abolish segregation in the public schools'. Davis demonstrated eloquence as well as sound legal knowledge. When he and his team put together their brief, he told the Court,

> We relied on the fact that this Court had not once but seven times ... pronounced in favor of the 'separate but equal' doctrine. We relied on the fact that the courts of last appeal of some sixteen or eighteen states have passed upon the validity of the 'separate but equal' doctrine ... We relied on the fact that Congress has continuously since 1862 segregated its schools in the District of Columbia.

It was, he suggested, 'late indeed in the day' to alter the view of 23 of the states that had ratified the Fourteenth Amendment that it effectively allowed for segregation.[58]

On the eve of the *Brown* decision, then, apologists for southern segregation were faced with a paradox. On the one hand, many of the bulwarks of segregation and the separate but equal system appeared to be holding up well, despite specific setbacks in terms of voting rights.[59] Davis and his colleagues proved that it was still possible, in the post-Second World War context, to present arguments in favour of a racially segregated society that demanded the full attention of the highest court in the land. Indeed, Klarman's recent historical analysis of the Supreme Court argues that, as late as December 1952, when the nine justices first convened to consider the *Brown* cases, four of them believed segregation was unconstitutional, but two did not and three others were 'apparently ambivalent' and in theory could have swung the decision either way.[60] Segregationists from the refined to the red-neck believed that history, the Constitution, and legal precedent were all on their side.

On the other hand, the very fact that Davis and his colleagues had been forced to defend the South's position in the Supreme Court exemplified the growing pressures under which segregation was being forced to operate. For decades, African Americans had been ratcheting up their willingness to fight Jim Crow segregation, not just on a personal, day-to-day level, but in an increasingly organized and structured manner. From the 1930s onwards, the NAACP had also begun to win important legal victories over segregation that hinted at a frontal assault on the constitutionality of segregation itself in the near future. Buoyed up by changes in society that ranged from the psychological (such as the collective boost of witnessing and participating in the Allies' victory against Aryan supremacists in the Second World War), to the more concrete (such as the existence of a greater number of trained black lawyers and the apparent support of President Harry S. Truman), a number of southern blacks were increasingly moved to brave the worst excesses of southern racism and take their fights against segregation to the courts. Dr

L. K. Jackson, pastor of St Paul's Baptist Church in Gary, Indiana, exemplified blacks' growing anger in an open letter to Fulton Lewis, Jr., whose regular radio show was broadcast from Washington DC. A strong supporter of Truman's Committee on Civil Rights, Jackson bemoaned the fact that, since the end of a war

> that was fought at a cost of over 2 hundred billion dollars and hundreds of thousands of American lives in the name of democracy, whole families of innocent helpless Negroes have been lynched. Negro soldiers' eyes have been plucked out by officers of the law and in some instances the perpetrators of this barbarity have stood in the courthouse and acknowledged their guilt and were freed.[61]

African Americans were increasingly unwilling to stand for such oppression. Southern whites were going to have to fight hard to maintain the institutions of white supremacy that had been constructed over centuries, and the systems of segregation that had sustained them since slavery.

THE TIMING AND TRAJECTORY OF 'MASSIVE' RESISTANCE

The rich history of trenchant white resistance to racial change in the southern states poses a delicate question: if resistance was an ever-present, when, precisely, did something that might accurately be called 'massive' resistance first emerge? Casting around for a single date that neatly delineates the start of massive resistance is problematic, not least because it is heavily dependent upon the way in which the phenomenon is viewed and defined. In what is the most consummately crafted contribution to the ongoing debate on the timing of massive resistance, Michael J. Klarman has put forward the 'backlash thesis'. As part of a wider project to understand the development of southern race relations in the post-*Brown* era, Klarman created a tidy chain of causation in which he argued that the impact of the Supreme Court's schools decision on the civil rights movement was merely an indirect one. *Brown*'s fundamental achievement was in catalysing southern resistance from its 'relatively limited scope' before 1954 to a 'tidal wave of racial hysteria that swept the South' afterwards. That in turn created a situation in which the region's politicians could – and did – make political capital out of appeals to the region's rekindled racial extremism. The result was that those politicians brazenly defied federal authority and brutally suppressed civil rights campaigns in the knowledge that they had a willing constituency that supported their actions. It was in the context of that cycle that *Brown* 'crystallized southern resistance to racial change'. 'While the civil rights movement did not require *Brown* as a catalyst', Klarman has argued, 'the massive resistance movement did.'[62]

The decision to cite a single, tangible event as a clearly defined starting point for massive resistance – in this case *Brown* itself – hints at a deeper misunderstanding of what it was, exactly, that such resistance entailed.

There is no doubt that *Brown* played an important part in the genesis of massive resistance, and equally it is clear that the decision had an important role to play in ripping out the middle ground of southern politics and throwing political debate into the radical margins of the region's political spectrum. Massive resistance, though, was more than just a political phenomenon played out at the elite level of congressional and senatorial politics. As well as the actions of high-profile politicians, it was born of the concerted efforts of concerned segregationists at the grassroots who strove to hold on to a long-cherished, segregated way of life in the face of not only federally mandated desegregation edicts and pressure from successive presidential administrations, but also from increasingly well-organized indigenous civil rights activists.

The southern whites who were sufficiently moved to mount that defensive action were a disparate group, and the movement that they created was often disordered, complex and even muddled. Different sections of southern society, and different communities in different geographical locales took up resistance at different times. They often had varied goals within the overall objective of resisting desegregation, ranging from a desire to elevate the terms of the debate over racial segregation so that it might appeal to a wider, non-southern audience to maintaining office by playing upon the prejudices of a particular political constituency, and, at the most prosaic, to ensuring economic and social supremacy over 'uppity' blacks near whom they lived and worked in small towns and rural areas throughout the southern states.

Resistance, in other words, was an amorphous beast, which in many ways explains why pinpointing the date of its inception has been – and continues to be – so problematic. As will be seen, while anti-integration fever raged in some areas, there were other white communities whose members simply showed themselves to be unwilling to countenance continued segregation in the face of a Supreme Court decree. Elsewhere, those put in charge of official legislative responses to *Brown* in many of the southern states remained wracked with indecision at the same time as Citizens' Council organizing suggests that there were considerable numbers of grassroots segregationists who were willing, and able, to mobilize effectively and efficiently. The overall result of such vagaries is that massive resistance must be seen as a phenomenon that was too sprawling, and simply not sufficiently obedient, to have been ushered into existence by a single landmark event, whether it be the *Brown* decisions of 1954 or the statement of southern political intent that became known as the Southern Manifesto of March 1956.

Almost inevitably given such a context, the elegant flow of Klarman's thesis replaces some of the more awkward aspects of massive resistance with simplified generalities that wash over the intricacies and complexities of resistance history.[63] Other historians have found the temptation of looking to the Southern Manifesto for a definitive starting date too great to resist. Francis Wilhoit, for example, has claimed that, 'If one can set a date on which the South's resistance to Brown [sic] turned into something close to a political counterrevolution, the date would have to be March 12, 1956.' Dewey Grantham, meanwhile, has argued that the Southern Manifesto provided a 'dramatic indication of the South's mounting political defiance'.[64]

Given the fluctuations in southern segregationists' defences of their position, it is more useful to chart massive resistance in terms of the resisters' outlook and approach than in strictly chronological terms, although the two are clearly interlinked. To that end, three broadly distinct periods of resistance activity can be identified. The first was indeed sparked off by the *Brown* decision, but rather than signalling the arrival of a prefabricated massive resistance movement, the months immediately following the Supreme Court's decision on schools highlighted the discrepancies that existed between political and grassroots approaches to maintaining segregation. During those months, segregationists' political representatives appeared bereft of tangible ideas and curiously reserved in their denunciations of *Brown*, with the result that it was locally organized groups and societies which began to bring much needed momentum to the cause. The second period of resistance was ushered in with the signing of the Southern Manifesto. That is not to say that the Manifesto represented the start of massive resistance per se; rather, its unveiling signalled the start of a period during which resistance was very much on the front foot. From 1956 until 1960, resisters were by and large on the offensive, with segregationists setting the tone for resistance and defining its character and many of its parameters.

The third period, from 1960 to 1965, followed setbacks at the hands of federal forces, in the federal courts, and in the face of a tactically astute civil rights movement. As a result, those years saw massive resistance in long-term decline. There were a number of occasions when resistance appeared to be at its most brutal in that third period, but, rather than representing an upsurge in segregationist fortunes and spirit, they more accurately represented the final death throes of a cornered beast. It was a period that saw segregationists losing the initiative, and, crucially, reacting to an agenda set by others, most notably the activists and tacticians of the civil rights movement but also the federal government. By 1965, massive resistance appeared defeated. It did not disappear altogether, however, for while 1965 saw the end of the most openly abrasive, hostile and violent episodes of southern resistance, and while civil and voting rights legislation in 1964 and 1965 respectively saw a diminution in the most public forms of white supremacy, other more subtle forms of resistance saw their stock increase rather than decrease. This applies in particular to those segregationists who had always striven to elevate their arguments above the maelstrom of demagogic racist appeals and segregationist police brutality that pervaded the South. Their alternative approach attempted to construct what they believed to be 'respectable' resistance strategies capable of a wider appeal to those outside the confines of the region's borders. As a result, they were not left isolated by the failure of resistance, but rather were brought seamlessly into the new currents of developing national conservatism; a theme that will be discussed further in the final chapter, 'The Confederate Chameleon'.

2

BROWN AND ITS AFTERMATH, 1954–1956

POLITICAL RESPONSES TO *BROWN*: DIFFIDENCE AND INDECISION

All nine Supreme Court justices sided unanimously with the plaintiffs in the *Brown* decision on 17 May 1954. Given that the Court's ruling threatened to overturn the social structure of a region that had clung to racial separation through centuries of slavery and over 50 years of 'separate but equal' segregation, the very least that could be expected from the segregationist South was a robust and sustained response to *Brown*. Instead, the South's political leaders registered their regret at the Court's ruling but failed to take decisive action. South Carolina's Jimmy Byrnes reported that he was 'shocked' at the decision. North Carolina's William B. Umstead claimed that he was 'terribly disappointed', but surprisingly added the caveat that because it was the highest court in the land that had spoken, the decision ought to be obeyed.[1] Nowhere was that indecision more apparent than in the press release that emanated from the office of the individual who many came to see as the personification of southern resistance, Harry Flood Byrd. At times, Byrd seemed to be urging caution and restraint: those in positions of authority and those who had children of school-going age 'should exercise the greatest wisdom in shaping our future course. Whatever is done', he proclaimed, 'should be based on our most mature judgement after sober and exhaustive consideration.' In amongst his words of moderation, however, were veiled threats. The Court's decision, he warned, 'will bring implications and dangers of the greatest consequence', and his home state of Virginia was 'now facing a crisis of the first magnitude'.[2]

Beyond such initial verbal sparring, however, the South's political leaders seemed to be at a loss as to where to turn. On a regional level, there appeared to be uncertainty as to the tone that should be adopted. A number of segregationist political leaders appeared to be willing to take measures to shore up their own respective state's position against federally mandated desegregation, but were equally reluctant to put their names to South-wide strategies of resistance, either because they feared the political consequences of being closely associated with a regional strategy that might fail in the face of federal obduracy, or because they remained unsure of the temper of the South and the sacrifices that southerners would be willing to make in order to cling to segregation. That unwillingness to suggest a decisive course of action is all the more surprising given the fact that the cases that coalesced in *Brown* had been working their way through the judicial system for nearly four years: the decision in the original Kansas cases had been handed down in the district court in August 1951, and in the South Carolina cases, *Briggs v. Elliott*, in June of the same year. What is more, the southern governors had specifically taken time during their annual conference in 1953 to discuss the organization and operation of state school systems at both elementary and secondary levels.[3] As retired attorney and Southern Regional Council vice-president Marion A. Wright commented, the *Brown* decision 'should have surprised no one', but the responses of southern political leaders suggested otherwise:

> Many of our politicians assail the decision as though it were a bolt from the blue, taking by surprise a completely unforewarned South. The facts are quite to the contrary. Beginning with the Court headed by Justice Hughes through the court headed by Justice Vinson – those were no left-wingers – there was a series of decisions which should have prepared the South. They foretold as clearly as words could that, upon a proper case, the court would strike a mortal blow at legalized segregation.[4]

North Carolina's Guy Benton Johnson was more succinct. As he explained to a Washington DC audience a full 11 months before the decree, 'the Supreme Court is about to make a momentous decision on the question of the constitutionality of compulsory segregation in the public schools. This decision', he predicted, 'may precipitate a grave crisis in the relations of the races in the South.'[5]

Charting the initial reaction of regional leaders to *Brown* on a South-wide basis is complicated by the fact that, in the run-up to the decision, some states had taken measures to try to eliminate the most glaring inequalities that existed between white and non-white schools. Most of the plans were enacted in the states of the Deep South, where those inequalities were most conspicuous. In South Carolina, Byrnes himself ordered a school equalization programme in 1951, a year after his election to the governor's mansion. In what was a tacit admission that 'separate' had not meant 'equal' in the state's public education system, a 3 per cent sales tax was instituted to raise the estimated $75 million necessary to bring African American schools up to the level of their white counterparts.[6] In Alabama, there was a move in some quarters to end the disparity in the pay of black and white teachers, which, for the 1950–51 school year saw white teachers earning an average of $232 more than their black equivalent, even though black teacher salaries had risen by 212 per cent between 1939 and 1951.[7] In Mississippi, too, school equalization measures predated the *Brown* decision by two years.[8]

Strategically minded segregationists believed such measures to have an obvious shortcoming, for they were designed to forestall a Supreme Court decision on racial segregation rather than to respond to a decision once it had been handed down. As Harry Byrd noted in conclusion to his remarks on *Brown*, it was one of the 'cruel results' arising from the Supreme Court's 'about face' that the White South had 'in recent years expended hundreds of millions of dollars for construction of new Negro school facilities to conform with the policy previously laid down [in *Plessy v. Ferguson*]'.[9] Once 'separate but equal' as a policy had been struck down in its entirety, there was little relief to be had from attempting to equalize school facilities, at least in the eyes of the federal courts. What remained very apparent was that, in the immediate aftermath of *Brown*, southern leaders failed to devise or even outline plans for the maintenance of segregation that were as rational as the school equalization plans that had been drawn up prior to the decision. Although all of the southern states were faced with fundamental changes to their established way of life, there was a marked absence of strategic thinking on a regional level, and certainly nothing sufficiently coherent to be described as a 'southern response' emerged in the immediate aftermath of the Supreme Court's decision.

While that lack of a detailed, synchronized response to *Brown* initially appears surprising, it can be explained by a number of different factors. Most obviously, the states that came together to make up 'the South' formed a far less coherent whole than was often portrayed in both historical and contemporary press accounts. As political activist Allard Lowenstein explained to the editor of the *New Republic*, 'In so many articles ... the South is painted with a simplicity of stroke wondrous to behold.'[10] The states of the Old Confederacy lacked the sort of homogeneity that was necessary to agree upon a central, unified plan of resistance. Most could boast of their own peculiar electoral and legislative rules as well as local political traditions, and had different population densities, racial ratios and professed ideological outlooks.

In one sense, however, what contributed to the lack of an organized response was the lack of a need for such a response. In carefully choreographing a unanimous decision in *Brown*, Chief Justice Earl Warren ensured the transmission of a strong message to the White South. Warren's critics looked askance at the paucity of his legislative experience, but once he had managed to unify a potentially divided court for the schools decision, few could doubt the strength of his interpersonal and political skills. As the most recent history of the decision has noted, in December 1952 there was still 'no secure majority' that favoured overturning *Plessy v. Ferguson*, and certainly no likelihood of unanimity.[11] What the Supreme Court justices had not been able to agree upon in May 1954 was the manner in which segregated schools should be desegregated, and the timetable under which such actions should take place. A number of those justices were wary of a white backlash and thus preferred a gradual timetable to desegregation, while others saw segregation as increasingly incommensurate with the American creed and therefore pushed for 'immediatism'.[12] In order to bridge that divide, Warren devised a course of action by which the Court deferred any such decision to what became known as the separate 'implementation' decree, or *Brown II*, which would not be decided until the Court's next term.[13] The result was that segregationists spent the 12 months following *Brown* in the knowledge that their segregated way of life was effectively unconstitutional, but they had not been told how or when that way of life would be dismantled. As North Carolina's Governor William Umstead told the NAACP's Kelly Alexander in June 1954, in his mind 'the schools in North Carolina will open in September on the same basis upon which they have been operating'.[14]

Given that delay, what remains unexplained is the fact that the leaders of the segregationist South did not use the time available between the two parts of the *Brown* decision to formulate detailed proposals and workable rejoinders. They knew that an implementation decree was coming, but while many talked of defiance in oratory that was a wonder of bluster and indignation, the lack of detailed defensive planning was startling. Racial policies in some states simply atrophied. As Tennessee Governor Frank Clement noted in October 1954, his state chose to avoid any official discussion of *Brown*'s ramifications. 'It has been our thinking that until the final decision is handed down by the Court that it would probably be best to defer the appointment of a Study Commission', he concluded.[15]

Many states did set up commissions with specific mandates to devise appropriate responses, but a close look at the correspondence of those involved suggests that many were little more than talking shops and holding operations. Thomas Jenkins Pearsall was put in charge of North Carolina's Special Advisory Committee on Education in autumn 1954, and candidly admitted not only that it was 'a tremendous responsibility' but also that he felt terribly inadequate. 'The distressing part', he continued 'is everyone on the Committee, as well as the Governor, seems almost lost as to where to turn.' Pearsall clung to the nebulous hope that either time or Providence would provide the solution.[16] In South Carolina and Virginia the pressure was even more intense than it was in Pearsall's Tar Heel State of North Carolina, as both states had been named in cases brought before the Supreme Court as part of the *Brown* arguments, *Davis v. County School Board of Prince Edward County* in Virginia and *Briggs v. Elliott* in South Carolina. In Virginia, Garland 'Peck' Gray was charged with the same task as Pearsall but he, too, could think of no immediately workable solutions.[17] One of the few decisive joint tactical decisions taken by those states affected by *Brown* came when Georgia, Louisiana, Alabama and Mississippi all turned down the invitation to file *amicus curiae* briefs for *Brown II*. Had they agreed to do so, they would of course have been tacitly accepting the first *Brown* decision.[18]

The work of those southern segregationists charged with responding to *Brown* was greatly facilitated by the terms of the 'implementation' decision which was handed down by the Court just over a year after the first decision, on 31 May 1955. Those intent upon resisting desegregation could draw two distinct pluses from *Brown II*. Although the decision required a 'prompt and reasonable start toward full compliance' with the original *Brown* decision, the exact timeframe that was demanded for school desegregation was nothing more than the abstract requirement for it to take place with 'all deliberate speed'. Supreme Court Justice Hugo Black, himself a southerner, later rued the vague wording of the implementation decision. 'All deliberate speed', Black said in retrospect, was 'language for lawyers and that had been a grievous mistake'.[19] Given the intemperance of segregationist polemic, especially in the Deep South, it was very obvious just how deliberate the speed of their desegregation was going to be. Black's Supreme Court colleague, Justice Brennan, recalled that, 'several times later at conference, [Black] said sadly, "... We made a mistake"'.[20] Not only had the Court failed to impose a strict timetable on desegregation, it had also placed responsibility for implementing the decision in the hands of local school boards, many of which were composed of the very whites who were intent upon forestalling desegregation.

MIXED MESSAGES FROM THE GRASSROOTS: REFERENDUMS IN LOUISIANA AND GEORGIA

The fitful attempts of states to establish effective legislative rejoinders to federally mandated segregation were, however, only part of the battle. At the grassroots level, the constituents that had elected the South's leaders also battled to make sense of, and to come to terms with, the Supreme Court's decisions on segregation. The majority of white southerners favoured a path between the two extremes of total integration and steadfast segregation. In explaining his position on the issue, one native Tennessean wrote to the offices of the NAACP to note that he 'knows segregation must come to an end', and was 'willing to see it ended'. Nonetheless, he felt impelled to add the major caveat that any such change should be 'at a pace that is commensurate with local conditions and bigotry on either side [is] overruled'. He concluded that there were two types of people who were the greatest hindrance to the peaceful settlement of the issue in the South, those who were for integration without qualification and those who were against it without qualification.[21] Those southerners who were moved to explain their outlook in such letters were not necessarily reflective of southern opinion, however, and there are dangers inherent in attempting to judge public opinion through such correspondence. As Sarah Patton Boyle admitted to the noted author Lillian Smith, for example, she had personally been responsible for writing 14 of the 18 pro-integration letters that had appeared in the *Richmond Times-Dispatch* by the beginning of September 1951, many under assumed names.[22]

A series of referendums that were held in certain southern states on the subject of the forced desegregation of public schools offers a more accurate appraisal of the public mood in the region than those provided by letters. Most importantly for historians of white resistance, the referendums provide a wide sweep both geographically and chronologically, for they took place in seven southern states, the first was held before *Brown*, three were subsequently held between the two decisions, and three after *Brown II*. In all seven, southern whites were actively encouraged to vote by their political leaders. A close examination of the campaigns that led up to those referendums and the results of the popular votes sheds light both on the voting public's attitude towards the preservation of segregated schooling and on the measures that legislative leaders were willing to take as they attempted to shape public opinion to their own advantage.

In Louisiana, the referendum of 2 November 1954 followed a burst of legislative activity. A range of resistance laws was quickly passed by the state legislature, one of which, according to the Louisiana *Times-Picayune*, 'would invoke the police power of the state to legalize retention of separate schools' if those schools were deemed to be threatened by *Brown*. It was a drastic proposal, and signalled such a change in the running of public schools in the state that a change to Louisiana's Constitution was needed before it could come into operation. For that to happen, it would have to be passed by a popular vote. Here, then, was a chance for Louisianans to show en masse the strength of their attachment to a racially separate public school system.[23] The passage of what became known as 'Amendment 16' was deemed to be so important to the segregationist cause that the newly formed Joint Legislative Committee to Maintain Segregation was charged with ensuring its success. The Committee, in the words of historian Adam Fairclough, 'rapidly became the spearhead of opposition to *Brown*' in the state, and was led by William M. 'Willie' Rainach, 'the most conservative member of the Louisiana Senate'.[24] The importance of the vote to those who, like Rainach, were committed to the preservation of segregation at all costs was clearly reflected in the high-profile campaign that the Joint Legislative Committee underwrote. Rainach himself appeared on local television station WDSU-TV, and immediately took the offensive. In explaining the need for the passage of so drastic a measure as Amendment 16, Rainach chose to vilify the NAACP. He claimed openly that the Association's members were 'driving their wedge between our white and colored people', and had thus 'forced us to assert our leadership'. The Joint Legislative Committee was sufficiently worried about the result to place a newspaper advertisement on polling day itself, which played to many of the traditional fears of the segregationist South. 'Do you realize that mixing races among young children in schools will lead to serious racial problems?' it asked, before noting that Amendment 16 would 'continue separate public schools — in the interest of public health, morals, better education, peace and order'. Echoing the paternalism of

Rainach's television address, the advertisement concluded with the statement that the Amendment 'will permit continued progress, peace and harmony, and better education for all our children, regardless of race or color'.[25]

Just over 82 per cent of voters cast their votes for the Amendment. On first appearance, it is a vote that suggests a ringing endorsement for massive resistance to *Brown* in theory, and for Rainach's hard-line resistance proposals in practice. Such an analysis is again overly simplistic, however, for there were a number of other factors playing upon voters' minds. Despite the Joint Legislative Committee's claims that every individual's vote was necessary for the adoption of the Amendment, less than a third of Louisiana's registered voters were sufficiently moved to cast ballots. Many of them were clearly perplexed by the exercise, for Louisianans were being asked to vote on 31 separate proposals, of which Rainach's resistance measure was only one. As one local newspaper editorial put it, those citizens 'who faced up to the task of trying to understand and register their convictions' ought to be commended.[26] On closer inspection, Amendment 16 also posed other thorny issues for Louisiana's voters, and it was certainly not as clear-cut a resistance measure as Rainach and the members of his committee were attempting to suggest. The Amendment had passed through both houses of the Louisiana legislature with relative ease, but that masked the indifference that a number of legislators felt towards the small print of Rainach's proposal. State Senator Robert A. Ainsworth, for example, admitted to voting for Amendment 16 not because he believed that the state should have the police powers that it prescribed, but because he disagreed with *Brown* and 'voted for the measure on the Senate floor in the interest of borrowing time to work out the problem. I feel we needed time', he conceded, 'so that the people could approach the subject in a sane manner and work things out for themselves'.[27] Among the general public, there were those who were opposed to desegregation, but who were not sufficiently wedded to segregation to vote for wide-ranging police powers to enforce its maintenance. Louisiana's voters were witness to the fact that turning a theoretical stand for maintaining segregation into explicit executive acts designed to do just that was a difficult task indeed.

In Georgia, the pattern was remarkably similar. Again, an amendment to the state constitution was necessary, this time for a plan devised by Governor Herman 'Humman' Talmadge, which planned for the creation of a state-wide private school system in the event of the enforced desegregation of state schools. In a deft mixture of ideology and practicality that was emblematic of southern legislative politics throughout the resistance era, Talmadge's proposal was certainly born from his single-minded attachment to segregation, but was also the direct consequence of complicated wider political manoeuvres that were designed to protect his traditional political powerbase – Georgia's rural constituencies – from the state's increasingly cosmopolitan urban areas.[28]

'Amendment 4', as it became known in Georgia, was not as clearly defined as its Louisianan counterpart, but was more draconian. In very simple terms it furnished the state legislature with the authority to abolish the public school system if threatened with desegregation, and provided for 'grants of State, County or Municipal funds to citizens of the state for educational purposes'.[29] Again, it was accompanied by a coordinated propaganda campaign, this time under the aegis of the Georgia Education Commission whose most vocal members were Talmadge himself, Attorney General Eugene Cook and Lieutenant Governor Marvin Griffin. The Commission expended state funds on a campaign which, according to one historian, included a mail shot of 9,000 pamphlets, cards and letters at a cost of $13,000.[30] That literature was once again bolstered by television appearances, with Cook particularly vocal. If the Amendment were passed, he proclaimed in a 90-minute television programme, traditions of segregation in the state would be secured for the foreseeable future. Once it had passed, he explained, if the Supreme Court justices were to attempt to roll back one of the state's segregation statutes, Talmadge would simply 'call the Legislature and pass another one. Thus', he concluded chillingly, 'we can keep substituting plans until doomsday'.[31]

Unlike Louisiana, the vote in Georgia was remarkably close. At the end of polling day, only 753 of the state's 1,810 precincts had finished counting their votes, but nonetheless the statistics were startling. In a state of the Deep South, just six months after *Brown*, the Associated Press reported that 118,411 had voted for the segregationists' amendment, but 121,268 had voted against. Once counting had been completed in all precincts, the Amendment was passed, but the margin of victory was far from comfortable and the final tally showed that less than 54 per cent of those voting supported it.[32] As Talmadge himself later surmised, it was chiefly the counting of rural votes, many of which came in later than their urban counterparts, that finally spirited the amendment to victory.[33] He was clearly taken aback at just how close the outcome had been, and chose not to dwell upon it in his later attacks on desegregation. In 1955's *You and Segregation*, for example, Talmadge noted that

> the day the United States Supreme Court orders Georgia to integrate its public schools ... will be the day Georgia's public school system will be legally destroyed ... However, the citizens of Georgia have looked ahead and provided for this day by amending the Constitution.

He did not add that 46 per cent of Georgians voting in the referendum had chosen not to do so.[34]

In the rather more accurate words of Ralph McGill, 'the decision does not at all resemble a mandate'.[35] In traditional histories of massive resistance, however, neither the closeness of the vote in Georgia nor the fact that the chance to vote on a similar measure in Louisiana failed to inspire a respectable turnout have received detailed comment or analysis.[36] Such results must be

used to refine the historical understanding of the ebb and flow of segregationist resistance in the post-*Brown* South, for they demand adjustments to
any understanding of the pervasiveness of resistance sentiment, and the
extent to which the majority of white southerners were willing to sacrifice
other freedoms in a bid to cling to rigidly segregated systems.

Part of the reason for the close nature of the Georgia vote in particular
was the network of opposition groups that came together to oppose
Talmadge's plans. The main thrust of that opposition was the contention that
it was more important to have an academically successful public school
system than it was to have a segregated schooling system. The former chairman of the Southern Association of Colleges and Secondary Schools, James
R. McCain, went head to head with a number of the Georgia Education
Commission's most high-profile members in the build-up to the Georgia referendum. At the very least, Georgia would be greatly damaged by the successful passage of the Amendment, McCain warned, because it would lead to
Georgia's university system losing its accreditation. Other educators, such as
State School Superintendent M. D. Collins, joined the nascent alliance against
the segregationist proposal, but so too did dissenting legislators, labour
representatives, church groups and a number of women's groups. Most
conspicuous among the Amendment's opponents was the *Augusta Courier*'s
Roy Harris. Unlike his fellow opponents, Harris was wedded to continued
segregation at any cost, and his opposition centred on what he perceived to
be the weakness of the bill. His solution was to intimidate African Americans
with such threats of violent reprisal that they would not attempt any form
of desegregation.[37]

AN ALTERNATIVE MODEL: HOXIE, ARKANSAS

Drawing attention to the extent of opposition to the segregationists' 1954
amendments underscores important aspects of massive resistance. Not only
does it serve to emphasize the lack of homogeneity within southern white
ranks throughout the resistance era, but it also gives an early indication of
the groups around which such dissent to the rigid segregationist line tended
to coalesce. There were also a wide number of issues that caused concern
among the amendments' opponents, lending further credence to the
argument that white southerners were uncertain how best to respond to
Brown. In Louisiana, for example, one state senator maintained that he did
not think 'segregation is a Christian thing to do', and that it was 'not proper
to relegate people to second-class citizenship'. A state representative, on the
other hand, believed that it was 'a very dangerous precedent', on the
grounds that 'education should never be under police power'.[38]

The most prevalent opposition groups to the amendments were not
organized by politicians but by teachers, members of Parent Teacher
Associations, and by women's groups. That was not a coincidence.
Throughout the resistance era it was teachers, parents and concerned women

— many of them mothers — who were at the forefront of dissent whenever segregationists' resistance methods directly threatened the operation of public schools. They may not have complained vocally against some of the other, more forthright measures of massive resistance, such as the brutal policing tactics of Birmingham's Bull Connor or Selma's Jim Clark, but they did exert significant pressure when the continued provision of free public schools appeared in doubt.

As a number of recent historical analyses have suggested, there was a point at which many southerners' antipathy towards the principle of federally mandated desegregation was overturned by the harsh realities of the measures that they would have to undertake in practice to derail desegregation. When resistance strategists proposed the closure of public schools, many southern women and many of the region's teachers recognized that, from their personal point of view, that point had been reached.[39] In Louisiana, the Independent Women's Organization (IWO) was unequivocal in its denunciation of Rainach's proposed police powers amendment, and, when Rainach characteristically attempted to dismiss the organization's members as 'subversives', they were even more acerbic in their denunciations of him. They were 'astonished' by his outbursts against the IWO, and 'For the sake of restoring the level of public debate in Louisiana to a higher plane' hoped that Rainach would have 'the courtesy to withdraw his ill-considered remarks'.[40]

If the outlook of such groups necessarily complicates our understanding of the trajectory of resistance, then so too does the existence of a number of white communities in the South that, upon hearing the Supreme Court's decision in *Brown*, decided simply to abide by the decree and desegregate. The NAACP's Thurgood Marshall was able to report in November 1955 that several locales in the peripheral South had desegregated with little fuss. In Kentucky, for example, 24 school districts had already desegregated rapidly and peaceably, in Delaware the total was 21 school districts, and all of Baltimore and eight counties in Maryland had also desegregated.[41] In Big Springs, Texas, the pastor of the First Baptist Church was able to report that the high school was integrated and, moreover, that 'No unwholesome incident has been observed that I know about in the two years of integration in the school'.[42] In Arkansas, the towns of Charleston and Fayetteville quietly desegregated, as did Hoxie, a town that lay a mere 100 miles north of Little Rock.

As recent historical analyses have shown, the case of Hoxie, in particular, has drawn out the wide discrepancies that existed in the responses of different southern white communities to *Brown*. At a July 1955 meeting of the Hoxie school board, Superintendent Howard Vance and the five other members of the board, Guy Floyd, Leo Robert, Leslie Howell, L. L. Cochran and Howard's brother K. E. Vance voted unanimously to desegregate the school. In terms of the rhythms and cadences of southern resistance, what is most interesting about the school board's decision is the rationale that lay behind that decision.[43]

The Hoxie board took their decision in order to 'uphold the law of the land'. Vance remembered simply that they had heard news of the *Brown* decision, and therefore decided that it should be implemented. To place their decision in context, Mississippi Senator James O. Eastland told an audience at Senatobia, Mississippi the month after the Hoxie board's decision that 'You are not required to obey any court which passes out such a ruling. In fact, you are obligated to defy it.' Eastland was serving as chairman of the Senate Judiciary Committee at the time of his pronouncement.[44] Clearly, there was an ideological chasm separating Vance and Eastland. The sharp differences in the approach of these two southern white men to the Supreme Court's decision can, on the surface, be explained by factors of geography and demography. Hoxie nestled in the rural northwest corner of Arkansas where there were relatively few African Americans, whereas Eastland represented Sunflower County, in the heart of Mississippi's Black Belt. What is equally significant in the task of unravelling the complexities of southern attitudes to segregation in the mid-1950s is Vance's stated rationale for implementing *Brown*. He later claimed that he arrived at his decision to desegregate Hoxie's school on moral and Christian grounds, as well as on legal grounds. 'I was raised to obey the law', he revealed, and in this particular case felt that God was helping him in adhering to the tenets of his upbringing. 'I know that I couldn't have done it without Him', he recalled, 'He strengthened me so that I could go out and do what was right'. The Hoxie school board, he believed, acted 'because they thought it was the right thing to do: because it was right, lawfully, and right, morally, and it was right all the way round'.[45]

Many white southerners shared Vance's belief that what they were attempting to do was morally, legally and religiously correct. The sharp difference, however, was that their concepts of law, morality and religion led them to support continued segregation. While Vance argued for the morality of desegregated schools, for example, one of his fellow white southerners argued for the morality of segregated schools: integration, it was claimed, would lead children to 'sink in delinquency, degradation, filth, total sin and the early destruction of the white race'.[46] Christian theology was clearly an integral strand of the fabric of segregationist ideology post-*Brown*. Where Vance believed that integrating Hoxie's schools was the will of God, pastors in southern churches such as Reverend James F. Burks believed that such a move was 'but another stepping stone toward the gross immorality and lawlessness that will be characteristic of the last days, just preceding the Return of the Lord Jesus Christ'.[47]

If the actions of Vance's school board offer evidence that, at least in the Border South, white communities were perfectly willing to desegregate their schools in the summer of 1955, much of the reaction that its decision elicited gives a clear indication that others remained deeply hostile to implementing

Brown. Photographers from *Life* magazine were present to record Hoxie's first day of desegregated schooling on 11 July 1955, and published their work shortly thereafter. Hard-line segregationists were mortified not only by the fact that a southern town would desegregate so quietly and peacefully, but also that such action was being drawn to national attention. Apart from the problems they associated with desegregation per se, such national exposure threatened to undermine two central tenets of the ideology of segregationist resistance: the segregationist mantra that desegregation was simply not possible because the people of the South would not stand for it, and that it was imperative for the maintenance of segregation that the White South appeared united in its efforts to stave off desegregation. There was a pressing need, as constituents continuously told their political leaders, for the South 'to try to solve the problem as a unified whole instead of State by State', and that the 'southern states must stand together'.[48]

The reaction to *Life* magazine's coverage changed the complexion of race relations in Hoxie dramatically. Hard-line segregationists began to flood the town with handbills and broadsides, and Amis Guthridge, an attorney from Little Rock who rose to become a prominent grassroots resistance leader in Arkansas in the late 1950s and early 1960s, was sent to Hoxie by an organization with the unequivocal moniker of White America, Inc.[49] A coterie of anti-integration whites formed around Guthridge and Albert Brewer, and Brewer himself attended meetings where such segregationist luminaries as Senator Eastland, Judge Tom P. Brady and James D. 'Jim' Johnson exhorted white southerners to more and more intemperate stands of defiance. On 17 September, Johnson hosted a well-advertised segregationist rally in nearby Walnut Ridge, having driven around the county to drum up support. In Hoxie, which Johnson also visited, Brewer managed to organize a boycott of the still desegregated school and a petition with over 1,000 signatories. By the end of the year, Johnson was openly arguing for the school system in Hoxie to be replaced by an all-white private school because of what he termed the 'unwarranted and unnecessary action of the school board', and because he wished to avoid the damage to the school-aged population's 'future development of character' that, to his mind, the integration of Hoxie's schools would bring.[50]

Although Hoxie was a small town in the geographic periphery of the South, events surrounding the desegregation of its school reveal themes of central importance to massive resistance on a South-wide basis. Its story reveals subtle twists in the complex ideology of southern segregation, not just because Vance defended the Board's decision to desegregate using the same touchstones that many massive resisters used to call for the maintenance of segregation. It also uncovers other ironies in white segregationist reaction that are often overlooked. When massive resistance was at its most intemperate, hard-line segregationists often made reference to 'outside agitators' who had come south to disrupt what they paternalistically termed the 'fine state' of race relations in the region. Indeed, 'outside agitators' became one of the catchphrases of resistance rhetoric, and attempting to lay the blame for disturbances at their door was an enduring motif of the campaign against desegregation. In Hoxie, outside agitators again aggravated the local racial situation, but this time they were white, they were southern, and they were segregationist. As Vance himself remembered, 'It wasn't local people. Our local people didn't care that much.'[51] Indeed, Johnson admitted that 'there's no question about the fact that I was a part of the outside advice and agitation. There's no question about that.'[52] In a bid to offset the impact of Johnson's particular form of outside agitation, the school board secured the services of maverick lawyer Bill Penix. As well as obtaining an injunction against Johnson's activities in the short term, Penix fought a protracted legal battle on behalf of the Hoxie board. It was a case that few judges appeared willing to take in the circumstances, but when retired Federal Judge Albert Reeves finally agreed to do so, he ruled that attending an integrated school was a civil right protected by the Constitution.[53]

THE CITIZENS' COUNCILS: AIMS, ORGANIZATION AND PROPAGANDA TACTICS

The nascent organizing of grassroots southerners in opposition to desegregation in Hoxie – albeit led by 'outsiders' – reflects a crucial development in the history and timing of southern resistance more broadly. For, in the summer of 1954, segregationists began to organize themselves into groups that soon became known as Citizens' Councils. The first such group was organized in Indianola, Mississippi, in July 1954. It was officially titled the White Citizens' Council, and was co-founded by the president of the Indianola Bank, Herman Moore, local lawyer Arthur Clark, Jr. and plantation manager Robert 'Tut' Patterson. Their overall design was to maintain rigid segregation in the South, and they sought to do so by vetting political candidates, countering the threat of the NAACP, and stifling internal dissent – or, in the words of Moore at that first meeting, to ensure that 'various agitators and their like could be removed from the communities in which they operate' in a bid to ensure unanimous local support for segregation. Contemporary observers were quick to latch on to the success that Citizens' Councils had in suppressing dissenting white voices, noting on one occasion that 'This is perhaps their most alarming achievement – to have robbed the South of the open discussion of the torturing problems that it so desperately needs', and on another that 'The whites, too, are subjected to the same terror [as blacks] if they dare to stray from the most rigid segregation line. The domination is total.'[54] This was to be no return to the open violence of the Ku Klux Klan, however, for the Councils' goals were to be achieved 'through the careful application of economic pressure upon those men who cannot be controlled otherwise'. As journalist Stan Opotowsky wrote in 1957, it was 'the start of a new network of racists that was to blanket the South'.[55]

To an extent, the Citizens' Councils and their influence did indeed come to blanket the South. Historian Neil McMillen has noted that there were some 90 Citizens' Councils and Council-related organizations in the region, and that those groups could lay claim to over a quarter of a million members just two years after *Brown*.[56] Many of those organizations chose to highlight their links to the Council movement directly by calling themselves the Citizens' Councils of, for example, Mississippi, Alabama, Arkansas, Florida, Louisiana and Georgia respectively. Others chose names that were felt, in some way, to reflect the White South's glorious and chivalric past, such as Louisiana's Southern Gentlemen, Inc., the Patrick Henry Group of Richmond, Virginia, and the Paul Revere Associated Yeomen, Inc. of New Orleans. Still others, such as the Citizens Grass Roots Crusade of South Carolina, attempted to use their name to indicate what they hoped would be the breadth of their appeal.

As the Charleston-based Grass Roots Crusade's title suggested, the Citizens' Councils collectively professed – at least outwardly via their myriad publications – to be grassroots organizations with local power bases. Some deliberately attempted to attract a blue-collar constituency, such as the North Alabama Citizens' Council, which was run by Asa 'Ace' Carter, a vitriolic racist and anti-Semite. Writing in *The Southerner*, the official organ of his group which he both edited and published, Carter attacked the region's leadership elite in numerous articles and editorials. If those leaders were to take up the reins of the Citizens' Councils, he argued, 'it will lead down the path of "gradual" surrender' and take the South 'down a gradual incline to the bottom of that mongrelizing abyss'. For too long, he believed, the working men of the South had 'allowed the politicians to handle us', offering ineffective and evasive bills that left the White South prone to attack but which kept those politicians 'in their secure position in office'. Such political forces, he concluded, 'kill every grassroots White people's movement that lifts its head'.[57] It was a line that a number of contemporaries took at face value, such as Hodding Carter III, who in 1959 referred to the Councils as a 'grass roots organization of Southern whites'.[58] The reality, however, was somewhat more complex. In the specific case of Asa Carter's North Alabama Citizens' Council, the emphasis on non-political grassroots membership was a direct result of a battle for members and influence with Sam Engelhardt's Citizens' Councils of Alabama, a battle which one historian has described as leading to 'rancorous infighting'.[59]

There was, in fact, little overall pattern to Citizens' Council membership and different groups' relationships to established power structures. The leadership of a number of Citizens' Councils was intimately bound up with the membership of the state legislature, especially in the Deep South. In Louisiana, for example, W. O. 'Willie' Rainach was chair of both the Louisiana Joint Legislative Committee and the Associated White Citizens' Councils of Louisiana, Inc. In Florida, the legislature had established a committee under Charlie E. Johns that had as its official remit the investigation of subversion. In practice, the Johns Committee was effectively used to delay the onset of desegregation, and the make-up of its membership overlapped so greatly with the Citizens' Councils that by 1961 the NAACP's Bob Saunders referred to it as 'a real Citizen Council Committee this year with no liberals'.[60]

In other areas, councillors followed Carter's lead and froze out local political leaders, especially where they were forced to operate in areas boasting relatively moderate, progressive power structures. It was not until the early 1960s that a Memphis Citizens' Council was established, for example, and even then its incorporation was largely the result of efforts made by Louis Hollis, head of the Citizens' Councils of America from the neighbouring state of Mississippi. Towards the end of 1961, 200 people answered personal invitations to attend the inaugural meeting at Memphis's aptly named King Cotton Hotel, where they were assailed by local attorney Marvin Brooks Norfleet, who 'blistered and scorched' against the local power structure. As the 'Editorial Opinion' of *The Citizen* later spelt out, 'The door to race mixing' in Memphis had been opened 'by a clique of politicians and moderates', in what was another example of a coup being pulled off 'by a small group of self-serving moderates against an unorganized and apathetic majority'. Indeed, the Memphis Council's animus towards local elected officials proved to be so strong that the local sheriff, Milbourn A. Hinds, was denied all access to Council activities, and was eventually forced to send an undercover informant to meetings to keep an eye on developments.[61]

Analysing the way in which the Citizens' Council movement was established and later grew reveals a number of themes that are essential to the salient debates surrounding the history of massive resistance. If the diverse nature of the Councils leaves some uncertainty as to their real constituencies, and in particular whether they truly represented grassroots southern support for resistance or were rather the product of shrewd state-level political elites, then the literature that they produced clearly does not. Citizens' Councils appeared in many different incarnations in numerous geographical locations and represented subtly different constituents, but they all shared a propensity for the massed distribution of pamphlets, broadsides, newssheets, newspapers, posters, booklets and reprinted speeches. Indeed, their collective ability to disseminate pro-segregation material was so great that the editor of Greenville, Mississippi's *Delta Democrat-Times* referred to their main tactic as 'offensive by duplicating machines'.[62] The content of that published material forms a rich historical source. Not only do the Councils' printed works reveal much about the networks that were forged between different resistance groups both across and within state lines, but they also reveal crucial information about the constituencies to which the Councils were attempting to appeal. Their style and content strongly suggest that the various Councils and Council-affiliated groups of the resistance-era were attempting to appeal to two different audiences. There was not one single dialogue of resistance between segregationists, but a number of quite separate conversations of resistance that ran concurrently. One such dialogue was deliberately designed to appeal to the lowest common denominator of base racial fears, and reflected a clear attempt both to impose solidarity and homogeneity on working-class white southerners and to keep their morale high throughout the long battle against the federal foe. The other most notable stream reflected a far more refined attempt to court those southerners who were segregationists in principle but unsure of their commitment to massive resistance in practice. With that second approach, a limited number of pro-segregation propagandists even hoped to convert those beyond the Mason–Dixon Line to the southern cause.

The clearest example of those two separate approaches is provided by two of the most cherished documents of Citizens' Council propagandists, Judge Tom P. Brady's *Black Monday*, and the rather less catchy *Congressional Committee Report on What Happened When Schools Were Integrated in Washington D.C.* The latter was a clear attempt to broaden the appeal of resistance by emphasizing the national aspects of the United States' racial problems, as well as to impose a sheen of respectability on resistance by quoting excerpts from a federal document. It reproduced excerpts from a federal subcommittee that was asked to 'clarify the many conflicting reports, rumors and misleading information about conditions in Washington schools' that had arisen since the District of Columbia board of education's decision, just eight days after *Brown*, to desegregate them.[63] It was no coincidence that the pamphlet's biggest distributor was the lofty sounding 'Educational Fund' of the Greenwood, Mississippi Citizens' Council, nor was it surprising that the publishers encouraged their readers to 'read and pass on' the pamphlet.

As well as being part of a calculated attempt to deflect blame from the South for wanting to hold on to segregated schooling, the decision to focus on the report on Washington's schools was also a vivid attempt to bring southern resistance into the national mainstream. The Educational Fund's stated aims were to 'publish and distribute nationwide' what it termed 'factual literature' putting forward the South's position, as well as to 'initiate a movement to enter the national propaganda media such as the national press services, television, radio, national publications and the motion picture industry' in the face of what it termed an NAACP-led propaganda campaign for the South to accept integration.[64] For those segregationists that were sufficiently astute to identify the need for national credibility, the report could not have better suited to their purposes if they had scripted it themselves. It included the president of the District of Columbia school board's testimony that he opposed the 'quick action' taken in integrating the schools. It noted that Washington offered 'the most favorable choice as an integration experiment most likely to succeed' but revelled in providing statistics on IQ, truancy, juvenile delinquency, 'sex problems', 'discipline', and white flight from the public school system which strongly suggested that the experiment had roundly failed. Furthermore it alluded to the fact that the NAACP had acted nefariously in trying to silence the subcommittee's hearings. In conclusion, it found not only that the model of desegregation followed in Washington was 'not a model to be copied by other communities', but also that it could not be copied 'by those who seek an orderly and successful school operation'.[65] Other publications followed in the same vein. Speeches delivered on the Senate floor by the South's segregationist representatives proved to be particularly popular, with reams of them distributed and redistributed by Citizens' Councils and their affiliates throughout the resistance period.[66]

The *Black Monday* pamphlet served different segregationist ends. Certainly, the decision to disseminate it so widely was taken for different purposes and to fulfil a different remit. The pamphlet's first incarnation was as a speech delivered by Mississippi Circuit Judge Tom Pickens Brady to the Greenwood Chapter of the Sons of the American Revolution. In its most polished form, it drew its title from the terminology used by John Bell Williams in the Mississippi state legislature to characterize the day on which the *Brown* decision was handed down, and was known as *Black Monday: Segregation or Amalgamation ... America Has Its Choice*. Brady himself later remembered that 'several men came up and said, "Judge, you ought to write that in a book." I told several men in public office that I was going to wait until June [1955] and if nothing was done about the problem, I was going to publish it.' In an indictment of the lack of early leadership offered by his political leaders, Brady concluded that 'Nothing was done, so I put it out.'[67] An expanded edition appeared in print under the auspices of the Association of Citizens' Councils as a 92-page booklet that sold for one dollar, and soon became what a number of historians have referred to as the 'handbook' of the Citizens' Council movement.[68] In the words of one of the NAACP's confidential informants in the Citizens' Council movement, 'This book is the segregationist case.'[69] Unlike the reprints of the congressional subcommittee's report on Washington DC, *Black Monday* was a clear attempt at a populist appeal to grassroots southerners. Brady himself admitted as much in a later interview with journalist and writer James Graham Cook, when the judge admitted that, at the time in which he was writing the expanded version, 'an appeal was needed in words of one syllable'.[70] The aim of that appeal was to ensure – in Brady's language – that something was done to counter federally mandated segregation in the South. More specifically, he argued that white southerners should unite in a spirited display of homogeneity, providing 'solid adverse public opinion' to ensure that the provisions of *Brown* were not enforced.

Throughout *Black Monday*, Brady's tone was so paternalistic and redolent of the Old South that even he must have realized that its potential audience was narrow, and certainly that it would do little to promote the segregationists' cause beyond the region's borders. Within its pages, Brady extolled the accom-modationist Booker T. Washington as the 'first great American Negro this country has produced' and claimed that it was 'ridiculous' to suggest that African Americans had played any part whatsoever in the historical processes that led to American Independence, before falling back on the region's pater-nalistic traditions to characterize the period between the 1870s and 1930s as one of 'peace in the South between the races'. This was not a proselytizing segregationist looking for new recruits, but one who was preaching to the converted. Brady exhorted southern whites to stand in defiance of the Supreme Court, and maintained that it was both their 'moral' and 'patriotic' obligation to resist *Brown* because the decision could only be part of a wider international plot to bring chaos to American society, and, ultimately, to ensure its downfall. *Black Monday* signalled the start of a cavalcade of printed segregationist polemic aimed squarely at the basest fears of working-class southern whites that lasted for over a decade. It was widely read and widely copied. Albert Brewer remembered reading it shortly after resistance began to congeal in Hoxie. In Greenwood, Mississippi, one resident remembered that Byron de la Beckwith, a white supremacist who murdered the NAACP's Medgar Evers, had previously 'stood on the street corner one day selling copies'.[71]

Organized resistance groups began to publish newspapers designed to keep morale high and to convince their audience that resistance remained viable, some of which appeared regularly while others were more fitful. The White Citizens' Council of Arkansas, for example, produced *Arkansas Faith*, which featured photographs depicting the integration of a federal school in Oak Ridge, Tennessee, asking readers to 'look at the leer on the negro's face as he socializes with the white girl'. In Alabama, the Montgomery Citizens' Council produced the *States' Rights Advocate* complete with grainy images of an inter-racial couple dancing under the headline of 'Results of Integration'. In Jackson, Mississippi, the Citizens' Council of America produced *The Citizens' Council*, littered with crude cartoons stereotyping blacks as avaricious, communist-duped simpletons, and with self-consciously populist editorials such as 'Pinkos in the Pulpit'. Elsewhere, Newport News' Virginia League produced *The Virginian*, a broadsheet newspaper which specialized in decrying the movement for civil rights reform as being backed by communists and led by the Kremlin.[72] Each newspaper urged its readers to maximize its respective paper's circulation, be it through calls to 'order extra copies of this issue of *The Virginian* for your friends, neighbors, employees!' or the *States' Rights Advocates'* simple command to 'Read and Pass On'. Many offered discounts for issues bought in bulk, notably *The Citizens' Council*, which offered a basic subscription rate of $2 a year, but, clearly anticipating something of a rush, discounts of 100 copies at $108 a year, 250 copies at $216 a year, and 500 copies at $415 a year.[73]

The Citizens' Councils may well have been able to boast solid membership numbers soon after their inception, but that did not necessarily mean that they had a monopoly on the dissemination of grassroots resistance sentiment. Throughout the region, imaginative and energetic small groups and individuals created their own news-sheets, often no more than one or two pages long. Such enterprises might not have been large in scale or in scope, but, as John Bartlow Martin revealed in June 1957, even Engelhardt's Citizens' Council of Alabama operated out of a single bedroom in a motel on Jefferson Davis Highway with little more than bundles of literature, 'a copying machine and a postage meter'.[74]

Before a Citizens' Council had been formed in South Carolina, Stanley F. Morse had established the Citizens' Grass Roots Crusade of South Carolina, with Charleston businessman Micah Jenkins as the group's energetic 'Religious Affairs Committee Chairman'. It soon mutated into the Grass Roots League, which, as one historian has noted, was 'highly vocal' but 'numerically insignificant'.[75] Certainly, its activities stand as testament to the fact that the numerical strength of an organization in the resistance-era South did not necessarily directly equate with the height of its profile. Starting two months before *Brown*, Morse and Jenkins released the grandly titled 'Research Bulletin No. 1', the first in a series of mail shots aimed at stirring the White South into action against African American civil rights protesters. In keeping with its pretensions, the bulletin was fully footnoted and aimed to guide its readers through the intricacies of the 'red plot' which, they believed, was driving civil rights agitation.[76]

Further to the West, Horace Sherman Miller pursued a one-man campaign to spread his views on white supremacy and launched a news-sheet reflecting his white supremacist and distinctly anti-Semitic views from Waco, Texas. Its piecemeal nature was reflected in the variable printing quality and constant switching of typesets between issues of *White Man's News*, but he did have ambition, asking readers to 'help me put out ten million' copies.[77] Miller was a different voice, clearly closer to the Ku Klux Klan than the Citizens' Councils, but he relentlessly pursued a similarly populist agenda, venting his fury at the Warren Court and Eisenhower's plans to force integration in the Armed Forces.[78]

Although the Citizens' Councils could count within their ranks 'corporation lawyers, bankers, industrialists, large farmers, judges of court law, local and state politicians', as well as 'several governors, United States Senators and members of the House of Representatives', they remained at heart a grassroots organization and their actions offer the clearest indication of working-class white activity within massive resistance. A contemporary *New York Times* journalist's research into the Council movement highlighted 'the essentially local origin of the units; and the fact that at least in their early stages, organization and operation have remained largely localized'.[79] The tone of much of the Councils' propaganda suggests that they were aiming to appeal to working-class sentiment, both in the style of the articles and cartoons that were continuously published and reprinted, and in the manner in which that material depicted the segregationist South's foes. Further evidence of the extent to which the Councils appealed to white working-class sentiment is presented in a confidential memo drafted in late January 1956, in which former Southern Tenant Farmers' Union secretary and notable civil rights activist H. L. Mitchell outlined the findings of months of research.[80] Mitchell reported that he was 'convinced' that the Citizens' Councils were also directed against trade unions. Having followed the December 1955 gathering of Citizens' Council members in Memphis, Tennessee, where an attempt had been made to unite the often disparate Council and Council-related groups into a united Federation for Constitutional Government, Mitchell could not help but note an anti-union theme. 'Nearly all of the members of the various committees of the Federation for Constitutional Government are anti-union', he concluded, 'and many of them can be identified as sponsors of state right to work laws' and as supporters of the Taft-Hartley Act of 1947, which had seriously curbed many of the rights that organized labour had been granted during the New Deal.[81]

In several incidents across the South, white workers affiliated with Citizens' Councils were reported to have been involved in breaking up attempts to organize bi-racial unions, and to have intervened in attempts to organize black and white workers who were employed together. At the Manhattan Raybestos plant in Charleston, South Carolina, for example, Citizens' Council members used a single campaign to attack the twin targets of bi-racial unionism and proposed integration on a wider scale. An estimated 80 per cent of black and white workers were enlisted in the rubber workers' union, but were still defeated in elections by a skilfully targeted segregationist campaign. Citizens' Council chapters published the names of black union members who had signed a petition to desegregate a local school along with the simple question, 'Do you want to belong to the same union as these Negroes who want their children in school with yours?' Other pamphlets distributed among the workers contained not a question but the statement, 'The AFL-CIO gives money to the NAACP so your child will have to go to school with niggers.'[82] For those business executives who had chosen to affiliate with the Citizens' Councils, such as North Carolina's Dallas Gwynn, the rewards of maintaining a non-unionized workforce in the South were obvious at a time in which northern industries were being lured South by the promise of cheaper labour. For white working men, the economic imperatives of ensuring that blacks had few rights in the workplace were equally important.

Across the South, the segregationist zealots who established Citizens' Councils and other similar groups saw dramatic increases in their membership levels either when particular locales felt that their segregated way of life was being specifically threatened, or when membership drives were organized to boost numbers, often by white supremacists from elsewhere. That is not to say that the Citizens' Councils were moribund when no particular threat presented itself – the incessant volume of printed propaganda is testament to that – but what was termed 'agitation', especially by the NAACP, did have a galvanizing effect on previously unaffiliated individuals in local white communities. When Council groups were first incorporated across the South, it became apparent that there were a number of whites in the region who, while favouring a segregated way of life, were either insufficiently committed to it or simply too busy to become active Council members, in much the same way as they proved unwilling to vote for segregationist measures that were too punishing on the public school system itself. For many, *Brown* posed a serious threat to their way of life, but it was a curiously ethereal threat, especially when timetables for desegregation were yet to be ascertained. When the NAACP began the process of suing individual school boards to force them to accept desegregation, Council membership levels increased significantly. After 15 months of intensive research into local Council activity, *Nashville Tennessean* reporter David Halberstam noted in October 1956 that towns such as Clifford, in the 'flatlands' of southwestern Alabama, had little membership to speak of. 'So far the Negroes have taken no official action to implement the Supreme Court decisions', he reported, but 'when they do, membership in the Council will climb.'[83]

THE CASE OF EMMETT TILL

Grassroots forces were mobilizing in the South by 1955, even if, in some cases, they needed to be physically roused into taking action. It was also becoming increasingly difficult to mask the fact that certain elements of the White South were openly at odds with the rest of the nation, especially where federal policy on race was concerned. Events in Mississippi in late August 1955 did little to dismiss that notion. On 28 August, a 14-year-old black boy from Chicago, Emmett 'Bobo' Till, was abducted and murdered while visiting his grandparents in Money, Mississippi. The disappearance of an African American in Mississippi in the 1950s was such a regular occurrence that it was assumed, rather than feared, that murder was responsible when Till's whereabouts first became uncertain. Just two weeks before Till's disappearance, for example, Lamar Smith had been murdered in broad daylight on Brookhaven's courthouse lawn.[84] For a number of reasons, however, Till's case attracted attention beyond the borders of the 'Magnolia State' of Mississippi to the extent that the details became well known across the nation in the months following his murder. Till, it was alleged, was unschooled in the racial etiquette of the South to such a degree that he had bragged publicly about his relationships with white girls in the North, and on 24 August wolf-whistled at 21-year-old Carolyn Bryant while she served him in a store in Money. Carolyn's husband, Roy Bryant, along with J. W. 'Big' Milam, whose wife Juanita also worked at the store, picked Till up four days later. The 14-year-old was pistol-whipped with Milam's army issue .45 revolver before being driven to the banks of the Tallahatchie River. There,

Milam shot him in the head with the same weapon, before tying a three-foot wide cotton ginning fan around his neck with barbed wire. The teenager's corpse was then thrown into 20 feet of water, and even though the fan weighed 74 pounds, his body was spotted three days later, 8 miles downstream.[85]

Many of the details of the case are known despite, rather than because of, the trial of Milam and Bryant. The details emerged because both men met *Look* journalist William Bradford Huie in the offices of their lawyer, John Whitten, when they had been acquitted of murder by an all-white jury but remained under bond on charges of kidnapping Till. It was Whitten who pushed the men for their side of the story, but Huie who published their recollections in a series of *Look* magazine articles. Aspects of the case were embellished and distorted by the time that they appeared in print, but they were nonetheless important in drawing national attention to the rationales of the two assailants. They defended themselves with arguments that were stoutly within the traditions of southern segregationist ideology. *Look*'s readership could therefore see for themselves the deep-seated mixture of rage and fear that the possibilities of miscegenation stirred in segregationists, for it led Milam to reveal that 'when a nigger even gets close to mentioning sex with a white woman, he's tired o' livin'. I'm likely to kill him.' He also clearly exemplified the segregationist South's ongoing and enduring fear of 'outside agitators', recounting that he had said to Till, 'Chicago boy ... I'm tired of 'em sending your kind down here to stir up trouble. God-damn you, I'm going to make an example of you.'[86]

A number of historians have argued for the Till case's importance in the history of the South. Stephen Whitfield, for example, has lucidly argued that Till's murder was an important catalyst in the civil rights movement, for it roused many African Americans ranging from Ann Moody to Cleveland Sellars to take action against such blatant injustice.[87] There can be little doubt that the tone of articles exacerbated black militancy. They were run under the sensationalist headline, 'The Shocking Story of Approved Killing in Mississippi', and included a photograph of a smiling Milam reclining insouciantly above the description, 'The man who shot Emmett Till relaxes in the cotton fields of the Delta'. As James T. Patterson has argued, the case vividly exposed the ultimate weapon in the segregationists' arsenal, that of the sanctioned murder of blacks below the Mason–Dixon Line. What is more, Patterson notes, the case brought to a wider audience the particular sensitivity that school desegregation – and the resultant social mixing that such a move would entail – held for white southerners, especially given Till's alleged crime against white womanhood and the fact that he was of school-going age.[88]

In the context of massive resistance, Till's murder and its after-effects had further ramifications. Huie's description of the attack, and in particular his detailing of the actions and later responses of the assailants, had a chilling effect on the American public. The inequities of Mississippi's judicial system were placed starkly under the national spotlight, not least when Bryant and Milam's attorney summed up their defence by telling the jury of his certainty that 'Every last Anglo-Saxon one of you has the courage to free [the defendants]', and the jury proceeded to do just that in a little over one hour.[89] Liberal northern sensibilities were further bruised by segregationist groups' widespread dissemination of leaflets and flyers that sought to deflect blame for the teenager's murder away from the White South via such proclamations as 'Emmett Till is Alive', that he was 'whisked away into hiding by the NAACP', and that he was happily living 'in California where his mother is now visiting'.[90] Till's mother did play a prominent role in the aftermath of his death, but in a very different way from that suggested by such segregationist propaganda. She magnified the brutality of the murder by taking the brave and dignified decision to afford his battered and bloated corpse an open-casket funeral in Chicago. Given the press coverage of the funeral, and, later, the revelations of Huie's *Look* articles, American citizens North and South were forced to confront issues that were often glossed over or ignored. The murder of Till made it starkly apparent that the most hardline of the South's resisters had effectively isolated themselves from the American mainstream. Indeed, Milam and Bryant were held in such disdain that they were even reported to have been shunned by many of their fellow white Mississippians.[91]

For historians seeking to examine the ebb and flow of southern resistance, Bryant and Milam's actions also serve as an important indicator of a separate development: the growing sophistication of certain sections of the resistance movement. Within a year of Till's murder, Mississippi's state-sanctioned propaganda agency, the Mississippi State Sovereignty Commission, took active steps to limit the damage that the murder, trial and subsequent reportage had inflicted upon the South's image. As Yasuhiro Katagiri's detailed research into the previously unopened Sovereignty Commission papers has revealed, a small-town newspaperman and political activist, Hal C. DeCell, was appointed public relations director of the organization in May 1956. By mid-summer, DeCell had managed to secure an unlikely appointment as 'technical director' to a documentary film by James Peck and George M. Martin, Jr. Their subject was race relations, and the pair were working under the auspices of the Fund for the Republic. By the time the film was canned, DeCell had proved such a successful lobbyist for the southern cause that the film's title was transformed from *Crisis in the South* to *Segregation and the South*. More significantly, perhaps, DeCell himself boasted that he had 'managed to make them remove the Till case'.[92] Here was clear evidence of a new approach from segregationists in one of white supremacy's heartlands.

DeCell's lobbying shows conclusively that, at least in certain segregationist circles, the realization had dawned that public opinion outside the South could not be ignored. As such, it is indicative of a major cleavage within segregationist strategy for it suggests that there were a number of southern resisters who had not only begun to comprehend the importance of managing the image of the segregated South beyond the region's borders, but, more importantly, had begun to identify the tools necessary to reshape that image. Where some southerners rigidly maintained the view that their northern counterparts' only detectable role in resistance was as 'outside agitators', here was a segregationist agency that clearly understood that such reductionism was no longer sufficient, and that the dynamics of the desegregation debate had to be recalibrated.

THE SOUTHERN LEGISLATIVE RESPONSE TO *BROWN*: THREE CASE STUDIES

It is testament to the multi-stranded fabric of resistance that, while grassroots resisters were beginning to establish themselves in Citizens' Councils, and while Mississippi's segregationist propaganda agencies were beginning to hone their work, a very different aspect of southern resistance was also slowly coming to fruition. During the final months of 1955, it became clear that the commissions and committees that had been set up by a number of southern states to formulate legislative rejoinders to *Brown* were readying themselves to make their reports public. Seven states had entrusted their responses to what was euphemistically called the 'segregation issue' to specially created legislative bodies: Alabama, Georgia, Louisiana, Mississippi, North Carolina, South Carolina and Virginia. The task was an exacting one, for each committee or commission had in essence been charged with finding ways to override, or at least circumvent, a Supreme Court decision. Unlike the Citizens' Councils, those legislative bodies were also hidebound by the constraints of the law. As most – but by no means all – commission members agreed, there was little point in agonizing over the crafting and subsequent drafting of legislative acts that would in due course quickly be overturned by the courts.

It soon became apparent that there were common themes in the ways in which those seven states' committees had designed their official responses to *Brown*, but it was equally clear that each of them had been acting under a different set of constraints. The internal political dynamics of the states in question, as well as a range of broader external factors, inevitably led each respective state to come to a subtly different answer to the question of how best to respond to the desegregation decision. In some states, notably Virginia and South Carolina, committees toiled under the added pressure that came from the knowledge that both states had been named in the original *Brown* cases. Elsewhere, states found that they could not effectively isolate resistance to racial desegregation from other pressing concerns, especially economic ones. That was particularly true of states in the Border South, where political leaders had begun to see the logic in presenting themselves as 'progressives' in a bid to attract much-needed northern financial investment to their respective state economies.

North Carolina and the progressive façade

North Carolina offers perhaps the clearest example of a state whose resistance plans were constantly tempered by thoughts of the image that the state was projecting north of the Mason–Dixon Line. State legislatures in the Border South had their eye not only on investment from private industrial firms, but also on federal coffers. As David Cecelski has argued, it was federal military installations in the Tar Heel State, especially in its eastern areas, that had been vital in extricating North Carolina from the pre-war Depression.[93] Racial upheaval and agitation were anathema to both sets of investors, and North Carolina's strategists did their utmost to avoid it. The first Pearsall Plan, as state Senator Thomas Jenkins Pearsall's first raft of proposals became known, was announced in January 1955. From its inception, the plan was carefully presented so as to appear reasonable in both tone and content. It remained devoid of the bluster of the Deep South's demagogues and avoided the political grandstanding of Senators Eastland or Thurmond. Instead, it decided to respond to the call to desegregate the state's schools with 'all deliberate speed' by quietly devolving the assignment of school pupils to local school boards. Such a resistance plan was not conspicuously demagogic or defiant, but benefited the state's segregationists nonetheless for it ensured that any legal attempt to desegregate Tar Heel schools would have to tackle each school individually on a one-by-one basis. Desegregation by those means, it was widely assumed, would not only take generations to complete but would also stretch the NAACP's resources to breaking point.

Governor Luther Hartwell Hodges, a former mill executive, proved himself to be well versed in the demands of progressive business politics. Indeed, the governor's office managed to present North Carolina's plans to maintain rigid segregation in public schools in such a way that they appeared to be the only reasonable way forward. Segregation was cast as a controlling mechanism on chaos, not because blacks were innately inferior or posed any specific threat to white womanhood, but merely because 'the mixing of the races forthwith in the public schools throughout the State cannot be accomplished and should not be attempted'. As the 1955–56 academic year began, Hodges was pointedly referring to the ongoing segregation of North Carolinian schools as being in line with the state's code of 'voluntary segregation'. As though to reinforce the message, a summary of Hodges' statements and actions was printed and widely disseminated, drawing attention to the fact that North Carolinians were merely 'acting in the tradition of their forefathers', and, in what amounted to a public rebuke of the unrefined activities of the region's more militant segregationists, that they 'have for the most part approached the problems created by the Supreme Court's decision calmly and without irresponsible and intemperate statements and actions'.[94]

By April 1956, Hodges had been so successful in controlling the terms of the debate that he was able to refer to Pearsall's proposed second tranche of legislation, which would permit local communities to close down their public schools by popular vote if threatened by imminent desegregation, as a 'safety valve' that would ensure that 'we don't have trouble'. Anyone who opposed the plan, whether on grounds of its excessive caution or its insufficient assertiveness, was labelled 'extremist' by a governor who appeared to have successfully positioned himself in the middle ground:

> Those who would force this State to choose between integrated schools and abandonment of the public school system will be responsible if, in the choice, we lose the public school system ... and find, to our eternal sorrow, the personal racial bitterness which North Carolinians of both races have avoided so successfully.[95]

Early historical accounts of massive resistance in North Carolina were taken in by the canard of gentility and progressivism that Hodges and Pearsall managed to construct.[96] It was not until a succession of case studies chose to focus tightly on North Carolinian resistance that historians began to peel away the veneer of respectability that Pearsall's plans had managed to attain. In a ground-breaking case study of Greensboro, William Chafe was sufficiently concerned by the illusory quality of the state's progressivism to refer to North Carolina's 'progressive mystique'. Others have been even blunter. Jack Bass and Walter De Vries, for example, termed it a 'progressive myth' and expressed surprise that it continued to be believed by both politicians and constituents 'despite ample evidence to the contrary'.[97] In a study that concentrated more intently on segregationist resistance in the Tar Heel State, Jonathan Houghton tellingly and convincingly described North Carolina's avoidance of the central tenets of *Brown* as 'sly resistance' to the Supreme Court's decision.[98]

The extent to which Pearsall and Hodges were able to manufacture an obdurate defence of segregation is reflected in the lack of desegregation that took place in the state's public schools, and reveals that the notion of the state as anything other than committed to the rigid maintenance of its segregated systems is misleading. Moreover, the evidence from North Carolina also exemplifies the fact that resistance did not have to be abrasive, brutal or demagogic to be successful. A decade after *Brown*, for example, fewer than 1.5 per cent of North Carolina's black pupils attended schools with white children, a figure which – in segregationists' eyes – compared favourably with over 5 per cent in Tennessee and Virginia, nearly 8 per cent in Texas and over 2.5 per cent in Florida.[99]

Virginia and the role of personal politics

If North Carolina provides a vivid example of the unexpected constraints under which segregationist legislatures in the Border South were forced to work when formulating resistance plans, then the state's northerly neighbour, Virginia, provides a clear indication of the added pressures that came with being named in the original school cases argued before the Supreme Court: the state's public schools were under specific court order to desegregate.[100] On one level, there were clear similarities between the paths to resistance that both states chose. Just as North Carolina's Pearsall Plan had been designed around a central strategy of local option and devolved pupil assignment, so the plan that Peck Gray presented to Virginia Governor Tom Stanley on 11 November 1955 had local option at its heart. Documents that have recently come to light suggest that such similarities were no mere flukes. In May 1955, the sometime counsel for the Gray Commission, David J. Mays, had met a cabal of high-ranking North Carolinians including Governor Hodges, the governor's administrative assistant Paul A. Johnstone, State Attorney General Harry McMullan, Pearsall, members of his Advisory Committee, and a scattering of state legislators to discuss possible strategic avenues for legislative resistance. Such intra-state discussions were far more prevalent than has often been realized. Two months after the meeting with the North Carolina delegation, for example, Virginia's attorney general was involved in over three hours of fevered discussion with T. N. Gare, Jr., secretary of Mississippi's Legal Education Advisory Committee. As one eye-witness account reported, the two men were 'trading ideas over possible courses to follow in the segregation issue'.[101] Mays' main conclusion from his May 1955 meeting with the North Carolinians was that the uncertainty that had dogged the initial musings of the two states' respective resistance strategists had yet to be dispelled. In fact, he believed that 'the leaders know of no solution which will retain both the public school system and segregation'. What they had come to realize was that local option assignment plans remained the best option for circumventing *Brown*, albeit as merely 'a stop gap, not an ultimate solution'.[102]

In other respects, however, the character and tone of legislative resistance in the two states could not have been more different. Although both states began on an equal footing with local option plans in the first half of 1955, Virginia's resistance soon veered off on a different trajectory altogether. By November 1955, Gray had added a significant codicil to his initial local option plan which transformed his commission's report into the first comprehensive, systematic examination of the possibilities that existed for legal defiance of *Brown*. If desegregation were to be forced on any Virginia school district, Gray proposed that state-funded tuition grants should be made available to white students who wished to attend private schools rather than endure desegregated public education. In late August 1956, Governor Stanley guided a package of bills through the Virginia Assembly that created a State Pupil Placement Board, which effectively centralized resistance powers by taking them away from local school boards and placing them instead in the hands of the governor. Stanley therefore had the authority to close any schools under direct court order to desegregate and to cut off state funds to any school threatening to integrate upon reopening.

In 1957, former Attorney General J. Lindsay Almond, Jr. ran a campaign for the Virginia governorship that was peppered with declarations of out-and-out segregationist intent. He pronounced that, under his leadership, white Virginians would 'oppose with every facility at our command, and with every ounce of our energy, the attempt being made to mix the white and Negro races in our classrooms. Let there be no misunderstanding', he continued, 'no weasel words, on this point: We dedicate our every capacity to preserve segregation in the schools.'[103] An effective and often colourful campaign speaker, Almond memorably raised his arm before Virginia's electorate and maintained that, if elected, he would see it severed from his body before allowing any integration to take place in the state's public schools.[104] North Carolina's governor had fought continuously to present his state's resistance strategies in progressive terms, but by the time of his campaign, Almond was clearly intent upon following a different course altogether. He romped to victory with 63 per cent of the vote.[105] By September 1958, the rigidity of Virginia's stance on resistance led directly to the closure of nine white schools threatened with immediate court orders to desegregate in Warren County, Charlottesville and Norfolk. Virginia was being led into an era of truly massive resistance.[106]

It is impossible to come to a complete understanding of the pushes and pulls that shaped resistance on a South-wide level without first arriving at a detailed understanding of how – and why – politicians in Virginia took the decision to shut down a number of the state's white public schools, for it was a decision that represented the ultimate circumvention of *Brown*. Historians have long been intrigued by the way in which Virginia's resistance strategies underwent such hasty changes of direction, and have sought to explain why the state's early resistance was transformed from something akin to legislative resistance plans in other states to something altogether more intransigent. As a direct result, the tenor and trajectory of resistance in the Old Dominion has been subjected to what is – in massive resistance terms – an unprecedented breadth of interpretation, counter-interpretation, and re-interpretation.[107] The end result is that three distinct schools of thought have emerged to try to explain why events unfolded as they did in the Old Dominion. The first looked to what V. O. Key, Jr. famously referred to as a 'political museum piece' for answers, namely what was known by its allies as Harry Flood Byrd's political 'organization', and by its foes as Byrd's 'machine'.[108] By the 1950s, it has been argued, Byrd had wielded political power for so long that his methods were increasingly anachronistic, and he and his leading lieutenants were simply unable to cope with the demands being made upon a modern state. As many of Byrd's core voters began to search for a political alternative to the Senator's old-fashioned *laissez-faire*, pay-as-you-go conservatism, massive resistance came as a revitalizing tonic for his regime and Byrd seized upon it with relief. As one historian memorably put it, with the issue of school desegregation 'the Byrd machine quickly refueled its spluttering engines'. In the same vein, *Richmond Times-Dispatch* reporter James Latimer opened a retrospective piece on massive resistance in 1996 with 'perhaps the most famous anonymous quote in mid-century Virginia politics: "This will keep us in power another 25 years"'.[109]

The second interpretation focuses not on V. O. Key's museum piece itself, but on the man who might accurately be referred to as the museum's curator, Harry Flood Byrd. In a less cynical view of events, it is argued that Byrd and his closest lieutenants were driven to favour all-out resistance not because it made practical political sense in the aftermath of the two *Brown* decisions, but because they were ideologically driven to maintain segregation at all costs. Byrd simply could not envisage a Virginia that was not segregated, and he was instrumental in driving massive resistance strategies to their most rabid extremes.[110] As historians of the civil rights movement in general have become ever more interested by developments at the grassroots, so too have historians interested by Virginia's patterns of resistance, and the third interpretative model to emerge has suggested that resistance thrived because it faced little concerted opposition. Many whites in the state were perfectly willing to go along with whatever resistance strategies were decided in the legislature, but only as long as schools in their localities remained open. Thus, there was no clear grassroots opposition to the strategic planning of figures such as Byrd and Stanley until 1958, when the decision was taken to shut schools rather than allow them to desegregate. As historians Matthew D. Lassiter and Andrew B. Lewis argued in a ground-breaking collection of essays, too many historians have lazily equated opposition to segregated schools with support for massive resistance.[111] An examination of what they termed the 'interplay between political events at the state level and the actions of ordinary citizens at the community level' gives a clearer picture. If it came down to a straight choice between resisting federally mandated desegregation edicts or closing public schools, the schools would stay open.[112]

While there is certainly truth in such an argument, grassroots sentiment for desegregated schools was strong in some areas of Virginia from the outset. White newspaper editor Lenoir Chambers, for example, consistently opposed massive resistance through the editorials of his *Virginia-Pilot*, and in doing so not only provided sustenance for the morale of those opposed to massive resistance at the local level in Norfolk, but also served as a rallying point for other pro-public school groups. Local teachers, organized associations such as the Norfolk Committee for Public Schools, committed individuals such as local naval base commander Rear Admiral Massie Hughes, and other 'well-meaning but less influential groups' such as the League of Women Voters, were able to operate as an effective coalition against school closures, thanks to the thoughtful guidance offered by Chambers. As one of Chambers' associate editors later wrote, throughout the school crisis he 'said and said again in his editorial column what the law was, and what justice was, and what reality was. He never wavered.'[113]

When Gray modified his original resistance plan by suggesting that state-funded tuition grants should be made available to white students wishing to attend private schools rather than having to endure desegregated public education, he began a move to a more staunchly segregationist position. His proposals signalled such a shift in the state's provision of public schooling that, under the terms of Virginia's Constitution, they could only be made if they were approved by a majority of the voting public. In January 1956, Virginia therefore became the fifth southern state to hold a referendum. In keeping with the character of Virginian resistance up until that point, many of the state's political leaders saw the referendum as little more than a rubber stamp for a relatively moderate resistance plan. Harry Byrd certainly gave every indication that he did. An official statement released by the senator in the run-up to the vote was almost conciliatory. There would be, he claimed, 'no occasion for precipitous action in the immediate future', and 'we will succeed better by going forward on a flexible basis', albeit for the time being.[114]

As with those referendums that had already taken place in Virginia's sister states, the vote was preceded by a concerted propaganda campaign. Two stalwarts of Byrd's political organization, Dabney S. Lancaster and Henry T. Wickham, masterminded the segregationist campaign from their base in the Richmond Hotel, from where Byrd was later to spark the debate over 'passive' or 'massive' resistance. Byrd surprised a number of people who knew him well not only by endorsing Gray's relatively moderate proposals, but by doing so in a calculated, public manner. Virginius Dabney, for one, told Byrd that he was 'glad you have thrown the weight of your great influence behind the Gray Commission's report. I am sure that will go far to put it over, but we will still have a lot of work to do.'[115] The patterns established by popular votes on massive resistance measures in South Carolina, Georgia, Louisiana and Mississippi were further repeated with the appearance of concerted opposition, again from women's groups and organized labour. This time, it was led by the Virginia League of Women Voters, the Virginia Society for the Preservation of the Public Schools, branches of the American Association of University Women in Virginia, and the state chapters of the Federation of Labor and Congress of Industrial Organizations.

Dabney had greeted Byrd's decision to lobby for Gray's proposals with mild surprise because the senator was not in the habit of lending his support to any measure that was not a clear, ringing endorsement of segregation. He was certainly not cast from the same mould as North Carolina's avowedly progressive Luther Hodges, and it was difficult to find any part of Byrd's outlook that could not be accurately labelled conservative, whether that conservatism was political, fiscal or racial. That position appeared to place him at odds with the moderate proposals that Gray had put forward, and it was even more surprising that Byrd's hard-line political machine campaigned so ferociously to obtain a resounding 'yes' vote in the referendum. In January 1956, Virginians approved the calling of a constitutional convention to ratify Gray's commission by a vote of over two to one.[116] Seven months later, the reasons for the hard work of Byrd's political organization became clearer. When Governor Stanley and the Virginia Assembly convened in a special legislative session in August 1956, they used the overwhelming public mandate for moderate resistance measures to argue that the public will was on resistance's side, and thus as an excuse to pass the bills that formed the basis of Virginia's most draconian resistance strategies. It was that legislation that gave Almond the legal wherewithal to close public schools for the start of the 1958 academic year.

The greatest anomaly in those school closures is not that they came after such a moderate start to Virginia's legislative resistance plans, but that when schools were closed it was on the orders of Almond. For, throughout his involvement in the early designation of Virginia's strategic take on resistance, Almond had remained hidebound by his legal training and, along with David Mays, shared the view that any resistance plan had to be workable rather than wishful. It was because of that stance that both Almond and Mays opposed Stanley's hard-line resistance plan in 1957. Fourteen months before he made the decision to close Virginia's schools, Mays recalled that he and Almond 'told the Governor that his stance would not stand up [in Court]' when it came to school closures. As Mays went on to recollect, 'it was that reason that the Governor quit consulting either Lindsay or me on the subject'.[117] Almond's shift from legal-minded conservative to zealot of massive resistance clearly needs to be explained. Somewhat absurdly given the circumstances, his bold change of direction had little to do with race, but everything to do with a deeper malaise that lay at the heart of Virginia's resistance politics. At every stage of the development of Virginia's official legislative response to *Brown* and *Brown II*, the tactical decisions and strategic thinking of the major players involved were bedevilled by interpersonal rivalries, individual ambition, and political fawning. Moreover, the impact of those personal rivalries was magnified because they were played out right at the heart of the legislative decision-making process, within the ranks of Gray's commission.[118] The Byrd organization's descent into outright resistance exemplifies the fact that not all of the decisions taken to maintain segregation during massive resistance were taken on racial grounds. Indeed, there were times at which concerns about race and the maintenance of segregation were wholly subsumed by factional infighting and personal political ambition. To certain figures at the forefront of Virginia's campaign, the successful prosecution of massive resistance strategies was not always an end in itself, but became a useful and evocative means to altogether different political ends.

Those involved in deciding the course of Virginia's legislative response to *Brown* were split into two camps. On one side was Peck Gray, who was supported by many of the central cogs of Byrd's political machine, including Governor Tom Stanley and two senators from the traditional segregationist heartland of Southside Virginia, Watkins M. Abbitt and Bill Tuck. On the other side was Almond, ably supported by Mays, who had managed to position himself close to the centre of political power but yet had always cultivated and maintained a discreet distance between himself and the closest ranks of Byrd's organization. At a time in which the members of Gray's commission ought to have been pooling the resources of their not inconsiderable talents and working through the efficacy of possible legal and legislative rejoinders to *Brown*, they were instead so at odds with one another that members of the two camps at times refused even to communicate. For, as well as being allies in the legislature's fight to stave off desegregation, Almond and Gray were also arch rivals in the race to succeed Tom Stanley as state governor. As early as November 1954, for example, David Mays was carefully noting the fact that, 'Involved in the whole segregation affair [is] a backstage fight for the next governorship.' It was not simply a passive contest in which the more talented of the two would rise to preeminence, either, for Gray and his allies were 'busily trying to undermine' Almond. As any commission insider could see, both men, in Mays' words, were 'trying to use the school issue to win high office'.[119] By the summer of 1955, that rivalry was clearly beginning to hinder the commission's ability to carry out its original assignment. Even Tom Stanley (the state governor) was refusing to ask Almond (the state attorney general) for advice, trying vainly to use Mays as a go-between. Mays would have none of it, and at one stage pointedly told the governor to speak to Almond face to face.[120]

The feud between the Gray and Almond camps was further complicated by a central paradox that lay at the heart of Virginia's legislative attempts to combat the two *Brown* decisions. Senator Byrd was the accomplished puppeteer of Virginia politics, responsible for placing his 'favoured' candidates in political offices across the state from courthouse to governor's mansion. Given the fact that, in historian V. O. Key's words, Virginia was the one American state that could accurately lay claim to being thoroughly controlled by an oligarchy, receiving Byrd's backing for nomination as a Democratic candidate was tantamount to electoral victory.[121] Generations of aspiring gubernatorial candidates in Virginia had needed 'the nod' from Byrd before running successfully for office, a fact that escaped neither Almond nor Gray. Both men were well aware that the most likely route to obtaining the senator's assent for their gubernatorial bid – and thus to become the 'organization candidate' – was to formulate an effective resistance plan that conformed to Byrd's own perception of segregation's future. The central problem that they faced, however, was that Byrd would countenance no deviation from absolute segregation. Even tokenism, which formed the successful basis for North Carolina's 'sly resistance' to *Brown*, was a step too far for the senator. The dilemma encountered by those entrusted with transferring that ideological position of maintaining all-out segregation into practical legislation was that none of them had any idea how it might be accomplished. The end result was that both protagonists, Gray and Almond, were forced to take public positions on the segregation issue that they would not by choice have normally taken. Gray was so intent upon pushing the entire Commission to a stance that was sufficiently radical to placate Byrd's zero tolerance approach to desegregation that he came close to resigning in disgust when his fellow members urged at least some caution in their final report.[122]

By late 1956, Almond's personal ambition to become governor and his rivalry with Gray was proving to be a greater force on his political decision-making than his legal judgement. It was strongly rumoured – and Almond himself believed – that he had only narrowly missed out on Byrd's 'nod' for the 1953 gubernatorial race that had brought Tom Stanley to power, and he clearly did not want to be denied a second time. There were even attempts by the Byrd organization to repair internal division and disharmony by offering Almond an appointment to the Court of Appeals in order to clear the way for Gray's gubernatorial run.[123] He refused. He was, therefore, leaving himself the unenviable task of having to outflank Peck Gray for the governorship, or risk disappointment for the second time in his career. The usual form for anyone connected to the organization was to clear their candidacy with Byrd before they publicly announced that they were running. Realizing that he had to outmanoeuvre Gray to stand any chance of electoral success, Almond broke ranks and failed to notify Byrd of his intended candidacy before announcing it to the media. He seized upon the opportunity presented by a trip that Gray had taken to Mexico, and declared his intention to run on 17 November 1956 while Gray was still out of the country. By the time Gray returned, public support had flooded in for Almond, leaving Gray to conclude that he had no realistic future in the race. On 6 December, Gray let it be known that he would not be running in the Democratic primary.[124]

The political sleight of hand that Almond had to play to secure the Democratic nomination for Virginia's governorship does not altogether explain why he went on to run such a rabidly segregationist campaign, especially one that ran counter to his own legal-minded instincts. Historians have, unsurprisingly, struggled to account for that apparent incongruity. For Ira Lechner, the attorney general turned governor was, simply, 'shrouded in contradiction'. Benjamin Muse could only note that Almond was a man who 'may himself have contributed to the malevolent hysteria' of the school closures.[125] The answer was far more prosaic, however, and once again had far less to do with ideology than with the exigencies of personal ambition. Having effectively stolen a march on Gray to gain the Democratic nomination, Almond was in turn himself effectively outmanoeuvred by Republican candidate Ted Dalton. Dalton had run exceptionally strongly against Stanley in 1953 during a campaign that saw him focusing not on race, but on issues such as the inequities of the poll tax and the flaws of Byrd's taxation system. Since it had proven to be a successful tactic, it was widely thought that he would repeat it for his platform in the 1957 race. As soon as he made his intention to run public, however, Dalton immediately made his primary issue the need to keep the public schools open. Mays described the fallout of Dalton's tactical decision, which 'immediately puts Lindsay in a deep hole since he must now go for "massive resistance" without stint, backing the Governor's statute that would cut off school funds in any county or city where any integration took place', even though, Mays continued, 'both Lindsay and I told the Governor that his stance would not stand up'.[126]

Such insight reveals that, in this instance, the traditional historiographical view is not irrelevant, but equally does not explain events in their entirety. The Byrd machine certainly was crumbling, and no doubt did latch on to massive resistance to provide a political panacea. Had it been less vulnerable, Almond or any other anointed Byrd candidate would hardly have needed to campaign. It is only when that vulnerability is viewed in conjunction with the atrophying political imagination of those segregationists attempting to devise resistance plans, as well as the skill of Dalton's political acumen, and the scale of Almond's personal political ambition, that the reasons for his adoption of what was, for him, such an uncharacteristically radical stance on resistance become clear.[127]

Louisiana: 'neo-populism' versus 'neo-Bourbonism'

As segregationists in other states begin to attract the breadth and depth of historical attention that Virginia's have received, the long-established view of massive resistance as the product of an elite, neo-Bourbon political campaign appears increasingly simplistic and untenable. What has become most apparent is that the calibre and tenor of massive resistance were greatly affected by the idiosyncrasies of state politics and the peculiarities of local conditions. That was not simply the case for the more subtle, delicate strategies practised in the Border South, either. As one historian has recently argued by way of example, the 'cultural and political distinctiveness' of Louisiana had a marked effect on the Pelican State's attempts to resist the provisions of the *Brown* decisions. Where the path to Virginia's resistance was shaped to a certain extent by factional fighting within one dominant political organization, Louisiana's struggle to maintain segregation was affected throughout its development by an ongoing battle between two competing political groups: the neo-populists under Governor Earl K. Long and the hard-line segregationist axis of state Senator Rainach, Leander 'The Judge' Perez and Attorney General Fred LeBlanc.[128] That battle was informed by, and played out against, a backdrop of great geo-political variance within the state, which saw Perez turn his bailiwick in Plaquemines Parish into a personal fiefdom of deference to white supremacy on the one hand, but colleges in Lake Charles, Lafayette and Hammond desegregate in time for the 1954–55 school year on the other.[129]

Earl Long evoked comparisons with his elder brother, Huey, both in his preference of avoiding the race question whenever possible, and in his attempts to expand the franchise wherever practicable, both of which set Louisiana at immediate odds with the traditions of the South's more conservative white supremacist regimes. While the Byrd organization's continued stranglehold on Virginia politics was predicated on the regime's ability to limit the franchise to like-minded whites from the state's Southside, Earl Long ran a gubernatorial campaign two years after *Brown* that avoided dwelling on the racial question and actively attempted to court African American votes. He won with 51 per cent of the ballots cast, which included the majority of the 160,000 blacks then registered. It was, in the words of historian Adam Fairclough, 'a resounding triumph of neopopulism over neo-Bourbonism'.[130]

Just as the continuing presence of deep pockets of reactionary political conservatism in North Carolina should not be masked by Luther Hodges' notionally progressive stance on massive resistance, so Long's victory in the gubernatorial race should not divert attention away from the coterie of committed white supremacists who remained entrenched in Louisiana's legislature. Indeed, it was the constant interplay between Long and hard-line segregationists such as Perez, Rainach and LeBlanc that gave Louisianan resistance much of its character. Long managed to shore up the foundations of his powerbase in the wake of his electoral victory by engineering the cancellation of all resultant run-offs, thus ensuring the election of his entire ticket – a 'remarkable piece of political legerdemain' by anyone's standards.[131] In response, Rainach embroiled himself in a range of underhand activities that was designed to erode black political strength in the state and improve the hand of hard-line segregationists that centred around a concerted effort to eradicate black voters from the electoral rolls. The Claiborne parish senator also used his powerful position in the legislature and his chairmanship of the Joint Legislative Committee to pass a raft of massive resistance measures. Interestingly, Long chose not to oppose them. Where Mays and Almond had chosen not to endorse prospective resistance measures in Virginia on the grounds that they would inevitably fall foul of the courts, Long in contrast declined to offer any meaningful opposition to Rainach's legislative onslaught because he realized that, in time, the courts would surely repeal them.[132]

The result was an often bewildering political atmosphere, but one which ultimately favoured a strong pro-segregationist stance. Almost two years to the day after *Brown*, for example, the New Orleans-based *Times-Picayune* reported on a joint conference held by the newly elected Long and 'the state's foremost segregationist leader' Rainach at the governor's mansion. Long was quoted as subscribing to Rainach's announcement that his segregationist cadre 'expects to work with the governor in maintaining a firm policy of segregation in the state', while at the same time repeating his frequent assertion that he would 'continue to be a friend to the negro'.[133] It was no doubt the realization that Long reaped tangible benefits from such political friendship that motivated Rainach and his allies to attempt to purge blacks from Louisiana's electoral rolls.

RESISTERS IN SEARCH OF HOMOGENEITY: INTERPOSITION AND THE SOUTHERN MANIFESTO

The political processes that led to the passage of resistance legislation in Virginia, North Carolina and Louisiana serve as a reminder that southern states were beholden to disparate political traditions. Most importantly, in this context, those traditions necessarily affected the trajectory, potency and pace of resistance measures in each individual state. Regardless of those local conditions, however, the former Confederate states collectively passed more than 136 legislative measures in the first three years after *Brown*, each of which was designed to counteract some aspect of federally mandated desegregation. In a concurrent development, within two years of *Brown* the South's resistance strategists signalled their first real attempt to marry southern legislative intransigence to a coherent ideology by infusing resistance rhetoric with the idea of interposition. In essence, interposition represented the extreme limit of the states' rights doctrine, for its adherents claimed that the legislatures of individual sovereign states had the right – and the power – to intercede if the federal government overstepped its legitimate authority in a manner that threatened the citizens of those states.[134] Interposition was not a new theory, but was exhumed in the resistance-era in the hope that it might transform the southern response to *Brown* from defensive obfuscation to a more constructive, active approach. While historians have often pointed to the long tradition of interposition in American politics, they have failed to agree on its first use in the context of massive resistance. Some, for example, have pointed to discussions that Georgia's Herman Talmadge had with his advisers in May 1951, while others have asserted that the first relevant reference did not occur until 'The Committee of 52', a white supremacist group from South Carolina, issued a declaration of principles that included interposition in August 1955.[135]

Charting the evolution of interposition from a seemingly outmoded and apparently forgotten relic of previous centuries to an essential part of the doctrine of massive resistance again reveals much about the true diversity of southern resistance. Close inspection of the rise of interposition can be used to draw out some of the abiding themes of massive resistance. Once again, it was Virginia that was at the heart of the first concerted attempts to propose interposition as the 'identifiable doctrine' of massive resistance, and it was largely due to the long-established channels of segregationist communication in the Old Dominion that interposition was revitalized. The 'father of interposition', at least according to the segregationist *Richmond News Leader*, was Judge William 'Wild Billy' Old from Chesterfield, Virginia. Old was so assured of the constitutional status of segregation that he unashamedly kept reams of resistance polemic on his office desk, situated in Chesterfield's courthouse.[136] It was the editorial page editor of the *News Leader*, James Jackson Kilpatrick, who ensured interposition's rise to statewide, then South-wide, and ultimately nationwide prominence. In a series of three editorials that were timed perfectly to coincide with the delivery of Peck Gray's report on Virginia's legislative response to *Brown*, Kilpatrick drew upon the work and legacy of Jefferson and Madison to renovate interposition. The 'principles enunciated so forcefully' by the two men during the Kentucky–Virginia Resolutions, he wrote in the first of those three editorials, surely has 'great validity today'. By the second editorial, Kilpatrick was talking in terms of the 'Right of Interposition'. On the third day, there were five editorials espousing interposition, one of which stated unequivocally that 'Unless interposition is made now, in a desperate effort to halt this process of judicial amendment of the Constitution, the States inevitably will be reduced to non-entities; and the whole structure of our Union will be radically altered.'[137]

Although Kilpatrick was a journalist by trade, he was no political ingénue. By 1955, he was an essential cog in Byrd's political machine and the relationship between the two men undoubtedly had a positive effect on attempts to promote interposition as the ideological centrepiece of massive resistance.[138] When Byrd was first reported as calling for massive resistance in the *New York Times*, for example, it was no surprise that he was also heard making mention of interposition. 'In interposition', he said, 'the South has a perfectly legal means of appeal from the Supreme Court's order.'[139] By the end of 1956, Virginia, Alabama, Georgia, South Carolina, Mississippi, Louisiana and North Carolina had all formally adopted resolutions that linked them to interposition, ranging from Georgia's claim that it was nothing less than 'the duty of the state' to interpose its powers in such a flagrant abuse of federal powers as that borne out by the Supreme Court in *Brown*, to Alabama's assertion that the *Brown* decisions were 'as a matter of right, null, void, and of no effect', and that, as a result, 'this State is not bound to abide by them'.[140] Ever the populist, Mississippi's James O. Eastland sought to broaden interposition's appeal, and to introduce it to the massed ranks of segregationists. It was, he told an audience of 4,000 at the inaugural meeting of the South Carolina Association of Citizens' Councils, not just a hopeful tactic but the only solution to protect the South from the desegregation decisions.[141]

The mounting exuberance with which Kilpatrick wrote on interposition was not always shared by those who were charged with the responsibility of transforming resistance ideology into legislation. Indeed, there is convincing evidence to suggest that a number of segregationist leaders were far from comfortable with the idea of passing interposition laws. As late as January 1956, the four southern states whose legislatures were then in regular session sent representatives to a meeting held behind closed doors in Richmond, Virginia, which 'observers' from North Carolina also attended. Governors

Coleman, Griffin, Timmerman, Stanley and Hodges, and such prominent segregationists as Walter Sillers, Roy Harris, Marion Gressette, Thomas Pearsall and Peck Gray could not reach agreement, however. They struggled in their efforts to come to a unified position on interposition, or indeed to formulate any coherent strategy for what Stanley euphemistically called 'problems of mutual concern in the field of public education'. Interposition was high on the agenda, but was by no means universally embraced. Some, such as Georgia's Marvin Griffin, were adamant that interposition was the way forward, but many more were far less certain. Referring to interposition's ability to 'nullify' federal edicts, Luther Hodges curtly announced that 'I do not believe our people will support nullification'. South Carolina's George Bell Timmerman, Jr. was equally nonplussed. 'We do not believe nullification will help us in South Carolina', he proclaimed. Whilst the state was willing to close down such public amenities as its parks, he reported, 'We are not prepared to bring a crisis in our schools.' Mississippi Speaker Walter Sillers remained more concerned by the legal position of nullification, which he believed left the South 'on thin ice'. In the end, the governors released a statement that outlined a four-point plan, but it was clear that accommodations had been made to those wary of the interposition route.[142]

The eventual, widespread adoption of interposition measures should not be allowed to hide the underlying unease with which many segregationists, especially those with legal training, approached the issue. Its rise to prominence does, however, reveal a number of important aspects in the segregationists' struggle. As well as demonstrating the impact that close political connections could have on the promotion of possible ideologies for resistance, the prominence that interposition attained in the southern segregationist canon is also a clear reflection of the many different agendas that individuals pursued within the framework of massive resistance. Kilpatrick, in particular, was clearly attempting to provide a rationale for resistance that transcended the savage polemic of many of his peers; one that would tackle the Supreme Court's decisions on segregation head-on without ever referring explicitly to race. In 1960, Kilpatrick reviewed his 1955 decision to rejuvenate interposition in a personal letter to Harry Byrd. 'Circumstances were completely different then, and the South most desperately needed a rallying cry of some sort', he noted. 'We needed also to get this dispute on a high ground of constitutional principle, and away from the muck of the race issue as such.' The Virginia General Assembly's interposition resolution of 1956, he concluded, was 'a temperate and dignified request to our sister States to join us in opposing and reconsidering palpable encroachment upon the constitutional rights of all States'. A number of Byrd's fellow politicians joined him in his enthusiastic embrace of the possibilities that interposition promised as a constitutional solution to the segregation problem.

It became increasingly obvious, however, that although the interposition campaign brought a number of pluses to massive resistance, a sound legal basis was not one of them. By 1960, even Kilpatrick was trying to explain to Byrd that 'It is absolutely futile to revive this business of "interposition" now, with any idea that it will result in a legal unscrambling of eggs.' His explanation for its unravelling was somewhat disingenuous. From Kilpatrick's point of view, interposition failed because Virginia's 'sister States proved as deaf as stones'. Clearly trying to dissuade Byrd from attempting to resurrect it, he went on to remind the senator that 'There is not the slightest reason to believe that their hearing has improved in the meantime.'[143] Historians have been less charitable. Referring to the 'legal charade' staged by the proponents of interposition, Jack Bass and Walter De Vries correctly surmised that, 'Once examined calmly, interposition was legal nonsense.'[144] Dale Bumpers, who served as Charleston, Arkansas city attorney through the massive resistance years before running successfully for that state's governorship in 1970, believed segregationists' use of interposition to be 'palpable nonsense'. It was, he recalled, 'One of the most outrageous doctrines ... that's what we fought the Civil War about!'[145]

Nevertheless, when southern resisters did fall upon interposition, the way in which they did so bordered on relief. It was a relief born from the realization that here, finally, was a binding agent that might be able to unite the disparate strands of the southern battle to maintain segregation. That resisters shared common aims had never been in doubt; what they had not previously identified was a common strategy that would allow them to achieve their goals. Within four months of Kilpatrick's editorials, a number of the South's political leaders sought to build upon the momentum generated by interposition. On 12 March 1956, Senator Walter F. George of Georgia presented a document to the Senate that had been drafted by three of the grandees of the southern political scene, Richard Russell, Strom Thurmond and Harry Byrd. The document's title, 'The Declaration of Constitutional Principles', immediately set the tone of its message, although it was deemed too unwieldy a title for popular use, and it was initially referred to as the 'Washington Manifesto' before quickly becoming known as the rather more colloquial 'Southern Manifesto'.[146]

Just as interposition had attracted Kilpatrick because of its ability to raise resistance out of the mire of racial rhetoric and into matters of constitutional principle, so the Southern Manifesto sought to defend the segregationist South's position via steadfastly American touchstones that included shared historical memory, the Founding Fathers, the Constitution and the judicial system. In that respect, it was a shrewdly pitched document, although its drafters patently could not resist descending into a paternalism redolent of the Old South with the claim that, as a result of *Brown*, the federal government was 'destroying amicable relations between the white and negro races that have been created through 90 years of patient effort by the good people of both races'. More substantively, the Manifesto argued that the Supreme Court had overstepped its constitutionally defined role when handing down the *Brown* decision, for in doing so it had taken on the mantle of lawmaker and thus had brought what many segregationists saw as a growing trend of judicial power abuse to a dramatic climax. The document also highlighted ongoing states' rights concerns by reiterating the southern segregationist belief that there were no explicit mentions of a federal right to interfere in state education systems in any of the nation's founding documents, and thus that individual states should have total control over their provision of public schooling. Its authors argued that segregated schooling was historically a northern phenomenon that had its origins in the 1849 case *Roberts v. City of Boston*, and that 1896's *Plessy* decision had established such a strong legal precedent for segregation that it had 'become a part of the life of the people' not just in the South, but in 'many of the states'. In continued recognition of the need to appeal to a broader constituency than those already wedded to segregation, the Manifesto 'commended the motives of those States which have declared the intention to resist forced integration by any lawful means', and, as if to reinforce that message, pledged to use 'all lawful means' to bring about a reversal of *Brown*.[147]

Under the close eye of Harry Byrd, the Manifesto went through a number of drafts in a bid to make it acceptable to the maximum number of southern politicians. By the sixth draft, the Manifesto was demonstrably less acerbic than it had been in its original formulation, with the result that it was able to appeal to a greater number of signatories. The breadth of that appeal was apparent when the document was first brought to public attention, for it boasted the signatures of 101 of the 128 politicians that the South sent to Washington.[148] On the surface, the Southern Manifesto had a galvanizing effect. The redrafting process had softened the harsh edges of segregationist ideology that had permeated the original versions of the document to the extent that it had become a useful tool for promoting the southern cause beyond the Mason–Dixon Line. Veteran civil rights activist A. Philip Randolph certainly feared the impact that the Manifesto might have, for he believed that it would both galvanize white resisters and suppress northern white liberal support for southern racial reform, and as a result would be potentially damaging for the African American struggle for equality. Writing to the NAACP's Roy Wilkins just four days after the Manifesto's release, Randolph noted that:

> In my opinion, the manifesto of the 100 Southern Congressmen is not to be taken lightly so far as its probable influence in weakening the liberal forces in the North in their support for the fight for desegregation. Already influential publications in the North are beginning to dilute and greatly water-down their expression of interest in the fight for desegregation and civil rights.

Randolph's fears shed considerable light on the purpose of the Southern Manifesto. It was designed to show conclusively that resistance was not simply a 'down home' southern election issue, and crucially that to view resistance to federal desegregation edicts as a peculiarly southern phenomenon based in racial politics was to fundamentally misread the situation. This was not about issues surrounding race, the Manifesto's signatories were suggesting, but rather was a reflection of broader national concerns over constitutional interpretation and states' rights. It was no coincidence that the Manifesto was first introduced to the public consciousness on the Senate floor, for its setting on such a national stage was seen as integral to its appeal.[149]

It would, however, be as inaccurate to claim that the Southern Manifesto was produced to fulfil that lone objective as it would be to reduce southern resistance to a single strategy. For, while it certainly improved the validity of certain segregationist arguments in northern eyes, it also played a role in strengthening segregationists' resolve within the South. The document, and in particular its published list of signatories, presented clear evidence to southern constituents – both black and white – that their political representatives were not about to waver in their commitment to segregation, and thus contributed to the eroding of the middle ground of southern politics. As Randolph continued in his letter to Wilkins, 'Of one thing we may be sure, that is that the 100 Congressmen and the White Citizens Councils in general are not kidding the Negro about their intentions to fight to the finish all efforts for civil rights.'[150] The signatories were not leaving southern whites in any doubt, either. The Citizens' Councils to which Randolph made mention latched onto the Manifesto without a second bidding. Virginia's Defenders of State Sovereignty and Individual Liberty, for example, dedicated a radio broadcast to the document which loudly proclaimed just how proud the people of the South were of each and every one of the Manifesto's 101 signatories. The Defenders also saw the document as its authors had intended, viewing it as a document steeped not only in southern traditions but also in national 'American' ones. 'In signing this statement', the radio address pronounced, southern congressmen were displaying not just personal courage but 'patriotism of a high order'.[151]

The apparent unity of cause that the Manifesto represented was an important facet in resisters' attempts to present a unified and homogeneous façade, but even such a high-profile document could not smooth over the uneven surfaces of southern politics. From a regional perspective, the presence of 101 signatories did indeed represent an impressive aggregate, and lends some credence to the thesis that the Southern Manifesto signalled the start of what could for the first time accurately be labelled truly 'massive' resistance. There is, however, also significant evidence to suggest that there was less homogeneity and more inconsistency in the White South's pursuit of resistance in this period than many contemporaries were willing to allow to be acknowledged publicly. Taken in total, over 20 per cent of the region's national representatives refused to sign the Manifesto at a time in which the segregation issue was a vital part of southern politics, yet historians are still content to label the document 'highly successful'.[152]

The reasons for such an analysis are deceptively complex. As historian Tony Badger has argued, the Manifesto had a significant impact in coercing a number of wavering political moderates into making a public stand against the Supreme Court – moderates who, given other circumstances, might have faced up to the segregation issue with rather more circumspection.[153] Although the number of *bona fide* moderates in southern politics was distinctly limited by the spring of 1956, Badger has argued that the promoters of the Manifesto were beset by a feeling which, if not quite paranoia, might best be described as a crisis of confidence in the strength of their position. In one of the ironies of the resistance era, 'both conservatives and moderates believed that public opinion was on the other side'. Nevertheless, Badger's analysis has shown that failure to sign the Manifesto was not necessarily political suicide, even in the segregationist states. While a number of notable liberals were coerced into signing against their better judgement, such as Alabama's Lister Hill and Arkansas' William Fulbright, a significant number refused. Two of those non-signatories, North Carolina's Charles B. Deane and Harold Cooley, faced elections in the immediate aftermath of the Manifesto in which they were repeatedly challenged by rivals who preyed upon their failure to sign. Whereas Deane was comfortably beaten, Cooley survived.[154]

Clearly, southern politicians faced a number of difficult choices when it came to deciding whether or not to add their name to the Manifesto's signatories, not least of which was the calculation of whether or not it would imperil their political futures to do so. That was an easier decision for some to make than others. North Carolina's Kerr Scott, for example, was so bewildered by the ramifications of signing that he at first said that he would, before changing his mind on the morning of the Manifesto's release. By the time his vacillating had finally come to an end and he had come to a firm decision not to sign, it proved to be too late to have his name removed. It is also doubtful that the Southern Manifesto ever conferred the national appeal on resistance that many of its drafters and supporters had hoped that it would. Those southerners who held ambitions of election to national political offices, for example, were never expected to put their name to the document, even by their most committed segregationist peers. In what was a tacit admission that close links to the Southern Manifesto would damage a southerner's bid for the presidency, vice-presidency or even leadership of the National Democratic Party, there was little pressure on either Texas's Lyndon Johnson or Tennessee's Estes Kefauver to sign. In that light, the drafters' attempts to use the document to transform the image of the segregationist cause from one of base-level racist reaction into something with truly national appeal had failed.

There were also mixed messages below the lofty level of the national political scene. The Manifesto's effect was sufficiently galvanizing to worry civil rights proponents such as A. Philip Randolph, but there are also strong suggestions that the concerns of local politics and attendant factional infighting remained a more pressing concern to many segregationists than the issue of promoting a united regional front on race. In Texas, for example, the state's peculiar political circumstances and traditions created a climate in which only five of the state's national political representatives actually put their names to the document, despite widespread support for continued segregation there.[155] In some of the states of the peripheral South, too, the suggestion is that racially progressive politicians underestimated the extent to which they would have been able to retain the support of their electoral base had they refused to sign the segregationist charter.[156] By spring 1956, almost two years after the first *Brown* decision, and five drafts after the Southern Manifesto had first been conceived, the South's political leaders were still finding it difficult to present a unified political front on the issue of segregation to the rest of the nation.

3

RESISTANCE RAMPANT, 1956–1960

MASSIVE RESISTANCE AND THE COLD WAR

'What I find appalling – and really dangerous', commented African American writer and activist James Baldwin, 'is the American assumption that the Negro is so contented with his lot here that only the cynical agents of a foreign power can rouse him to protest.' Given the pervasive Cold War atmosphere of the 1950s and 1960s, there was no need for Baldwin to elucidate further, for his readers would have understood immediately that those 'cynical agents' represented communists, and that 'foreign power' was an oblique reference to the Soviet Union. As his allusions made clear, there was a growing belief in certain quarters that the notable increase in post-war civil rights agitation was driven, in contemporary parlance, by the democratic West's new Cold War foes in the totalitarian East. Baldwin was, however, quick to recognize that the realities of the apparently simple, bilateral Cold War world also produced a number of complex and competing impulses. For, while certain segregationists strove to curtail African American ambition by tainting civil rights protest with the claim that it was financed, organized and led by communists, black activists were not slow to bring out the ironies involved in living as an oppressed minority within the borders of the self-appointed leader of the free world. 'At the rate things are going here', noted one of Baldwin's characters, 'all of Africa will be free before we can get a lousy cup of coffee.'[1]

Although Baldwin made his remarks in 1961, it took more than a quarter of a century for historians to begin to bring in-depth scholarly analysis to bear on the effects of the Cold War on US race relations. In an article published in 1988, Mary Dudziak argued persuasively that the precipitating Cold War had a marked effect on the federal drive for desegregation in the United States, and that the global conflict produced a climate in which it proved imperative for successive US governments to end the practice of segregation. Such pressures, according to Dudziak, formed a compelling part of the rationale for *Brown*. A number of scholarly works have gone on to highlight the various ways in which successive federal governments attempted to exert control over domestic race relations, and, more importantly, attempted to manage the outside world's image and understanding of internal US racial policies, as part of a bid to minimize the embarrassment that continued domestic racism might cause in the national arena.[2] Any State Department attempt to woo the non-white nations of the world into the United States' Cold War sphere was clearly incommensurate with the continued practice of open white supremacy within the nation's borders. In a remarkable, if unintentional, parallel with the development of the historiography of the African American civil rights movement, those initial works collectively focused on the top echelons of presidential administrations and Washington's elite policy-makers and power-brokers. Only recently have historians attempted to shift their focus to an analysis of Cold War concerns away from federal policy, looking first at regional political leaders and subsequently at the grassroots. That second tranche of work also differs from previous studies of Cold War civil rights by focusing not upon civil rights policy per se, but upon the southern white opponents of civil rights reform.[3]

Conspicuous evidence of continued domestic racism within the United States clearly had the potential to damage the nation's international image in the Cold War environment. It was not civil rights demonstrations themselves that roused the ire of newly independent non-white nations in the late 1950s and early 1960s, however, for non-violent demonstrations for greater civil rights were, and remain, an essential part of vibrant democratic life. Rather, it was the violent and often brutal suppression of those demonstrations by southern whites that shocked worldwide audiences: for successive US governments, it was not the civil rights movement that proved a weeping sore, but clear and ongoing evidence of the strength and persistence of massive resistance. For their part, massive resisters did not passively accept the new exigencies of the Cold War. Many segregationists were fully cognizant of the demands of the international climate and actively sought to maximize the potential that the conflict could offer the cause of continued white supremacy. As both sides knew full well, neither *Brown* nor southern resistance to it occurred in domestic isolation.[4]

It was in that context that the Cold War offered segregationists a rare forum to showcase an ingenuity and adaptability for which they are rarely credited. Resisters were faced with an increasing volume of calls to curtail their continued segregationist practices in order to placate newly independent, non-white nations in Africa, Asia and the Caribbean. In response, a number of segregationist spokesmen took to portraying events in those nascent states as clear evidence that, wherever they resided, Africans were simply unable to govern themselves. The strictures of white rule in apartheid South Africa, it was often argued, were all that allowed that nation to remain as a bastion of civility and law and order in an increasingly barbarous and ill-governed continent. As Thomas Noer has shown, one of the essential texts of southern resistance, *The Citizen*, strove to point out that 'Africans were not just unprepared for independence, they were unable to govern themselves.'[5] The clear inference was that the chaos of the Belgian Congo and the violence of the Mau Mau insurgency in Kenya would be transported to the southern states of the United States if African Americans were not to remain under white control.

As the central ideological and rhetorical precepts of southern resistance continued to be refined in the post-*Brown* 1950s, a number of segregationists exhibited such skill and dexterity in adapting to the demands of the global conflict that they appeared to revel in the new challenges that it presented, and viewed its strictures as offering opportunities rather than constraints. In the broadest of terms, the Cold War offered succour to segregationists in three distinct ways. First, as Baldwin suggested, it allowed them to expand upon existing claims of nefarious, communist involvement in the promotion of civil rights. Second, it handed southern resisters the ability to recast many of the region's long-held, traditional arguments in a new light, thus renovating a number of defensive strategies that were in danger of looking increasingly tired and anachronistic. Finally, it offered at least the possibility of transforming what was perceived to be, in essence, a southern sectional problem of race relations into an American problem of national security. Many segregationists seized the opportunity that presented itself, and turned anticommunism into a mainstay of massive resistance. Although a number of segregationists refused to red-bait their civil rights opponents on point of principle, to claim, as one historian has done, that southern segregationists refrained from using anticommunism against the civil rights movement until they were beset by a dramatic change of heart in 1964 is patently absurd.[6] Massive resisters inherited rich traditions of deploying anticommunism as a means of attacking the region's enemies from previous generations of white southern apologists. Birmingham's Theophilus Eugene 'Bull' Connor, for example, had made anticommunism a major plank of his initial election platform in 1937. When Mississippi Senator James O. Eastland used his chairmanship of the Senate Internal Security Subcommittee (SISS) to intimidate pro-civil rights campaigners, he drew strongly upon the template for domestic anticommunist witch-hunts and harassment that had been forged by federal red-baiters such as Hamilton Fish in the 1930s, and which were then perfected by Wisconsin Senator Joseph 'Tailgunner Joe' McCarthy in the early 1950s. From 1954 to 1958, Eastland served subpoenas to high-profile civil rights proponents throughout the South in the hope that appearing before his committee would taint their reputations. McCarthy's fall from grace had largely discredited such formalized anticommunism by 1954, however, and Eastland was rarely successful. Nevertheless, more informal pamphlets and broadsides were produced by anticommunist resisters which boiled with exposés of the supposed underlying pro-communist bent of the Supreme

Court, and questioned who was *Behind the Plot to Sovietize the South*.[7] In short, from the grassroots to the floor of the US Capitol, the rhetoric of resistance was infused with anticommunism.

Other staple arguments from the southern defensive tradition were also updated to reflect the new climate of the 1950s. That renovation is probably most clearly seen in the development of the states' rights doctrine, although it also affected arguments concerning miscegenation and religion. For centuries, first southern slaveholders and then the region's segregationists had argued that they should be governed from their respective state capitals, and not by the federal government in Washington. Most often, they predicated the validity of those arguments on the guarantees afforded by the Tenth Amendment, which stated that powers not delegated to the federal government should be retained by the individual states. By the 1950s, however, as contemporary fears of a Soviet-led invasion of the United States magnified, they were able to argue that the presence of strong individual state governments was of positive benefit not just to southerners, but to the nation as a whole. As one Citizens' Council radio broadcast put it, 'It is much easier for those who would overthrow our form of government to subvert and infiltrate centralized government than it is to go into 48 separate states and do the same thing.'[8] For the less blinkered supporters of massive resistance, and in particular for those who had sufficient objectivity to realize that the southern cause had to make inroads into northern public opinion to stand any chance of long-term success, the possibility of reformulating the former Confederacy's struggle against desegregation as a struggle of truly national importance was too opportune to ignore. It was a strategy that managed to amalgamate all of the race-related concerns of the Cold War. In much the same way as it was argued that splintering the seat of government across all the individual states would retard a communist invasion, so it was argued that, because communists or communist sympathizers underpinned all aspects of civil rights activity, keeping such activity at bay was an effective way of repulsing a Soviet onslaught. Defying civil rights 'agitation' in that context became nothing short of a national priority.

Given that segregationists had to find some explanation for the rapid changes that were threatening the fabric of their carefully crafted social systems in the post-*Brown* South, the resort to anticommunism is perhaps less fanciful, and less cynical, than is often suggested. The Supreme Court, which handed down *Brown*, and the Constitution, which formed at least part of the basis for the justices' decision in the case, were, after all, as much the segregationists' Supreme Court and Constitution as they were other Americans', whether northern white liberals or southern African Americans. In some way or other, segregationists had to explain – to themselves as much as to anyone else – why those central pillars of Americanism had conspired against them to such drastic effect. The belief that the Court was staffed by 'communists', 'red sympathizers' or 'parlour pinks' went at least some way to offering just such an explanation. That still left resisters with troublesome and largely unanswered questions concerning racial change, however, especially since the vast majority of segregationists had been brought up steeped in the paternalistic belief that the region's blacks were content with their lot. The 101 signatories of the Southern Manifesto had signed a document that publicly proclaimed 90 years of 'friendship' and 'understanding' between the races. Such 'amicable relations' were clearly incommensurate with the wave of civil rights 'agitation' that swept the southern states.[9] Something was upsetting the region's blacks, those paternalists believed, and it could not have come from within. As Baldwin's writing made plain, segregationists needed to believe that outsiders must have been at work.

By the mid-1950s, both the civil rights struggle and massive resistance were saturated in the concerns, ideology and rhetoric of the Cold War. It was a conflict that created a climate in which mistrust between East and West abounded. The understanding that most Americans had of communism and the activities of the Communist Party was filtered through a prism of propaganda, resulting in widespread inaccuracies and stereotypes. In the South, many of those stereotypes were purposefully shaped to reflect the region's traditional demons, and by the 1950s most segregationists shared a common set of fears about communists. 'Reds' were held to be purveyors of 'international brotherhood', a term that was sufficiently ill-defined to allow segregationists to equate it with racial equality. It was commonly believed that communists were not only content for members of different races to marry one another, but were also intent upon actively forcing that intermarriage upon the South. Finally, much play was made of the fact that communists were godless, accusations that were of particular importance given the centrality of the church to the southern way of life.

MASSIVE RESISTANCE AND RELIGION

Recent scholarship has been at pains to emphasize the importance of religion to the way in which massive resistance developed, although it is testament to the upsurge in historical interest that segregationists have begun to attract in recent years that two distinct schools of thought have emerged in respect to the church's position in massive resistance ideology. On one side of the debate lies the claim that, in stark contrast to the positives that African American civil rights activists were able to draw from both the organizational skills and spiritual nourishment provided by their church communities, religion exposed a fault-line in the ideology of massive resistance. Where slavery's apologists were able to look to the scriptures to provide chapter and verse justifications and biblical precedents for the institution of slavery, the region's segregationists struggled to find coherent scriptural rationales for societal separation based on race in the post-*Brown* South.

In such a formulation, the civil rights era can be understood not by seeking to understand why or how the forces fighting for racial equality came to triumph, but conversely why the White South failed to cling on to its long-established segregated way of life. The primary reason for that failure was the lack of direction afforded to segregationists by certain southern institutions, notably the region's churches. The South's religious leaders failed to espouse a unity of purpose and 'did not live up to the expectations generated by their elected political leaders' and that religion itself 'turned out to be utterly disappointing to the segregationist movement as a whole'.[10] It was in the often angry letters and tracts produced by laypeople and among ministers' congregations that biblical arguments were most frequently found as a justification for continued segregation, the most common of which were stories relating to the Curse of Ham, the Tower of Babel, and a passage in Acts 17 in which God set out the 'bounds of habitation' for separate nations. With one or two notably rabid exceptions, such as the Reverend G. T. Gillespie, ministers themselves were prone to be more moderate than their congregants, and on the whole segregationists had neither great confidence in, nor great use for, theological arguments in support of their position.[11]

The other contrasting side of the religious debate seeks to suggest that religious arguments did indeed contribute to massive resistance, most notably – though never solely – in terms of ideology. Where any such success was observed, however, it was within narrowly defined parameters and within equally narrow chronological confines. For, in the immediate aftermath of the first *Brown* decision in particular, massive resistance's proponents developed what amounted to a sexualized theology. The federal judiciary's insistence on selecting school-age children to be at the forefront of the drive for legally mandated desegregation served only to exacerbate segregationists' historical fears over miscegenation, for surely, segregationists reasoned, the social interaction of white children with non-whites would be the unavoidable consequence of their enforced educational mixing. In the segregationist mind, the social mixing to which naïve and innocent young white southerners would thus be exposed would inevitably accelerate the dilution and, therefore, eventual destruction of the purity of the white race. It was that deep-seated fear that led segregationists to return to the Bible to try to buttress their long-held social, racial and historical arguments against miscegenation with divinely sanctioned ones. 'The argument that God was against sexual integration', argues historian Jane Dailey, 'was articulated across a broad spectrum of education and respectability, by senators and Klansmen, by housewives, sorority sisters, and Rotarians, and, not least of all, by mainstream protestant clergymen.' An important subtext of the battle between integrationist and segregationist forces, then, was 'the monumental conflict between the integrationist Christian theology of liberation and its venerable counterpart, the theology of segregation'.[12]

Despite some obvious differences between what appear to be two competing interpretations of the role and efficacy of religion in massive resistance, there are nonetheless a number of salient points that can be drawn from both theses. The tone of the debate masks the fact that there is broad agreement between both sides on a number of issues, notably that it was civil rights activists, rather than their segregationist opponents, who were able to appropriate religious imagery and doctrine most successfully in the pursuance of their campaign objectives. It is also apparent that it was the segregationist South's religious leaders rather than their congregants who were most responsible for that predicament. Members of southern congregations were more than able to construct biblical justifications to buttress their position, if not in a way that supported massive resistance ideology in general then certainly in a few specific cases, most notably that of miscegenation. In an interesting twist to the traditional argument espoused by Numan Bartley that massive resistance was the product of the region's neo-Bourbon elites and thus was – in its origins at least – an elitist phenomenon, the focus on segregationists' use of religion makes it quite clear that, at least where religion was concerned, it was the South's grassroots congregants rather than their religious leaders that were more willing to push a hard-line segregationist agenda.[13]

MASSIVE RESISTANCE IN ALABAMA: SETBACK AND SUCCESS

While southern segregationists at both grassroots and leadership level continued to develop and finesse their intellectual and ideological arguments in response to *Brown* and the imminent threat of federally mandated desegregation, it was becoming increasingly obvious by 1956 that the White South would soon be faced with a full-scale confrontation on the segregation issue, and that the strength of the region's resolve in maintaining segregation would be tested. In one sense it had already been tested, albeit within the narrowly demarcated confines of the segregation of public transport in Montgomery, Alabama. Where historians have, justifiably, concentrated on the Montgomery bus boycott as the launching pad for Martin Luther King, Jr.'s meteoric rise to prominence as a nationally recognized leader of the African American freedom struggle, the episode also sheds important light on the actions of Alabama's segregationists. If the early musings of those legislators charged with leading southern states' respective responses to *Brown* revealed deep uncertainty in southern legislative ranks over how to proceed, the bus boycott in Montgomery revealed conclusively that segregationists at the grassroots and municipal levels were equally unsure of their tactics. Segregationists were originally faced with nothing more than a one-day boycott aimed at establishing a more equitable system of segregation on the city's buses. As J. Mills Thornton has argued, the transformation of a protest that was originally designed to work within the parameters of segregation into a 381-day campaign for integrated transport was largely the result of segregationist shortcomings, notably the intransigence of white municipal officials such as Montgomery's Clyde Sellars, and the 'no compromise' approach of the bus company's lawyer, Jack Crenshaw.[14] It soon became clear that local segregationists' established patterns of oppression had done little to curb the enthusiasm of this new generation of protesters. The arrest of boycott leaders at a time when African American morale was waning also proved ill-conceived, as it served to rejuvenate the flagging spirit of protesters, as did the local Citizens' Council's decision to bomb the homes of two boycott leaders, including that of King. As the preacher and Montgomery Improvement Association leader himself wrote in the wake of the Councilmen's violence,

> Threats and violence do not necessarily intimidate those who are sufficiently aroused and non-violent. The bombing of two of our homes has made us more resolute. When a handbill was circulated at a White Citizens' Council meeting stating that Negroes should be 'abolished' by 'guns, bows and arrows, sling shots and knives,' we responded with even greater determination.[15]

Montgomery segregationists' attempts to maintain systems of Jim Crow segregation on their municipal transport networks proved unequal to the resourcefulness of their African American opponents. In the sphere of education, however, Alabama segregationists proved themselves to be better equipped. In 1956, a young African American student named Autherine Lucy responded to the Supreme Court's 1950 *Sweatt v. Painter* decision by applying to attend, and thus by implication desegregate, the University of Alabama. Although Lucy had sued for admission in the same year that *Sweatt* had been handed down, it had taken five years of legal bartering to force the university – reluctantly – to admit her in February 1956. As Lucy arrived, so did a 1,200-strong white mob, consisting, in one journalist's account, of both University of Alabama students and 'outsiders', many of whom were said to have been recruited from a nearby rubber plant.[16] Although historians later estimated that it took 'two weeks' for a Citizens' Council to be established in response to Lucy's admission, her attorney, Arthur Shores, reported incessant telephone threats from callers purporting to be Council, and even Klan, members.

Almost as soon as the mob began to gather at the university, the scene became violent and increasingly uncontrolled. Jeff Bennett, who was assistant to the president of the university at the time of Lucy's attempts to enrol, recalled being pelted by 'eggs, rocks and mud balls containing rocks'.[17] It was the mob that was so clearly fomenting the unrest at the university, but when the board of trustees finally decided to take action three days after the violence had begun, it was not against the mob that they turned but against their only black student. Lucy was suspended on the grounds that it was not safe for her to continue her studies. When she responded by launching contempt proceedings against the trustees, she was expelled by the university despite the fact that the court had ordered her reinstatement. The one positive that desegregationists could take from the Lucy incident was that the university had been served with a court order to admit its first non-white student, but as victories go this was a pyrrhic one. The Lucy affair was far more important in the context of massive resistance for the fact that a segregationist mob had managed to secure a de facto victory for segregation, however piecemeal and however short-term it might have been in the first instance.

The Lucy affair also provided the first hard evidence of the extent to which Cold War concerns had permeated the mindset of both sides of the desegregation debate. Southern segregationists had previously sought to taint the *Brown* decision as communist-inspired, and the NAACP attorneys who had brought the *Brown* cases before the Supreme Court as 'Red dupes', but this was altogether different. As the prominent players in the disturbance stepped up their arguments, it became clear that what was developing was little short of a rhetorical battle for the right to claim the one, truly 'American' position, and therefore by association a concerted effort to label respective opponents 'un-American'. As one observer reported it, Radio Moscow wasted little time to press the claim that the action of the mob demonstrated that 'while the US in effect is attempting to impress a respect of equality and freedom on other peoples of the world, we cannot do so at home'. Martin Luther King, Jr. pointedly used the episodes of violence that had surrounded Lucy's attempts to enrol to remark that 'Until we come to the point that we in the south, as well as over the nation, will respect the laws, the finer law of the land, we will never have the type of democracy that will make our nation the leader of the free world.'[18] A number of segregationists, in stark contrast, strove to expose what they believed to be Lucy's own un-American credentials. Some believed that she and her supporters were being underwritten by East German communists, and that, in the words of *The Citizens' Council*, 'The Comrades Love Lucy'. Others echoed one southern woman's simple belief that 'Autherine Lucy was a paid plant I feel sure.'[19]

GRASSROOTS MILITANCY: MANSFIELD, STURGIS, CLAY AND CLINTON

The mob's apparent ability to stave off a single student's attempts at attending a previously all-white university took on added significance in the summer of 1956, when groups of angry white protesters managed to halt federal attempts to force the desegregation of Texarkana Junior College and Mansfield High School, both in Texas, and further schools in two Kentucky towns, Sturgis and Clay. Again, though, the numbers attempting enrolment were small, with only three blacks at Mansfield High and thirteen in Sturgis and Clay combined. Events in Mansfield were orchestrated by the local Citizens' Council, whose members wrote defiant letters to the editor of the *Mansfield News*. In response to the filing of a suit to desegregate Mansfield High, the Council demonstrated its ability to act as a hub of local discontent by organizing an open meeting which attracted an audience that contemporaries estimated to be 100 strong. School officials showed more sympathy with the Council than with their three prospective black students, with Mansfield High's principal refusing at one point to take down an effigy of a hanging African American that dangled over the school's entrance. 'I didn't put it up there', he was reported to have said, 'and I'm not going to take it down.'

In a clear display of segregationists' ongoing will to supplant Supreme Court authority with state power – and one that was not reversed or even queried by President Eisenhower – Texas Governor Allan Shivers ended the desegregation attempt at Mansfield by reassigning the three pupils himself, although not before he had made it clear that, to his mind, it was the NAACP and not the Mansfield mob who were the villains of the piece. Eisenhower had the option of trying to reinstate the primacy of federal authority by force, but chose not to. For the forces of massive resistance, there was little evidence that *Brown* would be given teeth by the federal government. In Clay, states' rights proponents showed a similar disregard for federal power. The town's long serving mayor, Herman T. Clark, openly mocked the Supreme Court's authority and supported a white crowd that had gathered to try to prevent desegregation there. 'The Supreme Court may say that integration is the law of the land, but as far as I'm concerned', he proclaimed, 'and 98 per cent of my citizens agree, the law of the state of Kentucky is the law here. When the chips are down', he concluded, 'I'm going to stand with my own people.' It was those people who had ensured his re-election for the previous 20 years. As it had in Texas, so the primacy of states' rights prevailed in Clay. Although the National Guard was deployed to restore order, Kentucky's attorney general later declared the four black students' enrolment illegal on a technicality, and they were summarily returned to their original school in Dunbar.[20]

In the late summer and early autumn of 1956, then, it looked very much as though concerted and well-organized local agitation, coupled to a governor or a state attorney general harbouring a strong states' rights sensibility, would be a match for the federal government's ability – or at the very least, its willingness – to enforce the Supreme Court's will as far as school desegregation was concerned. The visceral power of local grassroots intransigence was further evident in Clinton, Tennessee, where the National Guard had to be deployed as a last resort to quell the anti-integration violence stirred up by an itinerant rabble-rousing racist from New Jersey, John Kasper. The imminent desegregation of Clinton High School by 12 black students led to a five-day period in which tensions increased until massed white crowds of up to 2,000 people gathered regularly in the town square, and an estimated 50 pupils formed 'a teenage counterpart to the Citizens Council'. Order was only restored by the arrival of 650 National Guardsmen and a phalanx of tanks.[21] Nevertheless, as the Hoxie situation so clearly demonstrated, the overall South-wide pattern was complex. As one of Tennessee's two *Southern*

School News reporters observed in 1957, 'Communities almost next door to one another have reacted to the school segregation–desegregation issue as though they might be a continent apart'. Where Clinton boiled in the heated atmosphere stoked by Kasper, the Tennessee Federation for Constitutional Government was established as a Citizens' Council affiliate with the specific purpose of maintaining segregation in Oak Ridge, a mere 20 miles east of Clinton. It failed. Oak Ridge's school served the families of Atomic Energy Commission personnel, whose itinerant workers' regard for federal authority was clearly higher than that of the average southern segregationist.[22]

THE 1957 LITTLE ROCK SCHOOLS CRISIS

Towards the end of the 1956 school year, it was increasingly obvious that such community-by-community drift could not be allowed to continue. What is perhaps surprising, however, is that, when matters did come to a head – or, as a noted southern newspaper editor put it, 'when the chickens finally fluttered in to roost' – they did so in Little Rock, Arkansas, a city that has been described as 'among the least likely scenes for a dramatic confrontation between state and federal power'.[23] The city itself had the reputation of being relatively progressive on matters of race and the state's governor, Orval Faubus, appeared to possess all the credentials of a thoroughgoing southern liberal. Moreover, former governor Sid McMath was an avowed progressive, and Harry Ashmore and his *Arkansas Gazette* had a nation-wide reputation for reasoned moderation. Under the surface the situation was far more ambiguous, however, for Faubus balanced any such progressive idealism with a hard-headed and ultimately self-serving political pragmatism.[24] Arkansas' reaction to *Brown* was also complicated by an east–west divide in the state that was so pronounced that Dale Bumpers, elected governor in 1970, later recalled that, 'I thought I was governor of two states, as the cultures were so different.' The northwest corner of Arkansas had been a seat of Union sympathy during the war, and was thus fairly amenable to the prospect of gradual desegregation; the rest, however, 'was hardcore southern'.[25] It was a position reflected in the reaction to the Supreme Court's 1954 decision. Incumbent Governor Francis Cherry pronounced boldly that 'Arkansas will obey the law', and that his constituents would not react in a way that might see them branded as 'outlaws'. Many of his constituents in eastern Arkansas begged to differ, and attempts to desegregate a school in Sheridan in time for the start of the 1954–55 school year ended in ignominious defeat.[26]

The result of Arkansas' potent blend of progressivism and hard-line segregation sentiment was a genuine debate between legislators in the Arkansas General Assembly over the implementation of a Pupil Assignment Law. It was a debate that was absent from most other southern states, where legislatures simply accepted pupil assignment plans as what might best be described as the default setting of legislative resistance. Little Rock had a symbolic role to play in defining the state's reaction to *Brown*, not only because it was the state capital but also because its school system was the largest in the state, and because it sat astride the geographical divide that separated Arkansas' two political extremes.[27] At first, the signs were positive. Those entrusted with decision-making powers planned assiduously and planned early in a move that should have avoided the ad hoc mob pressures that had prevailed the previous year in smaller communities across the peripheral South. Two years before the Supreme Court had reached its verdict on the segregation question, for example, a plan to implement limited desegregation had been proposed by the Little Rock Council on Schools, an inter-racial alliance backed by local NAACP, Urban League and Southern Regional Council chapters. A day after *Brown*, the Little Rock school board instructed the Superintendent of Schools, Virgil T. Blossom, to devise a plan for compliance with the Court's edict. Just four days after the decision, however, the first hints of prevarication were discernible in Blossom's first official pronouncement. Rather than seizing the initiative, he placed Little Rock in a holding pattern and declared that the school board would wait to hear the Supreme Court's own implementation strategy before taking further action.[28]

Within a year, Blossom had formulated a coherent plan. The Phase Programme, or the 'Blossom Plan' as it became known locally, was as careful as Faubus had been in its attempts to appeal to a broad cross-section of the public. It called for the commencement of slow and limited desegregation at the start of the 1957 school year, but mollified hard-line segregationists by presenting no tangible or immediate threat to the city's separate school systems. Only Central High School was set to be desegregated for the start of the 1957 school year, to be followed by a phased system of tokenism that would take in junior high schools in 1960 and elementary schools three years later. The omens for a peaceful resolution to the desegregation issue in the city appeared to augur well. It was therefore genuinely surprising that the start of the 1957 school year witnessed a gathering of zealous opponents of Blossom's token desegregation plan outside Central High. On 2 September, the day before nine African American students were scheduled to attend classes to accomplish the de facto desegregation of the school, those segregationists had coalesced into a mob that was deemed to pose such a risk of lawlessness that Governor Faubus announced that he had no plan to deal with the situation effectively, and called in the National Guard to preserve order and, by implication, segregation.

Unravelling the reasons for the decay in Little Rock's racial situation, or more accurately in the collapse of the city's planned route to a peaceful solution to *Brown*, is complex. It is also essential, not just for comprehending events in Little Rock itself but also for coming to a full understanding of massive resistance more generally. Eisenhower's *laissez-faire* attitude to desegregation in small communities such as Clay and Sturgis offered no long-term solution to southern attempts to resist *Brown*, and it was clear that the appearance of concerted resistance in a city the size of Little Rock – and a seat of state government – required more than indecision and drift from the White House. As well as providing the most unambiguous sign to date of the federal will to enforce the Supreme Court's desegregation decision, Little Rock also presents a microcosm of the factors that shaped the strength and depth of resistance in communities across the South. Race was indubitably a prime motivating factor for the disturbances, but it was not the only one and could not always be disentangled from other stimuli such as local politics, deep-seated class antagonisms and gender concerns.

Events in the city provide further examples of the centrality of both political elites and grassroots constituents to massive resistance, for they were each important players in the build-up and eventual denouement of the desegregation crisis at Central High, and at times constituents and politicians were equally responsible for stoking the other's racism and demagoguery. The emergence of the Capital Citizens' Council (CCC) as a potent force exemplified the impact that highly motivated grassroots activists could have on the desegregation question. In stark contrast to a number of Citizens' Councils in the Deep South, whose executive membership lists were often indistinguishable from lists of elected state legislators, the CCC remained quite separate from the city government. The CCC's leader, Robert E. Brown, was an active agent in the escalation of tensions in Little Rock and openly courted controversy. In an attempt to inflame latent tensions over race relations and states' rights, for example, he published an open letter that simultaneously taunted Faubus's weak leadership and roused local states' rights passions by making reference to Texas Governor Shivers' earlier decision to override federal demands for desegregation in Mansfield.[29] If one southern governor could refuse to bow to *Brown*'s strictures, Brown was effectively arguing, then so could all the others.

The majority of the CCC's membership was working class. Many of them were spurred into active resistance by one of the provisions of Blossom's original plan for gradual, tokenistic desegregation. Blossom and the city's leaders had decided to delay desegregation until 1957 to allow for the construction of a third high school, Hall High, which was intended to take in white pupils from Little Rock's most affluent neighbourhoods and spare them from the traumas that most white parents associated with school desegregation. It was only Central High that was to be integrated as a result of the plan, although, as later historians have revealed, Blossom readily told the city's NAACP leaders that all three schools would be desegregated.[30] Once Hall High had come on line and opened its doors to the affluent whites of its surrounding neighbourhood, the children of blue-collar workers would predominate at Central High. Working-class families would therefore be at the front line of school desegregation while the children of the city's leaders and business elites would both be isolated and protected from the direct consequences of racial upheaval.[31] Where such class-based issues were central to the appeal of the CCC, gender concerns were vital to the establishment of a second grassroots resistance group in Little Rock, the Mothers' League of Central High. The Mothers' League's members supplemented the CCC's work with their own attempts at mobilizing support for continued segregation at the school, and, crucially, claimed to do so in avowedly respectable terms with non-violent, Christian appeals for the maintenance of segregation.[32]

Although gender-based anxieties formed the centrepiece of the Mothers' League's appeal, they were not confined to members of that organization. The working-class membership of the CCC freely mixed racial concerns with those of blue-collar workers more generally, and they included issues surrounding gender. As historian Karen S. Anderson has concluded, 'the stakes of the desegregation struggle included white womanhood itself', and it was the feelings of emasculation that accompanied many CCC members' inability to secure blue-collar jobs that spurred their resistance. Many feared that they would no longer be able to compete successfully for the affections of white womanhood, not only because they were unable to provide financially for their families, but also because they were unable to protect their white daughters from mixing together with black boys in the maelstrom of high school social events. There was an undercurrent of aggression beneath the masculine concerns of the CCC, but it was not one that was shared by the Mothers' League. A veneer of 'maternalistic respectability' was crucial to the Mothers' League's appeal, for it allowed the leadership to portray its members as eschewers of all forms of violence at the same time as they were depicted as hard-line segregationists. The Mothers' League's insistence on purging open calls to violence from the rhetoric of the group's supporters and members paid dividends. It attracted a broader base of support from local concerned whites, and was even sufficient to sway the Federal Bureau of Investigation's J. Edgar Hoover, who explained to Eisenhower that he should not send federal troops in to quell the crowds gathered at Central High. The presence of so many women and church ministers in the midst of those crowds suggested – to Hoover at least – that they could not be seen as legitimate targets.[33]

While the grassroots continued to raise their profile, Faubus began to look for ways of appealing to their segregationist sensibilities. His early response to impending desegregation in Little Rock's schools can only be described as one of benign drift, but as his campaign for re-election began to take shape in early 1956, he became far more animated in his defence of segregation. In part, he was driven to take a more radical stance by the avowedly segregationist candidacy of one of his opponents, the rabidly demagogic Jim Johnson, who was fresh from his attempts to whip up pro-segregationist sentiment in Hoxie. Wider events also conspired to convince Faubus that he had little to gain from enforcing desegregation, most notably the Supreme

Court's judgment in *Brown II* and Eisenhower's reluctance to become person-ally involved in enforcing the original *Brown* decision in Texas. Ever the pragmatic and resourceful political operator, Faubus was even able to couch his new-found harder line on the maintenance of segregation in terms that would appeal to his moderate support base, much as Luther Hodges was able to do in North Carolina. Faubus moved first to set up a five-man committee under State Board of Education Chairman Marvin E. Bird. When the commit-tee produced a far less progressive plan than Blossom's, the governor quickly endorsed it. By doing so, he managed simultaneously to impinge upon parts of Johnson's natural constituency as a supporter of segregation and to portray himself as merely adhering to the sensible course outlined by a state legislative committee.[34]

If Faubus's creation of a segregationist edifice was built upon the shifting sands of political pragmatism, other leaders descended upon Little Rock determined to shore up segregation on more solid ideological foundations. Little Rock furniture dealer Amis Guthridge and Dallas radio's Reverend J. A. Lovell provided vocal support for the segregationist rationale of the CCC, while Georgia's Governor Marvin Griffin and Council leader Roy V. Harris performed their duties as 'roving ambassadors of resistance', appear-ing at a CCC fundraiser in August, and puffing up Faubus's segregationist credentials by agreeing with his request that they stay at the governor's mansion.[35] There were attempts to rouse what one writer referred to as 'Faubus's rabble' to a tumultuous display of regional obduracy with dark, demagogic rhetoric, but there were also simultaneous appeals to broader national opinion aimed at explaining the reasons that lay behind the segre-gationists' determined stance at Little Rock.

The clearest example of the latter appeared at the beginning of the year when Thomas R. Waring, editor of South Carolina's *Charleston News and Courier*, strove to explain why, despite the Supreme Court's ruling, 'few White Southerners are able to accept the prospect of mingling white and Negro pupils'. Waring catalogued the reasons for those objections in five distinct categories: 'health', including whites' worry that 'the incidence of venereal disease ... is much greater among Negroes than among whites'; 'home environment', which, due to the slow growth of a black middle class, led to what Waring perceived as the continuation of master–slave relation-ships between blacks and whites in the home; 'marital habits', which, he claimed, were so lax among blacks that many did not bother to observe marriage conventions, resulting in such sexual profligacy that 'illegitimacy has little if any stigma'; 'crime', which, the author noted, 'has been more prevalent among Negroes than among white people in the South' for 'many years'; and finally 'intellectual development', which was held to be so low among African Americans that the first generation of whites to be schooled in mixed classrooms would surely suffer, even though whites were in the process of 'rubbing off white civilization onto the colored children'. Such was public opinion in the South, Waring reported. 'That opinion is a fact. It exists', he argued, before leaving readers with a simple rhetorical question in explanation of many white southerners' position on school desegregation. 'Which would you *really* put first: your theory of racial justice, or justice to your own child?'[36]

Faubus clearly believed he knew what the resounding answer to such a question would be among his constituents. By calling out the National Guard to, in his words, 'restore the peace and good order of this community', he was in effect interposing states' rights before the might of the federal judiciary, for the Guard blocked the admission of the nine African American pupils attempting to desegregate Central High and continued to do so for a further 18 days. Judge Ronald Davies, sitting on the federal district court in Little Rock, attempted to redress the balance in favour of the federal judiciary, ordering the US attorney general to file a petition for an injunction against the obstructive behaviour of Faubus and the National Guard on 9 September. On 20 September, after a day of hearings, Davies formally enjoined the governor and the Guard from any further attempts at avoiding desegregation.[37] That contact between the federal judiciary, in the guise of Davies, and state-centred power, personified by Faubus, was not the only direct clash between the contested ideologies of state and federal primacy during the Little Rock campaign. For, as soon as it became clear that the situation in Little Rock was heading towards a crisis of state–federal relations, Faubus began what became an ongoing – if sporadic – dialogue with the White House. Eisenhower, however, was reluctant to get actively involved, not least because he was himself drawn towards the doctrine of states' rights, and had been cautioned by his close friend, South Carolina's Jimmy Byrnes, that chaotic violence would surely follow any desegregation in the South that was forced through by agents of the federal government.[38]

That dialogue with the presidential administration had been initiated by Faubus in August 1957 as part of an attempt to deflect blame for Little Rock's impending crisis away from the governor's mansion. The fallout from those discussions provides a clear picture of the extremely delicate position in which the region's political leaders found themselves in the massive resistance years. Faubus was clearly unwilling to be the first such leader to put his name to a concrete strategy of defiance in the face of concerted federal attempts to ensure the desegregation of schools under his control. His only viable alternative was to consort with the federal government or, at the very least, to try to ascertain from federal representatives the extent to which they were minded to enforce the provisions of *Brown* in the face of concerted resistance. Such a move appears safer in theory, but in practice was fraught with dangers. When, for example, details of Faubus's conversations with the Justice Department's Arthur B. Caldwell were leaked to the press, the governor found himself facing altogether different pressures, this time from his own constituents as they tried to come to terms with the fact that their anointed leader appeared willing to broker secret deals with the federal authorities on matters of race. It was a political gamble, and, for Faubus, it was one that failed at every level. The leak compromised his authority locally, and the conversations themselves gave him little succour, since the subtext of Caldwell's response was that the federal government was as ill-prepared and bereft of clear plans as Faubus himself appeared to be. A president that had never publicly endorsed the *Brown* decision clearly did not want to become embroiled in Faubus's crisis.[39]

Nevertheless, on 24 September, Eisenhower was moved to federalize the National Guard to fill the void left by Judge Davies's decision. The federal authorities were working on the assumption that the removal of Faubus's control over the troops stationed at Little Rock would ensure the quiet enrolment of the nine African American students who had been assigned to Central High. Any hope of such a peaceful resolution was fast thwarted by the continued presence of an angry white mob outside the school. By the morning of 24 September, Mayor Woodrow Mann reported that the city was close to chaos, and Eisenhower sent in a 1,000-strong battle group from the 101st Airborne. As if the troops themselves were not a sufficient symbol of the deployment of the federal government's might, one native Arkansan onlooker also reported an invasion of 'so many FBI agents [that] they created a problem of hotel accommodations'.[40] Faubus, it appeared, had lost the battle to maintain segregation in the city's schools.

There are a number of disparate arguments that can be made to suggest that Little Rock was not the tragedy for the segregationist cause that has long been described, however. Taken together, those arguments make a compelling case. Faubus, once a genuinely moderate and progressive governor, was re-elected to an unprecedented third term as governor because of his new-found segregationist streak, and went on to manage a further three successful runs at the governorship after 1958. In doing so, he showed that there were votes to be gained not from overseeing the implementation of *Brown*, but in ensuring that Blossom's smooth plan of token integration was unceremoniously derailed. There is also increasing evidence to suggest that Blossom's long-term goal was never the one of smooth, phased desegregation over a number of years that his plan – on the surface at least – suggested, but was instead a far more malevolent ruse to ensure 'minimum compliance' with *Brown*. Whilst Little Rock's superintendent of schools never tired of explaining publicly to black audiences that his Phase Plan provided a workable framework for delivering the provisions of *Brown*, in private he reassured concerned whites that his plan would provide 'the least amount of integration over the longest period', and quickly devised ways of diluting its effectiveness.[41]

From a wider perspective, the Little Rock crisis demonstrated to grass-roots segregationists across the South that their actions could have a significant impact on the course of their political masters' defence of segregation.

Certainly, the members of the Mothers' League of Central High were prime movers in the dissemination of rumours that violence was imminent in Little Rock as desegregation approached, and they also played a vital role in encouraging the mob to gather outside the school. It was also the political authorities' inability to grasp the real fears of many of their constituents that precipitated organized segregationist action. As journalist Roy Reed explained, the 'fatal flaw' in Blossom's Phase Plan lay in the domineering school superintendent's neglect of white working-class mothers' concerns. Although it was those mothers' children who were to be at the coal face of school desegregation, they were never properly consulted on their apprehensions by Blossom as he was drawing up his strategy, and, as a result, their greatest fears were never assuaged.[42]

From a segregationist point of view, Little Rock also provided a collective historical experience from which a rich source of rhetoric and symbolism emerged. The obvious similarities between the post-Civil War Reconstruction period and the deployment of federal forces in the Arkansas capital simply could not be missed by southern advocates of states' rights, many of whom had begun to draw lurid parallels between the two 'invasions' long before Faubus's National Guard had been federalized.[43] As historians have begun to concentrate on the rhetoric and ideology of segregationists, so Little Rock's importance to the tone of massive resistance in general has started to become clear. For some, it was central to the creation in resisters' minds of a potent amalgam of fears based round white emasculation, inter-racial sex and the loss of parents' ability to protect their children. The ubiquitous presence of 'Remember Little Rock' stickers, stamps and decals from 1957 onwards, coupled with the emotive silhouetted insignia of infantrymen, bayonets at the ready, fending off young schoolgirls, provided a shorthand précis of many of those fears and seared them into the segregationist South's collective consciousness and imagination. A local newspaper editor, for example, noted that the image was carved into a seal that adorned every envelope that left the headquarters of the Southern Citizens' Councils, stuffed with segregationist propaganda.[44]

Historian Karen S. Anderson has also argued that events surrounding attempted school desegregation in Arkansas helped to define a 'masculinist rhetoric of honour and power' as segregationists played upon the helplessness of male parents, defenceless against a brutal external force intent upon ensuring the integration of their children's schools. Combined with those fears of masculine powerlessness, the state's leading segregationists also strove to create a 'sexually freighted fear of racial change' by highlighting the fact that the integration of schools would inevitably result in social intermingling, which, given the South's long-held stereotype of black men as sexually predatory, could only lead to miscegenation. The ceding of white supremacy to any form of equality with African Americans, Anderson argued, was nothing short of a 'humiliating capitulation' for white segregationist men.[45]

For Anderson, then, issues of gender had an important impact on the tenor of Little Rock-related resistance rhetoric. For others, it was the concurrent development of Cold War concerns that lent added piquancy to the debates surrounding desegregation at the time of the Little Rock crisis, not least because on 4 October, less than a fortnight after Eisenhower had federalized the National Guard, the Soviet Union successfully launched its Sputnik satellite into orbit. Little Rock and Sputnik shared front pages in the South, across the nation and throughout the world. To some Americans, it was a coincidence that caused great embarrassment, for it vividly contrasted the success of the Soviets' space programme with the ignominious failure of US racial policies. Contemporary commentators, noticeably *Arkansas Gazette* executive editor and Pulitzer Prizewinner Harry Ashmore, drew attention to the way in which the desegregation struggle in Little Rock had attracted an audience from across the global theatre of the Cold War. Ashmore admitted to feeling as though he had himself been turned into part of a sightseeing tour for 'a seemingly endless stream' of visitors who came 'to view the scene of the Battle of Little Rock – small, brown men from the Orient, lady parliamentary members from Norway, [and] earnest students from Eastern universities'. With Soviet propaganda reaching the crest of a wave of scientific advancement, Little Rock was, in contrast, 'about as handy a package as the Russians have had handed them since they set out to woo the colored peoples of the earth'.[46]

On a more prosaic level away from the larger contextual picture painted by Ashmore, segregationists sought to come to terms with the exigencies of the Cold War and the federal 'invasion' of the Arkansas capital. As the Autherine Lucy episode had demonstrated some seven months earlier, the Cold War had become an essential part of the arguments surrounding massive resistance, and in the wake of the federal enforcement of the provisions of *Brown*, a number of segregationists turned the new discourse of the global conflict to their own advantage. For many, it became imperative to prevent Eisenhower's deployment of troops at Little Rock from becoming a symbol of the futility of southern resistance in the face of overwhelming federal might. In attempting to do just that, a number of resistance supporters showcased the extent of their ingenuity and rhetorical flexibility. When Florida's Senator George Smathers spoke publicly about Little Rock in October 1957, for example, he managed to combine fears generated by the Cold War with the South's scarred historical memory of Reconstruction, the presidential administration's neglect of states' rights, and the dangers of social engineering, all in just two sentences:

> I know that it is thought-provoking to each of us to contemplate that here, in the year 1957, some 90 years after the end of the war between the States in this day of satellites circling our world in 96 minutes ... that we should find Federal troops parading up and down the inside of a high school building

enforcing a Supreme Court order which in essence seeks to make one group of people like another ... Surely all of us should have learned by this time that neither courts, nor troops, nor decisions, nor force, can make one group of our citizens wish to associate with another.[47]

Others sought to deflect blame from the South for the apparent disintegration of race relations in the region simply by casting Little Rock as the product of a concerted communist campaign. Virginia's most prominent Citizens' Council, the Defenders of State Sovereignty and Individual Liberties, dedicated an entire edition of their official publication, *Defenders' News and Views*, to what they perceived to be the communists' influence in Little Rock, in an eight-page exposé that included such chapters as 'Communists' Basic Goal: To Incite Racial Strife', 'Reds Goad NAACP to End Moderation', '*Daily Worker* Led the Cry for Federal Intervention' and 'Red Intrigue and Race Turmoil'.[48]

SELECTING THE ENEMIES OF RESISTANCE: THE CAMPAIGN AGAINST THE NAACP

It was no coincidence that, when the *Defenders' News and Views* invoked the list of demons that its authors believed to be behind desegregation campaigns in general and Little Rock specifically, the NAACP appeared at its heart. In the Deep South, the pattern was identical. A membership card issued in late 1955 by one Alabama Citizens' Council pledged the cardholder 'to help defeat the NAACP, Integration, Mongrelism, Socialism, Communist ideologies, FEPC and One World Government'.[49] The majority of segregationists, whether members or leaders of Citizens' Council groups, serving in state legislatures, or simply 'concerned citizens' at the grassroots of southern resistance, recognized the potential threat that the NAACP posed to their established way of life and were deeply fearful of the Association's capabilities. Given both the dominant segregationist mindset of the 1950s and the way in which their long-held social structures and racial mores were being quickly eroded, such a fear was not groundless. Indeed, it is worth emphasizing that the NAACP was not merely caught up in a blanket attack of reactionary conservatism, but rather was singled out with scalpel-like efficiency by segregationists as an enemy that needed to be combated.

In the wake of *Brown*, all manner of segregationists struggled to explain why their Supreme Court had issued a verdict that effectively outlawed the basis of their established way of life. A grassroots segregationist from Florida, for example, who was trying to come to terms with that decision a month after it was promulgated, wrote that 'If I understand simple English, this body of Justices of the Supreme Court are now making laws, a power only delegated to legislative branches of government. If I am correct in this, then this decision ... is a violation of the law.'[50] Five years later, North Carolina's ranking senator and avowed constitutional expert, Samuel J. Ervin, Jr. was essentially repeating that point, albeit in the assured language and cadences of a lawyer. 'The Constitution makes it clear that the laws of the United States are acts of Congress and not Court decisions. As a matter of fact the Supreme Court itself held way back in 1842 that a court decision is not law, but merely evidence of law', he continued. The justices had, he believed, 'ignored the judicial process and usurped power to amend the Constitution when they handed down the school segregation decision'.[51]

The clear inference for massive resisters was that some external force must have acted upon the Court in order to force it to alter what they believed to be its clearly defined constitutional role. The NAACP's lawyers were one of two likely instigators of that force for change, along with the Supreme Court justices who had sided with the Association's lawyers. At the same time, the Association was held responsible for what many resisters believed to be the logical outcome of the implementation of *Brown*, namely miscegenation, especially since the Court had ensured that it was to be the region's school children at the forefront of desegregation. 'To force a 6-year-old child to live in school for 12 years with negroes in every social relation fixes his thinking and attitude for life', wrote one former junior high school principal as the 1954–55 school year approached. 'This force is more powerful than the atom and hydrogen bombs.'[52]

It is symptomatic of the energetic early years of the segregationist South's campaign to maintain segregation that, rather than waiting passively for the NAACP to bring further legal suits against segregation and, thus, to accelerate the erosion of segregation, massive resisters instead formulated a number of aggressive and active strategies that sought to pre-empt the Association's activities in the hope of rendering them ineffective.[53] The devices that segregationists formulated in order to aid their quest of disabling the NAACP reflected the subtly different agendas that the separate strands of the South's resistance campaigns held, but almost all were imaginative and intelligent. They ranged from the concrete, including specific legislative bans on the Association's activities and, for example, threats to make public its membership lists, to the more ephemeral, such as rhetorical campaigns aimed at sowing distrust as to the Association's provenance and its precise aims and objectives, as well as the McCarthyite smearing of its members and supporters, as exemplified by the *Defenders' News and Views*. When the NAACP's Roy Wilkins wrote in the summer of 1957 that segregationists 'will have to bring out something better than the thin contentions thus far advanced', he was either being bullish in the face of adversity, or greatly underestimating the resourcefulness of his southern foes.[54]

By 1956, the NAACP's legal resources were already stretched to the limit by the decision of a number of southern legislatures to adopt 'local option' assignment plans as part of their massive resistance measures. By devolving the decision on the composition of the student body to individual school boards, segregationists knew full well that lawyers would be forced to bring suit against each board individually if they attempted to enforce the provisions of *Brown*, which many also knew was likely to stretch the limited resources of the Association beyond breaking point. It was as NAACP lawyers were attempting to adjust to those new strictures that southern legislatures compounded their difficulties by passing a bewildering array of laws aimed at further curbing the efficacy of NAACP activities. As a number of historians have noted, it signalled a 'ferocious legal assault' on the organization and, significantly, a 'massive counterattack' by the White South.[55]

By the spring of 1960, the Southern Regional Council was reporting that some 230 laws aimed at 'the muzzling of individuals or organizations who would speak out for desegregation' had been passed by southern legislatures in the previous four years, most of which were specifically designed to inhibit the NAACP. The attorney general of Arkansas, for example, claimed openly that an act passed by his state's legislature in 1959 'was designed to harass the NAACP and', he concluded, 'it has accomplished its purpose'.[56] In Florida, too, little attempt was made to obscure the intimidatory intent of the anti-NAACP measures. In 1956, the state legislature authorized the creation of a Legislative Investigation Committee under the chairmanship of Senator Charlie E. Johns, a staunch segregationist and, it was widely rumoured, a former Ku Klux Klan member. Although the committee was created with an absurdly broad remit which included the investigation of organizations 'whose operations are not to the best interest of the majority of Florida's citizens', Vice-Chairman Dewey Johnson was open in his assertions that the NAACP was the committee's primary target.[57]

The campaign against the NAACP also offers clear evidence of southern senators' eagerness to use the seniority that they had built up in Washington over the preceding decades to the advantage of the resistance cause. In March 1959, for example, Virginia's Harry Byrd confidentially informed Governor Almond that he had for some time been using his position as vice-chairman of the Joint Committee on Internal Revenue Taxation to work upon 'the question of canceling the tax exemption that has been granted on the contributions to the NAACP'. After a particularly long session with Revenue representatives, Byrd believed 'some progress was made'.[58]

The fact that so many of the anti-NAACP laws passed by southern states were so similar, both in legislative detail and in their proposed objectives, exemplifies the fact that, alongside the huge variability that could be found in resistance strategies across the region, there were also abiding commonalities. Certainly, in this instance, there was no obvious difference in the behaviour of states in the Border or Deep South. Taken collectively, those laws aimed to intimidate the NAACP's officers and members, to restrict the Association's financial viability and legal opportunities, and in some cases to ban it from functioning altogether. In order to achieve those objectives, new bills were passed but a number of old ordinances and laws were also renovated in the hope that they might have some relevance to the situation as it existed in the 1950s. In 1956, for example, a Louisiana law first passed 22 years earlier to restrict the activities of the Ku Klux Klan was resuscitated and turned on the NAACP, while in Mississippi segregationists attempted to revive two laws that had been passed in the middle of the Second World War, one of which forbade the promotion of 'arguments or suggestions in favor of social equality or of intermarriage', and the other that made it an offence to conspire 'to overthrow or violate the segregation laws of this state through force, violence, threats, intimidation, or otherwise'.[59]

Of the new laws, many were aimed at tightening up procedures against existing common law offences, especially the mediaeval sounding trio of barratry, champerty and maintenance.[60] Georgia, Mississippi, South Carolina, Florida, Tennessee and Virginia all passed laws in that vein, while Virginia, Tennessee, Texas and Arkansas specifically targeted the funding of the NAACP. Arkansas Attorney General Bruce Bennett, for example, presented state NAACP president Daisy Bates with 14 demands at the end of August 1957, which included the handing over of a list of donations made to the Association from within the state, a list of local branch members, and, in a clear example of the way in which the organization's life was fast being made intolerable, the 'exact address in Arkansas where the records, files, papers, correspondence, deposit slips, cancelled checks, reports and all other papers and/or correspondence' of the state chapter were held.[61] Similarly, in Virginia the state required certified statements from all NAACP chapters operating within its borders listing the names of officers, their addresses, monetary transactions that had been made, contributions that had been donated, and 'copies of all correspondence between your organization and persons in Virginia to whom your organization has rendered legal aid directly or indirectly'.[62] The Texas legislature, so often overlooked as an active participant in massive resistance, mulled over a bill that would simply have made it unlawful for any member of the NAACP to be employed 'by the State, any school district, any county, or municipality'.[63]

In order to make their counter-attack as sustained and tenacious as possible, a number of southern states added to the impact of their anti-NAACP laws by establishing committees whose members were given the specific remit of investigating the NAACP's members and activities. Alongside Florida's Johns Committee, a State Sovereignty Committee established in Arkansas as part of Faubus's drive for segregationist votes was specifically empowered to collect data on the NAACP in March 1957.[64] The Virginia legislature established two committees in its special session on massive resistance in 1956: the Legislative Committee on Law Reform and Racial Activities, and the Legislative Committee on Offenses Against the Administration of Justice, the second of which was known more popularly as the Boatwright Committee after its secretary, John B. Boatwright, Jr. Boatwright was so assiduous in his task that just a year later his committee produced a report on the NAACP that consisted of 22 pages of evidence and a further 50 pages of appendices.[65] Mississippi, too, passed a law that authorized the General Legislative Investigating Committee to carry out specific research into NAACP activities. On 18 November 1959 it duly did so 'in an effort to determine their "means, methods, associates, affiliations and ultimate objectives in this state"'.

Those investigative committees did not always have the desired effect, however. The first witness called by the Mississippi committee was J. B. Matthews, who was already known across the nation as something of a freelance anticommunist in the McCarthyite tradition. His appearance immediately lent credence to accusations of a witch-hunt. As Medgar Evers reported to the NAACP's director of branches, Gloster B. Current, 'very few people expressed any unusual interest in the proceedings, because it was all too obvious to everyone that it was "rigged"'.[66] In Florida, too, the gloss was taken off the Johns Committee's investigations when a newspaper exposé revealed that R. J. Strickland, a former Tallahassee police sergeant employed as an investigator for the Committee, had spent more than $2,000 of state funds to buy information about the NAACP from private individuals. Other reports referred to Matthews' 'dubious distinction' of having worked closely with McCarthy, and that the revelations from the hearings were so stale and 'hardly startling' that a Florida taxpayer 'will begin to suspect that all he is getting for his money is a re-reading of history'.[67] There were other side-effects to a number of the legislative acts that their segregationist sponsors had clearly not envisaged. In Louisiana, for example, a 1922 anti-Klan law that was recast as an anti-NAACP statute required the yearly compilation of complete membership lists for all organized groups in the state, with the exception of the National Guard or church affiliated groups. There were, however, a number of hard-line segregationist groups who were equally loath to comply with such a request and make their own lists public. In an indication of the increasing guile evident within certain elements of the southern resistance movement, the Reverend Perry Strickland, a Baptist minister from Livingston Parish, sought to make use of that ecclesiastical loophole and wasted little time in incorporating the National Christian Klan Kingdom to 'protect the ideals of the white race'.[68]

The legislative cavalcade that southern legislatures unleashed against the NAACP between 1956 and 1959 was specifically designed to cripple the Association, and in many cases it did so. In a number of states, such as Louisiana, Texas and Alabama, the Association was forced to shut down its operations altogether, most seriously in Alabama where the NAACP remained inoperative from 1956 to 1964. Membership numbers were also decimated, further depleting both the Association's manpower and its ability to raise funds through subscriptions. As one legal scholar has noted, the southern states 'proved enormously creative at translating white hatred of the NAACP into legal mechanisms for shutting it down'. Indeed, a number of the laws devised by segregationist legislatures were so ingenious in their conception that Supreme Court judges had to show immense 'creativity' in defending the NAACP and protecting the organization from their effects.[69]

Although historians of the segregationist South have consistently focused upon the anti-NAACP strategies that were so popular among southern legislators in the resistance era, they have – equally consistently – failed to examine the ways in which the legislative animus that was conceived and directed by the higher echelons of the South's political elites ran in parallel with altogether less high-brow attacks at the grassroots. By analysing the ways in which both southern elites and their grassroots constituents intertwined in their attempts to carry out the campaign against the NAACP, it is possible to unravel at least some of the complex questions that continue to surround the relationship that existed between resisters from different corners of the social, economic and, indeed, political spectrum. In what is perhaps the clearest example of the need for that broader focus, the success of many of the legislative proposals for suppressing the NAACP was entirely predicated upon the reaction that the bills' sponsors assumed they would elicit at the segregationist grassroots. From the segregationist perspective, there was little point in pressing the Association to release its membership lists and records of financial contributors unless it could be readily assumed that, once those lists entered the public domain, those who were named on them would be subject to acts of intimidation, whether overt or covert, financial or physical. It was a complex but ultimately symbiotic relationship. When those politicians assented to the passage of legislative acts against the NAACP as an organization, the grassroots interpreted their actions as legitimizing their own campaigns against the individuals that made up the Association's membership. As politicians relied upon their constituents, so in turn those constituents relied upon their elected representatives, leading to a situation in which all sides of the resistance movement roused and played upon the fears of their fellow resisters.

In one of the clearest examples of that process, Georgia's Attorney General Eugene Cook gave a speech on 'The Ugly Truth about the NAACP' to the Peace Officers' Association of Georgia in October 1955 which, when reprinted in pamphlet form, swiftly became a ubiquitous document in segregationist circles. Cook, who formed a cabal of leading segregationists in Georgia along with lawyers such as Charles Bloch and Carter Pittman, and fellow politicians such as Roy Harris and Marvin Griffin, was in the vanguard of Georgia's campaign against the state chapter of the NAACP.[70] Indeed, his reputation as a fervent white supremacist was so widespread that, when it first emerged that he had been invited to speak on the issue of segregation at Yale University in 1955, the decision was immediately condemned and opposed by six campus groups.[71]

Although Cook had written and published numerous segregationist tracts earlier in his career, such as 'The Georgia Constitution and Mixed Public Schools' which was issued in October 1954, they failed to make the same impression as his later work. It was, ironically, not Georgia's vehemently segregationist Commission on Education that distributed Cook's 'The Ugly Truth about the NAACP', but, in an apt display of the burgeoning publications network that suffused the southern states during the resistance era, it was the Patriots of North Carolina, Inc. who were responsible for its dissemination, at least initially. Other Citizens' Councils and Council-related groups followed the Patriots' lead with remarkable energy. Three years after its release, for example, Cook reported that 'more than one million copies of the address have been circulated in pamphlet form by the Citizens' Councils of several Southern states'.[72] The success of 'The Ugly Truth about the NAACP' was based primarily in Cook's ability to codify a number of pressing concerns that had long been central to the demonology of southern resistance, but which had existed up until Cook's intervention as little more than a series of vague assumptions, baseless claims and wild rumours. The importance of Cook's work was not in adding accuracy to those claims, but in cataloguing and cross-referencing accusations against the NAACP's provenance in such a way as to add a veneer of authenticity and legitimacy to them that had previously been lacking. By making reference to reams of House un-American Activities Committee (HUAC) citations, many of which were in turn entered into the *Congressional Record*, as well as to the work of fellow segregationist James O. Eastland's Senate Internal Security Subcommittee (SISS), Cook was able not only to claim erroneously that hard evidence had been found to implicate NAACP activists and officials in the seedy underworld of communist subversion, but, by putting aside his states' rights sympathies for just long enough to embrace the work of official US agencies whose power and status was derived from their inexorable links to the federal government, he was also able to bring a sheen of respectability to his claims.

It was exactly what resisters wanted to hear, and the pamphlet's impact was widely, and quickly, felt. As one female resister from Virginia told her governor in March 1956, the local chapter of the Defenders of State Sovereignty and Individual Liberty passed a resolution against the NAACP primarily because

> We had received indisputable information from Georgia's Attorney General Eugene Cook, as to the affiliation of this organization with the National Communist Party. I think we are all agreed as to the purpose and intent of this group, and that they are the chief cause of trouble between the races in the South and other parts of the country.[73]

Elsewhere, those opposed to desegregation took to quoting Cook's work verbatim, and both the language that he used and the accusations that he made soon permeated all aspects of resistance rhetoric. His status as Georgia's attorney general only added to the legitimacy that the references to HUAC and SISS had already conveyed. North Carolina's influential Senator

Sam Ervin, for example, was asked by one non-southerner why the states of the Old Confederacy allowed the NAACP to function in any form, since, she maintained, '[as] the Attorney General of Georgia declared, 75% of the NAACP leaders are Communists'.[74]

Even after the apparent success of Cook's attempts to brand the NAACP as communist-tainted, a number of segregationists in the Deep South clearly remained unconvinced that the NAACP's threat had been effectively neutered. As a result, they undertook an elaborate plan to link the Association publicly to another of the enduring demons of the segregationist South, the fear of miscegenation and intermarriage. It was a plan in which a number of leading southern legislators were clearly complicit, and equally clearly was an act of fraud and deception. The plan revolved around the widespread circulation in early 1956 of the transcript of a speech purportedly given by Roosevelt Williams, described as a high-ranking NAACP official and professor at Howard University, before a 'secret NAACP meeting' held in Mississippi in December 1954. The transcript began in even tones by gently needling southern white concerns, with Williams telling his audience that, because of NAACP pressure, 'the day of your complete emancipation is at hand'. Williams then upped the ante by inferring that whites were inherently unpatriotic and cowardly by proclaiming that 'Our people have fearlessly fought and died in the front lines while the white soldiers crouched in the back areas with the safety of their undeserved political commissions.' Moving on to claim that blacks were not simply equal, but in fact superior to their white oppressors, Williams reached a crescendo. 'We demand the abolition of all state laws which prohibit marriages of persons of different races', he was quoted as saying. Then, complete with bracketed remarks that were surely intended to bring further authenticity to the claim that this was indeed a hastily typed transcript, Williams was quoted as saying that

> It is simply [indistinct] that many of our discriminating negroes might be [not clear] to marry beneath their stations just because we simply demand the removal of laws that keep the barrier between us and complete equality. As many of you are aware, some of the most outstanding Americans ever produced were the products of white men crossed with generate negro women without benefit of clergy, and the whole world knows that the white man strongly prefers the negro women with its strong rich ancestors and warm, full blooded passions that recline in the spiritless women of his own race.[75]

By the time that Senator Sam Engelhardt had used a point of personal privilege to play a tape recording of the speech to the Alabama Legislature in January 1956, and Eugene Cook had distributed further copies of the transcript through the Georgia attorney general's office, the NAACP had embarked upon a frantic campaign of damage limitation. Reams of press releases and telegrams were produced pointing out that the Association had no one by the name of Roosevelt Williams on its books, and indeed never had done. Roy Wilkins wrote urgently to Alabama's most senior political figures, including the speaker of the house, the floor leader of both chambers, and the president of the Senate in an attempt to explain that 'We have a copy of this recording in our office as it is being peddled to anyone foolish enough to buy it and gullible enough to believe it. The recorded speech is a fake.'[76] In short order, responsible commentators began to distance themselves from such a blatant act of segregationist propaganda. The Columbus, Georgia *Ledger-Enquirer* branded Cook's actions a 'terrible public service', whilst the *Atlanta Constitution* believed claims of the Williams speech's authenticity to be 'as undocumented as the Protocols of the Elders of Zion'.[77] Less responsible sources remained unperturbed by Wilkins's strenuous denials. The speech was included in pamphlets which reportedly 'were distributed from house to house' in Hopeville, Georgia, and Engelhardt, whose loose grasp on constitutional rights was clearly exhibited in his comments to the Civil Rights Commission that 'slogans like *democracy* and *the brotherhood* of man are fine in their place but they don't solve practical, everyday problems', dismissed Wilkins's rebuttal as the 'obvious and expected defense to offer'.[78] The Citizens' Council of Tarrant, Alabama, which had rebranded the speech 'Negro Professor Demands Intermarriage between the Races', was still distributing it in April 1956, and in October Edwin J. Lukas of the American Jewish Committee received a copy, then titled 'The Ultimate Aim of the NAACP', which was distributed by the White Citizens Council, Inc. of St Petersburg, Florida, but which the Council had copied verbatim from the hard-line segregationist broadsheet, *The Dixie-American*.[79]

The importance of the Roosevelt Williams deception cannot be overemphasized for historians of massive resistance. Most readily, the ways in which transcriptions of the fake speech were continuously reprinted offer significant insights into the mechanics that lay behind the distribution of segregationist documents in the resistance era. One of Mississippi's Citizens' Council groups laid claim to the original tape recording of the Williams speech, but the emergence of separate editions of the document, each with subtle differences in the wording of the title, helps to reveal the ways in which other groups commandeered it and hastened its dissemination to grassroots activists all over the South. The changes to those headings from, for example, 'Negro Professor Demands Intermarriage between the Races' to 'The Ultimate Aim of the NAACP' also point to subtle differences in the outlook of separate segregationist groups, with the former drawing more attention to the end product, in this case miscegenation, and the latter to the progenitors of that miscegenation, the NAACP.

In a broader sense, the Roosevelt Williams episode is significant in aiding attempts to unravel the mind of the segregationist South in the post-*Brown* 1950s, or at the very least the mind of that coterie of segregationists that was drawn into the Citizens' Councils. In that respect, the fact that it was a forgery increases rather than lessens its impact: here was a document created entirely in the minds of segregationists, who, with no obvious template to follow, set about creating a document bristling with the issues and language that they believed was most likely to raise the ire of their fellow resisters. It was, in short, a compendium of the latent fears of grassroots resisters, but it also pointed to pragmatic political sensibilities. Alongside attempts to trigger deep-seated white supremacist concerns such as the imminent dilution – and resultant destruction – of the purity of the white race, and predictions that whites would soon be treated as second-class citizens in the wake of an unstoppable African American ascendancy, lay rather more specific, tangible concerns. The final paragraph was nothing short of a politically motivated assault on Arkansas' Orval Faubus, whom Williams was quoted as referring to as 'our friend', and who, it was claimed, had promised blacks numerous positions of authority in state government. 'Now hear this', the document concluded, 'we will absolutely control the next election in Arkansas.' It was a statement that one Citizens' Council saw fit to place in bold, underlined capitals.[80]

THE DAY-TO-DAY TERROR OF GRASSROOTS RESISTANCE

The evidence from the anti-NAACP campaigns suggests that segregationists at the ground level were more than willing to respond to the appeals of state legislators, Citizens' Council leaders, and the region's propagandists. The nature of the bills that were passed also makes it apparent that legislators were fully cognizant of their constituents' animus towards black activists. The daily acts of general intimidation and open violence that occurred throughout the South in the mid- to late-1950s certainly offered legislators clues to the ways in which their constituents would respond. Such violence formed an intrinsic part of massive resistance, although it often went unreported by a local press that was unreceptive to racial change, or undetected by a northern press with little insight into the realities of the southern life away from the region's urban hubs. A close analysis of that activity suggests that southern reprisals against civil rights activists fell into two categories, at times distinct from each other, but equally able to intertwine. First and foremost was the maintenance of an all-pervading climate of fear and insecurity, which, by ensuring that, for example, blacks could not trust local law enforcement officers, was designed to preserve the white power structure's near-feudal hold over all aspects of southern life, especially in isolated rural communities. Second was a far more intelligently targeted, incisive campaign specifically designed to confront and defeat explicit threats from within the black community. In many cases the intimidation that segregationists employed was designed to be pre-emptive rather than reactive, especially when civil rights organizers and demonstrators had been identified locally and were on the point of making inroads against white supremacy. In some cases, those inroads could be as minor as either attempting to register to vote, or more rarely actually trying to cast a vote. However slight the infraction, segregationists reacted swiftly to derail any such activity before it gathered momentum or before it garnered wider attention. In the majority of cases, members of local Citizens' Councils and their sympathizers managed to apply severe economic pressure to blacks, a trait which led many contemporary observers to refer to the Councils as purveyors of 'white-collar terrorism' or 'Economic Lynch Law'.[81] A number of local segregationists also proved themselves to be more than willing to resort to physical intimidation, and at times outright violence that was more redolent of the Ku Klux Klan than the pin-striped image of the Citizens' Councils.

Mississippi, which historian James C. Cobb memorably referred to as the 'most southern place on earth', was a hotbed of those grassroots pressures.[82] In a detailed case study of Sunflower County, the seat of Mississippi's ardently segregationist US Senator James O. Eastland, J. Todd Moye provides a rare glimpse into the networks that sustained the intensity of that intimidation. Eastland built a career on the maintenance of white supremacy, perhaps not surprisingly given the ways in which many of those living in his constituency brooked no dissent from a rigidly segregationist line. Local Council and NAACP branches 'circled each other warily' in the massive resistance era, each responding to a perceived increase in the strength of the other, creating a climate of mutual fear and suspicion that adds credence to Badger's view that both sides of the desegregation debate believed the other to be stronger.[83] When news filtered through to local segregationists that Theodore Keenan, an African American farmer in Sunflower County and former chairman of the Indianola NAACP, had, along with his wife, been the only person in the precinct to vote against Eastland in his 1954 campaign for re-election, the loans that Keenan had previously depended upon to sustain his farming livelihood were refused him. As the director of the local bank explained to Keenan in terms both threatening and typically paternalistic, the 'good white folk had been good to him and he had not shown proper respect by voting against Eastland and participating in [the] NAACP'.[84]

Across the state of Mississippi as a whole, the ability of Citizens' Councils and other local employers to enforce the denial of loans to African Americans and the foreclosure of their mortgages proved to be such a successful tactic that it forced black organizations to undertake drastic action. Led by the Regional Council of Negro Leadership's T. R. M. Howard, insurance companies, banks, labour unions, churches and other sympathetic organizations came to an accommodation with the Tri-State Bank of Memphis, whereby they regularly deposited money so that the bank had increased assets against which it could grant loans to black applicants denied them elsewhere. The decision to furnish loans remained squarely with the bank itself rather than with any of the contributing organizations, but it was made clear that 'the bank would give special attention to applications from Mississippi people who were being "squeezed" on account of civil rights'. By January 1956, the fund had accrued $307,000, which allowed for the provision of loans totalling $656,000.[85]

The economic pressure that was often applied through the sudden denial of bank loans was supplemented by the curtailment of employment. In February 1956, for example, two women were summarily fired from their jobs at Coahoma County Hospital in Clarksdale. The fact that the local hospital received federal funding did not perturb Reed Hogan, the hospital administrator, who apparently made no secret of the fact that the termination of Lurleaner Johnson's and Gussie P. Young's contracts was not related to the standard of their work. Instead, Hogan told both women that it was a direct result of a petition to end school desegregation in Clarksdale, which Young herself and Johnson's husband had both signed. Young claimed in an affidavit that Hogan also cited her 'activity with the NAACP', while Johnson claimed in a similar document that her husband's NAACP activity was also mentioned. Interestingly, Hogan himself was not a member of a Citizens' Council, but that did not allow him to avoid the ominous shadow that they cast. As both women attested, Hogan 'said that the pressure brought to bear against him by the Hospital Board and the White Citizens' Council left him no alternative'.[86]

The segregationist campaign against the activism of local NAACP members proved to be so ruthlessly efficient that the Clarksdale NAACP stopped operating under its usual moniker, and re-emerged instead as the Coahoma County Federated Council of Organizations in order, in the words of Roy Wilkins, 'to permit teachers and persons who cannot afford to be identified with us to participate'.[87] In Yazoo City, the reaction to a similar school petition was so intense that 38 of the 53 signatories fled the city, in no small part because the local Citizens' Council was sufficiently brazen to take out a full-page advertisement in the local paper publishing the names and addresses of each one of the petitioners. In a graphic indication of the rationale that underscored the passage of legislative acts aimed at bringing the NAACP's membership rosters into the public domain, retribution against those named was swift. Of those that chose to remain in the city, many were unable to secure employment, while others faced the same sanctions as Johnson and Young. Perrine Stephens, who petitioned on behalf of her 14-year-old child, was fired because her employer faced reprisals from the Citizens' Council if he failed to take such action, and she even had to resort to using firewood to heat her home and fuel her stove after the Yazoo Butane Co. terminated a contract to service her 150-gallon butane tank.[88] Clear markers were being set down, indicating in no uncertain terms that local attempts to enforce the desegregation promised by *Brown* would incur harsh penalties. Such actions may have lacked the finesse and bombast of the *Southern Manifesto*, but to those African Americans attempting to bring tangible racial change to their own local communities, they were far more imposing.

The ability of local white segregationists to muster fearsome – and fearsomely effective – resources against blacks, either because they were believed to be involved in the planning of coherent long-term civil rights campaigns or merely signing petitions intended to desegregate a single school, was by no means confined to Mississippi. African Americans employed in public schools were particularly vulnerable to the economic reprisals of resisters across the region, for reasons that ranged from the lack of explicit constitutional protection for those seeking a right to public employment, to the fact that teaching was one of the few professions that remained open to educated blacks in the South, and, thus, into which a disproportionate number of educated blacks entered.[89] By May 1956, South Carolina had taken the unprecedented step of inserting an 'anti-NAACP oath' into teachers' employment applications, following the passage of a state law prohibiting NAACP members from state, county or municipal employment. It was swiftly put into action. By July, there were reports from the executive secretary of the Palmetto Education Association that 24 teachers from Elloree, South Carolina, were on an official state 'black-list' because of their alleged links to the NAACP. 'In applying for a position', the executive secretary noted with some dismay, 'they have been told that they cannot get a job in this state'.[90]

Other segregationist reprisals, separate from the sort of state-driven actions that were exemplified by the South Carolinian black-list, were clearly well planned but often had little overall effect. In Montgomery, Alabama, for example, a group of 12 men who described themselves as a mix of 'union members and businessmen' staged an elaborate lynching of two life-size dummies, complete with full-size gallows, in the middle of the city's Court Square. One of the figures was white and carried a sash labelled 'I talked "integration"', the other was black and simply bore the letters 'NAACP'. Although a number of the men who staged the demonstration were Council members, it was made clear that the stunt was carried out under the auspices of the Committee on the Preservation of Segregation, whose acronym, COPS, was clearly intended as a very public suggestion of the way in which they believed civil rights 'agitators' should be policed. Although the scaffolding and effigies had been carefully constructed in a shed that belonged to one of the protester's unions, and that, according to one witness, the mock hanging had been rehearsed 'several times', its impact was probably best summed up by a small girl who, having watched the effigies being hanged, turned to her mother to ask, 'Mommy, is that all?'[91]

On other occasions, however, acts of intimidation were perpetrated on an almost ad hoc basis, often with far more profound effects. In Dawson, a rural black-belt town that served as the county seat of Georgia's Terrell County, for example, there was a studied nonchalance to the ways in which Police

Chief Edward L. Lee and County Sheriff Z. T. 'Zeke' Matthews habitually oppressed the town's African American community in the late 1950s. They succeeded in creating a climate of fear that was so pervasive that it effectively countered a nascent voting drive instituted by many of the town's blacks. The disproportionate power afforded to rural counties such as Terrell in many southern states, especially in the Deep South, added impetus to segregationists' historical campaign of ensuring the eradication of any vestige of black voting strength, even in small communities.[92]

Between 1956 and 1958, Lee and Matthews' campaign of extemporized terror had effectively reduced Terrell County's registered black voters from 105 to just 45. As one failed voter in the county told a reporter, 'There is an old joke about the Negro who was asked by the Georgia registrar what such-and-such section of the Constitution meant. "It means I ain't goin' to git to vote"', he replied. 'I used to laugh at that joke', concluded the interviewee, 'I don't think it's funny anymore.' It was no longer humorous because of the endemic police brutality that accompanied the campaign to continue the historic limitations placed on the enfranchisement of Terrell County's black population. On one day in April 1958, 30 blacks were refused the right to register to vote, one of whom, a graduate student from New York University, was denied because he allegedly slurred the word 'original' in a literacy test, and another, a civil servant working in Albany, was denied because he 'couldn't write'.[93]

It was no coincidence that the period was marked by an increase in anti-black violence. James Brazier, a Second World War veteran who held down two jobs, one of which was in his local Chevrolet dealership, died five days after receiving a beating from policemen who were attempting to arrest his father on trumped-up charges of drink driving. The inconsistencies that blighted official records of the attack on Brazier were so glaring that the Federal Bureau of Investigation sent agents to Dawson to carry out an investigation.[94] A month later, one of the officers implicated in the attack on Brazier, W. B. Cherry, shot another local African American man, Tobe Latimer, in the buttocks, before shooting dead a third black man, Willie Countryman, in his own backyard.[95] Lee and Matthews remained typically unrepentant. Indeed, when Lee was later accused of 'roughing up' another suspect that same weekend, he defended himself openly to a journalist by stating that 'Neither the arresting officers nor I had our blackjacks at the time, so I know it wasn't so.' Sheriff Matthews felt that further measures were needed to put an end to black 'agitation'. 'A man who knows the nigger can tell when dissatisfaction is brewing', he maintained. That dissatisfaction, he believed, stemmed from the greater communication ushered in by television, especially with the advent of news programmes 'telling what the Supreme Court has done and what the Federal Courts say and all about civil rights'. As a result, he believed, blacks 'begin thinking'. His response was simple. 'There's nothing like fear to keep niggers in line', said the sheriff, and 'we always tell them there are four roads leading out of Dawson in all directions and they are free to go any time they don't like it here.'[96]

The situation in Terrell County was not unique. Billie S. Fleming, an undertaker from Manning, South Carolina, and president of the Clarendon County Improvement Association, told the Senate Subcommittee on Constitutional Rights in April 1959 that, as well as the myriad forms of economic intimidation that black activists in the county had been forced to endure, the funeral home that Fleming ran had twice been 'severely shot up in the wee hours of the night'. Although Fleming had reported both attacks to County Sheriff T. K. Jackson, there had been no arrests and he was left with good reason to suspect that the sheriff was 'in sympathy with the Ku Klux Klan'.[97] Segregationist activity appeared to be particularly vigorous in Clarendon County, perhaps because of its infamous status – in the eyes of white resisters – as the county that begat the original suit in what were to become the *Brown* cases. As one of the primary targets of local segregationists' ire commented, an 'atmosphere favorable to persecution' was sustained by the activities of both grassroots resisters and a sheriff's department that was at best accommodating and, perhaps more accurately, an accomplice to anti-black oppression.[98] It was typical of the grassroots approach to resistance that the names and addresses of many of the petitioners involved in that initial *Brown* case were published in the front pages of local newspapers, leading to devastating economic reprisals, and Sheriff Jackson was able to engineer Fleming's arrest on charges of conspiracy to defraud an insurance company.[99]

The temptation to assume that such acts of economic and violent intimidation were confined to the Deep South must be avoided. Although resisters in states such as Mississippi, Georgia and Alabama could lay claim to the most concerted campaigns against segregation's foes, other southern states were by no means immune from such action. In Florida, for example, David Hawthorne, a well-known local segregationist and president of the Dade County Property Owners' Improvement Association, proved to be so efficient at organizing bomb attacks on a non-white housing project that threatened existing patterns of segregated housing in Miami that the area quickly earned the sobriquet 'Little Korea'.[100] In Somerville, Tennessee, local segregationist reaction to African American attempts to register to vote on registration day, 2 March 1959, took on what was by then an all too familiar guise. One would-be voter was refused gas for both his car and his farm, and was refused credit by the local bank after 17 years' worth of loans. Other farmers found suddenly that they could not persuade a local veterinarian to administer vaccinations to livestock, even though the jabs were provided free by the state, and that the local farm supply store – equally suddenly – refused to sell fertilizer, even for cash. A church minister who did manage to register to vote found that his wife was unceremoniously and suddenly fired from her job as a teacher at the local white high school.[101]

The supply of petroleum and gas appeared to be particularly susceptible to segregationist pressures, no doubt in part because local segregationists realized its importance to the maintenance of trade and commerce in rural communities. In Somerville alone, for example, those attempting to register to vote found that their supplies of Lion Gas, Gulf Gas and American Gas were no longer forthcoming because they were being blocked at source by the owners and operators of the local Amoco and Texaco gas stations.[102] Coincidentally, the petroleum industry also afforded Mississippi Governor Ross Barnett a rare opportunity to make the case for the economic desirability of segregation, when in September 1961 Standard Oil decided that their new $125 million oil refinery should be located in Pascagoula. In a wry comment on the prevailing wisdom that separate-but-equal codes and laws created extra expense for industries operating in the South, and that constant racial 'agitation' produced a climate that was incommensurate with the stable environment that successful industries were believed to need, Barnett stated in contrast that industrialists were attracted to Mississippi because it had become a 'symbol of successful segregation'. Despite the fact that Standard Oil rigidly maintained that the decision was made 'strictly on economic factors such as crude oil and product distribution', Barnett's sense of theatre and opportunism was not to be quashed. 'Who says segregation doesn't pay?' he asked rhetorically.[103]

THE INCREASING SOPHISTICATION OF RESISTANCE PROPAGANDA

As the grassroots campaign to maintain rigid white supremacy in the South continued, many segregationists proved that they were adept at making full use of the increasingly sophisticated communication systems that were available to them, and produced a propaganda campaign that buttressed their ongoing attempts at localized intimidation. In some cases, that meant little more than maximizing the impact of traditional printed materials by collating and distributing them in a more efficient way. The energy with which certain segregationist publications set about their task became an essential tool to their success. One resister from Tennessee who subscribed to the rigidly conservative, segregationist and anti-communist *Common Sense* was clearly impressed by the sheer range of other publications from which the newspaper's editors culled information. They 'seem to get information from *Congressional Record*, *US News & World Report*, various papers, magazines and books, foreign and domestic', she wrote in 1957, 'and they must have some *truth* in them to have been published for approx. 9 or 10 years.'[104] The presence of a copy of *The Virginian* in the files of Earnest Sevier Cox, a lifelong devotee of segregation who by the 1950s was based in North Carolina, is also indicative of the growing publishing network that sustained the written propaganda of resistance, especially when it is noted that Cox had not subscribed to *The Virginian* itself, but to a separate resistance body, the 'Keep America Committee' which issued reprints of the original to all its subscribers.[105]

There is also evidence to suggest that segregationists became increasingly sophisticated in the ways in which they attempted to target different sections of the white southern population, and in particular different demographic groups, with propaganda tracts that were specifically designed to ensure regional homogeneity. Louisiana's State Sovereignty Commission, for example, produced and distributed an eight-page cartoon that was designed to impress the segregationist agenda upon the region's children. The cartoon featured a stereotypical 1950s family unit that was tailored to fit the segregationist idyll. It depicted a be-suited, briefcase-carrying father, a mother happy in her home, an energetic respectful child, a faithful family dog and a neat suburban house complete with a white picket fence. Father and son are shown walking from the centre of town to their family home, all the while talking earnestly together. In the 24 frames of the cartoon, which take in scenes ranging from the busy town centre to bustling sidewalks, a municipal park, and even a voting booth, the serenity of their world is fortified by the absence of a single non-white figure. It is in the conversation between father and son, however, that the Louisiana Commission's message was delivered with the greatest clarity, for the strip's authors engineered a discussion of constitutional rights between the two figures. It is made clear to the boy that – 'so far' – he has been able to pick his own friends, both at school and in a secret club that he has formed with fellow white boys. 'But some federal judges have ordered races mixed in schools', the father explains, 'whether either wanted it or not', and that 'those same people in Washington ... want to regulate more and more things in our lives.' The only riposte, claims the father in the final frame, is a four-step solution of studying the Constitution, registering and voting, making sure to vote 'carefully' for 'good Americans', and, finally, telling the evil powers in Washington that 'we, the people, must govern ourselves'.[106]

Other groups reprinted white supremacist hymns, such as 'The Mongrel', written by the prolific isolationist poet Oliver Allstrom. The hymn included verses such as 'Gommorrah [sic], Sodom and Carthage, / Great cities in their day, / Were white, but joined with negro blood, / And so they passed away.' One of Allstrom's poems, 'The Saddest Story Ever Told', was equally popular and equally populist. It concluded a tale of inter-racial marriage with the lines, 'This black and white, prenuptial mess, this racial suicide, / Must be forbidden by the law [,] men must find racial pride!'[107] For others, the populist slant of their propaganda was more brazen still. One New Orleans resistance group, for example, chose to vent its disgust in January 1959 at recent Supreme Court decisions by publishing a list that mimicked the style of a baseball batting averages chart. The justices were each assigned a score that reflected, in the eyes of the Independent American organization, the extent to which they were carrying out the Communist Party's bidding.[108]

More significantly in terms of coverage, a number of resistance groups were able to use radio bulletins and television broadcasts in the hope of reaching a larger audience, although they did so with mixed results. Some of the radio stations, for example, were distinctly local in both outlook and in reach. Wesley Critz George, an Emeritus Professor of Histology and Embryology at UNC-Chapel Hill who, in the late 1950s, almost single-handedly breathed life into the moribund Patriots of North Carolina by using the group to popularize his theories of racial science, was approached by a family-run radio station based high in the North Carolina mountains which was eager to air segregationist views. Stuart Epperson, whose brother owned Station WPAQ in Mount Airy, reported to George that 'My father, brothers and I are trying to do our best to offset the "liberal" propaganda that has brainwashed so many persons in our country during the past few decades.'[109] In other states, Citizens' Council groups took the initiative, and broadcast their own regular radio slots. Virginia's Defenders of State Sovereignty and Individual Liberty were particularly proactive in that regard, broadcasting shows under titles that were designed to prick the consciousness of their southern audience, such as 'The Southern Manifesto', 'Mixed Blood and Mixed Schools', and, drawing heavily upon George's work on racial science, 'The Result of Integration' and 'Human Progress and the Race Problem'.[110]

It was in their use of television, though, that massive resistance's proponents were able to break new ground and utilize a medium that had not been readily available to previous generations of white supremacy's apologists. Initially, many of the segregationists' slots were piecemeal, and reflected successful opportunism on the part of individuals. At the start of the 1957 school year, for example, Dr I. Beverley Lake, a caustic segregationist from North Carolina, raised the profile of his hard-line stance with a slot on the discussion of 'Gradual Integration in North Carolina' on Raleigh's WRAL-TV. Lake was an avowed opponent of Hodges' 'progressive segregation'; he had presented North Carolina's *amicus curae* brief to the Supreme Court in the *Brown* hearings and had openly equated the NAACP with communism while serving as the state's attorney general. It was none too surprising that WRAL-TV had been drawn to Lake's militancy, given that the station's vice-president was Jesse Helms. Indeed, Helms was soon assuring North Carolina's foremost segregationist group, the Defenders of State Sovereignty, that his station would be willing to carry programmes for them free of charge, as long as he had a hand in their creation. As the Defenders' president, Reverend James P. 'Jimmy' Dees freely acknowledged, 'This can be a tremendous morale boost to our cause.'[111]

By the time of the Little Rock crisis, a number of segregationist legislators were fully appreciative of television's potential to reach a mass audience, and were also showing a growing awareness of the possibilities of staging what appeared at first to be television debates, but which were, in practice, little more than scripted propaganda slots. In one of the more brazen early examples, newsreader Dick Sanders hosted Mississippi's Governor James P.

Coleman and, among others, Senators James O. Eastland and John Bell Williams for what was advertised as a 'public service programme' on the Little Rock Crisis. All the contributors were fervent white segregationists, and were equally fervent in the paternalistic belief that they understood Little Rock's African American population, for they claimed to know exactly what they wanted to achieve.[112] It was the Citizens' Councils themselves, however, who were first responsible for attempting to bring a level of professionalism to regular segregationist propaganda broadcasts. The remit of coordinating and presenting the Councils' worldview on both radio and television was given to Richard 'Dick' Morphew, a graduate of the University of Missouri School of Journalism who was hired full-time by the Association of Citizens' Councils of America as its public relations director in 1958. As the anchor of the only regularly televised segregationist propaganda broadcasts, *Citizens' Council Forum*, Morphew hid what one commentator has referred to as his 'generously fleshed' frame behind a studio desk, from where he conducted interviews with a number of leading segregationist figures. The early programmes were plagued by poor production, Morphew's overly scripted, wooden approach and a succession of slightly bemused interviewees, but the professionalism of both Morphew and the series as a whole had improved dramatically by the time that he was able to announce, in 1961, that the *Citizens' Council Forum* was going 'coast to coast' for the first time. For Morphew, the programmes provided 'a long-needed expression of the Southern and conservative viewpoints'.[113]

As the *Citizens' Council Forum* gradually lost its parochialism and gained a proficiency more redolent of networked television productions, so it became an increasingly valuable tool for massive resistance propaganda. The fact that the *Forum* was established in the first place strongly suggests that certain well-placed individuals in the South's resistance campaign were cognizant of the need to reach a broader audience, not in place of the reams of printed propaganda materials that were already being aimed squarely at southern whites, but to run concurrently with them. Indeed, as the 1950s drew on, it became increasingly clear to a number of segregationists that massive resistance's long-term success was dependent on their ability to draw national public opinion behind the segregationist South's cause, or at the very least to ensure that northern public opinion remained apathetic where the implementation of *Brown* was concerned. If that could be achieved, some of the more cerebral resisters reckoned, then any presidential administration preparing to flex the muscles of federal power to enforce desegregation might instead allow those muscles to atrophy and take no firm action. What proved more difficult, however, was designing campaigns to achieve a change in opinion beyond the Mason–Dixon Line.

One such campaign, mounted by the Mississippi State Sovereignty Commission in October 1956, highlights both the difficulties that segregationists had in their attempts to temper northern public opinion and the glaring disjuncture that existed between segregationists' own view of the South and the perceptions held by interested parties from outside the region. From its inception on 29 March 1956, the Sovereignty Commission sought, in the words of its first official report, to 'give the South's side' to a national audience. Commission member and Mississippi House Speaker Walter Sillers expanded on the rationale that lay behind its formation when he noted, 'We can't win this battle in Mississippi or the South, [for] it must be won in 31 states north of the Mason and Dixon Line.'[114] As an important initial step in that campaign, the Sovereignty Commission's Hal C. DeCell invited 21 New England newspaper editors to see Mississippi first hand, in the belief that many of the prejudices that they held about the Deep South would be overturned by direct experience.[115]

It was an audacious plan that rested on the assumption that northern whites did not understand southern racial mores because they lived in a world in which they encountered very few, if any, African Americans on a daily basis. It failed. The response of William B. Rotch, editor and publisher of Milford, New Hampshire's *The Cabinet*, suggested that the Sovereignty Commission's central premise was flawed. For, rather than changing his opinion on Mississippi race relations because of what he had seen in the Magnolia State, Rotch was moved to reaffirm his status as 'a New Hampshire Yankee raised in a part of the country where this stuff about all men being created equal is believed'.[116] Rotch wrote of finding the trip 'deeply disturbing', while Richard P. Lewis, managing editor of *The Journal-Transcript* of Franklin, New Hampshire, 'found the situation in Mississippi somewhat worse than I had been led to expect'.[117] A number of the editors broke away from the official engagements that the Sovereignty Commission had organized, and heard first-hand accounts of the indignities that the state's non-white population had to suffer on a day-to-day basis.[118] It was Lewis, though, who offered the most eloquent summary of the editors' concerns and who most clearly exposed the conceit at the heart of the Sovereignty Commission's premise.

> The violence, the major oppressions, the dramatic injustices are the things that make the headlines up in this part of the country. We don't hear in New Hampshire, though, of the thousands of tiny indignities that add up, as I see it, to something far worse, far more vicious than such a simple thing as murder. I don't know, but there seems to me that there's a certain dignity in dying in violence, and there are worse things that can happen to a man than being killed. The systematic destruction of the basic dignity, of the fundamental human rights of a whole segment of the population, is something that has left me shamed and sickened.[119]

The Mississippi Sovereignty Commission's campaign to improve the image of southern race relations in the eyes of northern newspapermen failed because of a series of gross misjudgements. Most fundamentally, perhaps, the paternalism that was so in evidence throughout the segregationist South had clearly permeated the decision-making circles of the Sovereignty Commission. When one of the New England editors discussed the trip in some depth with a southern black correspondent, for example, it was suggested to him that the reports filed by his fellow editors 'confirm[ed] a strong impression: namely that the Southern segregationist finds it hard to believe that any white man can sincerely hold a contrary opinion ... They must have been quite sure that, once on the scene, you and your companions would see things as they do.'[120]

The naïvety and ineptitude that the Commission's members displayed should not, however, be allowed to detract from the importance of the initiative that they had taken. Within a few years a number of other segregationist groups were following the Sovereignty Commission's lead. In 1958, for example, Willie Rainach's Joint Legislative Committee took out a full-page advertisement in the *New York Herald Tribune*. Designed as an open letter 'To The People of New York City', it sought not to mollify northern critics of southern race relations as the Sovereignty Commission had done, but rather to warn northerners that the problems experienced by the South were heading northwards. Northern society should take steps to adjust to 'the more than one-half of the Negroes in this country who will live in the North by 1980', the text maintained, and the easiest way of achieving that adjustment would be to allow each individual community to alight upon its own model of race relations. As Rainach reiterated in a memorandum issued two weeks after the *Herald Tribune* letter, 'The North is waking up and finding that it has suddenly acquired another race in substantial proportion without acquiring the necessary corollary, a workable bi-racial system.'[121] Although the approach was significantly different from that pioneered by the Sovereignty Commission, the overall effect was similar. As one correspondent to the *New York Post* put it, the Legislative Committee's advertisement was unconvincing but nonetheless interesting, if only because 'it seems that these gentlemen from the South apparently are beginning to care what people in the North think'.[122]

A succession of ill-judged propaganda campaigns, from the Sovereignty Commission's New England initiative to the Roosevelt Williams fiasco, served as constant reminders to supporters of massive resisters of the difficulties inherent in putting a well-intentioned propaganda campaign into practice. Both of those examples were too heavy-handed and insufficiently sophisticated to make a case for the maintenance of southern segregation to an already sceptical northern audience. Rainach in Louisiana, Coleman in Mississippi, and Cook in Georgia, found it difficult to gain the objectivity that was necessary to view southern racial practices from a national perspective. As one contemporary African American activist remarked in 1956, 'Unfortunately, some [segregationists] are so much smarter than Cook – they are the difficult ones.'[123] The 'smarter' ones chose deliberately to tone down the brutal excesses of southern segregation, and replaced them instead with lengthy discussions of constitutional government, states' rights and rich historical precedent. William D. Workman, Jr.'s *The Case for the South*, published in 1960, stands out as one of the most erudite such works, but so, too, does James Jackson Kilpatrick's *The Southern Case for School Segregation*.[124]

Significantly, of the two it was only Kilpatrick who extended his expertise beyond the written word and made a series of compelling public appearances in an attempt to preserve the segregated way of life that, despite being a native Oklahoman, he held in such high esteem. Having established himself in the public consciousness with his stream of 'interposition' editorials in November 1955, Kilpatrick was content to ride the wave of publicity that had been created to further expand upon his defence of segregation. On NBC's long-running *Comment* show in the summer of 1958, Kilpatrick held forth before his national audience on the subject of what he pointedly and derisorily termed the 'judicial experiment' that was *Brown*, a decision which, he concluded, southerners feared 'would destroy both education and society in a single revolutionary stroke'.[125]

It was in a televised debate in 1960, however, that Kilpatrick was able to demonstrate before a nation-wide audience that being an avid segregationist was not necessarily incommensurate with displaying a quick wit, possessing fiery intelligence, and appearing both personable and eminently reasonable. Kilpatrick was called in to debate Martin Luther King, Jr. on the show after King's original opponent, Albany *Herald* editor James H. Gray, had pulled out at late notice. No doubt slightly relieved that he would not have to face King live on national television, and also trying to regain some of the moral high ground for segregationists that had been ceded to the civil rights movement, Gray cited King's recent violation of a Georgia court's parole and probation orders as the reason for his refusal to debate the minister. Kilpatrick had no such qualms. As the debate turned to one of the central concepts that underpinned civil rights groups' strategy of non-violent direct action, Kilpatrick, swathed in the smoke of his own cigarette, listened intently as King began his well-rehearsed argument that St Augustine had been essentially correct to argue that, while all citizens should obey just laws, 'an unjust law is no law at all'. In fact, King continued, 'when we find an unjust law, I think we have a moral obligation to take a stand against it'. When King then turned to Kilpatrick and announced that he would like to deal with 'the resistance of segregationists to the Supreme Court's decision of 1954', Kilpatrick was quick yet gentle with his response. 'We thought we were resisting an unjust law, you see ...' Although King went on to recover his poise and to differentiate between 'civil' and 'uncivil' disobedience, Kilpatrick had made his mark.[126]

Kilpatrick's performance on *The Nation's Future* encapsulated the confidence that had begun to permeate massive resistance's ranks at the close of the 1950s. Certainly, there had been setbacks for the forces of segregation, not least in the psychological blow provided by Eisenhower's belated decision to use federal force to implement *Brown* in Little Rock. Nevertheless, there was mounting evidence to suggest that resistance was still on a firm footing. At least some of massive resistance's leaders had realized that they needed to broaden their horizons to construct arguments and rationales that appealed to those who lived beyond the regional confines of the South, and who were only alienated by the basest segregationist appeals for continued white supremacy. What is more, after some early misjudgements by individuals and organizations that failed to come to terms with the nuances and subtleties involved in launching such campaigns, certain segregationists proved themselves to be adept, and on occasion even highly skilled at taking the message to other parts of the nation. The concurrent development of such a broad array of arguments specifically designed to appeal to grassroots segregationists within the states of the Old Confederacy reinforces the fact that massive resistance was not a monolithic entity. By the end of the decade segregationists had devised a broad panoply of resistance measures, many of which were designed to achieve very different aims, but all of which worked towards the same ultimate goal: the maintenance of segregation. Those multifaceted strands of ideological, rhetorical, legislative and often violently coercive resistance were also, by 1960, being buttressed by an increasingly sophisticated apparatus of resistance. Sovereignty commissions, investigative and legislative committees, Citizens' Councils and quasi-council groups brought both gravitas and efficiency to the resistance cause, but also aided in the establishment of a complex distribution and publication network that gave resistance much of its peculiar character.

4

RESPONSIVE RESISTANCE, c. 1960-1965

By the start of the 1960s, segregationists had accumulated a range of discernibly different tactics to resist federally enforced desegregation. Much of the legislative web of massive resistance that southern politicians had constructed in the 1950s remained in place, as segregationists continued to dominate the region's legislatures. The longevity of concerted opposition to *Brown* in the South meant that, by the 1960s, politicians at the local and state levels had all come to power in elections that had taken place against the backdrop of massive resistance. There were no longer any incumbents that had been voted into position in the pre-*Brown* era, who had not had to make their views on the Supreme Court's schools decision clear to their constituents. Legislatures, governors' mansions and local municipal posts were filled with politicians who openly and aggressively pursued resistance strategies. The result was that massive resistance had in effect become state sponsored, especially in the Deep South. In tandem with the political scene, localized day-to-day resistance continued in rural areas, towns and cities across the South, where it remained searing in its brutality.

There was little change to the circumstances in which the South's African Americans and civil rights proponents had to work on a daily basis, and massive resistance appeared deeply entrenched. That said, there was increasing evidence of a totemic shift in the balance of power in the wider struggle over desegregation, as the forces operating outside the immediate control of those local white communities and their elected representatives slowly began to reduce their tolerance for outright resistance. Sixteen months after Eisenhower sent the 101st Airborne into Little Rock, Virginia's school closing laws were overturned by both federal and state courts on the same day, 19 January 1959. The closing of white schools in any locality faced with imminent desegregation had formed the backbone of the massive resistance laws that Governor Tom 'Bahnse' Stanley had forced through Virginia's state legislature in the summer of 1956. Although only a small minority of Virginia's school-age children had been personally affected by the closures, the ramifications of the courts' decisions to reopen the schools were much wider. It was of course a coincidence that both decisions were delivered on the anniversary of Robert E. Lee's birth, but it added a certain symbolism to the occasion nonetheless: it took Stanley's successor in the Virginia governor's mansion, J. Lindsay Almond, Jr., over a week to come to terms with the courts' verdicts, but on 28 January 1959 he publicly consigned Virginia's school closing to the state's political past. He was, in effect, conceding defeat on behalf of Virginia's most hard-line segregationist legislators.[1]

An end to those staunchly hard-line resistance measures should not, however, be equated with a defeat of massive resistance in its entirety. Rather than complying meekly with *Brown* in the wake of the 1959 court decisions, the Old Dominion simply returned to its initial resistance strategy based around local option assignment plans. This was an organized retreat, not a rout. In the aftermath of Faubus's stand at Little Rock, Arkansas also turned to a tokenistic plan of 'minimum compliance' with *Brown* that was far short of wholesale desegregation, and the federal government appeared to signal the end of what segregationists referred to as 'interference' in the state's affairs when, in the months after the crisis, it chose not to bring legal cases against those who had been accused of fuelling the mob.[2] In broader terms, away from the specifics of school desegregation plans, many of the southern states' other legislative resistance measures remained on the statute books. The Supreme Court had begun to chip away at the litany of laws against the NAACP as early as 1958, when the justices forbade Alabama from making the Association's membership lists public, but the South's legislatures had collectively passed so many bills aimed at undermining the NAACP that the Supreme Court was still busy overturning them in 1963.[3] By the start of the 1964–65 school year, a decade after *Brown*, less than 3 per cent of the South's African Americans attended school with whites, and in Alabama, Arkansas, Georgia, Mississippi and South Carolina that number remained substantially below 1 per cent.[4]

THE 1960 NEW ORLEANS SCHOOL CRISIS

Although broad geographical divisions existed in the strength of resistance, notably between states of the Border and Deep South, any uniformity in the patterns of segregation and desegregation continued to be offset by peculiar local conditions. The particular circumstances governing racial separation in New Orleans serve to highlight the anomalies that were increasingly evident in the practice of segregation, as well as the forces that continued to be brought to bear on the resistance question into the new decade. For, although residential neighbourhoods had been integrated in New Orleans for 300 years by 1960, and the city's buses and parks had been desegregated by federal order with the minimum of fuss, a rigidly segregated school system remained in place. The continuation of school segregation in the Crescent City six years after the first *Brown* decision was not merely the result of a *laissez-faire* attitude by local resisters. The city's NAACP chapter had, for example, filed suit against the Orleans parish school board to commence desegregation as early as 1952, and African American activists had begun to petition for such a move two years before that. It was not until May 1960, when US District Court Judge J. Skelly Wright ordered the school board to implement a grade-by-grade desegregation plan for the coming autumn that the situation developed into what became known as the New Orleans 'school crisis'.[5] The multi-layered, sequential strategies that segregationists developed to hinder Wright's plans for the orderly desegregation of the city's schools serve as testament to the endurance of massive resistance beyond the 1950s.

The city's segregationists mixed an ongoing general displeasure over the idea of mixed schooling with a number of fears that were specific to the situation in New Orleans. Judge Wright's plan demanded that, in the long term, each child in the city would simply attend the nearest school to his or her home. New Orleans' historical patterns of non-segregated housing led to a situation in which, by the time his plan had been completed, two-thirds of the city's 48 white elementary schools would be integrated: this would be no token desegregation. The city's particular and peculiar religious mix also had the potential to add significantly to segregationists' woes, for while the city's public school system catered for 91,000 pupils, 54,000 of whom were black, a significant number of other children attended schools that operated under the control of New Orleans' Catholic Archbishop, Joseph Francis Rummel. In all, 49,000 pupils attended those Catholic schools, 8,000 of whom were black. As a result, many segregationists were concerned that a call by the Archbishop to desegregate those schools that operated in his archdiocese would lead inevitably and inexorably to pressure for the desegregation of public schools across the whole network.[6]

The most immediate and telling response to Wright's school desegregation plan came from Louisiana's segregationist legislature. In a gubernatorial campaign that straddled the 1959–60 New Year, Governor James H. 'Sunshine' Davis had been successful in wresting power from the dynastic first family of Louisiana politics, the Longs. Davis ran on a staunchly segregationist ticket, and throughout the school crisis was ably abetted by a phalanx of hard-line segregationists including Willie Rainach, Leander Perez, Attorney General Jack P.F. Gremillion, Secretary of State Wade O. Martin, Jr., State Sovereignty Commission Chairman Frank H. Voelker, Jr., State Superintendent of Education Shelby M. Jackson and Orleans parish school board member Emile Wagner. The legislature, top heavy with segregationist intent, was called into a series of five emergency sessions to deal with the looming school crisis. In what has been accurately referred to as a 'fast-moving and repetitive legal duel', Judge Wright moved quickly to establish legal rebuttals for the succession of obfuscatory plans that the legislature concocted. Davis and his coterie of segregationists attempted, among other things, to replace the school board with an eight-man committee that would operate under their control, before subsequently replacing that eight-man committee altogether by transferring its powers to the legislature. In evidence of their increasingly reactive, piecemeal approach, they then declared the first day of proposed desegregated schooling a school holiday and summarily fired superintendent of schools James F. Redmond from his job, replacing him with a 'sergeant-at-arms' equipped with a 'legislative police force' to stop desegregation. In turn, as part of his response, Judge Wright became the first man in legal history to enjoin an entire state legislature with a restraining order.[7]

The escalation of the crisis in New Orleans also serves as a case study of massive resisters' continued ability to inject extremism into what was, in southern terms at least, a relatively moderate situation. For, in the summer of 1960, it appeared as though even the most ardent of the city's segregationists were reconciling themselves to some form of limited school desegregation in the coming months. Resisters' actions appeared legally hidebound by the federal courts' decision in the Little Rock-inspired *Cooper v. Aaron* case, the outcome of which declared that schools that were about to be desegregated could not be closed on the premise that violence might erupt as a result. What is more, progressive groups such as the Southern Regional Council-sponsored 'Save Our Schools' and the 'Committee for Public Education' stole an ideological march on the city's segregationists by successfully recasting the terms of the debate over schooling from one of 'segregated schools versus integrated schools' into one of 'open schools versus closed schools'.[8]

Nonetheless, the city's massive resisters did not give up hope amid signs that desegregation would not progress smoothly. The school board selected the schools that were to be at the forefront of New Orleans' desegregation via a series of arcane criteria which played into segregationists' hands. As one historian has noted, the deprived working-class neighbourhoods of the city's Ninth Ward made it 'a most unlikely place to begin such a revolution in human behavior', especially given that those neighbourhoods bordered St Bernard Parish, where that most iconoclastic of southern resisters, Leander Perez, held court. What is more, two of the schools that were finally selected, McDonogh No. 19 and William J. Frantz Elementary, were situated in the same neighbourhood, thus allowing segregationists to concentrate their disruption in one locality.[9] The Citizens' Councils, too, refused to be deterred by the creeping fatalism that had infected some segregationist ranks, and campaigned steadily for the establishment of 'educational cooperatives' which they hoped would provide education for white students removed from desegregating schools.[10] When Judge Wright decided to stay his desegregation programme until November, it proved to be a pivotal movement. The time lag not only allowed the moderates' momentum to dissipate, but equally crucially allowed massive resisters vital time to organize.

Resisters' campaign to maintain segregation in New Orleans' schools can be separated into three distinct phases. The first revolved around the legislature's failed attempt to wrest control of the situation away from Judge Wright. Davis and his cohorts buttressed the construction of their legislative rejoinders to Wright with a concerted and intelligently directed media campaign, which focused upon all the familiar touchstones of southern resistance ideology. Governor Davis, whose earlier stint as a guitarist and author of the noted hit 'You Are My Sunshine' prepared him well for media exposure, told television audiences on 13 November that 'the Supreme Court, in attempting to prohibit the state of Louisiana from using its power to operate schools, has clearly usurped the amendatory power that is constitutionally vested in the states and their citizens'.[11] Where Davis preached the broader church of states' rights primacy, Leander Perez unrepentantly sought to reach a far narrower congregation. 'Don't wait for your daughter to be raped by these Congolese', he announced, stoking latent fears of miscegenation. 'Do something about it now!'[12] Perez's rhetoric, and in particular a meeting at the city's Municipal Auditorium at which both he and Rainach spoke to an estimated 5,000 Citizens' Council supporters, triggered the second discrete phase of segregationist activity. As four African American students enrolled at McDonogh No. 19 and Frantz Elementary, mobs gathered outside the two schools on a daily basis.

Of particular note was a group of women who became known collectively as 'the Cheerleaders'. Ostensibly made up of working-class mothers opposed to their children attending desegregated schools, the Cheerleaders gathered daily outside the affected schools. From there they confounded both contemporary and historical stereotypes by bringing heretofore unknown levels of spite and hatred into the realm of public politics, and, what is more, doing so accompanied by a level of profanity that might very well have shamed so seasoned a resister as Perez himself. The Cheerleaders appeared so intent upon derailing planned, phased desegregation, and so vituperative in their daily mobbing of those attempting to attend McDonogh No. 19 and Frantz Elementary, that they received widespread television coverage and attained what can only be described as celebrity status within hard-line resistance circles, but infamy among more objective viewers. They even caused the writer John Steinbeck to alter the course of his planned journey around the United States to view what he described as 'the most reported and pictured' incident in contemporary newspapers. What he saw was 'a group of stout middle-aged women who, by some curious definition of the word "mother", gathered every day to scream invectives at children'. This was massive resistance as street theatre. Crowds gathered not to involve themselves in the Cheerleaders' campaign, but simply to watch the drama created by the women — along with attendant local police and federal marshals — unfold. Steinbeck detected a certain tenor and cadence to the Cheerleaders' invective which, to his writer's ears, suggested previously prepared material and the recitation of lines learned by rote. He was also taken aback by the content of the women's rhetoric, despite the fact that television stations had seen fit to blur the language of the Cheerleaders so as to render its obscenities indistinct. The words he heard were 'bestial and filthy and degenerate', he later reported. 'In a long and unprotected life I have seen and heard the vomitings of demoniac humans before', but still these words filled him 'with a shocked and sickened sorrow'.[13]

The Cheerleaders' task was to intimidate both the students attempting to gain entry to McDonogh No. 19 and Frantz Elementary, and the parents who continued to escort them to their newly desegregated schools. In one glaring respect, the Cheerleaders were utterly blind to the colour line, for they targeted parents and children of all races in an attempt to enforce a total boycott of the schools as a sign that desegregated schooling was unenforceable and, ultimately, unworkable. On 29 November, for example, a crowd estimated at 400-strong followed one pupil and her mother from the school all the way home, with police officers watching complicitly as the mob 'swarm[ed] over them, shouting obscenities, and smashing windows in their house'. The victims of the attack were white.[14] In what signalled the third and final phase of resistance in New Orleans, the mobs shifted the focus of their harassment and attacks from outside the schools themselves to the neighbourhoods in which those attempting to desegregate the city's educational facilities lived. What has been referred to as the 'street battle' took the fight directly to the homes of those whites threatening to break the Citizens' Council-endorsed school boycott. Emile Wagner coordinated a campaign to furnish resisters with a list of the drivers' names and licence plate numbers of the cars that were increasingly being used to ferry schoolchildren through the mobs each morning and afternoon.[15]

The Citizens' Council emerged as a guiding force throughout the crisis and, in the Louisiana Advisory Committee on Civil Rights' phrase, became 'the dominant political force in the community'. To one historian's mind, 'more important still was the large body of white New Orleanians who, although not directly affiliated with the organized resistance movement, would support its demands to the point of sacrificing public education'.[16] As well as the widespread support that segregationists received from within New Orleans, their cause was bolstered by a distinct lack of leadership from any moderate source in the city, and there were few clear voices calling for a temperate, peaceful solution. A moderate member of the school board did win re-election by 55,000 votes against three avowedly segregationist candidates in November 1960, one of whom had received explicit Citizens' Council backing, suggesting that parents' will to resist desegregation indefinitely was waning, but in the short term at least the city's segregationists appeared to hold the upper hand.

As the crisis continued, however, the pre-eminence of massive resisters in New Orleans was unsettled by the emergence of new forces that, as the decade wore on, were to confront and ultimately peg back resistance across all of the southern states. A number of the decisions taken at the local level in New Orleans foreshadowed wider trends that were to emerge over the coming decade, and many of the stresses to which resisters were exposed in the Crescent City portended broader trends that were to befall the region as a whole. Certainly, Judge J. Skelly Wright's indefatigable campaign to uphold the legal ramifications of the *Brown* decision, and his refusal to be cowed by the extraordinary actions of Davis and the state legislature, signalled a judicial determination to enforce at least some measure of constitutional equality in the public school system in southern locales. When a three-judge federal court ruled on 30 November 1960 that the Louisiana legislature's attempts to nullify the two *Brown* decisions represented 'a preposterous perversion of Article V of the Constitution', it brought a tangible legal victory for those African Americans who had first sought redress with *Bush v. Orleans Parish Board* in September 1952. More auspiciously, it heralded the end of interposition as a possible legal tactic of massive resistance, although, in truth, the majority of resisters had discarded it years previously.

Louisiana's business elite also played an important role in the negotiations that led, finally, to the token desegregation of New Orleans' public schools, thereby confirming the emergence of business progressives as an important variable in the desegregation struggle. In some southern cities, notably Tampa, Dallas and Columbia, businessmen were in the vanguard of those preparing their communities for inevitable desegregation. In others, including New Orleans, they were far less proactive but nonetheless were aware of the harm that outward displays of racial hatred could cause to the local economy and, thus, to their own profits. In fact, the New Orleans crisis saw both sides of the desegregation debate taking economic factors into consideration. Davis and the legislature, for example, sought to withhold money from moderates on the school board and other apologists for planned desegregation in what amounted to little more than state-sponsored blackmail. For many of the city's businessmen, the campaign for segregation was seen primarily as an impediment to business expansion. Thus, on 14 December 1961, with the annual financial gold rush of Mardi Gras fast approaching, over 100 businessmen put their names to a three-quarter page advertisement in the *Times-Picayune* that appealed for the end of street demonstrations and open defiance of the school board.[17] Many of the signatories were segregationist by persuasion, but businessmen by profession.

When the pressure applied by those businessmen is seen in conjunction with the November court decision, it is clear that the segregationist stand in New Orleans was fast losing momentum. That was confirmed when, in March 1962, Archbishop Rummel was finally cajoled into announcing the desegregation of the parochial schools in his Catholic archdiocese. One week later, on 3 April, Judge Wright effectively invalidated Louisiana's pupil placement law by upholding the desegregation petition of 102 African Americans.[18] The campaign for the maintenance of absolute school segregation in New Orleans had failed. More importantly, the few segregationists who were willing or indeed able to view the long-term consequences of the New Orleans crisis with any sense of clarity were also faced with subtle – though nonetheless crucial – indicators of change in presidential attitudes to continued southern resistance.

The Louisiana crisis had escalated just as the main political parties were steeling themselves for the 1960 presidential elections. Eisenhower was unwilling to allow federal forces to become physically involved in a repeat of the Little Rock showdown so close to polling day, and did little more than offer vocal encouragement to Judge Wright. The Kennedys, in contrast, fresh from their electioneering coup of telephoning Coretta Scott King while her husband, Martin Luther King, Jr., sat isolated in Georgia's Reidsville State penitentiary, sent out a series of subtle signals that suggested a more 'hands-on' approach to the racial question might be forthcoming from a Democratic White House. Kennedy was wary of losing the support of those southerners whose long, uninterrupted careers in the capitol had seen them rise to the senior ranks of the Democratic Party, and there remains little to challenge the prevailing historical view that the Kennedy White House came late to the civil rights struggle. Nonetheless, when the new administration filed an *amicus curiae* brief in the *Bush* case and sought to enjoin obstructive state officials in relation to the case, it clearly signalled that segregationists had a foe to be reckoned with in the Kennedy White House. It may have been more discernible in the attorney general than in the president himself, but here was an impatience with southern officials who persisted in actively opposing *Brown* that had not been present in the somnolent Eisenhower regime.[19]

THE CONTINUING REFINEMENT OF THE RESISTANCE CANON

Of course, the legislative measures that were guided through state legislatures by segregationist-minded politicians throughout the post-*Brown* era formed but one of the many strands of massive resistance. They were continually reinforced and buttressed by the dissemination of ideological arguments and the development of intellectual defences of the segregated society that those legislative measures were designed to uphold. By the start of the new decade, that intellectual rationale had been refined considerably. Perhaps the clearest single indication of the breadth of those arguments, as well as organized segregationists' willingness to disperse them to as wide an audience as possible, can be found in the material that the Jackson, Mississippi Citizens' Council sent out to a northern correspondent in January 1961. Roxanne Kalb, a high school student from Connecticut, wrote to the Council for information that, she hoped, would help her in an upcoming school debate in which she had the task of opposing the resolution that 'segregation should be illegal now'. Sensing a propaganda opportunity, the Council sent her a veritable compendium of resistance, made up of 14 separate publications and reprints that defined the resistance canon: 'Mixed Schools and Mixed Blood' by Herbert Ravenel Sass, which had originally been published in *Atlantic Monthly* magazine; 'Where Is the Reign of Terror?' by Mississippi Congressman John Bell Williams, and 'Strength through Unity' by his state Governor Ross R. Barnett; Eastland's 'We've Reached an Era of Judicial Tyranny'; 'The Supreme Court Must Be Curbed' by South Carolina's James F. 'Jimmy' Byrnes; Tom P. Brady's 'Segregation and the South'; 'The Ugly Truth about the NAACP' by Georgia Attorney General Eugene Cook; 'The Mid-West Hears the South's Story', a reprint of 'Address at Elmira College', and a *Congressional Record* tear sheet of 'The Search for America', all by Citizens' Council stalwart William J. Simmons; two pieces by Carleton Putnam, 'High Court's Arrogance is Viewed by Northerner' and his 'Second Putnam Letter'; the religious arguments provided by Rev. G. T. Gillespie in 'Conflicting Views on Segregation'; and, finally, a reprint of the *Congressional Committee Report on Washington, DC Schools*.[20]

Here, then, were detailed arguments that sought to prove that *Brown* was the product of a politicized court working beyond the confines of its constitutional mandate. By acting beyond that remit, the writings collectively argued, the court was threatening what science had proven to be the purity of the white race and thus was also threatening whites' long-established position at the top of hierarchical pyramids of racial taxonomy. Racial science and a deeply paternalistic reading of history were fused together to suggest that racial purity was deeply embedded in the South's history and had acted as a primary contributor to the region's harmonious race relations. Much of that harmony had been built upon the civilizing instincts of whites, which had not only led to the creation of the South's own highly developed society but had also bestowed civility on blacks who, history was taken to have proven, were otherwise incapable of creating or sustaining civilized societies on their own. Bolstered by what was interpreted as a religious mandate for racial purity, segregationists also argued that they were being persecuted for what was not in fact a sectional problem at all, but rather was a localized outgrowth of an international battle against a godless, un-American foe. It was therefore outside agitators – who at best had little understanding of the South's peculiar historical practices and who at worst were paid members of the global communist conspiracy – that were most intent upon fomenting racial hatred in the region.

For some, the sheer expanse and diversity of those defences has been taken as a sign of the inherent weakness of the segregationist position because, it has been argued, such range came at the expense of a concentrated development on one or two arguments behind which a united South could rally.[21] There were certainly situations in which the lack of a single, coherent programme handicapped the segregationist South and some resisters did indeed latch on to any argument that was presented to them, notably those at the grassroots and particularly those who could not understand why it was that their established way of life was under such threat from their own government and judicial systems. Although such proponents of what might best be termed 'resistance at all costs' were present throughout the post-*Brown* era, there were times at which other segregationists chose to act very differently. In fact, tracing the ways in which the massive resistance canon developed and, in particular, the ways in which certain segregationists chose to highlight and promote different arguments from within that canon at different times, reveals much about the wider dynamics of the period.

Three distinct phases in the development of the rhetoric and intellectual rationale of resistance are discernible. Immediately after *Brown*, the South's segregationists appeared to be in disarray, and there was little solidity to the segregationist position and correspondingly little sign of the emergence of a coherent intellectual response. Many state officials knew that they ought to resist the decision, but were far less sure of how they might be able to do so to any great effect. By the end of the 1950s, however, the picture was rather different and a full panoply of resistance rationales and defensive weapons had been formulated. To claim that southern segregationists were in some way bewildered by the choice of intellectual rationales available to them in this period, however, is to misunderstand the way in which many segregationists chose to argue in defence of their position. Most resisters, especially those who were actively interested in trying to understand the position in which they now found themselves, were aware of the full range of resistance arguments that were being promulgated by their fellow segregationists. That did not mean that they were drawn to all of them. In contrast, most resisters in time alighted upon a single argument or set of arguments which they found to be most convincing, or which most accurately reflected their personal ideological position.

By the early 1960s, a third period of resistance was discernible, and it was one that shared many similarities with the period in the immediate aftermath of *Brown*. In the face of the growing federal pressure that was being exerted on their position, and as the civil rights movement developed increasingly sophisticated, dignified and ultimately successful lines of attack, massive resistance lost much of its new-found coherence. As they were forced into becoming increasingly responsive rather than proactive, segregationists once again struggled to find adequate weapons and tactics with which to tackle their opponents. As that rearguard action became increasingly desperate, so resisters increasingly flailed around in search of anything that might offer them an advantage.

Those segregationists who were sufficiently steeped in the paternalistic belief that southern blacks were content with their lot searched around for other external stimuli that could be blamed for fomenting radical racial change in the region. Some, such as Sunflower County's Mississippi Senator James O. Eastland, swiftly decided that the greatest spur was provided by the agents of communism. In that vein, he used the years after *Brown* to hone anti-communist attacks, drawing on the region's long traditions of anti-radicalism in order to find ever more ingenious ways to link the forces of desegregation to a broad communist insurgency. Beyond the rhetoric that questioned whether there was anything to stop Chief Justice Earl Warren 'citing as an authority in some future decision the works of Karl Marx', Eastland callously and calculatedly used his seniority position on the Judiciary Committee to chair a series of red-baiting hearings in the South that were designed with the sole intention of discrediting proponents of civil rights.[22] By 1961, one southern judge had taken it upon himself to warn the NAACP's headquarters that it was 'not doing any Negro any good to accept favors' from the liberal and progressive groups that Eastland had targeted.[23]

It was not the NAACP that formed the sole target of anti-communist attacks from Eastland's red-baiting committee and other committed southern segregationists, though. The South's biracial progressive organizations, such as the Southern Conference for Human Welfare, its educational offshoot the Southern Conference Educational Fund, and the Southern Regional Council formed the particular focus of such anti-communist attacks. For those committed segregationists such as Eastland who remained wedded to the importance of creating and subsequently maintaining a façade of southern white unity and homogeneity, such avowedly liberal groups presented a thorny dilemma. Not only did they stand as living proof that not all southern whites were avid followers of historical arguments for the pressing need for the paternalistic treatment of the region's blacks, but those organizations' meetings and conferences also vividly exemplified the fact that whites and blacks could occupy the same social spaces. The presence of a coterie of southern whites who looked for progressive solutions to the region's racial problems also threatened to render many of the central arguments of massive resistance obsolete. These were not 'outsiders', and they could not be brushed off with claims that they were ignorant of the specific ins and outs of the region's race relations. They could, of course, be attacked for being in the thrall of communism.

While Eastland and his cohorts persisted with loyalty hearings and anti-communist crusades, other resisters became utterly convinced that the only arguments that the South needed to put forward to justify continued racial segregation were those based in racial science, and they single-mindedly concentrated on their dissemination. A number of racial science's leading proponents were, on the face of it, unlikely bedfellows of massive resistance. Carleton Putnam, for example, was a Princeton-educated native New Yorker who had spent years employed as an airline executive, and who was initially – by his own account – unmoved by *Brown*. Little Rock, though, shook him from his torpor and he responded by producing some of resistance's most popular and widely disseminated works of scientific racism, notably *Race and Reason: A Yankee View*. His subsequent influence on resisters was sufficiently profound for Mississippi's governor to invite him to Jackson on 26 October 1961 for a dinner at which 'five hundred patriots' paid $25 a piece to attend, and for the day to be proclaimed 'Race and Reason Day'.[24]

Wesley Critz George provided a less unexpected source of scientifically based rationales for racism than Putnam, although he too was conspicuous as a non-native southerner. George boasted the clearer scientific credentials of the two. At the time of massive resistance, he was serving as an emeritus professor of histology and embryology at the University of North Carolina at Chapel Hill. He was so convinced that racial science held the answer to the desegregation debate, and that his long-held views on the inherent inferiority of non-white races was correct, that he effectively shunned all other arguments that were available to massive resisters. Moreover, he possessed both the strength of character and organizational skills required to run North Carolina's foremost Citizens' Council organization, The Patriots of North Carolina, Inc. as little more than a promulgator of his personal views on scientific racism. When it came to arguments over the separation of the races, George believed that he could 'do little more than present the facts', and as far as he was concerned by 1962 those 'facts' led him to believe that the races should not only be kept apart, but that white supremacy should reign unchecked in the South.[25]

Some – but by no means all – of the region's political grandees eschewed the greater excesses of resistance rhetoric altogether, and settled instead upon diplomatic statements that were bleached of the worst excesses of southern demagogic racism, relying upon coded references to race that their constituents would have readily understood. Such an approach was most popular with those segregationists that coveted a high profile in Washington, especially those that represented the South's border states. Virginia's Harry Flood Byrd, Sr., for example, retained a long and personal attachment to segregation at all costs. When he warned against a proposed civil rights bill, however, he belied his openly segregationist credentials by wording his opposition in such a subtle way that it appropriated the language of the Constitution while simultaneously heightening the racial fears of the majority of white southerners. 'Imposing Federal power in areas that have been reserved to the States', Byrd stated flatly, 'simply means an increasing bitterness against the destruction of states' rights by the federal Government, and the usurpation of power by the Supreme Court of the United States.'[26] South Carolina's Jimmy Byrnes, Virginia's David J. Mays, North Carolina's Samuel J. Ervin, Mississippi's John Satterfield and Georgia's Charles J. Bloch and R. Carter Pittman were all leading proponents of resistance arguments that were so firmly located in the language of the Founding Fathers and constitutional lawyers that they contributed to what one historian has called a 'cult of respectability' within white supremacist thought.

Pittman, who served briefly as the president of the States' Rights Council of Georgia, put so much faith in the Constitution and the founding documents of the Republic that he was averse to 'pure democracy', which he viewed as a system of government 'in which the will of the people is translated into action without regard to the constitution or laws'.

By the end of the 1950s, the release and liberal reprinting of a number of Pittman's written tracts on the judicial and legal position of segregation saw him firmly at the forefront of the constitutionalist strand of resistance thought. His attempts to elevate both himself and his arguments above the mob mentality of the baser racial rhetoric of many massive resisters was even visible in the small print of the pamphlets which he allowed to be distributed. *All Men Are Not Equal* identified the author at the bottom of the front page as 'the senior member' of law firm Pittman, Kinney & Pope, as well as 'an able lawyer and a historian and a scholar'. The front cover of a second work, *The Law of the Land*, proclaimed the tract as a reprint from Emory Law School's *Journal of Public Law*, and readers of *The Supreme Court, The Broken Constitution and the Shattered Bill of Rights* were reminded that it was a compilation of four addresses, including one that had been delivered at the annual meeting of the Georgia Bar Association, another that was read into the *Congressional Record*, and one that was first given as a paper to the Institute of City and County Attorneys.[27]

One of the clearest indications of the often very different approaches to resistance taken by southern segregationists comes from North Carolina's Sam Ervin. In 1961, Ervin wrote a letter to a member of the faculty at Duke University that clearly delineated between the senator's own brand of comparatively restrained, legalistic resistance and the more intemperate actions of some of his constituents:

> When Southern whites resort to interracial crimes of violence, or Southern law enforcement officers fail to protect those against whom such crimes are directed they do more injury to our cause than all the South's enemies are able to accomplish. In short, they lend aid and comfort to those who strive to defeat Southern Senators and Congressmen in their fight to preserve the basic governmental and legal rights of Southern States, Southern officials, and Southern people.[28]

Ervin remained a committed segregationist, and was fiercely resistant of *Brown* and the ramifications that the decision held for the segregated society in which he lived. He also personified the approach to resistance that saw no need to go beyond the legal framework that had long been in place in the South, and indeed the nation as a whole, and he certainly did not countenance violence. He simply believed that the changes being wrought on the South's racial practices were unconstitutional and should, therefore, be repealed. For resisters in his mould, the Supreme Court 'ignored the judicial processes and usurped power to amend the Constitution' with

Brown, which was the direct result of decisions that had been made in relation to the federal judiciary that were expressly political in nature and which had, for example, seen a former state governor appointed as chief justice. As Ervin told the audience of *The Citizens' Council Forum*, 'The constitution makes it clear that the laws of the United States are acts of Congress and not Court decisions.'[29]

MASSIVE RESISTANCE AND THE NORTH

By the start of the 1960s, the most eloquent and thoughtful of the South's resistance theorists had settled upon their chosen strategies. That is not to say, however, that the demonology of massive resistance had stagnated or was fixed. A number of resistance gambits drifted in and out of prominence, only to return in subsequent years as circumstances changed. The most notable example of such a shift is provided by the fluctuations in the argument that race and racism was not a peculiarly 'southern' problem at all, but was one that afflicted the entire nation. After the initial forays made by the judicious reprinting of the *Congressional Committee Report on What Happened When Schools Were Integrated in Washington DC* in the mid-1950s, resisters' attempts to draw attention to racial inequalities in the North calmed considerably. For a number of different reasons, the late 1950s and early 1960s saw an upsurge in the number of southern segregationists who attempted to revive the arguments put forward in that report and to recast the region's problems not as peculiarly sectional but as one example of wider, national issues. From Hal DeCell and the Mississippi Sovereignty Commission in the Deep South, to the work of James Jackson Kilpatrick and his fellow members of the Virginia Commission on Constitutional Government in the Border South, it was possible to detect a distinct and discrete tranche of resistance propaganda that was designed not to exculpate the South, but to expose the North's complicity in racial inequality.

That quest was greatly facilitated by the fact that neither civil rights activism, nor concerted segregationist opposition to that activism, was ever solely confined to the southern states.[30] In a ground-breaking study of urban racism in the North, historian Arnold R. Hirsch detailed the harsh realities encountered by those African Americans who attempted to desegregate Trumbull Park, a housing project in Chicago that was built during the New Deal. Although it was situated on the edge of South Deering, a 'heavily ethnic' neighbourhood, Trumbull Park remained all-white until a formal non-discriminatory policy was adopted in 1950. Once desegregation was transformed from policy into reality, a 'pattern of resistance' swiftly developed: new black residents were harassed day and night; any white resident who was seen to tolerate their presence was similarly targeted; and local shops that deigned to serve the project's non-white residents were quickly vandalized. Indeed, white resistance against the desegregation of Trumbull Park had become so organized by the summer of 1954, that, with uncanny similarities to a southern Citizens' Council, the euphemistically named South Deering Improvement Association (SDIA) was able to coordinate a terror campaign that saw explosions rock the homes of black residents every 30 minutes. Hate sheets and angry mobs became commonplace.[31] When the racial animosity that accompanied the attempted desegregation of the Trumbull Park project began to have a marked effect on local political campaigns, the similarities to events in the southern states became so marked that Hirsch saw fit to refer to 'South Deering's northern brand of massive resistance'.[32]

There is a temptation to cast such clear outbreaks of northern racism as somehow separate and distinct from those that continually punctuated southern life, perhaps because racism in the South received state sponsorship through laws, codes and ordinances that were largely absent from its northern incarnation. Such a temptation should be avoided, for although it was less pervasive above the Mason–Dixon Line, there is clear evidence that there were areas in which the state had an active hand in perpetuating racial inequality in northern states. In seeking to overturn what she has termed 'the prevailing views that dichotomize segregation as de facto in the North and de jure in the South', historian Jeanne Theoharis has used South Boston as a case study to show that vibrant civil rights struggles were underway in the North well before the *Brown* decision, and that such activism was not simply aimed at residual de facto segregation but also sought to roll back state-sponsored limitations on black opportunity.[33]

The per pupil spending of South Boston schools at the start of the 1950s was eerily evocative of schools in the southern states, and racially restrictive hiring practices meant that only 0.5 per cent of the district's schoolteachers were black.[34] The local chapter of the NAACP, which had supported local black mother Ruth Batson in her campaign to end desegregation as early as 1951, found that it could not avoid the concerted white opposition that was so redolent of its travails in the South. Most famously, the Association's St Patrick's Day float, which carried a sign declaring 'From the fight for Irish freedom, to the fight for American equality – NAACP Boston', and which was adorned with a photograph of John F. Kennedy, was hit by 'a barrage of stones, bricks ... eggs, beer cans, tomatoes, [and] white paint'. Local police made no attempt to arrest four youths 'who jumped in front of the float carrying a white banner saying "Nigger Go Home"'. The executive secretary of the local NAACP branch, Thomas Atkins, was highly critical of the police response to the episode, memorably remarking that the attack was carried out with a 'viciousness of the type you might expect to see in New Orleans or in the backwoods of Mississippi, but it happened in Boston'.[35]

The existence of such racial inequality and animosity, and the clear marshalling of support for continued segregation in the North, adds – on its own – an important dimension to any understanding of massive resistance in the South. The ways in which contemporary massive resisters in the South strove to turn such northern upheaval to their own advantage adds a further, vital element to any understanding of the segregationist campaign to resist desegregation. Resisters' attempts to highlight the extent of virulent northern racism, whether with broad brush strokes or in specific reference to the violent resistance encountered in areas such as Trumbull Park, have been continually neglected by historians. That is even more surprising given the central role that those attempts to highlight northern racism played in the teleology of massive resistance. Literary broadsides, from a glossy pamphlet by W. E. Debnam that had sold 215,000 copies by 1955 to 'The Case for the White Southerner' that Perry Morgan made in *Esquire* magazine in January 1962, drew unashamed parallels between the state of race relations on both sides of the Mason–Dixon Line.[36] Southern churchmen, such as the pastor of a Baptist church in Lake Charles, Louisiana, were keen to note that 'about the only difference' between the 'in-equalities, un-fair practices, and persecutions' that befell non-whites in the South and the North were to be found 'in the types and methods employed to bring them about'. Moreover, established resistance propagandists such as Kilpatrick continually strove to illuminate audiences to the fact that in 'one sense, the South has been the least segregated part of the country for generations; whites and Negroes have lived more closely together here, in far larger numbers, than anywhere else in the nation'.[37]

Privately, a number of high-ranking members of the NAACP did draw a distinction between racism in southern and northern states. It was black comedy, but a number of the Association's executive officers referred privately to the geographical dividing line between northern and southern states as the 'Smith and Wesson Line' on account of the open and outright violence which, they believed, was far more prevalent in the states of the South.[38] In contrast, their southern segregationist foes sought to limit any such difference, making much of rumoured racial antagonisms in the North with sharp and precise comments. One southern supporter of Senator Eastland berated the NAACP for omitting 'any reference to racial strife in the North' from their pronouncements, simply because segregation was not enshrined in law in the North. In addition to the well-known case of Chicago, massive resisters also sought to draw attention to Owosso, Michigan, and Fairborn, Ohio, where it was claimed 'Negroes are not even permitted to take up residence to say nothing of earning a living'.[39] *Arkansas Faith*, which served as the official publication of the White Citizens' Council of Arkansas, carried an article in April 1956 that made explicit comparisons between Little Rock and the 'completely segregated' city of Dearborn, Michigan. The article quoted liberally from an interview that the *Montgomery Advertiser*'s Tom Johnson had conducted with Dearborn's Mayor Orville L. Hubbard. Hubbard explained that it was a conscious decision to try to keep the 130,000 population of Dearborn so rigidly segregated that it was altogether free from blacks. 'It's the unwritten law', he said. 'They can't get in here. We watch it. Every time we hear of a negro moving in – for instance, we had one last year – we respond quicker than you do to a fire.' The Mayor's segregation-minded constituents had 'taken an open stand in our community', Hubbard concluded. 'We are for complete segregation with no ifs, ands and buts about it.'[40]

Many of the links that the South's massive resisters made to racial disturbances in the North were, at least in part, facilitated by information furnished by segregationists residing in the North. Historian Neil McMillen has argued that the Citizens' Councils' plans to extend their empire of organized resistance into northern states were largely inept, but the absence of coherently organized Councils should not be allowed to mask the presence of other groups who were intent upon destabilizing efforts at integration.[41] Alongside local organizations such as the SDIA in Chicago, two crosses – so redolent of the southern Ku Klux Klan – were burned in front of a black couple's house in Columbus, Ohio, in 1957; a white teenage gang known as the United Nordic Confederation was operating in the New York borough of Queens by 1958 'dedicated to propagating the idea of white supremacy'; and in Cincinnati in the same year, 'a heavy in-migration of Southern mountain whites' was blamed for an armed white gang's attack on black youths.[42] More importantly, the inability of resistance-minded segregationists to organize effective Councils 'beyond Dixie's frontiers' should not be equated with the failure of northern-based segregationists to impact upon massive resistance more widely. Asa 'Ace' Carter, that most vituperative of southern white supremacists, set aside regular column inches in his segregationist publication *The Southerner* for E. B. Girdley, 'an official of the Citizens Councils in Michigan' who lived in Detroit. Starting in the summer of 1956, Girdley used his articles to pass frequent comment on the dire state of race relations in the North in the hope of inflaming southern whites' sensibilities to the treatment that they were receiving from the federal government when, Girdley attested, northern whites' treatment of blacks was little different.

Some of massive resistance's supporters were clearly not content to stop at the passive dissemination of reports of decaying race relations in the North. In the summer of 1956, Roy Wilkins became so worried about a Citizens' Council-backed plot to foment greater racial unrest in northern cities that he wrote to the Federal Bureau of Investigation to outline his concerns. An informant was alleged to have tipped off the NAACP to Citizens' Council plans to call for 'the instigation of outbreaks of interracial violence this summer in certain northern urban centres', Wilkins told FBI director J. Edgar Hoover. 'Disturbances would be started at such places as picnics, baseball games, parks and playgrounds, excursion boats, bus and bus depots, and the employe [sic] entrances and parking lots of large industrial plants', Wilkins continued, noting that the Councils 'will bend every effort this summer to keep down any violence in the Southern states'. The plan's organizers hoped to achieve two distinct, though related, ends. First, to turn 'the attention of the North away from the South and toward its own racial problems', and second to provide '"evidence" that the Northern way of life which does not include state-imposed racial segregation produces racial clashes, whereas the Southern segregated system produces racial harmony'. The NAACP's informant reported that the Councils were willing to employ paid 'fomenters' if necessary, and believed that the cities of Detroit, Chicago and St Louis were particular targets. Almost immediately after Wilkins's warning to Hoover, the *Detroit Free Press* reported that Asa Carter's younger brother, James Douglas Carter, had rented an office and leased a post office box in Dearborn, and had 'established a beachhead' for a statewide Citizens' Council. The Citizens' Councils clearly had no intention of providing membership figures for their northern chapters that were any more reliable than those routinely provided for their southern ones: Joseph G. Cardinal, secretary of the Dearborn Chamber of Commerce, reported local rumours that 'the organization already has 125,000 members in Michigan and has set a goal of 300,000 members'.[43]

LOSING THE INITIATIVE: RESISTANCE, REACTION AND THE SIT-INS

It was not only the white segregationist side of the battle over southern desegregation that kept a watchful eye on events in the North and northern public opinion. As southern civil rights activists stepped up their campaign to end segregation in the region, they too took a tactical interest in northern affairs. The early 1960s appeared to witness an upsurge in the level of civil rights activity in the southern states, as African Americans ratcheted up the level of their ongoing protests against continued segregation there.[44] Closer analysis also suggests that the growth in the intensity of that black protest was not so much the result of increased activity per se as it was the result of an increasing sophistication in the design of civil rights protests. In close succession, the student-led 'sit-in' protests, the Freedom Rides, successive attempts to desegregate the Universities of Mississippi and Alabama, and mass direct action campaigns in towns and cities such as Birmingham, St Augustine and Selma all sought a head-on engagement with continued segregation in the South. Where segregationists sought to make use of the North to soften the specific focus on southern inequalities, civil rights proponents sought to use northern opinion to bring greater weight to bear on what they perceived to be peculiarly southern incarnations of racial oppression: each campaign, in other words, was designed specifically to bring national exposure to the ongoing oppression of non-whites in the post-*Brown* South. The calculations of Movement strategists held that tightly targeted civil rights protests would set in motion a chain of events that would, in the first instance, swing northern liberal, national and indeed international opinion behind civil rights protesters, and that as a result the White House would be left with no option other than to enforce constitutional notions of full equality for all citizens.

Massive resisters continued to operate in that new climate of militancy, but many found that the terms of engagement had changed. The underlying hum of intimidation, brutality and violence that had characterized many southern locales throughout the 1950s, especially in the region's isolated rural areas, did not abate in the early 1960s, and there was no sudden increase in the chances of redress for black victims from local white sheriffs. Where once segregationists had sought to take the initiative post-*Brown* by defining the ways in which they chose to respond to increased federal pressure to desegregate, however, they now increasingly found themselves in the position of having to respond to the initiatives of their opponents. The heady days of southern leaders attempting to coax the region's resisters into battle with clarion calls such as the Southern Manifesto were over, replaced by impromptu skirmishes in which southern forces tried desperately to repel breaches that civil rights protesters made in their increasingly fragile defensive lines. It was not an immediate change, and it was certainly not tidily heralded by a single defining moment, but as the 1960s unfurled it became clear that massive resistance was no longer following an agenda constructed by southern segregationists.

On 1 February 1960, four freshman students from A&T College staged a sit-in at the segregated lunch counter of their local Woolworth's department store in Greensboro, North Carolina. Their protest was not the first such sit-in, for the Congress of Racial Equality (CORE) had carried out pioneering sit-in demonstrations in the American context in the North in the 1940s, and there had been similar protests in Washington, Oklahoma City, Louisville, Tulsa and Miami. Nor was it an isolated instance of protest by Greensboro's African American community. While the four students themselves later claimed that they had acted without knowledge of CORE's earlier sit-ins, they were clearly participants in a long tradition of ongoing, local protest against Greensboro's Jim Crow laws. Their decision to block the segregated white-only lunch counter until they were offered service provided, in the words of William Chafe, 'the catalyst that triggered a decade of revolt', but it was a revolt that 'must also be seen as part of a continuing struggle to overcome racism'. In other words, this was not a radical departure from other expressions of blacks' displeasure at their ongoing oppression, but it did reflect a 'new language' of protest. As one commentator has put it, the sit-ins 'mobilized a previously inert generation'.[45] Those four A&T students, Ezell Blair, Jr., Joseph McNeil, Franklin E. McCain and David L. Richmond, had reignited a form of protest that – in terms of logistics if not courage – was relatively easy to stage, and which carried with it the potential to inflict huge damage upon systems of everyday segregation in the South. As the year ended, 100 southern cities had witnessed similar sit-in protests, in which 70,000 students had taken part.[46]

For a number of different reasons, the sit-ins posed questions that segregationists found very difficult to answer. By blocking service at segregated lunch counters, sit-in protesters managed to bring a harsh physicality to what had often remained a metaphysical idea, namely the issue of unequal rights. As David Goldfield has commented, the lunch-counter protests brought home the immorality of segregation to whites – both southern and northern – who might otherwise have continued to view segregation in terms of complex legal wrangles or as a problem that affected life beyond their immediate sphere, both of which had a tendency to leave the issue of greater civil rights as 'an abstract concept'.[47] In the specific context of massive resistance, then, the cold legal and constitutional arguments so carefully constructed by segregationists such as Sam Ervin and David Mays were in danger of being rendered ineffective by the emotion that such evocative protests were able to provoke. It was hard to concentrate on race-free matters of principle, in other words, when black protesters had found such a theatrical way of illustrating the deficiencies inherent in the daily implementation of those principles.

To add to segregationists' woes, there was also a clear disjuncture in the demeanour and appearance of the two sides involved in the sit-ins. It was not just that the local segregationists who regularly turned out to taunt, cajole or intimidate sit-in protesters could not compete with the reflective air of African American students who dressed in their best church-going suits and who carefully read college textbooks while waiting to be served. Merrill Proudfoot, a white Presbyterian minister who taught at Knoxville College, Tennessee, kept a diary of his participation in sit-ins at Rich's department store. In it, he noted that the grassroots segregationists who arrived at the scene of the demonstrations in which he was involved were 'poorly dressed' in 'dirty, tattered overalls', displayed 'crudely lettered signs' and were generally representative of 'what we call the hill-people'.[48] Proudfoot recalled a gang of about ten 'hoodlum boys' who maintained a menacing vigil outside Rich's, while in Greensboro 'members of white gangs who waved Confederate flags' appeared, and three whites were arrested by the end of the first week, one for setting fire to a black protester's coat.[49] Such activity contrasted starkly with that of the Greensboro four, who in the run-up to their first day of protest had asked themselves: 'At what point does the moral man act against injustice?' James Kilpatrick was quick to seize upon the problems of perception that such a contrast would bring. 'Here were the colored students, in coats, white shirts, ties, and one of them was reading Goethe and one was taking notes from a biology text', he wrote in a *Richmond News-Leader* editorial. 'And here, on the sidewalk outside, was a gang of white boys come to heckle, a ragtail rabble, slack-jawed, black-jacketed, grinning fit to kill.'[50]

The forces of massive resistance had to fight hard to counter the direct assault on Jim Crow that the sit-ins represented, as well as to repair the damage to the South's image that the coverage of the demonstrations had wrought. In Louisiana, the superintendent of education attempted a clamp down on the state's black colleges in an attempt to cut off the student-led sit-ins at source, but it proved futile as students took threatened expulsion in their stride and received assurances that the black community would put up bail bonds if they were arrested.[51] Most of the segregationists who maintained a keen awareness of the national picture in which southern segregation operated continued to favour legal and constitutional arguments: now, though, they were deployed defensively in reaction to black protest, rather than offensively to outline the basis of the southern position. By 1960, Kilpatrick served as chairman of the Virginia Commission on Constitutional Government's Publications Committee, and he oversaw the distribution of a pamphlet in April which maintained that, since the sit-ins took place on private premises, the actions of the protesters constituted trespass.[52] Unsurprisingly, it was an argument that found many supporters among those who attempted to rebuff the sit-in protesters. In Greensboro, for example, the manager of Woolworth's rejected an early compromise that was being discussed with protesters in late March 1960. As he told North Carolina's Governor Luther Hartwell Hodges, 'we are fighting a battle for the white people who still want to eat with white people'.[53] Proudfoot remembered being assailed by a segregationist making similar claims. 'The man who owns this store has not hurt your people in any way', the man proclaimed, even though Proudfoot was himself white. 'He tries to be a good citizen. He has a right to conduct business here in the free American way and choose whom he wants for his customers. Aren't you people ashamed to come in here day after day', he concluded, 'and try to ruin this man's business?'[54] If the owners of private premises wished to offer a service that did just that, then southern segregationists maintained that the Fourteenth Amendment gave them the right to do so.[55]

The sit-ins contributed to southern segregationists' growing discomfort by highlighting the ongoing discrepancies in the physical treatment that was afforded to blacks and whites in what was a supposedly 'separate but equal' society. At the same time, that new wave of protest also brought with it a concerted challenge to the ideology of the segregationist South. For those southern whites who had long predicated their support of Jim Crow on the paternalistic belief that 'their' blacks were content with their lot, and who believed the Southern Manifesto's claim that 'amicable relations between the white and the negro races' had been 'created through 90 years of patient effort by the good people of both races', the presence of so many southern blacks protesting against their second-class status appeared to create an insuperable intellectual paradox. After all, it was not until 1958 that *The Citizens' Council*, the self-styled 'official paper' of the Council movement, was first able to bring itself to admit that the majority of southern African Americans actually wanted integration.[56] Unlike the *Brown* decision, which, it could be argued, was the root cause of the crisis at Little Rock, this was not a distant, Washington-based Supreme Court that was trying to overturn entrenched southern social mores from afar, but was the work of aspirational African Americans who in many cases were born and brought up as southerners.

The most efficient way to overcome that paradox, segregationists soon learned, was to deny that the sit-in protesters were in fact southern, or, if their 'southerness' remained incontrovertible, to suggest that they were motivated by a pernicious external force. Those who wished to equate that external force with communism had a number of arguments to assist them. First and foremost, the fact that the sit-in protesters seemed intent upon causing friction between segregationists and their opponents was in line with the widely held view that communists' main tactic was one of 'divide and conquer', and that communists would only benefit from the societal chaos that segregationists believed would follow any breakdown in the region's racial patterns. Second, and as Virginia's Commission on Constitutional Government had attempted to convince its audience, certain segregationists also viewed the sit-ins as crimes against property rights, and the Communist Party was well known for abrogating any such rights.

Proudfoot himself recalled white youths outside Rich's store in Knoxville with handwritten signs asking rhetorically 'Is this a Communist Sponsored [sic] Organization?' to which one of his fellow sit-in protesters replied quick-wittedly by producing a sign stating that 'Khrushchev Could Eat Here – I Can't'. In Greensboro, Franklin McCain remembered that the Communist Party did try to get involved, offering the protesters money and even at one point extra bodies to help maintain the sit-ins' momentum, but the Party's advances were unequivocally rejected.[57] Most segregationists chose not to abide by the finer points of such arguments, though. As Proudfoot also found, segregationists failed to heed the fact that the NAACP had 'shown little interest in the lunch counter movement', at least in its early stages, and he grew weary of being hounded as a stooge of the Association – an Association which, elsewhere in the South, was being openly labelled the 'National Association for the Advancement of the Communist Party'.[58] The attempts to link communism with the sit-ins was explanatory as far as massive resisters were concerned, but also inflammatory. Georgia Governor Ernest Vandiver, for example, warned in February 1960 that any sit-ins occurring in his state would be met by the full force of state law. In March, when prospective demonstrators Lonnie King and Julian Bond took out an advertisement in the *Atlanta Journal and Constitution* to outline the rationale for their forthcoming protest, Vandiver thought the whole episode was the work of communists and was 'calculated to breed dissatisfaction, discontent, discord and evil'.[59]

Even after figures of high national profile such as J. Edgar Hoover, Harry S. Truman and James F. Byrnes had added their voices to concerns over the role of communists in the sit-in movements, the verbal attacks on those sitting-in did little to dull the ardour of their protests.[60] There were two further tactics available to massive resisters in their attempts to oppose the sit-ins, although they appealed to, and were utilized by, very different groups operating under the resistance banner. On the one hand, a number of southern legislatures instituted new legislative measures and empowered investigative committees in a bid to halt the rapid expansion of sit-ins across the region. On the other hand, grassroots resisters resorted increasingly to outright physical violence. In Georgia, Vandiver's response to King and Bond's newspaper article included a threat to pass a law making sit-ins illegal, while Louisiana's segregationist legislature went ahead and passed an 'anti-sit-in package' that spring.[61] In Texas, it was a nascent sit-in movement in the town of Marshall that provided the impetus for the state legislature to empower its General Investigating Committee (GIC) to follow the example of Congress's long-established investigator of suspected domestic subversives, the House un-American Activities Committee (HUAC). The committee was to act as a 'little HUAC', and it soon developed a mandate that amounted to little more than hounding civil rights activists in the state. The GIC's investigations centred on the role played by Doxie Wilkerson, an African American who had once belonged to the Communist Party but who had left when it became apparent to him that the Party's racial strategies were unrealistic and did not offer much concrete assistance to southern blacks. Despite the severing of Wilkerson's ties to the Party, the GIC pounced on his links with a black attorney, Romeo Williams, who had promised aid to the NAACP. In March 1960, the GIC published a report claiming that the Marshall sit-ins were the work of 'known Communists, Communist-fronts, and the NAACP', and, in the words of one historian, the information on Wilkerson was thereafter used to 'justify ongoing legal harassment of the civil rights movement in Texas'.[62]

At the other end of the spectrum from the state legislative agencies that responded to the sit-ins, whether in the form of Virginia's legalistic pamphleteering or Texas's red-baiting, a violent response remained the preserve of those massive resisters who thought little of the longer-term consequences of their actions, and who focused instead on what they saw as the need to deal out immediate retribution to those who were threatening the established mores of southern society. In Montgomery, Alabama, for example, where sit-ins had blossomed in late February, an all-out riot was only narrowly avoided when local police forces managed to intercede between supporters of the protesters who had congregated on the steps of Montgomery's capitol building and a crowd of angry whites, estimated to be some 5,000 strong, that was fast converging upon them. In Portsmouth, Virginia, too, the non-violence that characterized the sit-ins themselves was marred by violent confrontations between 'hundreds' of black and white students in February, and in Chattanooga, Tennessee, sit-ins dissolved into riotous confrontations involving an estimated 1,000 people. Alongside such mob violence, there was also evidence that smaller groups of vigilantes were intent upon disrupting sit-ins with violence. On 27 February, for example, a coterie of Ku Klux Klan members roamed the streets of Montgomery looking for demonstrators to attack, and found Christine Stovall. As the segregationist *Montgomery Home News* reported, 'The crisp crack of a hickory bat on a Negro head snapped the people out of their apathy into the realization that the steady, cold siege against their way of life was now breaking out in an obviously Communist-inspired racial strife.'[63]

Just as it had done during the Montgomery bus boycott, however, the violence that certain segregationists deployed against the sit-in protesters proved to be counter-productive. In Birmingham, for example, African American protesters decided on the less dramatic approach of holding a prayer vigil rather than sit-in demonstrations in March 1960. In response, eight members of the Ku Klux Klan forced their way into the home of one of those who had taken part in the vigil, beat him and his sister brutally, broke his mother's leg and finger and left her with further head injuries. It was an assault that, in the words of J. Mills Thornton, served only to 'radicalize' local students, and the planned prayer vigil was quickly replaced by sit-ins at five downtown lunch counters.[64]

The sit-ins caused desperate reassessments in parts of the South, especially among those southerners who routinely thought of themselves as morally upstanding and as good Christians. As well as highlighting the immoral aspects of segregation, the students who had manned the sit-in protests further succeeded by physically eroding one of the underlying assumptions upon which the South's separate societies had long been based: once Woolworth's had been forced into taking the decision to desegregate lunch counters, black patrons were able to eat in public spaces directly next to their white counterparts, and southern segregationists were thus no longer able to prohibit the close interaction of the two races in what many saw as a key social activity. The sit-ins also ushered in early signs of shifting momentum in the freedom struggle. A growing number of northerners were taking a direct interest in the conflicts over continued segregation in the South, and, worryingly for segregationists, they were choosing to align themselves behind the dynamic young protesters. By selecting local branches of national chain stores as the focus of their sit-ins, protesters such as the Greensboro four were – whether consciously or not – opening the way for northerners to instigate their own demonstrations in northern branches of the same stores as a show of solidarity with southern blacks' plight. That they did so in hundreds of cities, and that they raised considerable amounts of money to help pay the bail bonds of jailed southern protesters, indicated that national opinion was beginning its inexorable swing against segregationists.[65] Coupled to the speed with which the sit-ins gained momentum across the region, the edifice of segregation appeared to be cracking.

Nonetheless, the success of the new insurgency was not boundless, and there were counter-developments that offered segregationists hope. Initially, the forces of southern law and order appeared to have no idea how to police a non-violent, peaceful demonstration effectively. Policemen long trained in the art of suppressing violent upheavals and mob demonstrations were unaccustomed to being faced with what was, in Goldfield's memorable phrase, 'a still life' in which nothing appeared to be happening. As both the Virginia Commission for Constitutional Government and the Louisiana legislature were later able to show, however, there was considerable doubt surrounding the legality of staging sit-ins in places that many regarded as private premises, and, therefore, as exempt from the Fourteenth Amendment. Non-violent protesters were arrested for offences ranging from criminal trespass to disorderly conduct, and in Louisiana at least CORE's attempts to build upon the student-led demonstrations 'wilted under a barrage of injunctions and prosecutions'.[66] Once such legal action had been taken, it took almost two years for appeals to be heard and prosecutions to be overturned. It was not until May 1963, for example, that the Supreme Court decided that sit-in protesters could not be convicted of trespass if their protest had taken place in an establishment that was segregated by state ordinance.[67]

OPEN VIOLENCE ON A NATIONAL STAGE: MASSIVE RESISTANCE MEETS THE FREEDOM RIDES

In a subtle yet important contrast to the tactics adopted by the sit-in protesters, the participants in the Freedom Rides were not attempting to break down specific segregation ordinances. Instead, the two groups of volunteers – seven black and six whites – who boarded buses in Washington DC on 4 May 1961, did so with the intention of testing whether or not two decrees that the Supreme Court had already passed on matters involving segregated transport had actually been implemented at the state level. Where one member of the Greensboro four later recollected that, even in their 'wildest imagination' they could not have foreseen the full consequences of their actions, CORE's James Farmer was under no such illusions, remarking coolly that 'we were counting on the bigots of the South to do our work for us'.[68] The Supreme Court's 1946 *Morgan* decision had effectively outlawed segregation on inter-state transport, and the justices' decision in 1960's *Boynton* case had extended that ruling to apply to facilities within inter-state bus terminals. Farmer and the other Freedom Riders were, in effect, calculating that certain elements within the segregated South would be unwilling to allow inter-racial bus loads to travel through the region, and would not allow those passengers to make use of desegregated facilities in bus terminals as they did so. As a result, they hoped to bring to national attention the fact that segregation in southern transport continued unabated, despite two Supreme Court decrees that had emphatically ruled such action to be unconstitutional. In that respect, the Freedom Riders were not to be disappointed: although both buses, one Trailways and one Greyhound, made it as far as

Atlanta relatively unmolested save for assaults on John Lewis and Albert Bigelow in Rock Hill, South Carolina, both vehicles were met with open and brutal violence as their journeys progressed.[69]

The different ways in which segregationists struggled to respond to the Freedom Rides are testament not only to the tactical acumen of the journeys' planners, but also to the continued differences that existed within the heterogeneous world of massive resistance's supporters. All such resisters perceived the Freedom Riders to be a threat, but there was little agreement on the most appropriate way in which to meet that threat. That, again, was largely because those involved in formulating responses to the Freedom Riders were playing to different constituencies, and were thus interested in tailoring their resistance strategies to appeal to what were often very different audiences. As the most recent work on the Freedom Rides has shown, in total some 450 protesters took part, although historians have in the past focused most intently on those first two buses.[70]

In no small part, the continued focus on those initial buses is a direct result of the way in which grassroots segregationists greeted their arrival. Two white supremacist organizations that operated in Alabama, the National States Rights Party (NSRP) and local chapters of the Ku Klux Klan, conspired to halt the Freedom Rides in their tracks by coordinating violent attacks on the two buses. The original plan was for both buses to be attacked when they arrived in Birmingham, but when the Greyhound bus entered Anniston, circumstances changed. The original plans were susceptible to confusion, largely because, with four black and three white protesters on each bus, there was plenty of room for other passengers on board, and segregationists therefore had to make positive identifications of the Freedom Riders before the attacks went ahead. When the Greyhound reached Anniston, Alabama, a mob of agitated local whites and Klansmen was already waiting for it, and the bus lingered there just long enough for one of the men to puncture a tyre. Rather than wait for the bus to arrive in Birmingham, Klansmen realized that the Greyhound's tyre was fast losing air and pursued it in a motorcade estimated at 'some fifty cars'. When the bus driver was finally forced to a halt to deal with the tyre, his vehicle was viciously attacked. A firebomb was thrown through a window, and the passengers were only saved by a state investigator, Ell M. Cowling, who was riding on the bus incognito, and the arrival of highway patrolmen and a caravan led by local activist Reverend Fred L. Shuttlesworth. The Klan had been repelled, but, as Mills Thornton has noted, 'it had been a very close call'.[71]

When the Trailways bus reached Birmingham on 14 May, its occupants were met by a mixed group of NSRP members and Klansmen, armed with 'lead pipes, bats and chains'. For close to 20 minutes, the white supremacist mob attacked unhindered, save for a group of local blacks who, unschooled in the 'non-violent' arts of direct action, set upon three Klansmen and inflicted knife and head wounds. Again, the difficulties that the mob had in identifying and isolating the bi-racial Freedom Riders were apparent, for only two of the nine passengers on the Trailways bus who were seriously injured in the attack turned out to be Freedom Riders.[72] It later emerged that Theophilus Eugene 'Bull' Connor, Birmingham's newly re-elected public safety commissioner, had negotiated the 20-minute period as one in which his police forces would not arrive to restore order, and in which, therefore, the Klan and the NSRP would have free rein to terrorize those Freedom Riders that had made it to Birmingham. Furthermore, a network of inform-ants and double-agents, including Birmingham police sergeant Thomas H. Cook and Eastview Klavern Klansman G. Thomas Rowe, Jr., ensured not only that information could be passed easily between the police and the Klan to facilitate 'agreements' such as that which led to the 20 minutes, but also, given the fact that Rowe also worked as an informer for the FBI, that Hoover's men knew of such plans, too.[73]

As the most recent historical interpretation of these events persuasively argues, it was the 1961 Freedom Rides that heralded the 'nationalization' of what had previously been a localized and somewhat fractured civil rights movement.[74] The national – and indeed international – focus on the brutal attacks on the buses' occupants did little to ameliorate the national – and increasingly international – image of Birmingham as 'Bombingham', a city fuelled by racial hatred and violence. When the rising star of comedy and committed civil rights activist Dick Gregory swiftly incorporated 'Freedom-Rider Roulette' into his nightly routine, there was only a thin veneer of humour to his assertion that it was a game in which 'You pick from six bus tickets – five go to Chicago and one to Birmingham'.[75]

Given the circumstances, the open mob violence that filled the Trailways bus station might be seen as an embarrassment to the man charged with overseeing law and order in Birmingham. Instead, Connor remained bullish. When he was later asked by reporters to account for the fact that none of his officers were to be found anywhere near the bus terminus for the first 20 minutes of the mob's attack, he replied simply that 14 May was Mother's Day, and that his officers had consequently been visiting their mothers. Connor's actions in paving the way for the mob's attack, and his subsequent reaction to the national opprobrium that followed, were not miscalculations, and Connor had neither misread the gravity of the situation nor misjudged his response to the Freedom Riders' insurgency. Instead, it must be realized that the Freedom Riders' strategists and Birmingham's public safety commis-sioner were locked into a complex symbiotic relationship. The Freedom Riders' tactics were drawn up in order to elicit such a response from south-ern segregationists that national attention would be drawn to the fact that the Supreme Court's *Morgan* and *Boynton* decisions had effectively been ignored in the South. The protesters themselves may not have foreseen quite such visceral violence, but they were clearly under few illusions as to what awaited them on their journey.

Connor's response was equally tactical and equally calculated. Where the Freedom Riders were attempting to rouse national opinion, Connor was trying to appeal to the only opinions that mattered to him personally: those that belonged to his electoral base in Birmingham. As an avowed segregationist who relied upon an avowedly segregationist electorate, Connor knew that attacks on civil rights 'agitators' and meddling 'outsiders' played well in his constituency, and the Freedom Riders represented both. As Mills Thornton has argued in a brilliant history of municipal politics in Alabama, the local political situation was not only 'an essential factor' that shaped the thinking and actions of African American leaders, 'it was also frequently an important, and sometimes a decisive, motive in the actions of segregationist officials'.[76] Having lost a typically vitriolic run-off election to James 'Jabo' Waggoner in 1953, Connor spent four years in the political wilderness before an upsurge in local African American political activity effectively played into his hands. It roused white anxieties to such an extent that their votes ushered him back to office in 1957. As Birmingham's white middle classes used their increasing affluence to move to the suburbs, so Connor aimed to appeal to the working-class constituents who remained in his political heartland. By coincidence, he was again up for re-election on 2 May 1961, just two days before the Trailways and Greyhound buses left Washington. This time, he faced another avowed segregationist from the police department, T. E. Lindsey, who was reputed to be in receipt of the Ku Klux Klan's backing. Although Connor never admitted it himself, local FBI reports appear unequivocal in the belief that, in an attempt to win back Klan support, Connor conspired to use Cook as a go-between, and effectively swapped police intelligence for the votes of Klan members. Towards the end of April, that information included the proposed route of the Freedom Riders. The Klan knew when and where to attack their opponents, and Connor was re-elected handsomely.[77]

Connor perhaps best exemplifies the type of local segregationist who, while the civil rights activists around him sought long-term changes in constitutional interpretation, looked no further than his own political constituency to ensure short-term political success. Others higher up the political ladder shared Connor's attachment to the principles of a segregated society, but were unable to be quite so shortsighted in its advocacy. Alabama Governor John Patterson and the director of the state's highway patrol, Colonel Floyd Mann, both had to operate with one eye on their constituencies and the other on the White House. The complexities in the political relationship between Patterson and the Kennedy Administration were legion. The president and his attorney general realized the damage that further racially motivated violence could cause to the nation's image, but both were also well aware of the sensitivities involved in overriding a state governor with federal force. Eisenhower had belatedly done just that in Little Rock, but had paid a high political price with the powerful southern bloc in

Congress, and Kennedy was loath to lose their political backing yet further. At the same time, the president was sensitive to the fact that Patterson had to be seen to be protecting his state's rights by his constituents, and more importantly was aware of the political risks that Patterson had taken when, in summer 1959, he had been one of the first to endorse Kennedy's nascent political campaign.[78] The Freedom Riders were forced to pause after the flurries of violence in Birmingham as neither Trailways' nor Greyound's bus drivers proved willing to take them on to Montgomery, which had been planned as the next stage of their journey. In one sense, at least, it seemed as though the intimidatory tactics of Connor and the Klan had worked, for the buses had literally stopped in their tracks. The remaining Freedom Riders were forced to take up a Justice Department offer of flying to their planned final destination, New Orleans.

For neither the first time nor the last, however, southern segregationists were surprised by the commitment, obduracy and endurance of civil rights activists. No sooner had the CORE protesters departed than a group of SNCC students, corralled by original Rider John Lewis, arrived in Birmingham to complete the original itinerary. There was to be no respite. Patterson, in particular, found himself to be under increasing pressure, caught as he was by the Kennedy Administration on one hand, and his own ideological commitment – shared by his political supporters – to strong states' rights and the maintenance of segregation on the other. The Kennedys increased the pressure still further by sending members of the Civil Rights Division of the Justice Department, including the senior figures of John Doar and John Seigenthaler, to the scene of the chaos. Patterson eventually relented to the extent of guaranteeing the safety of a bus as far as the city limits of Montgomery, and both the governor and Colonel Mann believed that they had obtained a guarantee for the protesters' safety from Montgomery's city's Police Commissioner L. B. Sullivan. Sullivan, though, was in a similar position to Connor in Birmingham, and his political legitimacy would have been irreparably damaged if he was seen to be protecting 'outside' civil rights activists from violent white supremacists based in his own constituency. Perhaps unsurprisingly given Connor's behaviour, it later emerged that Sullivan had given a rather different assurance to the Klan than that he gave to Patterson and Mann, suggesting to local Klansmen that the city police would not intervene to protect the Freedom Riders in Montgomery.[79] The violence that greeted their entry into the city on 20 May was even more brutal than that which had occurred in Birmingham. White mobs attacked for well over an hour, unshackled by a complicit local police force, and even Seigenthaler was rendered unconscious by a blow to the back of the head.

Beyond confirming local Ku Klux Klan members' voracious appetite for racial violence, the attacks in Birmingham and Montgomery showed that grassroots massive resisters had the ability to enforce a pause in the progress of national civil rights protests, although they were unable to bring the Freedom Rides to a complete halt. While there is clear evidence that their local leaders exhibited a certain amount of political sophistication, notably in the cases of Connor and Sullivan, the violent episodes in the two Alabama cities also strongly suggest that the main perpetrators of the violence were either not concerned with, or more likely had not thought through, the long-term consequences of their actions. In Birmingham, for example, the front page of the *Birmingham News*, a newspaper which had endorsed Connor's election run earlier in the same month, asked 'Where Were the Police?' in the aftermath of the attacks on the Greyhound and Trailways buses, thereby ushering in a period in which the paper began to distance itself from the violent maintenance of segregation. Indeed, as historians such as Robert Corley and Glenn T. Eskew have argued, the attacks on the Freedom Riders saw something of a sea change in the attitude of many of those southerners who had previously supported segregation. The attacks followed a tradition in which local policemen worked 'in tandem' with armed mobs to preserve segregation, but it was clear in the aftermath of the attacks on the Freedom Riders that certain sections of the white community had grown uncomfortable with such violent methods, even though they retained a strong adherence to segregation. Most importantly, Birmingham's business progressives recognized that such scenes damaged their city's image considerably.[80]

Sid Smyer, who served as president of Birmingham's Chamber of Commerce in 1961, personified the increasingly complex and unforgiving position in which segregationist business leaders found themselves when faced with direct action campaigns. Smyer was, by one commentator's reckoning, 'the most influential man in Birmingham' at the time of the Freedom Rides, and was also a veteran of the Dixiecrat movement and occasional supporter of the Citizens' Council, although he had a long history of opposing the Klan.[81] He was also one of the first businessmen to recognize the wisdom of curtailing the kind of viciously violent massive resistance that was epitomized by Connor and the Klan, accepting that 'these racial incidents have given us a black eye we'll be a long time trying to forget'. As a result, Smyer instigated backroom discussions and negotiations with city officials, businessmen and at one point Attorney General Robert Kennedy himself, which effectively sought to circumvent Connor's power-base in a bid to bring greater racial harmony to Birmingham. As Smyer later acknowledged, however, those discussions had to be kept secret, for there were many segregationists who were yet to see the wisdom of placing 'a dollar-and-cents-thing' over and above an ideological commitment to continued segregation. Those who were involved in the discussions with Smyer, however, knew that 'If we're going to have good business in Birmingham, we better change our way of living.'[82]

In such a context, subjecting the South to progressive reform from within was the lesser of two evils. The alternative was to cave in to – and what is more to be seen to be caving in to – outside pressure from the federal authorities. Patterson's muddled reaction to the Freedom Rides acts as a clear example of the increasing difficulties that southern governors faced where civil rights was concerned. Once the Kennedy Administration had been forced to take an interest in civil rights, high-ranking southern politicians stood trapped between the will of the White House and the sentiment of their own constituents. Patterson may well have felt that he had been betrayed by Sullivan's duplicity in Montgomery, but of far greater long-term consequence for segregationists across the South was the Kennedy Administration's belief that it, in turn, had been betrayed by Patterson.

In direct response to Patterson's apparent inability to ensure the Freedom Riders' safety for the duration of their journey to Montgomery, some 400 US marshals were assembled by the attorney general and sent to the city to escort the buses to their final destination in Jackson, Mississippi. In a late display of acumen by southern resisters, Mississippi segregationists quietly arrested over 300 Riders in Jackson over the summer, but they did so for violating local segregation ordinances rather than for defying either the *Morgan* or *Boynton* decisions. In 1961, the Kennedys may have been willing to stage bruising encounters between federal forces and local state lawmen where Supreme Court decisions were concerned, and, more accurately, when they had been forced into doing so by the national and international attention provoked by well-directed non-violent activism. Where the political sums did not add up, however, or where local segregationist practices worked to curtail rather than exacerbate further violent incidents, they appeared willing and even somewhat relieved to turn a blind eye.[83]

The Klan may have had their day first in Birmingham and then in Montgomery, but they had also made a mighty contribution to an 'invasion' of the southern states by federal forces. Other segregationists saw the wisdom of treading more carefully. Virginia's immensely experienced senior senator Harry Flood Byrd was alive to the dangers that protesters such as the Freedom Riders posed to continued southern segregation, but was sufficiently canny to recognize that national coverage of the Ku Klux Klan's continued disregard for constitutional, legal, human and civil rights had just as much potential to damage the southern cause. Diplomatically, then, Byrd tried to carve out a middle ground. 'I deplore the violence which has occurred in Alabama', he began, 'but it must be realized that it was deliberately provoked by a mixed group of outsiders who went to Alabama to influence the people for propaganda benefits.'[84] The inference of the message that Byrd chose to deliver was clear if disingenuous: Americans had every right to be aghast at the violent scenes that had been reported from the bus stations, but they ought to see southern segregationists as victims rather than perpetrators.

The segregationist drive to demonize those protesting for greater constitutional rights, rather than those who had so very publicly tried to ensure that they were not granted, achieved greater momentum as increasing doubt was cast on the provenance of the Freedom Riders. Two days before Byrd had released his statement, first Orval Faubus and then South Carolina Governor Ernest Hollings demanded in quick succession that Kennedy investigate the 'agitators' that they presumed to be at the heart of the Freedom Rides. Both Patterson and his attorney general, MacDonald Gallion, assailed the White House with questions over the provenance of the 'invaders' whose one aim, they believed, was 'to create riots and breaches of the peace' across the region, and who had no understanding of a state's sovereign rights. Newspaper allegations of communist involvement in CORE and the Freedom Rides quickly followed, ranging from a predictable, populist red-baiting article in the *Citizens' Council* newspaper to rather more restrained journalistic pieces in the *Jackson Daily News, Memphis Commercial Appeal* and *Nashville Tennessean*.[85] Grassroots southerners besieged their political representatives with similar claims as massive resisters' response to the Freedom Rides coalesced into a solid campaign designed to draw attention away from the injudicious actions of white southerners by continuing to blame northern 'insurgents' for the violence of May 1961, by questioning the background of the 'outsiders' who had fomented that violence, and by inferring that the Freedom Riders were in some way linked to a wider foe of America's international Cold War struggle.

The widespread national revulsion at the brutal welcome afforded the Freedom Riders in Alabama, allied to the attempts by Birmingham's progressive business elite to eradicate such overt displays of racial hatred in the city should not, however, be used as indicators of an emerging tolerance in the approach of southern resisters more generally. Pressure from segregationist businessmen to moderate the greater physical excesses of resisters' behaviour was a feature peculiar to urban hubs and centres of commerce. In rural areas and small towns, any such moderating effect was inconsequential. Although historians have long been drawn to the drama of what might be termed the 'set pieces' of massive resistance in the 1960s, the day-to-day oppression experienced by African Americans throughout the South, and by others trying to eradicate existing racial inequalities in the South, continued more or less unabated. The shape and form of 1960s massive resistance was largely controlled by the agenda of civil rights activists, for it was to those activists' campaigns and forays that resisters increasingly found themselves forced to respond. At the same time, however, a parallel stream of resistance was clearly in evidence, as southern segregationists continued to place suffocating economic pressures at the local level upon those African Americans who remained intent upon fighting for their constitutional rights.

In Ruleville, Mississippi, for example, a Baptist church that functioned as the centre of attempts to register black voters found that its insurance policy was suddenly cancelled. It was a pattern repeated across the South. In Jasper County, South Carolina, an NAACP member found that his bank loan was foreclosed without warning, while in Snow Hill, North Carolina, the president of the local NAACP branch reported in May 1960 that his son and daughter-in-law had been summarily fired from their positions as teachers at the local high school, for no other reason, he reported, than 'because I am president of the NAACP'. The candour with which segregationists felt that they could impose such sanctions reflected a continued belief among local resisters that they could act with what amounted to impunity. In Georgia, for example, when Wesley W. Law was fired from his job as a post office employee on the grounds of spurious charges that had been brought against him, Congressman G. Elliott Hagan breezily informed a local Citizens' Council meeting that he had urged the termination of Law's employment himself because Law was also president of the Savannah NAACP.[86] The background hum of resistance and reprisal continued to be regularly punctuated by events that rose shrilly to grab national and, increasingly, international headlines and attention. It should not be ignored, however, for it was that form of day-to-day resistance that affected the greatest number of southern blacks, and it did so with an incessant monotony.

JAMES MEREDITH AND MASSIVE RESISTANCE AT OLE MISS

The Kennedy Administration's progress in the field of civil rights was slow before 1963, but it was nonetheless clear that both John Kennedy, as president, and Robert Kennedy, as attorney general, shared a greater desire to see constitutional rights being enforced in the southern states than their immediate predecessor in the White House. At the very least, they were keen to avoid a constitutional crisis such as that provoked by Orval Faubus's actions at Little Rock. By the summer of 1962, however, the Kennedy Administration had still failed to find a satisfactory state of equilibrium with southern state governors, each of whom viewed federal intervention as a violation of individual states' rights. More pressingly – and perhaps more practically – southern state governors realized that being seen to cave in to any such demands from Washington represented nothing short of political suicide.

When African American army veteran James Meredith applied for enrolment at the University of Mississippi in Oxford the day after Kennedy's inaugural address in 1961, it represented a minor irritation to segregation's supporters in the South. Conforming to long-established southern practice, the University produced a litany of reasons for denying Meredith entry, none of which was explicitly race-based but all of which were cited with the express purpose of keeping Ole Miss' student populace lily-white. As an example of that chicanery, the University first tried to maintain that the credits Meredith had received from undergraduate work at Jackson State College were unacceptable, although he also had credits from Maryland, Kansas and Washburn. Meredith was then accused of falsifying his application, for he had failed to declare that he had once attended Wayne University, although in his defence his academic career there had lasted for only two weeks. In what was an increasingly scatter-gun attack, the University's pre-emptive strike on Meredith's application also included an allegation of 'false swearing' by Meredith, relating to his attempt to register to vote in Hinds County. Although he was convicted *in absentia* by a Justice of the Peace Court in the county, ordered to pay a fine and spend a year in the county jail, Judge John Minor Wisdom of the Fifth Circuit Court in New Orleans threw out the charges. Wisdom was also forced to chastise Mississippi District Court Judge Sidney Mize for what he called the 'continuances of doubtful propriety and unreasonably long delays' in the process of enrolling Meredith, but it was not until 13 September 1963 that Mize ended months of legal wrangling by demanding that Meredith be registered immediately. All sides of the conflict recognized that it portended a major test of segregation's long-term viability.[87]

The governor of Mississippi, Ross Barnett, had been elected on a hard-line segregationist ticket in 1959. Although the governor's lack of political acumen has often been ridiculed, and he has been referred to as governing 'without purpose' and as 'a dull demagogue' who was 'just demagoguing it for the frivolous hell of it', Barnett was sufficiently astute to realize that the constituency that had elected him would brook no compromise with federal forces over Meredith's entry to the University.[88] Interviewed in December 1964, Robert Kennedy looked back on the events surrounding the Meredith episode and concluded that Barnett wanted nothing more than to avoid 'having to send federal troops and trying to avoid having a federal presence in Mississippi'. Meredith's attempted entry into Ole Miss quickly became a microcosm of the dispute between a state's right to maintain Jim Crow laws and ordinances on the one hand, and the federal government's duty to enforce the equal protection provision of the Constitution on the other. At the same time, it was also a crisis saturated in the concerns of state and national politics, and in the pragmatism of elected officials. Meredith, in effect, was a catalyst. As he later recalled in an interview, 'What I really did at Mississippi was to force the federal government to employ its troops on my side against the Mississippi troops.'[89]

As soon as Judge Mize ordered the University to accept Meredith, Mississippi's segregationist legislature rallied round the governor with defiant gestures that were calculated to express a unity of purpose among white resisters. Barnett went on television to proclaim that 'no school will be integrated in Mississippi while I am your governor' in a speech that received defiant praise from every member of Mississippi's congressional delegation bar the Delta moderate Frank Smith, who had recently suffered electoral defeat. More inauspiciously for the Kennedy Administration, Barnett's speech also included a directive to all state officials 'to interpose the State Sovereignty and themselves between the people of the state and any body-politic seeking to usurp such power'. Five days later, as Barnett called the legislature into special session, speaker Walter Sillers introduced a resolution pledging 'full support in the staunchest stand' that Barnett had taken, which was affirmed by all but two members. One of those two, Karl Wiesenburg, later wrote that 'the leaders of nearly every community, bankers, lawyers, businessmen and workers' rebelled with the governor.[90] On 25 September, state Senator Hayden Campbell took to the floor to liken admitting Meredith to opening the University's doors 'to murder and rape', while Mississippi's US Senator James O. Eastland completed a full card of political opposition by announcing in Washington that the upcoming showdown would 'determine whether a judicial tyranny as black and hideous as any in history exists in the United States'.[91]

The homogeneity displayed through the pronouncements of Mississippi's elected officials was buttressed by the actions of the region's Citizens' Councils and Council affiliates. Historian Neil McMillen has argued that, although the exact level of influence exerted by the Citizens' Councils in the Ole Miss crisis 'remains conjectural', it is clear that 'no group did more to create the miasma of defiance and bigotry' that enveloped the Oxford campus in late September. High-profile Citizens' Council members were prominent in the build-up at Ole Miss, including W. J. Simmons, who served as Barnett's personal representative in Oxford during the week preceding Meredith's attempted enrolment there, and even out-of-state figures of the calibre of Louisiana's Willie Rainach.

The Councils were certainly responsible for the fierce nature of the propaganda campaign in Oxford, too. *Rebel Underground*, a newspaper that was notionally anonymous but which was later found to have been run off on the same typewriter as that used by Robert Patterson, appeared with monotonous regularity to stir segregationist passions against Meredith, and an eight-page pamphlet, *Operation Ole Miss* was specially commissioned by the local Citizens' Council to popularize the premise that any institution financed by the state should close its doors immediately if taken over by federal forces. *The Citizen* took active steps to silence a number of moderate faculty members, whose vocal support for the desegregation of their institution threatened to derail the myth of unified southern opinion that the Citizens' Councils and others were trying so hard to instil. Equating the faculty members' receipt of their pay cheques with the acceptance of a loyalty oath, *The Citizen* claimed that 'This is no question of "academic freedom". It is rather, a simple matter of morality.'[92] Yet another broadside, *The Liberty Bulletin*, circulated around the campus. 'Place yourself under the direction of Gov. Barnett', it insisted. 'Do not engage yourself in force or violence *unless he calls for it.*'[93]

Two remarkable postcard campaigns were designed to export local segregationists' grievances to those who were held to be responsible for attempts to force the desegregation of the University. The first saw pre-printed postcards addressed to the University's chancellor and board of trustees, calling for the removal from the payroll of those faculty members who had urged desegregation to go ahead. The postcard identified each signatory as 'a taxpayer supporting state schools' and 'a loyal Mississippian promoting Americanism'.[94] The second represented the collusion that was often found in the Deep South between state government and non-state organizations. Over one million postcards addressed to President Kennedy were designed and printed by the Mississippi State Sovereignty Commission with the help of the owners of the *Jackson Daily News* and *Jackson Clarion-Ledger*. The cards urged Kennedy to refocus his attention on what was portrayed as the real threat posed by communist insurgents and the deteriorating situation in Cuba. More pressingly, the cards' signatories noted their resentment at 'the unnatural warfare being waged against the sovereign state of Mississippi'.[95] The Citizens' Councils did not, however, simply confine themselves to propaganda campaigns. As their members did in localities throughout the South, Council members in Oxford brought economic pressure and intimidation to bear on those individuals who proved to be unwilling supporters of their campaigns. Faculty members who were not sufficiently supportive of the resistance effort were warned that their names were being carefully logged, and conspicuous pronouncements were made to the effect that 'when this thing is over, some renegades are going to lose their jobs'.[96]

Early histories and contemporary accounts of the drama that developed into a full-blown crisis at Ole Miss tend to portray the lead-up to Meredith's installation in the University as a shambles, with none of the major players certain of their role, and a number of them equally unsure of their words. The first attempt to enrol Meredith occurred on 20 September, when he was escorted by John Doar from the Civil Rights Division of the Justice Department and James P. McShane, an equally high-ranking US marshal. They were rebuffed, as they were again on 25, 26 and 28 September. It was not until the fifth attempt, however, on 30 September, that Meredith's escorts succeeded in gaining him access to the university. Each failed attempt ratcheted up existing tensions, and, at least publicly, Barnett began to bask in the national attention that he was being afforded. On 29 September, the governor used the half-time interval of a football game between Ole Miss and Kentucky to whip the crowd into a frenzy of Confederate Flag-waving, 'Dixie'-singing belligerence with the simple yet heavily encoded chant, 'I love Mississippi! I love her people! I love her customs!' The fact that Barnett had been roundly booed by students at the same stadium during a similar football game in 1961 serves as a further indication of the changing mood on campus.[97] This time, Barnett was seen as the ringmaster of an increasingly ugly carnival. The white students watching the game were encouraged by the *Daily News* to sing a newly commissioned 'Mississippi song', which included the couplet, 'Ross's standin' like Gibraltar, he shall never falter; Ask us what we say, it's to hell with Bobby K' and the unambiguous refrain 'Never, Never, Never, Never, No-o-o Never Never Never'.[98]

What the crowd that were roused by such appeals most certainly did not realize, and what early accounts failed to detail, was that their defiant governor had in fact already been in detailed negotiations with their stated enemies for two weeks. Apparently sensing the ultimate futility of an open stand against the might of federal forces, and in an explicit display of the way in which the South's local demagogues and resistance-minded politicians were increasingly being forced to engage with the dynamics of national politics, channels of communication had been opened between the White House and the Mississippi's governor's mansion. Senator Eastland himself helped to engineer the talks, by using Thomas H. Watkins, a Jackson attorney and member of the Mississippi State Sovereignty Commission, as a conduit between the Kennedys and Barnett.[99] Between them, the two sides decided upon an elaborately choreographed sequence of events that would, it was believed, allow the situation in Ole Miss to be resolved with the minimum of fuss, given the circumstances. Barnett remained adamant that it would not be politically practicable for him to give in publicly to the federal forces that were shepherding Meredith, unless he was forced to do so. The governor felt that, at the very least, the federal marshals escorting Meredith should pull their guns on those barring their entry into the university's Lyceum building; federal officials thought this too risky, and a compromise was brokered whereby the marshals were merely to suggest that they were about to remove their weapons from their holsters, at which point Barnett would stand aside and – regretfully – allow segregation at the university to be compromised.

Barnett, though, was operating in a sphere far removed from the cosy world of small-town political patronage in which he felt most comfortable. His discomfort was first highlighted when, unsure of how to end one such intense telephone conversation with the president, he blurted his appreciation to Kennedy for the Administration's continued support for Mississippi's poultry programme 'and all those things'. Later, on 30 September, when Robert Kennedy tired of the lethargic pace of the ongoing negotiations, the attorney general telephoned Barnett and threatened to release details of the back-channel negotiations to the public unless Meredith's enrolment was expedited. Apparently unaware that he had left himself open to such pressure, Barnett agreed to allow Meredith's staged entry that afternoon. Sure enough, in a hastily written speech delivered live on television at 7.30pm that evening, Barnett signalled his capitulation to federal forces and announced that Meredith was already on campus. To mitigate that blow to his political prestige, Barnett declaimed that he was 'surrounded on all sides by the armed forces and the oppressive power' of the federal US government, and delivered a parting shot to Kennedy's US marshals and Justice Department officials: 'Gentlemen, you are tramping on the sovereignty of this great State and depriving it of every vestige of honor and respect as a member of the union of states. You are destroying the Constitution of this great Nation', he concluded, 'May God have mercy on your souls.'[100]

The news brought widespread – and widely reported – violence to Ole Miss. A crowd estimated to be 3,000-strong rampaged across the campus, besieging the small force of federal marshals protecting Meredith. The Kennedys had naïvely believed Barnett's earlier assurances that he could maintain order on campus, and, mindful of their own image in the South, had sent a small force of marshals to Oxford while a more aggressive force of 23,000 troops readied themselves for action in Memphis, just across the Tennessee border. One eyewitness recalled that the marshals were attacked by 'a minute-by-minute heavier barrage of lighted cigarette butts, stones, bottles, pieces of pipe, and even acid', while others reported that Molotov cocktails and bricks were also thrown.[101]

Sensing that the showdown at Ole Miss was a pivotal moment in the lifetime of massive resistance, segregationists flooded into Oxford from other states to swell the riot. James Silver, a professor of history at Ole Miss at the time of the disturbances, wrote to his daughter on 2 October to describe the events he had witnessed first hand during the riot while they were still fresh in his mind, and noted that he had 'talked with a professional agitator from Atlanta who had a small car with three rifles in it', and who dispassionately lent one of those rifles, 'what he called a 30:06' to a fellow rioter. The Justice Department later confirmed that roughly 300 people had been taken into custody, some of whom 'came from as far away as Los Angeles, California, and Decatur, Georgia'.[102] Major General Edwin A. Walker, who had led the federal troops in Little Rock before being forced into retirement in 1961, and who had become increasingly obsessed with conspiracy theories and the far-right John Birch Society, travelled from his native Dallas to maintain a visible presence in Oxford. On 26 September, Walker called in to Louisiana's KWKH radio station, and urged the station's listeners to 'volunteer' for the upcoming fight with federal forces.[103]

By the time that the troops arrived from Memphis to quell the disturbances, scores of protesters and 160 marshals had been injured, and two people had been killed. Meredith was ensconced in his dormitory, and went on to graduate successfully nine months later. As he did so, he poignantly and defiantly wore one of the resisters' 'Never' badges upside down on his lapel.[104] For massive resistance and southern segregationists, the broader ramifications were far more serious. Locally, the stock of those politicians who had been seen to be defending Mississippi's states' rights actively and aggressively rose significantly, but crucially – and surprisingly – only if their activities appeared to have been within the bounds of the law.

Hodding Carter, editor and publisher of the *Delta Democrat Times*, had been one of the very few contemporary southern voices to criticize Barnett's stand at Ole Miss, writing perceptively in the newspaper on 25 September that 'The nation cannot allow the governor to be successful.' He was also sufficiently well versed in the politics of Mississippi to note that, after his well-publicized stand against Kennedy's representatives at the university,

Barnett would be 'the dominant political figure in Mississippi as long as he lives'.[105] Mississippi's small-town newspapermen changed their view of Barnett almost immediately. Where, for example, the editor of the *Indianola Enterprise-Tocsin* had once thought of Barnett as 'a wind-bloated balloon who can be swayed by the last breeze to reach him', post-crisis he became a man 'standing up for the principles in which the people of his state believe and the laws of his state, against the firmly entrenched dictatorship of Washington'.[106] Lieutenant Governor Paul B. Johnson, who had 'stood tall' to physically block Meredith's first attempt to enter Ole Miss, won the 1964 gubernatorial election against former governor James P. Coleman with the slogan 'Stand Tall With Paul'.

In terms of propaganda for the southern cause, the way in which the crisis unfolded at Ole Miss allowed southern segregationists to lay the blame for the civil unrest on the federal 'invaders', and in so doing furnished them with sufficient material to renovate what were fast becoming the clichés of resistance rhetoric. In the belief that the violent usurpation of states' rights was an issue of national rather than purely regional concern, the State Sovereignty Commission patched together a 16-mm film, *Oxford, U.S.A.* Three expensive prints were made and did indeed receive widespread interest, culminating in screenings by groups in Iowa, Illinois, Massachusetts, New Hampshire, New York, California, Ohio, Indiana and Montana.[107] State officials such as congressman John Bell Williams referred to the 'bestiality, cruelty, and savagery' of the Justice Department officials who had acted in Oxford, and even drew parallels between them and Hitler's Gestapo. The Mississippi Junior Chamber of Commerce sent out 500,000 copies of *Oxford: A Warning for Americans*, a 24-page pamphlet dedicated to blaming the Kennedys for the disturbances.

The Women for Constitutional Government, a segregationist group who were as vociferous and almost as vitriolic as the Cheerleaders in New Orleans, were gathered together by the sister of the speaker of Mississippi's House and adopted a 'bill of grievances' which highlighted 'the collusion of the President of the United States, the Justice Department, and the federal courts' and their 'unwarranted and unlawful use of military force' in support of Meredith.[108] Earl Lively, Jr. produced a booklet unambiguously titled *The Invasion of Mississippi*, which proved to be so popular that it appeared in American Opinion's 'Reprint Series' for only one dollar, and which was so insistent upon rendering a segregationist history of the crisis that its words and phrases soon permeated the letters of other grassroots segregationists. The federal government, Lively claimed, had sought to 'create a false image' of 'a proactive and benevolent administration, flaunted by a rebellious state and mobs of insurrectionists who had no regard for law and order'. Both the crisis itself and the management of its memory were 'a sobering lesson on the evils and dangers of government by brute force'.[109]

Local, grassroots segregationists' brutality towards Mississippi's African Americans continued unabated after the defeat of resistance at Ole Miss.

Indeed, on 2 October 1962, the NAACP's Mississippi field secretary, Medgar Evers, reported that '[w]hile tension has lessened in the Oxford area it has increased in other parts of the state'. Driven by what was seen as the audacity of the 'uppity' Meredith, local resisters fought back hard against blacks who were suspected of fighting against the status quo. In his report, Evers documented Molotov cocktail attacks that had taken place in the brief period that had elapsed since the rioting, with targets ranging from the clinic run by Dr Gilbert R. Mason, president of the Biloxi branch of the NAACP, to the service station owned by the president of the Gulfport branch of the Association, and the home of a lifelong supporter and board member of the Association's Columbus branch.[110]

The 1962 disturbances also served to rouse Jackson, Mississippi, Mayor Allen Thompson from complacency. Realizing that concerted attacks on segregation were becoming increasingly insistent and ever more regular in his state, Thompson planned a two-year campaign to equip and train his police force to resist assaults on all aspects of Jackson's segregated practices. By 1964, he boasted of a $2.2 million budget, stockpiles of tear gas, 'three canvas-canopied troop lorries' and a 13,000-pound armoured battlewagon known locally as Thompson's tank. The psychological fears stirred in civil rights protesters' minds by the idea of confronting such a vehicle were assuaged somewhat when, on its first outing, a tear gas shell went off inside the tank and reduced all 23 occupants to a tearful flight through the tank's doors. Nevertheless, Thompson and his force were ready for 'a massive confrontation'. 'They are not bluffing and we are not bluffing', he concluded by 1964. 'We're going to be ready for them ... They won't have a chance.'[111]

The disparity between state-level success and national failure could not, however, have been any starker. Away from Mississippi state politics and the exhaustive propagandizing of segregationist groups, the crisis at Ole Miss proved decisively that outright and open defiance of the federal government would only end in defeat for the forces of massive resistance. Eisenhower had prevaricated and procrastinated before sending troops to resolve a schools crisis in a relatively progressive state of the Border South; Kennedy might also have prevaricated, but he nonetheless proved willing to dispatch federal forces into the heart of the Deep South, and did so with an overwhelming show of strength. Moreover, because Mississippi's Citizens' Councils had gambled upon being able to withstand federal pressures at Ole Miss and had contributed so greatly to the antics of the assembled mob, Kennedy's intervention was indirectly instrumental in the decline of Council fortunes in the Magnolia State.

As the Citizens' Council historian Neil McMillen has noted, Barnett's governorship ushered in an era in which the Council and its members became integral to Mississippi's legislative structure. Council leader William J. Simmons embodied that influence, and was widely rumoured to have Barnett 'in his hip pocket'. Such a state of affairs clearly antagonized both

Simmons' rivals and moderate voices in the state. The failure to halt Meredith was the catalyst that was needed to loosen the Citizens' Council's stranglehold on Mississippi's legislative processes and the Barnett administration.[112] What Ole Miss history professor James W. Silver scathingly referred to as Mississippi's 'closed society' was being forced gradually, yet significantly, ajar.[113]

GEORGE C. WALLACE AND THE SCHOOLHOUSE DOOR: THE APPOMATTOX OF SEGREGATION?

Less than a year after Barnett had stood in the schoolhouse door at Ole Miss in an ultimately abortive attempt to preserve the university as an all-white institution, his fellow southern governor, George Corley Wallace, became embroiled in segregationists' attempts to prohibit the desegregation of the University of Alabama. There had been no desegregation at the Tuscaloosa campus since Autherine Lucy's three-day stint there in 1956, but a federal court had ordered the university to admit two African American students on 11 June 1963. Although there were clear similarities between the two situations, there were also sharp contrasts. Most notably, where Barnett had made his stand drawn upon political calculations based on his in-state fortunes, Wallace knew full well that, by blocking the enrolment of Vivian Malone and Jimmy Hood, he was inviting national and international attention and appeared to thrive on it. Indeed, Wallace's stand at the University of Alabama was more about his own political fortunes and future ambitions than it was about the maintenance of segregation in the university's halls.

By 1963, Wallace had become a canny political operator. Both the state and the governor had histories and traditions of racial progressivism to call upon if they so wished. James 'Big Jim' Folsom, Lister Hill and John Sparkman had all been elected to high-profile political positions on New Deal, progressive tickets, and Wallace had himself been an early disciple of Folsom's maverick progressive rule. In an abrupt piece of political pragmatism, however, Wallace emerged from a rancorous defeat in Alabama's 1958 gubernatorial elections as a hard-line segregationist. It was in reaction to the race-baiting of arch-segregationist John Patterson in that campaign that Wallace was said to have muttered his infamous line, 'John Patterson out-nigguhed me. And boys, I'm not goin' to be out-nigguhed again.'[114] Wallace was more astute in his next campaign for the governorship, in which he attempted to rouse segregationist passions and stated that he would defy desegregation 'even to the point of standing at the schoolhouse door in person'. It was his inaugural address of January 1963, though, that secured his standing among southern segregationists. 'In the name of the greatest people that have ever trod the earth', he declared, 'I draw the line in the dust and toss the gauntlet before the feet of tyranny, and I say: "Segregation now – segregation tomorrow – segregation forever".' Wallace basked in his position as the South's foremost political proponent of segregation. His first

out-of-state engagement was an appearance before the Mississippi state legislature and the Jackson Citizens' Council, and he was often heard publicly
to invite southerners 'to join with me in becoming an active member of your
local Citizens' Council'.[115]

The differences between the handling of the universities' desegregation in
Alabama and Mississippi were palpable. Where Barnett's administration had
allowed the situation at Ole Miss to spiral out of its control, Wallace and his
advisers strove to maintain command, or at the very least the public façade
of being in command. In that regard, he was greatly aided by the complicity of the local Citizens' Council chapters, who not only advised their
supporters to stay away from the campus but also used a board meeting to
minute the fact that 'we must not have violence'.[116] Segregationist violence
in Alabama certainly had the ability to undermine Wallace's attempts to
create an image of himself as a man capable of statesmanship. Bobby Shelton's
Ku Klux Klan Klavern was particularly active in the pursuit of a violent
defence of segregation, and the FBI received reports that a local resister had
started 'a collection for the purpose of buying a rifle with a telescopic lens'
for 'taking care of' Malone and Hood. In an astounding illustration of the
firepower available to such groups, on 8 June, just three days before the
students' planned enrolment, Ku Klux Klan member and FBI-informant Gary
Thomas Rowe drove towards the campus in a car loaded with 'five carbines,
four twelve-gauge pump shotguns with the clip unattached so extra shells
could be added, five boxes of .00 buckshot, four bayonets, a dozen or so
fragmentation grenades, six tear-gas hand grenades, a .45 caliber machine
gun, a dozen dynamite sticks with caps, and a bazooka with six rounds of
ammunition'. Never one to be ill-prepared, Rowe had also decided to carry
a switchblade.[117]

For their part, the Kennedys attempted to maintain a civil dialogue with
Wallace throughout the build-up to the desegregation of the university, in
the hope of avoiding a repeat of the violence that had dogged Meredith's
enrolment the previous summer. This time, however, the Kennedys had a
willing accomplice. Wallace even told his regular enforcer, Al Lingo, to use
his segregationist posse to ensure that no outsiders strayed onto the campus
and, as Wallace's aide Bill Jones reminded Lingo, from Wallace's point of
view 'the whole purpose of the confrontation was national publicity'.[118] On
11 June, Deputy Attorney General Nicholas Katzenbach began the carefully
choreographed display by approaching Foster Auditorium and reading a
federal order for Wallace and his administration to 'cease and desist' from
disrupting the court-ordered desegregation of the university. Katzenbach
then had to endure Wallace's prepared five-page rebuttal, before withdraw-
ing peaceably. As the evening drew in, he returned with 100 federalized
guardsmen, and Wallace calmly stood aside. Both sides claimed victory. For
the presidential administration, a university of the Deep South had been
desegregated without recourse to violent disorder; for Wallace, his support-

ers were able to believe that he had outmanoeuvred Kennedy in the morning, and for the duration of the potential crisis had transcended his role as a state governor and had gained national political recognition.[119]

E. Culpepper Clark's detailed history of the 1963 desegregation of the University of Alabama equated Tuscaloosa with the South's final capitulation in the Civil War. It was, he has argued, the 'Appomattox of segregation' and Wallace's actions denoted 'segregation's last stand'.[120] The seminal address that President Kennedy delivered to the nation only two hours after Wallace had ceded his position in the schoolhouse door certainly supports the view that a sea change had taken place in Washington's willingness to tolerate southern resistance. 'We are confronted primarily with a moral issue', the president declared, thereby marking what one historian has referred to as 'a turning point in the administration's public policy on race'.[121] Neil McMillen's analysis of the Citizens' Councils also strongly suggests that those vital organs of the organization of grassroots resistance were in terminal decline. After the events at Tuscaloosa, he reports, 'the Council in Alabama no longer had a mass following'. Too often, the Councils had placed their long-term credibility on the line either by organizing or simply backing resistance campaigns that dissipated under the full weight of federal intervention to the extent that southern segregationists were losing confidence in the Councils' ability to deliver meaningful resistance strategies.[122]

The battles of successive summers at Ole Miss and Tuscaloosa certainly showed that massive resistance's proponents were losing the battle to maintain segregated public facilities in the South, a notion that was not dispelled when South Carolina's Clemson College admitted its first African American student in January 1963.[123] Caveats must be added, however, to any analysis that suggests that resistance had simply disintegrated or succumbed. Although the entry of black students into those previously all-white universities was undoubtedly a symbolic victory, it must be remembered that only one African American had been allowed to enrol at Mississippi and Clemson respectively, and only a further two students had made it into the University of Alabama. None of these enrolments can be claimed as the product of reshaped, enlightened entrance policies designed to overturn decades of prejudice; rather they were the result of unprecedented pressure and attempts to forestall further incidents of mob violence.

RESISTING NON-VIOLENT DIRECT ACTION: LAURIE PRITCHETT, BULL CONNOR AND JIM CLARK

Any sense that the desegregation of the universities was an organic part of a homogeneous civil rights movement, whose fast-building momentum was rendering white resistance redundant, should also be treated with scepticism. As historians of Mississippi activism stress, Meredith was very much a loner, and, although backed by the legal prowess of the NAACP, few people thought of Meredith as being part of 'the Movement' in the South, least of all Meredith himself.[124] Certainly, Meredith was not involved in any of the grand campaigns of mass civil disobedience by which civil rights' proponents sought to bring national attention to the ongoing nature of segregation in selected cities of the South. In a series of southern locales, beginning with Albany, Georgia, in the winter of 1961 and climaxing with Selma, Alabama, in March 1965, the Southern Christian Leadership Conference (SCLC) sought to transform existing traditions of local protest into non-violent direct action campaigns that were capable of drawing national and international attention to both the longevity and the brutality of segregation in the region.

The campaigns in Birmingham and Selma, in particular, have long been central to the canon of civil rights historiography, for they showcased the bravery, determination and essential dignity of the black freedom struggle's participants, as well as the political acumen of the movement's tacticians. They are also important flashpoints in the history of massive resistance, not least because the success of those campaigns of civil disobedience was largely predicated upon the ability of non-violent protesters to elicit a violent response from local white segregationists. In essence, Martin Luther King, Jr. and the SCLC's hierarchy hoped that their presence would highlight local segregationist practices that had changed little since the end of slavery. In their most successful campaigns, they chose to target local segregationist leaders who, they believed, would be either unwilling to end their adherence to entrenched racist practices, or quite simply incapable of doing so.

In hindsight, the central strategy that underpinned those non-violent campaigns of mass civil disobedience appears deceptively simple: select a town or city in which blatant segregation was enforced by a particularly intransigent and brutal police force; use the presence of King to lure national and international news broadcasters to the site; organize demonstrations steeped in the Christian ethos of non-violence; and, finally, ensure that those members of the press were present to witness and catalogue local segregationist violence against what were peaceful demonstrations for constitutionally guaranteed rights. Unwittingly, those segregationists who brought outright violence into the fold of massive resistance had become crucial to the success of the African American freedom struggle. In reality, the non-violent strategy that came to be favoured by civil rights protesters was honed over time, and came from experience. It reached its most polished incarnation only after Albany's segregationist Police Chief Laurie Pritchett exhibited such guile in policing demonstrations in his city that the SCLC was forced into a thorough re-examination of the way in which it selected its campaign targets. Pritchett was undoubtedly a thoroughgoing segregationist and a white supremacist, and had no compunction in telling SNCC activist Charles Sherrod that the battle between police and demonstrators in Albany was 'just a matter of mind over matter. I don't mind, and you don't matter'. As veteran activist John Lewis remembered, however, Pritchett was also 'a cunning man, as deceitful as he had to be'.[125]

The root of Pritchett's cunning lay in his willingness to suppress his instinctive animus towards civil rights protesters in the short term, in the belief that such action would better serve the viability of continued segregation in the long term. King had published detailed accounts of his own advocacy of Gandhian protest methods, and Pritchett read them with some zeal in order to determine his best response to such tactics. He quickly deduced that the violent policing of non-violent demonstrations was a prerequisite to their success, and that mass arrests were often more detrimental to the police force attempting to process those arrested than to the prisoners themselves. In response, therefore, Pritchett devised his own blueprint for coping with mass demonstrations in his city and prepared assiduously to put his plan into action. In his own words, Albany's police chief later recalled that he used his extensive local contacts to secure jails for would-be protesters in a concentric circle that had Albany as its hub. 'I had made arrangements', he noted, 'and we had it on a map – Lee County, which was ten miles, and then we'd go out twenty-five miles, go out fifty miles, a hundred miles – and all these places had agreed to take the prisoners.' Buses were laid on, too, so that the arrested demonstrators could be shipped to those jails as soon as they had been processed by Pritchett's force, which brought the added bonus of diffusing those arrested to such an extent that 'there was never a central focal point for either the demonstrators or the reporters to fix on'. His advanced planning had the desired effect. As SNCC staffer Bill Hansen remembered pithily, 'We ran out of people before he ran out of jails.'[126] By the end of the campaign, the Albany police had found jail space for more than 500 men, women and children. Although there were isolated outbreaks of brutal police violence during the Albany campaign, the overall image was one of peaceful policing and the maintenance of law and order. *Time* magazine, for example, reported that Pritchett had dealt with the black demonstrators there 'unemotionally and with dignity', and Robert Kennedy, in his role of attorney general, sent a telegram of congratulations to Pritchett.[127]

It was to the great detriment of the resistance movement that Pritchett's methods did not find more advocates in the South, and many of the region's lawmen failed to follow his example. The ferocious white backlash against non-violent campaigns in Birmingham and Selma, both in Alabama, provided watching newsmen with particularly vivid copy of the ongoing nature of racial inequality in areas of the South. They also revealed the extent to which certain segregationists were still willing to deploy brutal methods in the defence of their unequal society. In coordinating the segregationist response to massed black marches in those two cities, Bull Connor, Birmingham's public safety officer, and Jim Clark, sheriff of Dallas County, came to personify the visceral violence of southern resistance in the national consciousness. Connor exacerbated his burgeoning reputation as a man hell-bent on segregation regardless of the consequences when, on 2 May 1963, he ordered his men to arrest hundreds of black children marching under the guidance of the SCLC and the Alabama Council for Human Relations; Clark provided many of the enduring images of the civil rights movement's long crusade by allowing his leading henchman, Al Lingo, to ride a posse of armed cavalry into peaceful demonstrators by Selma's Edmund Pettus Bridge in March 1965.[128] As the SCLC's Birmingham campaign gained momentum, Connor's police chief, Jamie Moore, invited Laurie Pritchett to Birmingham to explain the methods that had worked so well for segregationists in Albany. Pritchett was exasperated by Connor's inability to meet non-violence with non-violence, and came to believe that, had Birmingham's authorities shown the same restraint as he had managed in Georgia, the massed ranks of protesters corralled by the SCLC would 'never [have] got to Selma'.[129]

Once again, though, a closer examination of the rationales that under-pinned Connor's and Clark's responses to civil rights demonstrations suggests a slightly more complex picture. Massive resistance in southern towns and cities such as Birmingham and Selma was not a linear phenomenon, and, although both Connor's and Clark's instinctive reactions were to counter black protest with force, they were subject to a number of competing corollaries and distractions from which resistance could not be discretely and cleanly isolated. Where Connor, for example, had taken his electoral victory against the relatively moderate incumbent, Bob Lindbergh, in 1957 as a mandate to pursue outright segregation, his margin of victory stood at just 103 votes and signalled that there was substantial opposition to his candidacy. Much of that opposition had been marshalled by the progressive businessmen who had so opposed the violence that Connor had sanctioned against the Freedom Riders. Sid Smyer, his fellow real estate tycoon William P. Engel and James A. Head, who was chairman of the chamber of commerce's influential 'Committee of 100', were by now firmly convinced that open violence and racial unrest hamstrung the city's efforts to attract new investment and greater commerce.

In contrast, however, the curators of Birmingham's traditional industries, especially its iron and steel magnates, remained unimpressed by any form of business progressivism and continued to be both defiantly anti-unionist and resolutely segregationist. Internecine warfare among Birmingham's white business elites lurked in the background throughout the escalation of massed civil rights demonstrations, causing friction and disunity within the city's power structure.[130] As complex behind-the-scenes negotiations took place in secret between that faction of Birmingham's businessmen who supported a more progressive philosophy, or who were, at least, willing to sacrifice the most conspicuous aspects of segregation for economic gain, and the leaders of the black protest movement, many of the grassroots segregationists who were not aware of the full extent of those confidential negotiations began to feel increasingly alienated, bewildered and resentful.[131]

Clark, too, was operating in an atmosphere of heightened racial suspicion and widespread distrust. Where entrenched conservative business elites worked to stave off progressive change in Birmingham, organized white resistance groups ensured an air of extremism prevailed in Selma. The lines between the local Citizens' Council and the municipal power structure were so blurred in Dallas County that, for the first three years of the 1960s, the area's only television station aired Citizens' Council television programmes free of charge as a public service. It was also county officials who in February 1964 decided that existing obstacles to black enfranchisement were insufficiently burdensome, and thus instituted an ordinance requiring two testimonials of 'good character' from registered voters. At the same time, they reduced voter registration days to only two per month.[132] As Mills Thornton's comprehensive studies of municipal politics in Alabama have shown, Citizens' Councils in Selma had been so overwhelmingly successful that they had, effectively, 'skewed the center of public discourse so far to the right' that even modest reforms of racial practices were held to be anathema, and businessmen seeking slight but nonetheless progressive change that might otherwise have offset the forthcoming demonstrations were viewed with grave mistrust by the majority of local segregationists.[133]

Both Connor and Clark did try to rein in their natural tendencies towards violence in line with Laurie Pritchett's advice, and for a brief while they succeeded. On 7 April 1963, however, police dogs in Birmingham were seen lunging at a black protester, although ironically their victim was neither an active demonstrator nor particularly wedded to non-violence, but was instead an interested onlooker who most probably concealed a knife in his pocket. In Selma, public safety director Wilson Baker later attested that Sheriff Clark's restraint had held to such an extent that the SCLC was only one day away from moving its protest to more volatile grounds. On 19 January, though, Clark finally buckled. He arrested Mrs Amelia Boynton on the courthouse steps and, in the all-important words of a *New York Times* reporter, he 'grabbed her by the back of her collar and pushed her roughly for half a block into a patrol car'. The SCLC's decision to select Selma for the site of its protests had eventually proved fruitful. 'They went back to the church that night', recalled Baker, 'and voted him [Clark] an honorary member of SNCC, SCLC, CORE, the N-Double-A-C-P ... And from then on they played him just like an expert playing a violin.'[134]

When the SCLC's director of field staff, Hosea Williams, prepared civil rights protesters for the final throes of the Selma campaign in April 1965, his rhetoric laid bare the tactics upon which such protest relied. As he explained to congregants in Brown's Chapel AME Church:

> We must pray that we are attacked, for if the sheriff [Clark] does nothing to stop us, if the state troopers help us accomplish our long walk ... then we have lost ... We must pray, in God's name, for the white man to commit violence, and *we must not fight back*.[135]

If there were traces of cynicism in the tactics of either side in the campaigns that were so brutally played out in locations such as Birmingham and Selma, however, it was a cynicism more clearly displayed by the forces of massive resistance than by those advocating greater civil rights for all US citizens. Williams was not attempting to provoke retaliatory violence from Clark that was in any way out of character for the Dallas County sheriff, or in any way different from that which scores of other lawmen had routinely practised for decades across all southern states. Instead, he and the SCLC's other tacticians were merely waiting for Clark in Selma, and Connor in Birmingham, to revert to type so that the racist violence that had for so long been endemic in the imposition of white supremacy in the region could be revealed to wider public consciousness. In that respect, when Laurie Pritchett later commented that Martin Luther King, Jr. 'was instrumental in passin' the Public Accommodations [Act] but the people that were most responsible was "Bull" Connor and Sheriff Clark', he was not so much blaming the two men as individuals as using them to personify the visible violence that had come to characterize one of the many facets of massive resistance.[136]

5

THE CONFEDERATE CHAMELEON

RESISTANCE MOVES TO WASHINGTON: OPPOSITION TO THE 1964 CIVIL RIGHTS ACT

The attention that the national and international media drew to events in Birmingham in 1963 and Selma two years later proved to be key to the drafting and subsequent passage of federal legislation that was designed to curb the greater excesses of continued southern resistance. The impact that the visceral images of segregationist violence from those two Alabama cities had on public opinion was exacerbated by the knowledge that its perpetrators were acting in the name of local government and law enforcement, and that they were doing so against opponents who had succeeded in casting themselves as non-violent Christians wanting no more than the rights that had been guaranteed to them by the Founding Fathers almost 200 years previously. In that respect, the actions of Connor, Clark and their respective posses and police forces succeeded only in creating the national climate and political will for sweeping legislative change that sought the long-term redress of racial inequalities.

Historians have long argued that the SCLC's Birmingham campaign, and the 'children's crusade' in particular, were decisive in forcing the Kennedy Administration to act in favour of greater civil rights. Glenn Eskew, for example, defines the protest in that city as one that 'broke the stalemate on the national level as it forced the president and Congress to draft legislation that ended legal racial discrimination'.[1] While such an assessment offers a correct analysis of the impact of the Birmingham conflagrations in overall terms, it should nevertheless be stressed that it was the segregationist obstruction and violence that greeted the civil rights protesters in the city, rather than the protest per se, that forced the administration's legislative hand.

Kennedy's decision to initiate a civil rights bill marked the end of the first phase of his administration's attempts to deal with the race issue in the

South, which had in essence relied upon the ability of the region's white moderates to engineer gradual desegregation through a system of voluntary agreements. In so doing, Kennedy sought to avoid the political damage caused by the spectre of federal intervention in the former Confederate states, and the subsequent emergence of damaging splits within the Democratic Party.[2] If the decision to push for legislation signalled that the White House's commitment and attitude towards civil rights had undergone a transformation, there was little if any sign that the fervour of the South's resistance forces had in any way abated. The unveiling of proposed civil rights measures with the explicit backing of the president did not guarantee their safe passage. As soon as New York Congressman Emanuel Celler introduced Kennedy's putative civil rights bill to the House on 20 June 1963, the South's segregationist legislators were given an opportunity to showcase their disruptive skills. Celler triggered a period of intense obstruction and political obfuscation by those politicians that grassroots massive resisters had elected as their representatives in Washington. Using the congressional and senatorial seniority that was the by-product of decades of uncontested elections and one-party politics in the South, the region's senior political figures on Capitol Hill did their utmost to prolong southern segregation by hampering the bill's progress. Virginia's veteran Congressman Howard W. Smith, whose Washington office had provided the venue for a clandestine meeting of Byrd Organization stalwarts in 1956 as they hammered out an agenda for the Old Dominion's special session on massive resistance, used his position on the House Rules Committee to bottle up the proposed civil rights bill.[3] By the time it was finally released from the Rules Committee's clutches, Kennedy was dead and Johnson's investiture into the presidency had been completed.

The rearguard action that the South's representatives managed to mount in the Senate hindered its passage yet further. Members of the southern bloc had long mastered the art of the filibuster as a means of upsetting the smooth passage of legislative bills with which they were not fully in accord. Given the effect that Kennedy's civil rights proposals would surely have on southern life, few contemporaries doubted that they would be ensnared by a senatorial filibuster. The omens were certainly not good for supporters of the administration's bill. In 1957, for example, South Carolina's Strom Thurmond had been so affronted by what was a relatively weak civil rights bill that he defied the wishes of many of his fellow southern representatives by launching a filibuster to halt its progress. Indeed, Thurmond was so committed to defeating the proposed bill that he managed to set both a personal and senatorial record for filibustering by holding the floor for over 24 hours; it was a clear signal of both his own determination in adversity and of the problems that Kennedy's later bill was likely to encounter. When Thurmond closed his marathon performance by declaring solemnly that he intended to vote against the proposed bill, it elicited laughter from the gallery of assembled journalists who were charting his performance, as it became clear to them that Thurmond genuinely believed that his antiquated tactics might have succeeded.[4]

Faced with Kennedy's far stronger proposals, members of the southern bloc demonstrated the full extent of their political resourcefulness. Even those who appeared peripheral to the bill's legislative progress strove to exert their influence. Virginia's Harry Byrd wielded power as the senior ranking figure on the Senate Finance Committee, from where he preached his personal gospel of pay-as-you-go taxation and conservative fiscal policies. Although well known as a segregationist, Byrd was almost as aghast at the Keynesian economic proposals that underpinned Kennedy's 1963 budget and proposed tax cut as he was at the mooted civil rights measures. His status on the Finance Committee placed him in a strong position to undermine the administration's economic plans, but it also allowed him to exert considerable tangential pressure on the president to weaken his civil rights proposals. In a relatively short amount of debating time, Kennedy wanted to secure the passage of his civil rights proposals, his proposed budget, and concurrent negotiations for a nuclear test ban treaty with the Soviet Union. If Byrd's Finance Committee chose to draw out argument over the budget, there would be very little time indeed for the president's other proposals, and there was every possibility that the civil rights bill would be stifled. It was not until Byrd received what was commonly known as 'the treatment' from his long-time acquaintance Lyndon B. Johnson that he finally agreed to report the budget out of committee.[5]

While Byrd looked to arcane Senate rules and procedures to thwart the civil rights bill's passage, others took a less circuitous route. By the early 1960s, the southern bloc's influence in Washington was not as strong as it once had been, for its resolute conservatism had been diluted by the steady growth and increasing influence of youthful liberalism in national party politics. The success of the civil rights movement in evoking national sympathy had also made it more difficult to obstruct civil rights measures openly and wilfully. Nonetheless, Georgia's Richard Russell prepared once again to rally the White South's representatives around him. In what was a coldly calculating attempt to unite wider conservative interests from across both political parties, Russell sought to draw attention to the communist influences to whom, he believed, many of the civil rights movement's leading figures were beholden.[6] It was a line of attack that was designed to appeal to two different constituencies simultaneously: on Capitol Hill, Russell hoped that ardent supporters of domestic anticommunism from both parties could be united against Kennedy's civil rights proposals; across the nation at large, Georgia's senior senator hoped to undermine the broader credibility and standing of the forces that had fought so hard to place civil rights at the forefront of the national political agenda. More practically, Russell realized that he and his dwindling bloc of southern segregationist senators had little chance of defeating the proposed civil rights measures outright. If, however, they could fend off motions of cloture, Senate rules allowed time for unlimited debate, as Thurmond had so graphically illustrated in 1957. In what was essentially a form of legislative blackmail, Russell hoped that he could use the southern bloc's well-deserved reputation for filibustering to draw concessions from the bill's supporters.[7] He and other senior southern senators duly began a filibuster on 9 March, which, when it was finally brought to an end by a vote of cloture on 10 June, was the longest collective filibuster in Senate history.

Although southern legislative defiance was effectively overridden with what appeared to be a decisive 71 to 29 vote, it is worth noting that the bill's safe passage was still far from assured. Johnson, who urged his fellow southerners to pass the proposed bill as a memorial to Kennedy, was left with no illusions over just how tortuous its passage would become. He was clearly aware of the power that Russell still wielded, and even called his old Senate mentor into the White House for a personal hearing. 'Dick, you've got to get out of my way. I'm going to run over you', Johnson told Russell unequivocally. 'You may do that', replied the Georgia senator, 'but, by God, it's going to cost you the South and cost you the election.'[8] It was Russell's genial colleague from North Carolina, Samuel J. Ervin, Jr., however, who ultimately came closest to derailing the bill and thus extending the South's lifespan as a segregated society. Ervin was a master of both constitutional law and the realities of politics, and had long proven adept at using his skills to advance the White South's agenda. He effectively stalled anti-poll tax legislation proposed by Senate Leader Mike Mansfield in early 1962, for example, by offering complex arguments to suggest that Mansfield's proposals were unconstitutional, and was again on hand to try to subvert the passage of the civil rights bill two years later.[9]

Ever a proponent of strong states' rights and the limitation of federal powers, Ervin proposed what became known as a 'double jeopardy' amendment on the morning of the final cloture vote in June 1964, which effectively sought to rule out a second, federal trial for those cleared by a state court for the same offence. In practical terms, such a codicil would have emasculated the civil rights bill, for it would have robbed the federal judiciary of the opportunity of bringing to justice those segregationists who had been cleared of racial crimes by all-white juries. As close analysis of the Senate records makes clear, Ervin's 'double jeopardy' amendment was defeated by a single vote, but, propitiously for the civil rights bill of which it was to have been a part, those votes had been miscounted. The defeated amendment should have been enacted by 48 votes to 47. In the event, Ervin was forced to dilute his measure to a far more palatable amendment which merely stipulated that no one person could be tried twice under United States law. As one top Democratic aide noted, the passage of Ervin's amendment 'would have gutted the [civil rights] bill'.[10] It was, therefore, neither the open posturing of the South's more militant segregationists, nor the red-baiting attacks such as those launched by Richard Russell that came closest to derailing the landmark 1964 Civil Rights Act, but the careful legislative plotting of one of the South's most enduring segregationist senators.

On 20 June 1964, the Civil Rights Act was passed, and President Johnson signed it into law on 2 July. The tide had turned against the southern filibuster on 19 May when senate minority leader Everett Dirksen swung his support behind the bill. The civil rights measures desperately needed bi-partisan support to succeed, and Dirksen's decision brought undecided Republican legislators in line behind him.[11] Over the course of the follow-ing year, Johnson chose to identify himself with the movement for racial change so closely that he amazed many black activists – and further ostra-cized swathes of white southerners – by purloining the language of the movement to declare that 'we *shall* overcome'. Southern dissent in the face of proposed voting rights legislation was muted in both houses, in no small part because the televised brutality meted out in Selma by Sheriff Jim Clark, and in particular by Al Lingo's horseback posse, made it quite clear to a national audience that the Civil Rights Act alone had been an insufficient cure for the South's racial ills. President Johnson signed the Voting Rights Act into law on 6 August 1965.

Taken together, the 1964 and 1965 Acts had, in the words of one histor-ian, 'declared the two institutions of southern racism, segregation and disfranchisement, illegal'.[12] What is more, the actions and rhetoric that emanated from the former Confederacy in the wake of those two landmark legislative acts strongly suggest that a newly supine South had emerged. Most of the region's legislative leaders moved to distance themselves from a decade of open defiance and from the recent filibusters. For many, the newly enacted civil and voting rights provisions were accepted in ways that the two *Brown* decisions had never been: the former were the products of the due process of constitutional law-making, many segregationists believed, while the latter were no more than the arbitrary, autocratic decisions of a Supreme Court operating far beyond its constitutionally prescribed powers.

Richard Russell, fresh from directing the southern bloc's attempted obstruction of Kennedy's civil rights provisions, was quoted by the *New York Times* as declaring that 'As long as it [the 1964 Civil Rights Act] is there it must be obeyed.' Louisiana's staunchly segregationist Allen J. Ellender had fought hard to prohibit the Act's passage, but, having failed to do so, he too resolved that 'the laws enacted by Congress must be respected'.[13] Atlanta's Mayor Ivan Allen, Jr. provided what was an even greater apparent anomaly, for he went before the Senate Commerce Committee in June 1963 to argue for strong federal guidance on civil rights laws. A product of the city's progressive business culture, Allen went head to head with the Commerce Committee's Strom Thurmond to claim that desegregation in the 'city too busy to hate' would be greatly facilitated by 'a clear definition from

Congress' on how best to tackle entrenched segregated practices. Thurmond was, of course, incensed by what he saw as the heretical position assumed by a fellow southerner, but Allen was well aware that Atlanta's business successes had been built upon a fragile bi-racial consensus and he was loath to compromise on its successful formula. A year later, the city's Congressman Charles Weltner endorsed Allen's position when he said in reference to the 1964 Act, 'We must not remain forever bound to another lost cause.'[14] Where once massive resisters had freely invoked memories of the Civil War to bolster their position, here was an elected southern official warning openly of its dangers.

At the grassroots, the segregationist constituents who had elected those political leaders were equally affected by the impact of the 1964 and 1965 legislation. Even in the Magnolia State, where organized resistance had once been so pervasive that it was often impossible to delineate clearly between the activities of Citizens' Councils and state government, segregationists' will to continue with outright and open defiance visibly wilted. Mississippi's Citizens' Councils continued a slow decline that had been triggered by their close association with a number of massive resistance's clear failures, notably the abortive attempt to prohibit Meredith from enrolling at Ole Miss. As many of Jackson's motels and hotels began to desegregate within 24 hours of President Johnson signing the Civil Rights Act, 'continued defiance', in the words of Neil McMillen, 'became a practical impossibility'. Tom Brady, the author of the seminal resistance pamphlet *Black Monday*, had been appointed to the Mississippi State Supreme Court by former Governor Ross Barnett by the time the Acts were passed, and made an admission in 1965 that would have been seen as sacrilegious to the southern cause in his mid-1950s heyday. The Supreme Court, he stated unequivocally, was 'still the ultimate in judicial determination' and that it was 'imperative that this state operate under law and law alone'.[15]

Other organizations that had once done so much to sustain the economy of segregation at the local level followed the lead of many of the South's legislative figures by showing displeasure and remorse at the content of the 1964 and 1965 Acts, while simultaneously conceding that their firm basis in law meant that they had to be obeyed. In what amounted to a gross distortion of recent historical events, the Chamber of Commerce pronounced that Jackson – the seat of the Ole Miss disturbances earlier in the decade – and its citizens had 'earned a reputation as a law-abiding community', and that while 'We might not be in sympathy with all of the laws of the land ... we must maintain our standing as a community which abides by the law.' Perhaps predictably, the city's Citizens' Council condemned what it chose to refer to as the Chamber of Commerce's 'surrender statement', but, when the city's ardently segregationist mayor affected a surprising volte-face and sanctioned the Chamber's legal approach, it signalled what one historian has termed 'a major turning point in the city's history'.[16]

AN END TO MASSIVE RESISTANCE?

That apparent sea change in the attitudes of southern segregationists towards resistance in the aftermath of the 1964 Civil Rights Act and the 1965 Voting Rights Act has had a marked effect on the historiography's treatment of massive resistance. Early accounts of the civil rights movement tended to view those two Acts almost as historical bookends, neatly bringing to conclusion a struggle that was initially believed to have started just as tidily with either the first *Brown* decision of 1954 or the Montgomery bus boycott of 1955–56. While such a view has been rendered increasingly obsolete by ever more sophisticated works on the freedom struggle, the lack of detailed analysis that massive resistance and its proponents have received has kept alive the notion that, with the odd exception, federal legislation was sufficient to bring about the downfall of southern segregationist resistance. As Francis Wilhoit's study of massive resistance concluded in 1973: 'Most scholars who have probed the history of the South's counterrevolution in depth have assigned it a life span of about ten years, extending from the fall of 1954 to the summer of 1964.'[17] Others have disagreed with such an assessment, however, and there remains as much confusion surrounding accounts of the demise of massive resistance as there is surrounding Byrd's first use of the term in early 1956. The difficulties that historians have encountered in their attempts to chronicle the end of resistance accurately can, in fact, be linked to the problems associated with Byrd's initial use of the phrase. It is because there was such confusion over the ways in which Byrd's enigmatic phrase emerged and slowly pressed itself onto the national consciousness that many southern segregationists themselves differed over what precisely was meant by 'massive resistance'. That uncertainty has crept into the historical record, and the resultant lack of clear definition that has characterized massive resistance's treatment in the canon of civil rights historiography has led to discussions of its demise being as poorly focused and ill conceived as discussions of its origins.

One of the legacies of the relative lack of scholarly attention afforded to southern segregationists in recent years is that historians have yet to agree upon a consensus of what, precisely, massive resistance entailed. As a result, historians have fallen upon different definitions and, as a consequence, have brought their studies of the phenomenon of resistance to a close at very different times, often marked by very different events. Those who have taken the most restrictive view of massive resistance, for example, have tended to herald its collapse far earlier than those who have sought a broader reading of the phenomenon. Thus, for the historians that decided upon what might be termed the 'literal' definition, massive resistance was no more than the special session of the Virginia legislature that bore its name in the summer of 1956, and consequently was over almost as quickly as it had begun. For Ralph Eisenberg, then, a 'climactic fight' at the end of those legislative battles in the Old Dominion signalled that 'massive resistance had collapsed' by 1957. Likewise, J. Harvie Wilkinson III believed that, when 'Massive resistance was teetering' towards the end of 1958, the decisions of the state and federal courts in January 1959 to overturn the state's school closing ordinances 'gave it a final push'.[18]

Others, as Wilhoit's remarks suggested, have been drawn towards an understanding of massive resistance as an organic entity that first grew, and subsequently withered, in direct response to civil rights activity between 1954 and 1964. In what might best be termed the 'symbiotic' model, massive resistance was in essence viewed as a reaction against the increased militancy of the South's African American population and a resultant upsurge of civil rights activism that remained insatiate until the passage of the Civil Rights Act. Thus, as Wilhoit himself went on to conclude, 'both practically and symbolically, the 1964 act did signal the end of Massive Resistance as a respectable ideology and as an effective counterrevolutionary obstacle to the implementation of Brown [sic] in the South'.[19] Although Bartley's *Rise of Massive Resistance* was self-evidently more absorbed with the genesis and subsequent growth of southern resistance than with its conclusions, he does suggest that, having climaxed with the crisis at Little Rock in 1957, 'massive resistance lost the initiative in southern politics' towards the end of 1958 and the start of 1959, the time at which the courts were readying themselves to overturn Virginia's school closure laws. With the important caveat that 'The demise of massive resistance did not herald the inauguration of a new political order in the South', Bartley nevertheless surmised that 'First in the upper South and then, during the early 1960's, in the Deep South, the massive resistance front gradually collapsed.'[20]

The 'symbiotic' model of massive resistance was largely the product of the paradigm of civil rights activity that prevailed when analyses such as Wilhoit's and Bartley's were being written. Given the myriad ways in which that paradigm has subsequently been altered and refined, it is a model that now appears flawed. In general terms, as the view of the 'Montgomery to Selma' movement has been revised into a longer, less disjointed narrative of continuous and contiguous African American struggles, the belief that massive resistance simply dissipated in the face of federal legislation passed on a specific date appears increasingly untenable, however overwhelming segregationists may have found the central tenets of that legislation to be.

In more specific terms, recent local studies of civil rights protest in Birmingham have shown unequivocally that the root causes of the end of segregationist defiance in the city are to be found in local events rather than in national politics. That local focus increases the implausibility that a national event, such as the passage of federal civil rights legislation, could have as wide-ranging an effect on local protest as local events. Open segregationist resistance continued in the city beyond the victory that King and the SCLC claimed to have won there, and there is even significant evidence to suggest that many of Birmingham's segregationists actually increased their opposition to desegregation after negotiations between city officials and civil rights activists had been concluded in August 1963 and King had left the city. Three groups in particular, United Americans (UA), the Birmingham Regional Association for Information and Needs (BRAIN) and the National States' Rights Party (NSRP) attempted to corral different constituencies of disaffected segregationists in Birmingham to illustrate the continuing grass-roots antipathy and hostility towards desegregation. Amidst public shows of strength and intimidation, representatives of UA, BRAIN and the neo-Nazi NSRP all submitted petitions to officials to protest against looming school desegregation: the NSRP, which had been at the forefront of the violent campaign against the Freedom Riders two years previously, claimed that they had amassed 30,000 signatures for a petition that they handed to Al Lingo; UA representatives presented the names of 595 parents opposed to desegregation to the school board; and BRAIN claimed to have 12,000 names on a similar petition that was delivered to the superintendent of schools, the mayor and Governor George Wallace.[21]

Events at the start of the 1963–64 school year in Birmingham were eerily redolent of the clashes between federal and state forces of the mid- to late-1950s. On 4 September, officials enrolled two African Americans at a previously all-white school in the Graymont section of the city, which led to Wallace mobilizing state troopers in an attempt to fend off desegregation there and in three other Alabama locales. When Wallace mobilized the Alabama National Guard in response to district court orders to desegregate on 9 September, he went so far as to barricade himself into his own office so that federal marshals could not reach him to serve him with the court's papers. The NSRP attempted to heighten the unrest by organizing the boycott of white students from schools that had been desegregated, beginning with a walkout of 1,440 white pupils from a single school. Such a show of continued segregationist unrest at the grassroots was, as one historian has concluded, 'precisely what the Wallace administration' had hoped for.[22]

The rising unrest continued in Birmingham until Sunday 15 September, when a huge blast of dynamite tore through the basement of the Sixteenth Street Baptist Church, from where many of the mass non-violent demonstrations had been organized the previous spring. Four black girls attending Sunday school Bible classes were killed. As Glenn T. Eskew has commented, the blast 'revealed how little had actually changed in the city. Court ordered school desegregation provoked the act of vigilante violence.' Such an assessment accurately reflected the immediate aftermath of the bombing, for even once the full extent of the devastation had become known, white youths drove past crowds that had assembled at the scene with banners demanding that 'Negroes Go Back to Africa'.[23] In time, it was neither federal intervention nor the threat of strong federal legislation that ended organized white resistance to school desegregation in Birmingham, and nor was it massed civil rights rallies and marches. Ironically, it was the violent actions of segregationists themselves that proved resistance's undoing. Investigations later revealed that a 59-year-old truck driver, Robert 'Dynamite Bob' Chambliss, had planted the bomb. Chambliss's past actions indicated that his nickname had been neither difficult to bestow nor lightly earned. He was an ideologically driven white supremacist, and was clearly intent upon creating as much carnage as possible at the church. Indeed, he was reported to have told his niece on the day before the explosion, 'You just wait until after Sunday morning. And they will beg us to let them segregate.'[24]

The effect of the Sixteenth Street Church bombing was profound, and was entirely different from that which Chambliss had planned. As African American activist John Lewis recalled in his autobiography:

> There had been so many deaths by then. You never get used to death, you never get acquainted with it, you never really understand it. It's something I will never be able to understand, the concept of killing someone, of taking a life away. But this was beyond comprehension.

One white attorney who was based in Birmingham, Charles Morgan, could say only of the bombing, 'We all did this.' Morgan was an avowed progressive, but even Wallace – who was clearly not – was moved to condemn the attack, at least initially. 'I cannot understand the feelings of anyone', he confided to Al Lingo, 'who would put a bomb under a church.'[25]

A close reading of events in Birmingham, then, suggests that it was nothing so definitive as the planning of a national civil rights act or the passage of a corresponding bill that brought open resistance to a close. The fact that the worst excesses of open resistance were ended by the atrocity at the Sixteenth Street Baptist Church should not, however, be taken to mean that race relations necessarily improved after the event. As Mills Thornton concluded towards the end of his epic study of the city's race relations, 'To a black or white liberal who surveyed the status of racial progress in Birmingham in mid-1964, things would undoubtedly have seemed dark indeed.'[26]

From an ideological point of view there was little hope that the passage of federal legislation would dampen the ardour with which committed segregationists defended their way of life, immediately or otherwise. Even if forced to desegregate by judicial decrees and congressional acts, the most committed segregationists had long made it clear that they might accept tokenism to limit the extent of desegregation as far as possible, but they would certainly not embrace integration in any meaningful way. Peter A. Carmichael, a professor of philosophy at Louisiana State University, summed up the position in which many of the region's segregationists found themselves in 1965. Neither the civil rights movement's successes, nor the federal government's apparently new-found desire to enforce desegregation in the South had changed the philosophical outlook of the majority of massive resisters. As Carmichael wrote in 1965:

> If our authorities do not want civil dissolution and military tyranny, they can have peace, provided they are willing to heed the terms. These are the same terms the country has stood on all along until the 1954 reversal; the same that were instituted at the adoption of the Constitution, at the adoption of the Fourteenth Amendment, and through the long line of judicial decisions specifying and applying the provisions of the Constitution to race matters.

Reviewing the 'results and prospects' of the post-Civil Rights Act South, Carmichael was more defiant still, and equally pessimistic. Noting that whites had what he termed a 'primordial racial aversion' to blacks and vice versa, Carmichael concluded that 'Ignoring the primordial fact of white repugnance [at forced integration] and resorting to coercion is the opposite of a solution – it is the generation of more and harder problems.'[27]

A 'SECOND GENERATION OF SUBTERFUGES'

Given that many white southerners' attachment to segregation was historical, deeply rooted and heartfelt, it is clear that even if the most egregious and openly violent forms of resistance were muted either by local events or by the 1964 Civil Rights Act and the 1965 Voting Rights Act, other strands of massive resistance were bound to continue in one guise or another. At the grassroots level, segregationists' long-established antipathy to granting southern blacks the basic citizenship right of voting did not simply dissipate at one stroke of President Johnson's pen in 1965. As Assistant Attorney General Burke Marshall noted, there were parts of the Deep South in particular where an increase in black voters would mean that 'the political viability of white supremacy' was at stake.[28] Such legislation may have been specifically designed to counter what Steven F. Lawson has referred to as 'the structure of white supremacy built upon literacy tests, poll taxes, and intimidation', but structural alterations were far removed from deep-seated changes in the attitudes and ideology of diehard massive resisters. Johnson himself told newsmen that the Act would 'correct an injustice of decades and centuries', a belief closely echoed by Burke Marshall's assumption that 'Only political power – not court orders or other federal law – will insure the election of fair men as sheriffs, school board members, police chiefs, mayors, county commissioners, and state officials.'[29] At its heart, the Voting Rights Act was intended to pinpoint continuing injustices in the practice of southern electoral politics, so that federal forces could then be unleashed at the exact point of constraint on full black political participation. The act's proponents believed that the attainment of voting rights in the region would systematically allow the South's African Americans to flush the last vestiges of institutional racism from the southern political system.

In practice, however, the picture was very different. Black residents in many voting wards in the South witnessed segregationists doing everything in their power to protect white domination of the franchise, as even the greatest apologists for the 1965 Act must have feared they would. After an initial burst of black voter registration, segregationists managed to ensure that their political hegemony was not overly threatened. By 1966, for example, there were still four southern states in which the number of African Americans of voting age who were registered to vote was less than 50 per cent: in Georgia, only 47.2 per cent had registered, in Louisiana 47.1 per cent, in Virginia 46.9 per cent and in Mississippi 32.9 per cent. Such low figures could not be blamed on general political apathy in the southern states, either, since on average over three-quarters of the southern white voting population had registered and Louisiana boasted a white registration figure of over 83 per cent. By 1968, the figures had improved sufficiently to allow more than half the voting age black population to register in each southern state, although enrolment remained at less than 60 per cent in seven states, and South Carolina barely scraped the halfway mark with only 50.8 per cent of eligible blacks registered. Figures that define the gap that existed between white and black enrolment are perhaps the most instructive in this regard, for they best illustrate the ease with which whites could negate black voting strength. As of 1968, there remained a 33.3 per cent gap between such enrolment in Alabama, 28.1 per cent in Georgia, 26.3 per cent in Louisiana and 23.3 per cent in Mississippi.[30]

The continued attempt to restrict the franchise, or, more accurately, to ensure that a greater number of whites than blacks remained registered in voting wards across the South, was not the limit of resistance strategies post-1965. For, even as the federal government began to utilize elements of the new 1965 Act to step up attempts to remove the most openly unconstitutional barriers to voter registration in the former Confederacy, the keenest of the South's segregationists chose not to rest on their laurels. Instead, they displayed a remarkable, chameleon-like ability to adapt and react to their new surroundings. In the simplest of terms, the forces of southern resistance altered their tack from seeking to limit the number of blacks taking part in elections to altering the structure of those elections so as to minimize the effect that such numbers could have on their outcome. In other words, once segregationists had been forced under federal duress to accept an increase in black voter registration, however slight that increase may have been, they shifted their emphasis away from denying the vote to nullifying the potency of that potential vote. They became so accomplished at what became widely known as 'vote dilution' schemes that the US Commission on Civil Rights was moved to acknowledge the existence of a 'second generation of subterfuges' only four years after the Voting Rights Act had been passed. The most popular such measures ranged from the simple gerrymandering and annexation of electoral wards to more complex provisions such as full-slate elections, which, by requiring voters to cast a vote for every available seat being contested in a particular election, effectively denied blacks the opportunity of concentrating their resources in a 'single shot' vote for one minority candidate. 'At large' elections could also be used as buttresses for continued white political supremacy, either by allowing a majority to elect a full slate of offices, or, for example, by requiring a run-off election between candidates if no clear majority resulted from the first ballot.[31]

Across the region, in states of both the Border and Deep South, legislators fell upon dilution schemes to counteract the dents that the Voting Rights Act had made in the edifice of continued white political power. One of the clearest indications of the extent and willingness of southerners to concoct such dilution schemes came in Mississippi in 1966, where, in what one of the state's most accomplished civil rights lawyers referred to as a 'Massive Resistance session', 30 such bills were introduced in one sitting of the state legislature. In an example of the new vocabulary of southern resistance, and of the sophistication with which many segregationists were now operating, not one of the 30 bills directly denied anyone the right to vote.[32] There was no let-up in the Border South. In the same year that the Mississippi legislature introduced its tranche of voter dilution bills, a special session of the North Carolina General Assembly enacted similar measures in almost half of the state's counties. Indeed, between 1965 and 1979, 193 legislative Acts were passed in North Carolina alone that affected election schemes.

More surprisingly, southern states' massed use of at-large elections remained effectively unchallenged by the courts until 1975, when Alabama native Wiley E. Bolden brought suit against the city of Mobile for effectively excluding blacks from office in at-large elections. Judge Virgil Pittman's summary of the case not only openly sided with Bolden, but also tacitly confirmed the rationale behind the expansion of 'at-large' contests. As 'practically all active candidates for public office testified', Pittman noted, 'it is highly unlikely that anytime in the foreseeable future, under the at-large system, that a black can be elected against a white'.[33] Even then the Supreme Court deflated aspiring black hopes by overturning that decision in April 1980. Offering a strict interpretation of what he understood to be the relevant section of the Constitution, Justice Potter Stewart ruled that the right to vote did not necessarily equate with the right to hold political power. 'The Fifteenth Amendment does not entail the right to have Negro candidates elected', he declared.[34]

While a number of historians have rightly brought attention to the fact that continued civil rights gains, especially in the South, were greatly slowed by the dissipation of the liberal consensus on civil rights, by internal splits between the core organizations that collectively made up the civil rights movement, by the different challenges provided by racism in the North, and by the violence that began spilling from northern ghettos in the mid- to late-1960s, it is also clear that such progress was deliberately and effectively curtailed by the adaptability and resourcefulness of segregation's greatest apologists.

THE POLITICS OF SOUTHERN RESISTANCE ON A NATIONAL STAGE: GEORGE C. WALLACE

It is in the realm of national politics that historians have been keenest to note the residual value of massive resistance. Specifically, the transformation of Alabama's George C. Wallace from a bruising colossus of state-level demagoguery to an equally bruising transformative force in national politics has become firmly entrenched in the established narrative of the growth of what has been termed the 'new conservatism' of the late 1960s, 1970s and 1980s. Wallace was involved in four putative national campaigns, three as a Democratic Party hopeful, in 1964, 1972 and 1976, and one as the American Independent Party's candidate for high office, in 1968. His impact on first the southern and then the national stage made him, in the view of one southern historian, 'the most popular and influential segregationist ever', although beyond the sheer weight of service delivered by the centenarian Strom Thurmond, or the brief period in which Richard Russell was able to marshal the southern legislative bloc in Washington to decent effect, Wallace had little competition for that particular accolade.[35]

Unravelling Wallace's appeal is complex, and stands in stark contrast to the deceptive simplicity with which he attempted to deliver his message. He never looked far beyond a blue-collar constituency of disenchanted workers, and sought constantly to distance himself from Washington's established political elite by playing upon his folksy roots, and, in a sense, by bringing southern stump politics to the nation. Wallace undoubtedly played to his down-home image, but it was nevertheless a subtly different image from the one that he had built up so assiduously in Alabama. As historian Dan T. Carter has noted in summary of Wallace's appeal, 'For the age-old southern cry of "Nigger, nigger", he substituted the political equivalents of apple pie and motherhood: the rights to private property, community control, neighborhood schools, [and] union seniority.' That is not to say, however, that he toned down the acerbic nature of his rhetoric, and his colourful denunciations of 'left-wing theoreticians, briefcase totin' bureaucrats, ivory tower guideline writers, bearded anarchists, smart-aleck editorial writers and pointy headed professors' quickly became a hallmark of his campaigns.[36]

Wallace was instrumental in changing the landscape of US politics in two distinct ways. Most clearly, his forays above the Mason–Dixon Line made it quite clear that, while there could be no wholesale national acceptance of the ideology of massive resistance, a number of the guiding principles that had underpinned southern resistance in the post-*Brown* era could be used to find willing constituents in all 50 states. What was perhaps more muted in the short term, but of far greater consequence in the long term, was the effect that Wallace's campaigns had on the policies and platforms of a succession of his opponents. Wallace himself was often sanguine about his overall chances of success, but resolute that the message that he was trying to deliver was of great importance. 'I know I can't win', he said of the 1964 Democratic Primaries, but nonetheless thought the experience would 'give me a chance to let the people know ... the dangers they face from the encroachments of their own government'.[37]

By 1968, *The Nation*'s Washington correspondent, Robert Sherrill, was forced to admit that Wallace had made 'surprisingly successful forays into the North', but was clearly more surprised still to learn of the 'deep veins of intolerance' in all parts of the nation that the Alabama governor was able to bring to the surface.[38] Wallace's concentration on a potent cocktail of issues including an overbearing federal government, a related diminution in the power of states' rights, the need for a strong programme of anticommunism both domestically and internationally, staunch family values, the importance of individual property rights, and what has been memorably referred to as 'cultural nostalgia' brought Wallace a northern constituency that was as devoted as the one that had routinely feted him in the South. 'The appeal of Governor Wallace', explained one of his most ardent supporters in the northern state of Wisconsin, for example, 'is not particularly his civil rights position. His appeal is as a conservative – and an articulate one. He upholds the Constitution, believes in states' rights, and limited federal government.'[39] It was an appeal that was not lost on conservative campaigners from Barry Goldwater to Richard Nixon and Ronald Reagan, each of whose political platforms came to reflect, in some way, the substance of the former amateur boxer from Barbour County's idiosyncratic but deceptively intelligent political approach.

The concentration on such an ebullient figure as Wallace in historical analyses seeking to track the transformation from traditional southern demagoguery to the rise of a new national conservatism is understandable, given the impact that Wallace's fresh approach had on the stale and staid state of presidential electioneering. The widespread acceptance of Wallace as the 'alchemist of the new social conservatism' and a man whose 'essential views ... presaged official American policy, especially as embraced and practiced by President Reagan in the 1980s' has effectively closed the debate on the political legacy of massive resistance.[40] In so doing, however, it has contributed to the imposition of too narrow a focus on the final throes of the phenomenon of southern resistance, and has distilled what was a more complex state of affairs into a singular, unified narrative. The sheer theatricality of Wallace's rapid transformation from the infamy of his 'Segregation now, segregation tomorrow, segregation forever' inaugural address in January 1963 to a position in which one in every four voters in Wisconsin's primary election endorsed him as a presidential candidate in April 1964, has ensured his position in the historical record. At the same time, however, it has obscured the essential role played by another discrete group of massive resisters in the transformation from southern resistance to national conservatism: groups who had gone to great lengths to ensure that, to revisit

Carter's phrase, they had never cried 'Nigger, nigger' at any time in the resistance years as they pursued continued segregation, and thus needed neither to cleanse their recent past of brutal racist rhetoric nor to alter the fundamental tenets of their ideology in order to appeal to a nationwide, conservative audience.

STATE-LEVEL RESISTERS AND THE QUEST FOR A NORTHERN AUDIENCE

It was only once state-level politics had propelled Wallace into the limelight as Alabama's antidote to the increasingly interventionist Kennedy Administration that the state governor began to turn his attention to a nationwide audience. It was also only once he had begun trying to win over a new audience beyond his natural constituency in the segregationist South that Wallace began to purge his rhetoric of its rougher edges and most overt manifestations of racism.[41] What historians have collectively tended to ignore, however, are the other resistance-minded groups, organizations and individuals that had long trained their sights on securing northern, conservative allies. Most of those groups did so by ensuring that, from their very inception, they maintained a discrete distance from their most blatantly racist, demagogic peers. It was, in turn, precisely because such organizations prosecuted their own brand of more 'respectable' resistance from the outset that they were able to adapt more easily to the new language, style and exigencies of the post-Birmingham and post-Selma political landscape: where Wallace was forced, in effect, to rebrand himself before connecting with the emerging currents of national conservatism, there were others who were able to slip into them seamlessly.

Most of those groups were – at least in their earliest incarnations – either state-run propaganda agencies or their offshoots. The two most notable were Mississippi's Coordinating Committee for Fundamental American Freedoms (CCFAF), a relative latecomer to resistance with close ties to the Mississippi State Sovereignty Commission and run by John C. Satterfield, and the Virginia Commission on Constitutional Government (CCG), headed by David J. Mays and established by the Virginia state legislature in 1958. It was no coincidence that both Satterfield and Mays were trained lawyers, for both attempted to steer their respective organizations away from racial extremism, and sought to avoid the basest racial language popular among many of their segregationist peers wherever and whenever possible. They did so by effectively bleaching the central concerns of southern resistance from any detail that was obviously racial, and by replacing sectional concerns over race with matters of constitutional and legal principle which, it was argued, underpinned many of the decisions that concerned federal policies on race. It was a clear attempt to reach out beyond the limited sectional constituency of southern segregationists and to forge, in its place, a national conservative consensus. In the case of *Brown*, for example, the CCG published reams of material decrying it not as the harbinger of an inter-racial apocalypse or the catalyst for a communist takeover, as massive resisters from James Eastland to Tom Brady had long held, but as clear evidence of a Supreme Court that had begun to overreach its constitutionally defined powers, and of justices who were now seeking to make, rather than interpret, laws.[42]

The similarities between the Coordinating Committee and the CCG were stark, not least because concrete links were made between the two organizations. Indeed, the activities of the two groups offer one of the clearest examples of the communication lines that were forged between resistance organizations in different states across the South. Mays wrote to a number of Virginia's sister states, including Mississippi, in August 1959 in an attempt to unearth resisters with a similar outlook to his own.[43] James Jackson Kilpatrick, who served first as head of the CCG's publications division and later as its vice chairman, was initially disparaging of Mississippi's efforts to replicate the CCG's approach, commenting in 1961 that 'So far as I know, Virginia's Commission is the only one in the country truly concerned with all questions of constitutional government. There is a similar commission in Mississippi', he continued, 'but it appears to be entirely concerned with the school integration issue.'[44]

As Satterfield began to develop an approach to resistance that was more subtle and thoughtful than that propagated by the Mississippi Sovereignty Commission, however, the CCG's board began to take an active interest. Satterfield attended a series of secretive meetings in Washington DC in June 1963 aimed at undermining the progress of Kennedy's civil rights proposals, where he was joined by a coterie of national conservative thinkers including the CCG's former director Hugh V. White, Jr. In July, Satterfield established the CCFAF in Washington as an extension of that effort to defeat Kennedy's proposals, with Kilpatrick as its vice chairman. From the outset, the CCFAF maintained its clear attempt to reach out to a constituency beyond the Mason–Dixon Line, with William Loeb, the publisher of a conservative New England paper, elected as the Committee's first chairman.[45]

Both the CCG and the Coordinating Committee concentrated firmly on critiques of the expansion of federal power in their speeches, committee meetings and publications. When the CCG released a pamphlet entitled *Civil Rights and Federal Powers*, for example, subtitled 'A further critical commentary upon the pending omnibus Civil Rights Bill', there was no mention of the state of race relations in the South. Instead, the pamphlet's authors built a legalistic argument around one 'great foundation stone ... If authority for a particular act cannot be found in the Constitution, it can be found nowhere else, for Congress has no innate or inherent powers.' In an unmistakably similar approach, the Coordinating Committee produced its own pamphlet *Due Process of Law or Government by Intimidation?* which the Mississippi Sovereignty Commission's Erle E. Johnston, Jr. called 'one of our best mailing pieces as far as interest is concerned'. Satterfield, too, echoed an increasingly popular conservative refrain when he said of the Civil Rights Act that 'What purports to be an act to "equalize" civil rights is in fact, but 10 per cent civil rights; *the rest is a grasp for Federal executive power.*'[46]

Despite that early focus on what it characterized as excessive federal power, the Coordinating Committee proved unable to maintain the discipline required to expunge racism from its resistance rhetoric. Satterfield asked his Governor Paul B. Johnson, Jr. for assistance in creating 'permanent nation-wide organizations in the field of [advocating] race differences and [studying] race relations', presaging the slow waning of the Committee's influence.[47] The CCG, in contrast, flourished. All of the organization's members were committed to the rigid maintenance of the Commission's disciplined view of massive resistance as a matter of legal and constitutional principle, rather than a matter of race. It was, in other words, an approach that focused resolutely on the principles that underpinned the South's segregated society, rather than any explicit example of racial inequality. As a result, they avoided the quagmire of long drawn-out ideological battles over the efficacy and viability of continued white supremacy, and crucially made themselves more attractive to conservative interests outside the South. By releasing an avalanche of literature reflecting that simple premise, such as *'Civil Rights' and Legal Wrongs*, *'State Action' and the Fourteenth Amendment*, *Voting Rights and Legal Wrongs* and *One Man One Vote*, and by organizing fact-finding trips and seminars with other interested parties, the CCG actively courted northern support. By October 1963, for example, the Commission had received requests from every state for further copies of *'Civil Rights' and Legal Wrongs*, over 66 per cent of which came from states outside the former Confederacy.[48]

As early as 1961, the interest that the CCG began to receive from a group of disaffected Pennsylvanian Republicans strongly suggested that a new core of shared ideological precepts was fast emerging in US politics, and, moreover, that it was a core shared equally by southern segregationists and northern conservatives. In such a context, it became clear that massive resistance bodies did have the potential to reach out to a broader constituency than that found within the segregated South if, as the CCG was wont to do, they were able to portray traditional southern concerns as being devoid of any particular racial animus. Indeed, the CCG's involvement with the Pennsylvanian group offers a blueprint for the way in which proponents of massive resistance could select arguments that reflected their own peculiarly southern view which were simultaneously of interest to proponents of an emerging national conservatism. This also provides clear evidence that many of the key principles that had long been shared across the spectrum of southern resistance could – if packaged correctly – also appeal to non-southerners and non-segregationists.

Two arch-conservatives of the Pennsylvanian Republican Party, W. Stuart Helm and Albert W. Johnson, used much that they had learned from the CCG in terms of both ideology and the transmission of ideological arguments in a coordinated national campaign to rein in the power of the federal government. Having spent three weekends in the presence of David Mays, Jack Kilpatrick and other CCG stalwarts, and having read many of the CCG's publications assiduously, Helm and Johnson launched a campaign in January 1963 to pass what became known as 'the silent amendments' through sufficient state legislatures to alter the Constitution of the United States in favour of greater states' rights and, correspondingly, less federal power. It was a campaign coordinated through the National Legislative Conference (NLC), a bi-partisan organization composed of high-ranking, or highly regarded, representatives from all 50 states, of which Helm had assumed the presidency in the early 1960s.

In a three-pronged attack, NLC representatives proposed, first, to hand state legislatures the power to propose amendments to the Constitution on the basis of support from two-thirds of the states, instead of existing provisions that called for the approval of Congress or a specially conceived constitutional convention; second, to remove reapportionment cases from the jurisdiction of federal courts and make reapportionment a state matter; and, third, to establish a 'Super Court' of the 50 state chief justices with the power to overrule the Supreme Court on constitutional questions. All three of the 'silent amendments' were eventually defeated, though not before President Kennedy, Supreme Court Chief Justice Earl Warren, the American Bar Association and the American Civil Liberties Union had all been moved to speak out publicly against their passage. The list of those states that supported the 'silent amendments' is nonetheless important in illustrating the fact that, by 1963, many of the ideological issues that had been selected as being of central importance by massive resistance organizations such as Virginia's CCG, were shared by interested parties in other states across the nation. By April 1963, for example, at least one of the Amendments had been given approval by the state legislatures of Arkansas, Florida, Idaho, Illinois, Kansas, Missouri, Montana, New Hampshire, Nebraska, Oklahoma, South Dakota, Texas, Washington and Wyoming.[49]

Crucially, all three Amendments were centred on issues that the CCG had already identified as central to their cause and on which they produced publications. Relevant works ranged from *The Constitution of the United States*, which included 'an examination of the amendatory process', *Reapportionment* and *The Tennessee Reapportionment Case*, both of which argued against the Supreme Court's reapportionment decision in the *Baker v. Carr* case, *Did the Court Interpret or Amend?*, *Boundary Lines*, *Mr Justice Douglas Dissents!* and *Mr Justice Harlan Dissents!*, all of which examined the relationship between state and federal power and, specifically, the extent of the Supreme Court's constitutionally mandated powers.[50] Mays and the other members of the CCG board continued to prove themselves to be prescient indicators of national trends in conservative thought after the defeat of the 'silent amendments', producing, for example, a pamphlet on the decline of domestic law and order in 1966, a year before Republican presidential hopeful Richard Nixon launched his own assault on lawlessness.[51]

FROM MASSIVE RESISTANCE TO INDIVIDUAL RIGHTS

The energy and fervour of George Wallace's assault on the national political stage, and the precision with which the campaigns of first Barry Goldwater and then Richard Nixon pinpointed potential Republican Party voters in the South have led many to assume that the transformation of southern politics from a forum for open segregation to one of encoded conservatism was the result of top-down electoral strategy and presidential electioneering.[52] Close observation of the development of patterns of segregationist prejudice at the community and state levels, however, suggest that those top-down political successes were greatly facilitated by – and, indeed, reliant upon – changes that had already begun to occur within the South at the grassroots level.[53] By the mid-1960s, the most egregious forms of open racism that had once made up such a distinct part of the massive resistance canon had – with the odd notable exception – subsided, either because of tactical choices made by segregationists themselves, or because of the pressures and constraints that were placed upon them by the passage of federal legislation. Once the Civil Rights Act had been passed, all but a handful of the South's most ardent segregationists had come to the collective realization that the most violent and tactically myopic threads of massive resistance that had once been routinely unleashed on civil rights protesters in the late 1950s and early 1960s were no longer sustainable.

The most notable result of that change in segregationists' perceptions was that the race-free appeals to racist constituencies, which had long been the preserve of select groups such as Virginia's CCG, became far more prevalent in the general discourse of southern politics. There was no single jolting change between resistance in its pomp and resistance in its new, more subtle guise, but there was a slow evolution in the way in which tactics were selected and ideology was disseminated. Base, openly public appeals to lowest common denominator racism were increasingly marginalized, and appeals that were made in language that was thought to be more acceptable to a national audience were slowly moved to the foreground. In particular, calls for the enforced separation of races within the South that had once been commonplace were now replaced with calls for the rights of individuals to choose with whom they associated. Where individual massive resisters had once sought to air the collective grievances of the segregationist South, now segregationists collectively resorted to defending their rights as individuals. That growing emphasis on individual rights allowed segregationists to reposition themselves in the national consciousness and, to some extent, to reinvent themselves. Where once they had been viewed as massive resisters and thus as peculiarly southern, they were now able to place themselves squarely within the national parameters of the growing conservative movement in US politics.

Certain segregationists had long tried to assume a mantle of respectability by couching what were, at heart, battles to keep predominately white neighbourhoods all-white in terms not of racial subjugation but of 'individual rights'. Those attempts at respectability were often eclipsed by less subtle – and more blatantly racial – contemporary appeals for the maintenance of a segregated society, but they formed an important part of community politics nonetheless. As early as the late 1940s, for example, agencies with a distinct segregationist agenda in Atlanta were established to try to maintain white hegemony in a number of neighbourhoods, each of which was under increasing threat from black incursion. In an attempt to fit in with the city's progressive reputation, and as part of an effort to divest white resistance of the unsavoury undertones that local neo-fascist groups such as The Columbians, Inc. had begun to lend it, those groups transformed the language of resistance in Atlanta from collective calls for racial solidarity to race-free appeals to individual rights. Thus, a court case brought in spring 1952 argued not that blacks should be prohibited from buying homes in previously all-white neighbourhoods on grounds of the collective inferiority of their race, but because individual white homeowners had 'rights' to their own neighbourhood. Such rights, it was argued, applied not just to a neighbourhood's housing stock, but to 'a completely developed and established section of long-standing, with white schools, parks, churches, and shopping centers nearby'. Resistance groups with white supremacy as their bottom line thus sought to portray themselves as 'legitimate community activists'.[54]

Soon, coded appeals to 'community rights' were joined by what appeared, on the surface at least, to be similarly race-neutral calls for 'freedom of association' by segregationists. In Atlanta, that move was kick-started by a single court case in May 1961 involving the proposed transfer of a single student from an Atlanta school that had undergone token desegregation to an all-white school. 'The rights to equal education are inseparably connected with rights to freedom of association', argued the student's father. 'This freedom is the right to associate with whom one pleases and the right not to associate with whom one pleases.'[55] The transfer was eventually denied after a drawn-out appeals process, but, rather than increasing the prospect of substantial school integration, in Atlanta at least it did little more than accelerate white flight to the suburbs. In certain areas of the South, then, segregationists were fast learning that if and when they lost the battle to fend off the court-ordered desegregation of their local neighbourhood schools, the most simple solution was not to rant and rave against federal encroachment of states' rights, but instead to assert their individual rights by moving to new – and all-white – suburban neighbourhoods.[56] The numbers involved reflect just how popular a solution, and how potent a weapon, such flight could be in segregationist southerners' continuing battle to send their children to non-integrated schools. In Atlanta, for example, the public school system lost 1,627 white students and gained 2,668 blacks in the 1959–60 academic year, and in 1960–61 lost 1,072 whites and gained 3,064 blacks. Elsewhere, segregationists opted to withdraw their children from the public school system altogether in favour of private education away from the demands of court-ordered desegregation. In Mississippi, for example, private schools thrived as white parents sought to find places for their children in schools to which aspirant blacks could not gain entry. There were only 17 private schools registered in the Magnolia State in the year before the Civil Rights Act was passed, but by the end of the decade there were over 150.[57]

Such subtle shifts in the parameters of segregationist resistance to desegregation were facilitated by broader changes that were being forced upon the South at a regional level. The fast development of the affluent suburbs in which so many whites sought sanctuary was largely the product of the economic rise of the 'Sunbelt South' and the rapid expansion and development of metropolitan hubs such as Charlotte and Atlanta. Banking and high-tech industries brought an influx of external investment, middle-class employees and progressive business leadership, which in turn helped to stimulate a fundamental shift in the balance of southern political power. The sparsely populated rural wards that had served as traditional strongholds for the South's racial demagogues gently ceded power to the fast-growing populations of the new urban centres and their expanding suburban fringes, while the income generated by the attendant growth in the job market fuelled white flight away from the city centres. Once workers from the affluent white middle classes were comfortably ensconced in those suburbs, it led to what one historian has termed a 'suburban fusion of racial and class segregation'.[58] Because the new suburbs were predominately white, their residents could – and immediately did – clamour for local neighbourhood schooling for their children, rather than for separate schools based on their children's racial characteristics. They were therefore working well within the terms of the 1964 Civil Rights Act, which had effectively put an end to decades of de jure segregation in the South but had no remedy for the de facto historical inequalities that had confined many of the region's blacks to particular neighbourhood wards and denied them many of the educational and job opportunities that had allowed whites to escape to more affluent areas.

The notional removal of race from the public discourse surrounding individual rights, and specifically from discussions of the rights of parents and their school-age children, reached its apogee with the 'busing' crisis of the early 1970s. The Supreme Court signalled that, however briefly, it had tired of the widespread evasion of *Brown*'s implementation via convoluted freedom of choice plans in *Green v. County School Board* in 1968, and, in

1971, the Court sustained the validity of busing children across neighbourhoods in order to integrate schools in *Swann v. Charlotte-Mecklenburg County*. In that resolutely progressive decision, District Judge James McMillan had agreed with the NAACP's Legal Defense Fund that more needed to be done to break down the patterns of segregated housing in North Carolina's sprawling Charlotte-Mecklenburg County, in order to facilitate the desegregation of the area's schools. The NAACP's Julius Chambers made Judge McMillan aware that the continued de facto segregation of neighbourhoods was providing many whites with too easy a way of skirting round *Brown*'s provisions. 'The system of assigning pupils by "neighborhoods", with "freedom of choice" for both pupils and faculty, superimposed on an urban population pattern where Negro residents have become concentrated almost entirely in one quadrant of a city of 270,000', McMillan surmised, 'is racially discriminatory.'[59] Fourteen years after *Brown*, a district judge was finally bringing judicial weight to bear on the obfuscatory and tokenistic plans that southern states had implemented to circumvent the direct consequences of the decision. Black students would be bused into white neighbourhoods, and vice versa.

As one historian of massive resistance has argued, 'Put simply, the segregationists opposed busing because it had significantly reduced school segregation and for the first time brought thousands of poor black children the advantages of middle-class white schools.'[60] The enduring problem with such an analysis, however, is that the issues surrounding busing cannot be 'put simply'. Certainly, as sociologist Lillian B. Rubin has argued, race and racism were at the heart of the busing crisis, as segregationists realized that, finally, a system that would ensure more than limited, token desegregation was being widely implemented. Equally, though, Rubin has noted other factors at play, from the fatal indecision of liberal school boards to the angry backlash generated by a silent conservative majority that felt its views had been ignored and subsumed by those of left-leaning liberal ideologues for too long.[61] There is no doubt that the issue of busing stirred the passions of affected parents. As one angry anti-busing protester in Charlotte told the school board, 'I served in Korea. I served in Vietnam. I'll serve in Charlotte if I need to.'[62]

Anti-busing, though, blurred the boundaries between what would once have been seen as outright segregationist resistance to desegregation initiatives and what was increasingly viewed as a manifestation of a broader political conservatism. Class concerns were conflated with what had once been viewed as a purely racial matter, as whites in many of the South's new suburbs maintained that the children of black families would be welcomed into suburban neighbourhood schools, but only once they were able to buy their way into the neighbourhoods in question. The increasingly complex situation led to some unlikely alliances. In the Senate, for example, Mississippi's veteran segregationist John Stennis was supported by the thoroughgoing Connecticut liberal Abraham Ribicoff when, in February 1970, he introduced an amendment to a federal education bill that called for school desegregation to be implemented equally in northern and southern states. Where Ribicoff wanted to end what he saw as the open hypocrisy of allowing de facto segregation to continue unabated in the North while de jure change was forced upon the South, his southern colleague was far more mischievous. Stennis was attempting to resuscitate massive resisters' time-honoured attempts to minimize the perceived disjuncture between racial practices in the southern and northern states, but this time there was an added twist. Stennis now wanted to force northern states to encounter first-hand what he saw as the harsh realities of federally enforced desegregation in the hope that a national, rather than simply a southern, regional backlash would ensue. In the wake of such a backlash, he had calculated, all Americans would once again be allowed to exercise the euphemistic 'freedom of choice' when it came to selecting schools.[63]

By 1972, when Rubin's study was first printed, busing students across large areas to ensure the desegregation of neighbourhood schools was becoming a resolutely and highly politicized national issue. George Wallace, who openly referred to busing as 'senseless' and 'asinine', had sought to ensure that the issues surrounding busing were high on the political agenda for the 1972 presidential campaign. Sensing that his constituents were preternaturally opposed to the idea, Wallace pounced on Democratic challenger George McGovern's insistence that support of busing be made a 'litmus test for racial commitment'. When Wallace won in Florida, and a poll suggested that his strong showing in the Sunshine State was linked to voters' antipathy to busing, Nixon's White House counsel Charles Colson proclaimed it to be the 'only issue' in the forthcoming election.[64] Nixon had already seen the sense of satiating the 'silent majority' of whites who had voted for him in 1968 with the slow pedalling of the desegregation issue during his first term, sending a memo to his aide John Ehrlichman which suggested that the Administration '[d]o what the law requires and not *one bit more*' where desegregation was concerned. When the Department of Health, Education and Welfare took what Nixon interpreted as too keen an interest in the implementation of busing plans, he demanded acerbically that they 'Knock off this crap'.[65]

In both national politics and local protest politics, non-racial criteria were routinely used to rationalize objections to busing, whether on account of the high cost of the exercise, the excessive journey times for schoolchildren being transported long distances on a daily basis, or, for example, the resulting destruction of neighbourhood schools. There is evidence to suggest that a small percentage of white Americans did separate the issue of busing from the issue of desegregation in their own minds, and politicians became increasingly practised in the art of removing race from the issue of busing as far as possible in public pronouncements. Louisiana's Governor John

McKeithen, for example, proclaimed during one high-profile campaign that 'I will not allow my children to be bused ... to be treated like cattle.'[66] The suspicion remained, however, that the underlying issue was that of race. Where certain massive resisters had once sought to use 'states' rights' as a coded appeal for continued segregation, they could now ally themselves with those who had legitimate grievances with the imperfections inherent in the system of busing to call for its cessation. The lines between the ideologies of segregation and conservatism were blurred indeed.

THE DISSOLUTION OF MASSIVE RESISTANCE

The presence of massive resisters who were intent upon maintaining segregation in the South, but who chose to frame their calls for continued segregation in more subtle and – for northern whites, at least – more palatable ways than many of their peers, adds further complication to the view of massive resistance as a linear historical phenomenon. That is not only because the language and terminology that they used, and the approach that they undertook, separated them from the open racism of those that are more commonly thought of as massive resisters, whether demagogic politicians, Citizens' Council groups, angry mobs or local white law enforcement officers. It is also because, as the case study of the 'community rights' pioneers of Atlanta attests, a number of resistance campaigns predated such familiar signposts to the genesis of resistance as *Brown* or the Southern Manifesto by at least a decade. Furthermore, as the operations of the Virginia Commission on Constitutional Government made clear, massive resistance continued in one guise or another beyond the established finishing posts of the Civil and Voting Rights Acts. It is, therefore, only through the imposition of a third model that it becomes possible to gauge what happened to massive resistance in its final years with any sense of accuracy. For, if massive resistance is understood in its broadest form as a multilayered and multifaceted campaign to resist the concerted attempts of both federal forces and an indigenous civil rights movement to ameliorate the position of blacks in the South, then chronicling its final stages becomes far less problematic.

It is, in other words, essential to envision massive resistance not as a single homogeneous movement, but as a conglomeration of concomitant conversations of resistance. At its central, binding core was the preservation and continued maintenance of a segregated, white-dominated society. That core was sheathed by a number of different defensive measures, many of which developed at different times, and some of which were successfully peeled away through the achievements of black protest and the actions of the federal government. The multitude of groups and individuals who operated under the banner of southern resistance often had slightly different aims, and certainly sought to achieve those aims by often wildly divergent operating practices. As a result, they were brought to an end at different times. The most egregious forms of public resistance to desegregation and to the attainment of equal rights for southern blacks were slowly but surely halted forcibly by increased federal action. For some resisters, Eisenhower's decision to use federal might to enforce desegregation in Little Rock, and in particular the Supreme Court's resultant decision in *Cooper v. Aaron*, was signal enough that the White South would not be able to hold out indefinitely. Even in Virginia, where so much of the theoretical basis for multiple resistance strategies had been thrashed out, that much was acknowledged. By August 1962, even Jack Kilpatrick came close to conceding defeat, writing forlornly that,

> Until the time of the Supreme Court decision in *Aaron v. Cooper* [sic], the Little Rock case, I had cherished real hope for modification of the terms of *Brown v. Board of Education*. But when *Cooper* was decided, simple common sense compelled a reconsideration of the situation before the South. That was in September '58, four years ago ... Times change, they really do.[67]

So concluded the man who had once championed intemperate interposition.

Many of those responsible at the grassroots for the incessant acts of day-to-day oppression and intimidation that hindered black political and economic advancement, however, took longer to become reconciled to that changing climate. The establishment of the Civil Rights Division of the Justice Department at the tail end of the 1950s attempted to hurry them on their way, but it was still an achingly slow process of reform: the assistant US attorney general noted in March 1964 that the Justice Department would have to tackle many such acts of intimidation on a case-by-case basis, and was aware of 'the ease with which new practices aimed at restricting Negro registration can be put into effect', including the 'cancellation of sharecropper arrangements, refusal of credit by banks and stores, a retaliatory boycott of suppliers, physical violence by a sheriff, unwarranted arrests or other police intimidation, and loss of employment'.[68] For those resisters who continued to believe well into the 1960s that segregation was sustainable, despite the escalating attempts to consign it to history by both the federal government and the civil rights movement, the 1964 Civil Rights Act provided a further indication of their increasingly imperiled position. Title II of the Act, in particular, which authorized the use of federal power for desegregating areas of private commerce as well as public services and institutions, put paid to many of the most clearly identifiable examples of segregation in the southern states, and established a high watermark in the enforcement of the 'equal protection' clause of the Fourteenth Amendment.

By 1965 and the denouement of the Selma conflagrations, it was clear that what little national tolerance there had been for figures in the mould of Bull Connor and Sheriff Jim Clark had effectively dissipated, and, equally important in the short term, pressure from local businessmen and progressive city officials to avoid a repetition of such scenes was steadily mounting. That, though, was not the end of all facets of massive resistance. Those of its proponents who had had the breadth of vision and foresight to look beyond the South for willing allies and constituents in the post-*Brown* era were well placed to continue their work in the wake of the new strictures imposed by the passage of federal legislation. In effect, the façade of unified southern resistance crumbled into its constituent parts, leaving only those that were sufficiently subtle in their approach, or that had chosen to encode any overtly racist appeals in such a way as to make them palatable to a broader, non-sectional audience, to continue their work and to merge almost imperceptibly into a steadily evolving national climate of conservatism.

NOTES

Chapter 1 The Origins of Massive Resistance

1. Senator Harry Flood Byrd quoted in *Richmond Times-Dispatch*, 15 February 1956. Byrd was quoted as using the phrase 'passive resistance' again in the same newspaper on 19 February.
2. James Latimer Interviews with Former Governors Darden and Tuck, Program 7, p. 1, Albert H. Small Special Collections Library, University of Virginia; Earle Dunford, *Richmond Times-Dispatch: The Story of a Newspaper* (Richmond: Cadmus Publishing, 1995), p. 362; *Richmond Times-Dispatch*, 26 February 1956, 1A. The same story, with minor editorial changes, also appeared on that day's front page of the *New York Times*.
3. Workman laid out five possible options in an article of 30 May 1954: acceptance of *Brown*; nullification of the decision; the abolition of public schools; 'evasive action' such as the establishment of private schools; and finally 'passive resistance'. Workman quoted in Howard H. Quint, *Profile in Black and White: A Frank Portrait of South Carolina* (Westport, CT: Greenwood Press, 1958), p. 93. There is limited evidence that 'massive resistance' had been used, but just not by anybody with Byrd – or, for that matter, Workman's – profile. On 9 January 1954, for example, Jackson W. Stokes, from Elba, Alabama, wrote to Governor Gordon Persons to suggest convocation of 'Alabama's best constitutional lawyers' to work with the legislature to formulate a 'constitutional plan for massive resistance'. Stokes quoted in Edward R. Crowther, 'Alabama's Fight to Maintain Segregated Schools, 1953–1956', *Alabama Review*, vol. XLIII, no. 3 (July 1990), p. 210.
4. Dunford, *Richmond Times-Dispatch*, p. 362; Latimer Interviews with Darden and Tuck, Program 7, p. 1. Byrd's personal papers cast little light on this question. Undated notes that he made for his own use in speeches and public utterances include the ambiguous 'Massive resistance, passive resistance, based on firm determination to preserve sovereignty and scoolsystem [*sic*].' 'Bits and Pieces', Byrd Speeches – Drafts – Civil Rights, etc. for Reference 1956–60, Box 1, Harry Flood Byrd, Sr. Papers, Albert H. Small Special Collections Library, University of Virginia.
5. *Richmond Times-Dispatch*, 26 February 1956, 1A.
6. *New York Times*, 26 February 1956, p. 49.
7. Raymond J. Crowley, 'Thoreau Proposed "Passive Resistance",' *Richmond Times-Dispatch*, 27 February 1956, p. 13.
8. The exception here is a 1962 monograph that concentrates on Virginia's resistance policies for just two years. Robbins L. Gates, *The Making of Massive Resistance: Virginia's Politics of Public School Desegregation, 1954–1956* (Chapel Hill: University of North Carolina Press, 1962), pp. 117–19.
9. See, for example, press release, 4 June 1959, in Papers of the National Association for the Advancement of Colored People, ed. August Meier, microfilm, 28 parts (Frederick, MD: University Publications of America, 1982), Part 20, 'White Resistance and Reprisals, 1956–1965' (hereafter NAACP White Reprisals Papers) reel 13, frame 0051.

10. Marshall used the definition in the Gino Speranza Lectures that he delivered at Columbia University in March and April 1964, later published as Burke Marshall, *Federalism and Civil Rights* (New York and London: Columbia University Press, 1964), p. 7.

11. Numan V. Bartley, *The Rise of Massive Resistance: Race and Politics in the South during the 1950's* (Baton Rouge: Louisiana State University Press, 1969); hereafter *Massive Resistance*.

12. Bartley's *Massive Resistance* is the most notable such work, but see also Francis M. Wilhoit, *The Politics of Massive Resistance* (New York: George Braziller, 1973). Others have produced works that deal exclusively with one aspect of the resistance movement, including James W. Ely, Jr., *The Crisis of Conservative Virginia: The Byrd Organization and the Politics of Massive Resistance* (Knoxville: University of Tennessee Press, 1976); Gates, *The Making of Massive Resistance*; and Matthew D. Lassiter and Andrew B. Lewis (eds) *The Moderates' Dilemma: Massive Resistance to School Desegregation in Virginia* (Charlottesville: University of Virginia Press, 1997).

13. Charles W. Eagles, 'Toward New Histories of the Civil Rights Era', *Journal of Southern History*, vol. 66, no. 4 (November 2000), pp. 815–48; David L. Chappell, 'Religious Ideas of the Segregationists', *Journal of American Studies*, vol. 32, no. 2 (1998), pp. 237–62.

14. A notable exception here is Peter A. Carmichael, *The South and Segregation* (Washington, DC: Public Affairs Press, 1965). A professor of philosophy at Louisiana State University, Carmichael openly acknowledged that his objectivity was in question when writing on race. Referring in his introduction to the Supreme Court's *Brown* decision as seditious, he admitted that, 'In the presence of this sedition it is not easy for an attentive witness to maintain the attitude of detachment.' See pp. v–vi.

15. Bartley, *Massive Resistance*, pp. 17, 19 and 27.

16. See, for example, the tightly focused essays in Clive Webb (ed.) *Massive Resistance: Southern Opposition to the Second Reconstruction* (New York: Oxford University Press, 2005); Kevin M. Kruse, *White Flight: Atlanta and the Making of Modern Conservatism* (Princeton and Oxford: Princeton University Press, 2005); and J. Todd Moye, *Let the People Decide: Black Freedom and White Resistance Movements in Sunflower County, Mississippi, 1945–1986* (Chapel Hill: University of North Carolina Press, 2004).

17. Kruse, *White Flight*, p. 132.

18. Robert Penn Warren, *Segregation: The Inner Conflict in the South* (London: Eyre & Spottiswoode, 1957), pp. 71–2.

19. Hodding Carter III, *The South Strikes Back* (Garden City, NY: Doubleday, 1959), pp. 12–13.

20. Carter, *The South Strikes Back*, p. 12.

21. Williams quoted in Irwin Klibaner, 'The Travail of Southern Radicals: The Southern Conference Educational Fund, 1946–1976', *Journal of Southern History*, vol. XLIX, no. 2 (May 1983), p. 180. During the New Deal years, which represented Franklin D. Roosevelt's attempt to mitigate the effects of the Great Depression between 1933 and 1937 with a programme of economic and social reform, Williams served as deputy director of the Works Progress Administration and director of the National Youth Administration. Anthony P. Dunbar, *Against the Grain: Southern Radicals and Prophets, 1929–1959* (Charlottesville: University Press of Virginia, 1981), pp. 144 and 164.

22. J. Mills Thornton III, *Dividing Lines: Municipal Politics and the Struggle for Civil Rights in Montgomery, Birmingham and Selma* (Tuscaloosa: University of Alabama

Press, 2002). Thornton returns to the theme of the establishment of a white segregationist consensus throughout the book, but see for example pp. 6, 96–7, 112, 195 and 250–1.

23. The change from 'White Citizens' Councils' to 'Citizens' Councils' was, according to Anthony, 'a significant index to the striving for respectability'. 'Pro-Segregation Groups in the South: A Special Report from the Southern Regional Council', 19 November 1956, NAACP White Reprisals Papers, reel 8, frames 0044–57.

24. Quoted in James W. Silver, 'Mississippi: The Closed Society', *Journal of Southern History*, vol. 30, no. 1 (February 1964), p. 12.

25. 'The South yielded to change, finally, not only because of federal and civil rights pressures', one historian has written in regard to those business leaders, 'but also in response to the reordered priorities of significant elements of its own leadership.' Elizabeth Jacoway, 'Introduction' in Elizabeth Jacoway and David R. Colburn (eds), *Southern Businessmen and Desegregation* (Baton Rouge: Louisiana State University Press, 1982), p. 6.

26. David L. Chappell, *A Stone of Hope: Prophetic Religion and the Death of Jim Crow* (Chapel Hill: University of North Carolina Press, 2004).

27. In total 2,321,716 southerners cast their vote in the referendums. See W. D. Workman, Jr., 'The Deep South', in Don Shoemaker (ed.), *With All Deliberate Speed: Segregation–Desegregation in Southern Schools* (New York: Harper & Brothers, 1957), pp. 98–9.

28. The links between teen culture – and in particular rock and roll – and massive resistance are explored in Brian Ward, *Just My Soul Responding: Rhythm and Blues, Black Consciousness and Race Relations* (Berkeley: University of California Press, 1998), pp. 95–122.

29. As George Brown Tindall wrote, 'In the 1920's the new peculiar institution of Negro subordination had reached its apogee as an established reality in law, politics, economics, and folkways ... The question was settled.' George Brown Tindall, *The Emergence of the New South, 1913–1945* (Baton Rouge: Louisiana State University Press, 1967), p. 160. See also pp. 161–7.

30. White women became politicized by such campaigns, but ironically only to demonstrate that they were reliant upon white male protection. Glenda Elizabeth Gilmore, *Gender & Jim Crow: Women and the Politics of White Supremacy in North Carolina, 1896–1920* (Chapel Hill: University of North Carolina Press, 1996), quotations from pp. 73 and 88.

31. Grace Elizabeth Hale, *Making Whiteness: The Culture of Segregation in the South, 1890–1940* (New York: Vintage Books, 1998), quotation from p. 74.

32. As Smith notes, paternalism was so entrenched in the psyche of Virginia's progressive whites that the full extent of African American demands did not even occur to Colgate Darden until 1944. He also notes that 'The leaders of the Anglo-Saxon Clubs could not have succeeded ... if their views and policies had not resonated with a much broader swath of the white population.' J. Douglas Smith, *Managing White Supremacy: Race, Politics, and Citizenship in Jim Crow Virginia* (Chapel Hill: University of North Carolina Press, 2002), pp. 285–6 and 77. For the opposing view on the implementation of legal racial categories, see Richard B. Sherman, ' "The Last Stand": The Fight for Racial Integrity in Virginia in the 1920s', *Journal of Southern History*, vol. LIV, no. 1 (February 1988), p. 69.

33. V. O. Key, Jr., *Southern Politics in State and Nation* (new edition) (Knoxville: University of Tennessee Press, 1984), pp. 531 and 533.

34. All such provisions were designed so that they could not be ruled unconstitutional

on the basis of the Fifteenth Amendment. As Key notes, they were phrased 'to exclude from the franchise not Negroes, as such, but persons with certain characteristics most of whom would be Negroes'. Key, *Southern Politics*, p. 538.

35. As Wallenstein elucidates, 'Houston ascertained that grand jurors in the county were always drawn from the property tax lists; the lists were divided between white and black; and only the first list, the white list, was drawn from. Much the same', he concluded, 'seemed true of trial jurors.' Peter Wallenstein, *Blue Laws and Black Codes: Conflicts, Courts, and Change in Twentieth Century Virginia* (Charlottesville: University of Virginia Press, 2004), p. 101.

36. A succession of cases involving such discrimination were brought before the Supreme Court: *Gaines v. Canada* (1938), *Sipuel v. Oklahoma* (1948) and *Sweatt v. Painter* (1950). As Michael J. Klarman has noted, however, very little changed as a result of Gaines, whereas, within six months of *Sweatt*, 'roughly a thousand blacks were attending formerly white colleges and universities'. Michael J. Klarman, *From Jim Crow to Civil Rights: The Supreme Court and the Struggle for Racial Equality* (Oxford and New York: Oxford University Press, 2004), p. 254.

37. John Dittmer, *Local People: The Struggle for Civil Rights in Mississippi* (Urbana and Chicago: University of Illinois Press), p. 13.

38. In 1931–32, expenditure on black schools was 29.6 per cent of that on their white equivalents. By 1941–42, expenditure on black schools had risen to 44.0 per cent of that spent on white equivalents. Tindall, *Emergence of the New South*, pp. 500–1.

39. The average annual salary for a white teacher in the same period was $1,861. Dittmer, *Local People*, p. 35.

40. 'An address made before the Civic Clubs of Edgecombe County, N.C. by Spencer P. Bass, M.D.' Copy in 'Segregation – NC', Box 255.40, Nell Battle Lewis Papers, Private Collections, State Archives, North Carolina Office of Archives and History, Raleigh.

41. Using Louisiana as a case study, Fairclough has argued that whites there were 'not willing to dilute their political power', even in the face of increased black attempts at enfranchisement. Adam Fairclough, *Race & Democracy: The Civil Rights Struggle in Louisiana, 1915–1972* (Athens and London: University of Georgia Press, 1995), quote from pp. xii and 103; for an earlier case study that makes a similar case, if in less stark terms, see Robert J. Norrell, *Reaping the Whirlwind: The Civil Rights Movement in Tuskegee* (New York: Alfred A. Knopf, 1985).

42. So strong was the link in southern minds between Graham and Truman's strong stand on civil rights in general, and FEPC in particular, that one side of an election flyer for Graham's 1950 campaign was entirely devoted to his opposition to FEPC: 'Frank Graham Opposes FEPC: Frank Graham is against FEPC. Frank Graham has already been at work against FEPC in the Senate. Frank Graham is now working against FEPC. Frank Graham will speak against FEPC on the floor of the Senate; his speech will be packed with power ... A Vote for Frank Graham is a Vote against FEPC.' Election Flyer (nd), Folder 19, Box 36, Frank Porter Graham Papers, Southern Historical Collection, Wilson Library, the University of North Carolina at Chapel Hill.

43. For the fullest historical treatment of the Philadelphia Convention, see Kari Frederickson, *The Dixiecrat Revolt and the End of the Solid South, 1932–1968* (Chapel Hill: University of North Carolina Press, 2001), pp. 118–33.

44. Although Tuck confessed that he did not believe Dixiecrat candidate Strom Thurmond to be 'particularly a great man', he did think the South Carolinian 'espoused sound principles of government'. Tuck quoted in Program 1 of 8, James Latimer Interviews with former Governors Darden and Tuck. Interview with

Alexander Heard, Southern Oral History Program, Southern Historical Collection, Wilson Library, University of North Carolina, Chapel Hill.

45. Because Bartley begins his analysis of the Dixiecrats in 1948, for example, he has been accused of 'highlighting the "flash-in-the-pan" quality of a political movement whose roots ran deeper and whose impact was more lasting'. Frederickson, *The Dixiecrat Revolt*, p. 5. The author of one of the few earlier analyses of the Dixiecrats confesses that her study 'has been limited ... to a study of the 1948 manifestations of the movement'. Sarah McCulloh Lemmon, 'The Ideology of the Dixiecrat Movement', *Social Forces*, vol. 30 (December 1951), p. 162.

46. There were roots to the Dixiecrat campaign visible in both the early days of the New Deal, and in the Macon Grassroots Convention of 1936: Frederickson looks to the New Deal in her analysis; Lemmon to the 1936 Convention. Frederickson, *The Dixiecrat Revolt*, esp. pp. 11–27; Lemmon, 'The Ideology of the Dixiecrat Movement', p. 162. At the Macon convention, the Democratic National Convention changed its rules so that in future a simple majority was all that was needed to select presidential and vice-presidential candidates. Previously, a two-thirds majority had been necessary, but it was accurately surmised in 1936 that this gave disproportionate political power to the bloc votes of the 'solid White South'.

47. Indeed, Frederickson goes as far as to argue that 'Southern governors remained united only in their opposition to Truman's proposals; beyond that, cohesion broke down over the appropriate response', and suggests that it is more accurate to refer to the emergence of not one, but of 11 discrete strategies in the southern campaign to break away from the National Democratic Party. Frederickson, *Dixiecrat Revolt*, pp. 82 and 68.

48. The lack of support in Texas and Arkansas, for example, 'underscored the primacy of the peculiarities of individual political cultures in determining the success or failure of the states' rights bolt'. Frederickson, *Dixiecrat Revolt*, p. 117.

49. In Georgia, a three-way battle followed the death of Eugene Talmadge, in December 1946. Louisiana was once again mired in a battle between the supporters and opponents of Huey P. Long. Frederickson, *Dixiecrat Revolt*, p. 114.

50. As well as Bartley's top-down view, Lemmon also centres her analysis around the 'speeches, articles and books which appeared immediately before and during the 1948 presidential campaign', such as those produced by Fielding L. Wright, Strom Thurmond and William M. Tuck. Lemmon, 'The Ideology of the Dixiecrat Movement', quote from p. 162.

51. The meeting took place in Jasper County; resolutions were passed in Jasper and neighbouring Greenwood County. Frederickson, *Dixiecrat Revolt*, pp. 86, 5 and 9–10.

52. Lemmon 'Ideology of the Dixiecrat Movement', p. 171.

53. Neil R. McMillen, *The Citizens' Council: Organized Resistance to the Second Reconstruction, 1954–1964* [Illini Book Edition] (Urbana, IL: University of Illinois Press, 1994), pp. 17, 117–18. Quote from p. 189.

54. Upton Blevins to Governor Tom Stanley, 21 October 1954, 'Segregation November December 1954', Box 103, Thomas B. Stanley Gubernatorial Papers, Archives and Research Services, Library of Virginia, Richmond.

55. He was solicitor general from 1913 to 1918, and ambassador to Britain from 1918 to 1921. See Leon Friedman (ed.), *Argument: The Complete Oral Argument before the Supreme Court in Brown v. Board of Education of Topeka, 1952–1955* (New York: Chelsea House Publishers, 1969), p. 6.

56. Klarman, *From Jim Crown to Civil Rights*, p. 293.

57. Friedman, *Argument*, p. 55.

58. J. Lindsay Almond, Jr., attorney general of Virginia (and soon to be the state's gover-

nor) who was defending Virginia's segregated schools before the Supreme Court, told the justices that the plaintiffs in the cases were calling upon the Court 'to tear down the principle of stare decisis ... laid down by this Court and the courts of last resort of every State in this Union'. Friedman (ed.), *Argument*, Davis quoted pp. 214–15; Almond quoted p. 231.

59. In 1935, the Supreme Court had decided unanimously in *Grovey v. Townsend* that the Democratic Party was a private institution, and therefore that its state conventions were within their constitutional rights to decide upon state Democratic Party membership, even though in practice that had allowed several state parties to bar blacks from voting in what were termed 'all-white primaries'. In 1944, that decision was overturned in *Smith v. Allwright*, which stated that the Texas Democratic Primary's impact went beyond the private sphere, and that the party could no longer bar blacks from voting in primary elections. *Smith v. Allwright* therefore effectively overturned the legality of all-white primaries.

60. Klarman, *From Jim Crow to Civil Rights*, p. 298.

61. Dr L. K. Jackson's open letter to Fulton Lewis, Jr., Mutual Broadcasting System, Washington DC, 17 January 1949, Folder 17, Box 36, Graham Papers.

62. The final link in Klarman's causative chain asserts that the press coverage of that brutal suppression, notably in Birmingham and Selma, provoked both northern public opinion and the Kennedy Administration to take a stand against civil rights abuses that culminated in the Civil Rights Act of 1964 and the Voting Rights Act of 1965. Michael J. Klarman, 'How *Brown* Changed Race Relations: The Backlash Thesis', *Journal of American History*, vol. 81 (June 1994), pp. 81–118. Quotations from pp. 92, 82 and 91.

63. By deeming white resistance to be fragmented and civil rights progress relatively fruitful pre-*Brown*, Klarman erroneously downplays the extent to which African American activists had to struggle for meaningful gains in the decade before the Supreme Court's decision, and, equally erroneously, overstates the hold that a new breed of New Deal-inspired, racially liberal politician had over southern politics in the same period. For scholarly attacks on this element of Klarman's 'backlash' thesis, see Peter B. Levy, letter to the editor, *Journal of American History*, vol. 81 (December 1994), pp. 1427–9, and, more recently, Tony Badger, '*Brown* and Backlash', in Webb (ed.), *Massive Resistance*, esp. pp. 39–41.

64. Wilhoit, *The Politics of Massive Resistance*, p. 51; Dewey W. Grantham, *The Life and Death of the Solid South: A Political History* [New Perspectives on the South] (Lexington: University Press of Kentucky, 1988), p. 138.

Chapter 2 *Brown* and Its Aftermath, 1954–1956

1 Jimmy Byrnes quoted in Howard H. Quint, *Profile in Black and White: A Frank Portrait of South Carolina* (Westport, CT: Greenwood Press, 1958), p. 22; Umstead quoted in Raleigh *News and Observer*, 18 May 1954, p. 1.

2. 'Statement by Senator Harry F. Byrd (D – Va) May 17, 1954', in folder 'Statement on Supreme Court Decision to Abolish Segregation in Schools', Box 408, Byrd Papers.

3. The conference was held at the Homestead Hotel, Hot Springs, Virginia, 1–4 November 1953. The Southern Governors' Conferences leading up to and directly following *Brown* have yet to receive the full historical analysis that they clearly deserve.

4. Marion A. Wright speech before National Community Relations Council, Detroit, Michigan, 'Desegregation: Misc (un-numbered)', Box 2, Reed Sarratt Papers, Southern Historical Collection, Wilson Library, the University of North Carolina at Chapel Hill.

5. 'Segregation vs Integration and the Impending Supreme Court Decision: An Address Delivered to the Association of Former Interns and Residents of Freedman's Hospital, Washington, June 4, 1953', Box 106, Guy Benton Johnson Papers, Southern Historical Collection, Wilson Library, the University of North Carolina at Chapel Hill.
6. Quint, *Profile in Black and White*, p. 16.
7. Edward R. Crowther, 'Alabama's Fight to Maintain Segregated Schools, 1953–1956', *Alabama Review*, vol. XLIII, no. 3 (July 1990), figures quoted p. 208.
8. For analysis of Mississippi's school equalization programme, see Charles C. Bolton, 'Mississippi's School Equalization Program, 1945–1954: "A Last Gasp to Try to Maintain a Segregated Educational System,"' *Journal of Southern History*, vol. 66 (2000), pp. 781–812.
9. 'Statement by Senator Harry F. Byrd (D – Va) May 17, 1954', in folder 'Statement on Supreme Court Decision to Abolish Segregation in Schools', Box 408, Byrd Papers.
10. Allard Lowenstein letter to Michael Straight, 3 August 1950, Folder 10, Box 39, Graham Papers.
11. Michael J. Klarman, *From Jim Crow to Civil Rights: The Supreme Court and the Struggle for Racial Equality* (Oxford and New York: Oxford University Press, 2004), p. 312.
12. Waldo E. Martin, Jr., *Brown v. Board of Education: A Brief History with Documents* [Bedford Series in History and Culture] (Boston: Bedford / St Martin's, 1998), p. 32.
13. For the fullest account of the Supreme Court justices' deliberations, see Richard Kluger, *Simple Justice: The History of Brown v. Board of Education and Black America's Struggle for Equality* (New York: Vintage, 1977). Klarman offers a more compressed account and also speculates more than Kluger on the changing voting patterns of the justices leading up to *Brown*, but is no less authoritative. See Klarman, *From Jim Crow to Civil Rights*, pp. 292–312.
14. William Umstead's letter to Kelly Alexander, 24 June 1954, 'Segregation', Box 58, William B. Umstead Gubernatorial Papers State Archives, North Carolina Office of Archives and History, Raleigh.
15. Frank Clement's letter to Thomas Pearsall, 13 October 1954, 'Governors Advisory Commission Education, C-D, 1954', Folder 2, Thomas Jenkins Pearsall Papers, Southern Historical Collection, Wilson Library, the University of North Carolina at Chapel Hill.
16. Pearsall quoted in George Lewis, *The White South and the Red Menace: Segregationists, Anticommunism, and Massive Resistance, 1945–1965* (Gainesville: University Press of Florida, 2004), p. 125.
17. Lewis, *White South and the Red Menace*, p. 125.
18. Michael S. Mayer, 'With Much Deliberation and Some Speed: Eisenhower and the *Brown* Decision', *Journal of Southern History*, vol. LII, no. 1 (February 1986), p. 70.
19. Black quoted in Bob Woodward and Scott Armstrong, *The Brethren: Inside the Supreme Court* (New York: Simon & Schuster, 1979), p. 38.
20. Brennan quoted in Roger K. Newman, *Hugo Black: A Biography* (New York: Pantheon, 1994), p. 440.
21. Earle Thomas's letter to NAACP, 15 March 1957, NAACP White Reprisals Papers, reel 10, frame 0153.
22. Sarah Patton Boyle's letter to Lillian Smith, 9 September 1951, Sarah Patton Boyle Papers, Albert H. Small Special Collections Library, University of Virginia.
23. 'Rainach Begs for Amendment', *Times-Picayune*, 28 October 1954, p. 23.
24. Adam Fairclough, *Race & Democracy: The Civil Rights Struggle in Louisiana, 1915–1972* (Athens and London: University of Georgia Press, 1995), pp. 170 and 184.

25. Advertisement in *Times-Picayune*, 2 November 1954, p. 5.

26. Editorial, *Times-Picayune*, 4 November 1954, p. 18.

27. Of 264,921 votes cast, 217,992 of them were in favour of the Amendment. Figures from W. D. Workman, Jr., 'The Deep South', in Don Shoemaker (ed.), *With All Deliberate Speed: Segregation–Desegregation in Southern Schools* (New York: Harper & Brothers, 1957), p. 98. The measure passed through Louisiana's House by 78 votes to 11, and through the Senate on 28 June by 35 votes to 2. Ainsworth quoted in 'Solon's Views Unchanged on Segregation Proposal', *Times-Picayune*, 29 October 1954, p. 6.

28. For Talmadge's political balancing act, see Jeff Roche, *Restructured Resistance: The Sibley Commission and the Politics of Desegregation in Georgia* (Athens and London: University of Georgia Press, 1998), esp. pp. 16–20.

29. Amendment quoted in Herman E. Talmadge, *You and Segregation* (Birmingham, AL: Vulcan Press, 1955), p. 61.

30. Roche, *Restructured Resistance*, p. 20.

31. Cook quoted in 'Says Public Schools Safe under Plan', *Atlanta Constitution*, 2 November 1954, p. 13.

32. AP figures quoted in 'School Proposal Trailing Slightly', *Atlanta Constitution*, 3 November 1954, p. 1. Of 391,636 votes cast, 210,488 of them were in favour of the Amendment. Workman, 'The Deep South', p. 98.

33. As might be expected, it was not quite as clear cut as a simple rural/urban divide. The *Atlanta Constitution* reported that 'the vote "for" and "against" the Amendment was not as sharply divided on a city–rural basis as had been anticipated. The "big city" counties gave a larger vote for the proposal than was expected, although most went against it'. 'Legislature Fight Hinted as School Proposal Passes', *Atlanta Constitution*, 4 November 1954, p. 1.

34. Talmadge, *You and Segregation*, pp. 60–1.

35. Editorial, 'Amendment No. 4 Is a Grave Step', *Atlanta Constitution*, 4 November 1954, p. 4.

36. Bartley, for example, outlines the course of the Georgia vote in a run through of state-by-state action between the 1952 presidential election and reaction to *Brown*, but notes only that the 'state's voters ratified the private school amendment by a relatively close vote in November, 1954'. Numan V. Bartley, *Rise of Massive Resistance: Race and Politics in the South during the 1950's* (Baton Rouge: Louisiana State University Press, 1969), p. 55.

37. 'Conflicting Warning Highlights School Pleas before Today's Voting: Both Sides Appear on TV, Radio', and 'Close Vote is Forecast on School Amendment', both in *Atlanta Constitution*, 2 November 1954, p. 1; Roche, *Restructured Resistance*, pp. 19–20.

38. Senator David H. MacHauer and Representative Joseph S. Casey quoted in 'Solon's Views Unchanged on Segregation Proposal', *Times-Picayune*, 29 October 1954, p. 6.

39. See, for example, James H. Hershman, Jr, 'Massive Resistance Meets Its Match: The Emergence of a Pro-Public School Majority', in Matthew D. Lassiter and Andrew B. Lewis (eds), *The Moderates' Dilemma: Massive Resistance to School Desegregation in Virginia* (Charlottesville and London: University Press of Virginia, 1998), pp. 105–33.

40. 'Women Deplore Rainach Attack', *Times-Picayune*, 29 October 1954, p. 43.

41. 'Excerpts from address by Thurgood Marshall, NAACP Special Counsel, scheduled for delivery at 3 pm Sunday, Nov. 27, before the 15th annual convention of the South Carolina State Conference of NAACP Branches', NAACP White Reprisals Papers, reel 10, frames 0877–0880. Figures quoted p. 2.

42. Roy L. Johnson's letter to Roy Wilkins, 12 March 1957, NAACP White Reprisals Papers, reel 10, frames 0056–0057.

43. *Hoxie: The First Stand* (David Appleby, US, 2003); John A. Kirk, *Redefining the Color Line: Black Activism in Little Rock, Arkansas, 1940–1970* (Gainesville: University Press of Florida, 2002), pp. 97–8; Kirk, 'Massive Resistance and Minimum Compliance: The Origins of the 1957 Little Rock School Crisis and the Failure of School Desegregation in the South', and Karen S. Anderson, 'Massive Resistance, Violence, and Southern Social Relations: The Little Rock, Arkansas, School Integration Crisis, 1954–1960', in Clive Webb (ed.), *Massive Resistance: Southern Opposition to the Second Reconstruction* (Oxford and New York: Oxford University Press, 2005), esp. pp. 82–4 and 204–6; Elizabeth Jacoway, 'Jim Johnson of Arkansas: Segregationist Prototype', in Ted Ownby (ed.), *The Role of Ideas in the Civil Rights South* (Jackson: University Press of Mississippi, 2002), esp. pp. 142–3.

44. Eastland's infamous remarks, made on 12 August 1955, were reprinted widely in pamphlet form. For examples of these, see NAACP White Reprisals Papers, reel 9, frames 0835–65.

45. Interview with Howard Vance, Hoxie Interviews, Department of Communication, University of Memphis (hereafter Hoxie Interviews).

46. Upton Blevins's letter to Governor Tom Stanley, 21 October 1954, 'Segregation November December 1954', Box 103, Stanley Papers.

47. Jane Dailey, 'The Theology of Massive Resistance: Sex, Segregation, and the Sacred after *Brown*', in Webb, *Massive Resistance*, quote p. 154; Burks quoted p. 156.

48. Mrs C. E. Taylor's letter to Tom Stanley, 30 May 1954, 'Segregation, June 1954', Box 100, Stanley Papers; Walter Farrar's letter to Terry Sanford, 25 May 1961, 'Segregation F-J', Box 111, Terry Sanford Gubernatorial Papers, State of North Carolina Department of Cultural Resources, Division of Archives and History, Raleigh, North Carolina.

49. Kirk, 'Massive Resistance and Minimum Compliance', p. 83.

50. Jim Johnson, 'Let's Build a Private School at Hoxie', *Arkansas Faith*, vol. 1, no. 2 (December 1955), p. 12.

51. Interview with Howard Vance, Hoxie Tapes.

52. Interview with Jim Johnson, Hoxie Tapes.

53. Johnson belatedly appealed the decision, but the federal government then finally threw its weight behind the Hoxie school board's case. The end result was that a federal court handed down a decisive victory against local segregationists. Interview with Bill Penix, Hoxie Tapes; *Hoxie: The First Stand* (David Appleby, US, 2003).

54. David Halberstam, 'The White Citizens' Councils: Respectable Means for Unrespectable Ends', *Commentary*, vol. 22 (October 1956), p. 301; Stan Opotowsky, *Dixie Dynamite: The Inside Story of the White Citizens Councils* (New York: National Association for the Advancement of Colored People, n.d.), p. 4.

55. An account of that first meeting appears in Opotowsky, *Dixie Dynamite*, a reprint of articles that appeared in the *New York Post* in 1957. The best historical treatment of the Councils remains Neil R. McMillen, *The Citizens' Council: Organized Resistance to the Second Reconstruction, 1954–1964* (Urbana: University of Illinois Press, 1994).

56. McMillen, *The Citizens' Council*, p. 11.

57. Quotes from *The Southerner*, vol. 1, no. 6 (August 1956), vol. 1, no. 1 (March 1956) and vol. 1, nos 2/3 (April/May 1956).

58. Hodding Carter III, *The South Strikes Back* (Garden City, NY: Doubleday, 1959), p. 17.

59. A long article in a spring 1956 edition of *The Southerner*, for example, draws direct

comparison between the two Alabama groups, headed 'Compare These Council Records', and is heavily in favour of Carter's North Alabama Citizens' Council. *The Southerner*, vol. 1, no. 2/3 (April/May 1956). McMillen, *The Citizens' Council*, p. 56.

60. The committee was made up of Charlie E. Johns, Huston W. Roberts and Ed Fraser from the Senate; George Stallings, Ben Hill Griffin, Dick Mitchell and William C. O'Neill from the House. See Bob Saunders' memo, 20 September 1961, NAACP White Reprisals Papers, reel 7, frame 0656.

61. On the formation of the Council in Memphis and its stance against the local city authorities, see clippings from *Commercial Appeal*, 26 December 1961 and *Memphis Press-Scimitar*, 8 November 1961, both in Folder 432, 'Memphis Citizens Council 1961', Box 13, Milbourn A. Hinds Papers, Mississippi Valley Collection, University of Memphis; and 'Editorial Opinion', *The Citizen*, October 61, p. 2. On the running of Hinds' informant, a man named 'Muldoon' who was known variously as 'Operator D' and 'Operator A', see 'Operator A Report from Shorthand Notes', 8 November 1961, and Hinds' letter to Frank Ahlgren of *Commercial Appeal*, 10 November 1961, both in Folder 432, 'Memphis Citizens Council 1961', Box 13, Hinds Papers.

62. Hodding Carter, editor of the *Delta Democrat Times*, quoted in Carter, *The South Strikes Back*, pp. 48–9.

63. The full title of the group was the Subcommittee of the House of Representatives on the District of Columbia to Investigate the District of Columbia Public Schools and Juvenile Delinquency in the District of Columbia. Their report was released on 28 December 1956 and was widely reprinted by various Citizens' Council organizations. The one cited here is *Congressional Committee Report on What Happened When Schools Were Integrated in Washington, D.C.* (Greenwood, MS: Educational Fund of the Citizens' Councils, n.d.), copy in NAACP White Reprisals Papers, reel 13, frames 0494–0504.

64. The Educational Fund's officers were W. C. 'Chuck' Trotter, from Indianola, P. F. 'Mr Pete' Williams, Sr., from Clarksdale, Ellis W. Wright, from Jackson, and Ellett Lawrence and Robert 'Tut' Patterson, both from Greenwood. *The Educational Fund of the Citizens' Council* (Greenwood, MS: Educational Fund of the Citizens' Councils, n.d.), copy in NAACP White Reprisals Papers, reel 13, frames 0846–50.

65. *Congressional Committee Report on What Happened When Schools Were Integrated in Washington, D.C.* (Greenwood, MS: Educational Fund of the Citizens' Councils, n.d.), quotations from pp. 4, 13, 14 and 17.

66. To give but one example, the National Citizens' Protective Association studiously reprinted Senator James O. Eastland's speech in the Senate on 26 May 1955, in which he called for a resolution asking the Senate to endorse an investigation of the 'alleged scientific authorities upon which the Supreme Court relied' in *Brown*. Copy in 'National Citizens' Protective Association' folder, Box 29, Earnest Sevier Cox Papers, Special Collections Library, Duke University, Durham, North Carolina.

67. Brady quoted in Carter, *The South Strikes Back*, p. 26. Tom P. Brady, *Black Monday* (Winona: Association of Citizens' Councils of Mississippi, 1955).

68. McMillen refers to it as 'the inspiration and first handbook for the Council movement', and Numan Bartley as 'the handbook of the movement'. McMillen, *The Citizens' Council*, p. 17; Bartley, *Rise of Massive Resistance*, p. 85.

69. Herbert Hill, 'Confidential Conference with Informant', Monday, 10 October 1960, 9.30 am, NAACP White Reprisals Papers, reel 13, quote from frame 0862.

70. Brady quoted in James Graham Cook, *The Segregationists* (New York: Appleton-Century-Crofts, 1962), p. 15. Unusually for a document so central to southern resistance, Brady also revealed to Cook that he had written most of the 92 pages in Colorado.

71. Interview with Albert Brewer, Hoxie Tapes; unnamed Greenwood, Mississippi resident quoted in Jane Riggers, 'Neighbors Recall Beckwith as Outspoken Marine Vet', 24 June 1963 clipping in NAACP White Reprisals Papers, reel 15, frame 0944.

72. 'Will Your School District Be Next?', *Arkansas Faith*, vol. 1, no. 2 (December 1955), p. 3; 'Results of Integration', *States' Rights Advocate*, vol. 1, no. 4 (28 June 1956), p. 3; see for example cartoons entitled 'Sugar Daddy' 'While We Slept' and 'Future Unemployed?', *The Citizens' Council*, vol. 2, no. 3 (December 1956), pp. 1, 2 and 4; see, for example, 'Long-Suspected Facts Revealed: SRC Drew Leadership from Commie Group', *The Virginian*, vol. 2, no. 3 (March 1956), p. 1, or vol. 4, nos 5/6 (May/June 1958), which boasted 17 pages devoted solely to 'The US Supreme Court: An Instrument of Communist Conquest'.

73. *The Virginian*, vol. 2, no. 3 (March 1956), p. 1; *States' Rights Advocate*, vol. 1, no. 4 (28 June 1956), p. 3 ; *The Citizens' Council*, vol. 2, no. 3 (December 1956), p. 2.

74. John Bartlow Martin, 'The Deep South Says "Never!"' Part III, *Saturday Evening Post*, 29 June 1957, p. 54.

75. Quint, *Profile in Black and White*, p. 44.

76. '"Negroes Menaced by Red Plot"', Citizens' Grass Roots Crusade of S.C., Research Bulletin no. 1', 18 March 1954, Folder 11, Box 2, Welsey Critz George Papers, Southern Historical Collection, Wilson Library, University of North Carolina, Chapel Hill.

77. Horace Sherman Miller, *White Man's News*, October 1954, copy in NAACP White Reprisals Papers, reel 13, frames 0806–8.

78. See, for example, 'Open Letter to the Supreme Warrenification's Supreme Court', and 'Now Hear This', NAACP White Reprisals Papers, reel 13, frames 0808 and 0749.

79. Milton Bracker, 'Segregation Conflict: Role of the "Councils"', *New York Times*, 26 February 1956, p. E9. Historian J. Todd Moye has drawn attention to the essentially local nature of those who came together at the first Council meeting in Indianola. The participants represented 'the perfect cross section of a small-town power base in the rural Jim Crow-era South', he wrote, since those present were the 'town mayor, the county sheriff, a farmer with large landholdings, a smaller farmer, the town banker, a farm manager, a dentist, a Harvard-educated lawyer, a gin operator, a farm implement dealer, two auto dealers, a druggist, and a hardware merchant'. J. Todd Moye, *Let the People Decide: Black Freedom and White Resistance Movements in Sunflower County, Mississippi, 1945–1986* (Chapel Hill: University of North Carolina Press, 2004), p. 65.

80. 'A Preliminary Report by H. L. Mitchell: On the Rise of the White Citizens Council and its Ties with Anti-Labor Forces in the South', copy in NAACP White Reprisals Papers, reel 13, frames 0324–35. Quotations on Council membership from frame 324.

81. 'A Preliminary Report by H. L. Mitchell: On the Rise of the White Citizens Council and its Ties With Anti-Labor Forces in the South', copy in NAACP White Reprisals Papers, reel 13, frames 0324–35. Quotations on Council membership from frame 327. Anti-union Citizens' Councillors included Eastland, who loudly denounced the AFL-CIO in his plenary address, and Joe Jenkins, Jr., who was on the board of the 'National Rights to Work Committee' alongside Fred Hartley, Jr., the co-author of the Taft-Hartley Act.

82. Opotowsky, *Dixie Dynamite*, pp. 4, 16.

83. Halberstam, 'The White Citizens' Councils', p. 299.

84. McMillen, *The Citizens' Council*, p. 217.

85. Details of Till's murder appear in William Bradford Huie, 'The Shocking Story of Approved Killing in Mississippi', *Look*, 24 January 1956. An advanced copy of the

article appears in NAACP White Reprisals Papers, reel 1, frames 0826–32, and a follow-up *Look* article in reel 1, frames 0935–41.

86. Milam quoted in Huie, 'The Shocking Story of Approved Killing in Mississippi', p. 50.

87. Huie also sent a copy personally to Martin Luther King, Jr. See Stephen J. Whitfield, *A Death in the Delta: The Story of Emmett Till* (Baltimore: Johns Hopkins University Press, 1988), pp. 88–107.

88. James T. Patterson, *Brown v. Board of Education: A Civil Rights Milestone and Its Troubled Legacy* [Pivotal Moments in American History] (Oxford and New York: Oxford University Press, 2001) pp. 87–8.

89. Quote from Patterson, *Brown v. Board of Education*, p. 88.

90. See, for example, 'Emmett Till is Alive', flyer produced by the 'American Anti-Communist Militia', copy in NAACP White Reprisals Papers, reel 1, frame 0905. 'This entire incident was a hoax', it proclaimed, 'created by the Jewish inspired NAACP to implement racial hatred'.

91. Huie reported in a second *Look* article that the Money, Mississippi store had been forced to close, and both men were attempting to retrain in order to find work. William Bradford Huie, untitled *Look* article in NAACP White Reprisals Papers, reel 1, frames 0935–41.

92. DeCell quoted in Yasuhiro Katagiri, *The Mississippi State Sovereignty Commission: Civil Rights and States' Rights* (Jackson: University Press of Mississippi, 2001), p. 14. The Commission's files remained closed to the public until 1998, when Judge William H. Barbour, Jr. ruled that those records of the Commission that were not subject to ongoing litigation proceedings should be made available and were subsequently opened.

93. David Cecelski, *Along Freedom Road: Hyde County, North Carolina, and the Fate of Black Schools in the South* (Chapel Hill: University of North Carolina Press, 1994), pp. 18 and 181, fn. 40.

94. *The Segregation Problem in the Public Schools of North Carolina* (Raleigh, NC: n.p. , 1957). Quotations from pp. 2, 5 and 1. Copy in Folder 8, Box 82, Basil Lee Whitener Papers, Special Collections Library, Duke University, Durham, North Carolina.

95. *The Segregation Problem in the Public Schools of North Carolina*, pp. 9 and 11. Historian William Chafe is correct in his assertion that, '[b]y the time he had finished the speech, Hodges had succeeded in creating a situation where anything he proposed – short of an outright endorsement of the Ku Klux Klan – could be portrayed as "moderate"'. William H. Chafe, *Civilities and Civil Rights: Greensboro, North Carolina, and the Black Struggle for Freedom* (New York: Oxford University Press, 1980), p. 52.

96. Bartley, for example, labelled them 'lesser segregation measures' than those adopted by Virginia. Bartley, *Rise of Massive Resistance*, p. 78.

97. Chafe, *Civilities and Civil Rights*, p. 6; Jack Bass and Walter De Vries, *The Transformation of Southern Politics: Social Change and Political Consequence Since 1945* (New York: Meridian, 1976), pp. 218–22.

98. Jonathan T. Y. Houghton, 'The North Carolina Republican Party: From Reconstruction to the Radical Right', dissertation, Chapel Hill, 1993.

99. The exact figures are: North Carolina, 1.42 per cent; Tennessee, 5.35 per cent; Virginia, 5.15 per cent; Texas, 7.84 per cent; and Florida, 2.67 per cent. Figures from *Southern School News'* 'Segregation–Desegregation Status Table', reproduced as 'Table B' in Francis M. Wilhoit, *The Politics of Massive Resistance* (New York: George Braziller, 1973), p. 289.

100. *Davis v. County School Board of Prince Edward County* was one of the original cases brought together in argument before the Supreme Court. As David J. Mays stressed at the time, the pending federal suit placed Virginia under added pressure when it came to resisting *Brown*. In July 1955, while noting that North Carolina had 'followed our lead in declaring the policy of segregation for the 1955–56 school year', he noted that North Carolina's strategists 'have a better chance of getting away with it since no federal suit is pending against any NC locality'. 11 July 1955, David J. Mays Diaries, Virginia Historical Society, Richmond, Virginia.

101. 21 July 1955, Mays Diaries.

102. 3 May 1955, Mays Diaries.

103. Almond quoted in Ira M. Lechner, 'Massive Resistance: Virginia's Great Leap Backward', *Virginia Quarterly Review*, vol. 74, no. 4 (1998), p. 633.

104. Almond was therefore deliberately echoing the words of nineteenth-century Virginia Governor Edmund Randolph, who, as a delegate to the 1787 Constitutional Convention, had pointed to his arm and threatened to 'assent to the lopping [off] of this limb before I assent to the dissolution of the union'. Randolph quoted in *When Virginia Joined the Union: A Backward Look at the Powerful Prophecy of Men Who Foresaw in 1788 the Trend of Events in 1963* (Richmond: Virginia Commission for Constitutional Government, n.d.), p. 8.

105. Figures quoted in Benjamin Muse, *Virginia's Massive Resistance* (Bloomington: Indiana University Press, 1961), p. 44.

106. Not even Arkansas' Orval Faubus took such a hardnosed approach to resistance: when he ordered the closure of Little Rock's schools on 12 September 1958, Faubus's decree was aimed at ensuring law and order in all of the city's schools, rather than simply isolating those white schools faced with imminent desegregation. For Faubus's actions see Kirk, *Redefining the Color Line*, pp. 132–3.

107. For examples of scholarly focus on massive resistance in Virginia, see Muse, *Virginia's Massive Resistance*; Robbins L. Gates, *The Making of Massive Resistance: Virginia's Politics of Public School Desegregation, 1954–1956* (Chapel Hill: University of North Carolina Press, 1962); J. Harvie Wilkinson III, *Harry Byrd and the Changing Face of Virginia Politics 1945–1966* (Charlottesville: University Press of Virginia, 1968); James W. Ely, Jr., *The Crisis of Conservative Virginia* (Knoxville: University of Tennessee Press, 1976); Alexander S. Leidholt, *Standing before the Shouting Mob: Lenoir Chambers and Virginia's Massive Resistance to Public-School Integration* (Tuscaloosa and London: University of Alabama Press, 1997); Lassiter and Lewis (eds), *The Moderates' Dilemma*.

108. V. O. Key, Jr., *Southern Politics in State and Nation* (Knoxville: University of Tennessee Press, 1984), pp. 19–35.

109. Wilkinson, *Harry Byrd*, p. 112; James Latimer, 'The Rise and Fall of ... Massive Resistance', *Richmond Times-Dispatch*, 22 September 1996, A1, A9–A12. Quote from p. A9; see also Ronald L. Heinemann, *Harry Byrd of Virginia* (Charlottesville and London: University Press of Virginia, 1996). Both Wilkinson, in 1968, and Byrd biographer Heinemann, some 30 years later, argued that Virginia's massive resistance policies were manufactured and engineered by an ailing political organization, in a last-ditch attempt to extend its increasingly frail grip on power by falling back on the tried and tested formula of what was, in effect, race-baiting, albeit with a sheen of conservatism that removed it from the greatest excesses of southern demagoguery. Byrd's fiscal conservatism and pay-as-you-go financial vision were simply unable to deal with the demands of the post-war world. Evidence for this view is provided by Francis Pickens Miller's anti-organization run in 1949, and, in

particular, Republican Ted Dalton's explosive showing in the 1953 gubernatorial election, in which he challenged Byrd's anointed candidate, Tom Stanley, to the very last.

110. Historians that have promoted this argument believe the much-mooted demise of the organization to have been grandly overstated. Muse, for example, argued that, once the tricky gubernatorial elections of 1949 and 1953 were out of the way, 'opposition in the legislature was insignificant and nearly all public offices throughout the state were filled by loyal followers [of Byrd]'. Muse, *Virginia's Massive Resistance*, p. 25.

111. They point to Ely's *Crisis of Conservative Virginia* as a particularly egregious example. See Matthew D. Lassiter and Andrew B. Lewis, 'Massive Resistance Revisited: Virginia's White Moderates and the Byrd Organization', in Lassiter and Lewis (eds), *The Moderates' Dilemma*, p. 10.

112. Lassiter and Lewis, 'Massive Resistance Revisited', pp. 12–16.

113. Leidholt, *Standing before the Shouting Mob*, both quotes from p. 127.

114. 'Statement – December 18, 1955, on the referendum', Box 409, Byrd Papers.

115. Virginius Dabney's letter to Harry Byrd, Sr., 21 December 1955, Box 3, Byrd Papers.

116. The final figures were 304,154 in favour, 146,164 against. Quoted in Workman, 'The Deep South', p. 98.

117. 5 July 1957, Mays Diaries.

118. For a number of reasons, the factional infighting that constantly undermined that Commission's work has remained absent from the historical account of massive resistance: those involved attempted, wherever possible, to confine their actions to committee rooms beyond the watchful eye of Harry Byrd himself; had the extent of that internecine warfare come to the attention of Byrd, it would have been subject to the first unspoken rule of his organization, which demanded that any such internal squabbling should never be allowed to reach the general public; and, in large part because of that final proviso, it was not until previously unreleased private accounts of those clashes were made available to historians that it became possible to document exactly what had taken place. The most important source for revealing those tensions are the diaries of David J. Mays. They were finally opened to researchers at the Virginia Historical Society in 1996. It was rumoured for many years that they contained revealing, behind-the-scenes information on Virginia politics, not least because Mays repeatedly told veteran political reporter James Latimer of their existence, but denied him – and all others – access to them until 25 years after his death. For Latimer's first response to them, see Latimer, 'The Rise and Fall of Massive Resistance', *Richmond Times-Dispatch*, 22 September 1996, A1, A9–A12.

119. They were, as Mays went on to state, 'rivals for the governorship.' 19 November 1954, 6 January 1955, 13 June 1955, Mays Diaries.

120. 15 June 1956, Mays Diaries.

121. Key, *Southern Politics in State and Nation*, p. 19.

122. 'Peck is much upset that he has not been able to drive his commission to a more radical course', Mays wrote in June 1955, 'and is threatening [as a result] to resign from it'. 24 June 1955, Mays Diaries. There is great irony in the fact that, when the Gray Plan was finally unveiled on 12 November 1955, one of two dissenting members was the man who had given his name to both the Commission and its report, Peck Gray. Heinemann, *Harry Byrd*, pp. 331–2

123. Ely, *Crisis of Conservative Virginia*, p. 54; 19 May 1956, Mays Diaries.

124. Ely, *Crisis of Conservative Virginia*, p. 54.

125. Lechner, 'Massive Resistance', p. 639; Muse, *Virginia's Massive Resistance*, pp.

131–2; Most recently, Klarman noted simply that 'Governor Almond changed his tune virtually overnight', because, Klarman reasoned, federal action in Little Rock jolted the White South into a recalculation of the amount of suffering that it was willing to undergo for the sake of continued segregation. Michael J. Klarman, 'Why Massive Resistance?' in Webb (ed.), *Massive Resistance*, p. 31. Heinemann pictures a pragmatic politician, who had 'correctly judged the rising tide in favour of public education and had counted his votes well'. Heinemann, *Harry Byrd*, p. 349.

126. 5 July 1957, Mays Diaries.

127. Wilkinson, *Harry Byrd*, p. 112; see also Heinemann, *Harry Byrd*. In the same vein, James Latimer, who served as the *Richmond Times-Dispatch*'s political reporter throughout the resistance period, opened a retrospective piece on massive resistance in 1996 with 'perhaps the most famous anonymous quote in mid-century Virginia politics: "This will keep us in power another 25 years"'. Latimer, 'The Rise and Fall of ... Massive Resistance', quote from p. A9.

128. Adam Fairclough, 'A Political *Coup d'Etat*?: How the Enemies of Earl Long Overwhelmed Racial Moderation in Louisiana', in Webb (ed.), *Massive Resistance*, p. 68. As Fairclough also argues, the geographical distinctions that demarcated support for, and opposition to, massive resistance in Bartley's thesis were not rigidly followed in Louisiana, either; see pp. 56–7.

129. Fairclough, 'A Political *Coup d'Etat*?', pp. 57–8. For more on Perez, see Glen Jeansonne, *Leander Perez: Boss of the Delta* (Baton Rouge and London: Louisiana State University Press, 1977), esp. pp. 222–4 and Fairclough, *Race and Democracy*, esp. pp. 21–2 and 33–4.

130. Fairclough, *Race and Democracy*, p. 193; Fairclough, 'A Political *Coup d'Etat*?', p. 59.

131. Fairclough, 'A Political *Coup d'Etat*?', p. 59.

132. Fairclough, 'A Political *Coup d'Etat*?', p. 66.

133. Rainach and Long quoted in 'Leaders Agree on Segregation', *Times-Picayune*, 18 May 1956. Clipping in NAACP White Reprisals Papers, reel 9, frames 0456–7. Long often lost patience with Rainach's segregationist cabal, and was later reported to have yelled at Rainach himself, 'I'm sick and tired of you yellin' nigger, nigger, nigger! People aren't with you, they're just scared of you!' Long quoted in Robert Sherrill, *Gothic Politics in the Deep South* (New York: Grossman Publishers, 1968), p. 28.

134. An editorial by James Kilpatrick later described interposition thus: 'The right of interposition, as enunciated by Jefferson, Madison, Calhoun, Hayne, Randolph and many others, is seen historically as the States' right to interpose their sovereignty between the federal government and the object of its encroachments upon powers reserved to the States. This right rests in the incontrovertible theory that ours is a Union of sovereign States; that the Federal government exists only by reason of a solemn compact among the States; that each respective state is a co-equal party to this compact; that if the compact is violated by the federal government, every State has a right to judge of the infraction; and that when an issue of contested power arises, only the States themselves, by constitutional process, may finally decide the issue.' Kilpatrick quoted in Workman, 'The Deep South', p. 100.

135. For the Talmadge view, see Bartley, *Rise of Massive Resistance*, pp. 128–9; for the South Carolinian one, see Workman, 'The Deep South', p. 100.

136. Dunford, *Richmond Times-Dispatch*, pp. 364–5. *News Leader*, quoted p. 364.

137. Kilpatrick's three editorials appeared on consecutive days starting on 21 November 1955. Excerpts from all three quoted in Dunford, *Richmond Times-Dispatch*, pp. 360–1.

138. Wilkinson comments on Kilpatrick that 'No more ideal spokesman for the view of the organization could be found.' Wilkinson, *Harry Byrd*, p. 127; Ely noted that 'So influential had Kilpatrick become by the mid-1950s that Virginia liberals viewed him as the power behind the throne, the man who set the tone of the debate and effectively determined the course of public policy.' Ely, *Crisis of Conservative Virginia*, pp. 14–15.
139. *New York Times*, 26 February 1956, pp. 1 and 49.
140. Workman, 'The Deep South', pp. 101–2. As Bartley has noted, 'By mid-1957 eight states [Mississippi, Louisiana, Alabama, Georgia, South Carolina, Virginia, Florida, and Arkansas] had approved interposition measures; Texas had endorsed the doctrine; and North Carolina and Tennessee had voiced protest against the *Brown* decision.' Bartley, *Rise of Massive Resistance*, p. 131.
141. James O. Eastland quoted in Nadine Cohodas, *Strom Thurmond and the Politics of Southern Change* (New York: Simon & Schuster, 1993), p. 282.
142. The final resolution included a number of caveats, including, for example, the agreement to adopt a resolution of interposition 'or protest in appropriate language' against federal encroachment on state sovereignty. 'Resumé of Discussion at Conference of Governors of Virginia, North Carolina, South Carolina, Georgia and Mississippi, Richmond, Virginia, January 24 1956', Segregation K-L, Box 119, Luther H. Hodges Gubernatorial Papers, State of North Carolina Department of Cultural Resources, Division of Archives and History, Raleigh, North Carolina.
143. Kilpatrick's letter to Byrd, 18 January 1960, 'Misc. correspondence with Byrd, 1958–1963', Box 11, James J. Kilpatrick Papers, Albert H. Small Special Collections Library, University of Virginia.
144. Bass and De Vries, *The Transformation of Southern Politics*, pp. 346–7.
145. Dale Bumpers Interview, Hoxie Tapes.
146. Virginia's Governor Tom Stanley, for example, referred to it as the 'Washington Manifesto'. 'Comment by Governor Thos. B. Stanley on Washington Manifesto, March 12 1956', Governors' Speeches (Segregation), Box 109, Stanley Papers.
147. In reinforcing the essentially lawful nature of southern resistance, the Manifesto's authors sought to pin the blame for any violence not on native southerners, but on 'agitators and trouble-makers invading our States' and appealed to southerners 'to scrupulously refrain from disorder and lawless acts'. 'Declaration of Constitutional Principles.' Press release copy 'For release Monday a.m. March 12, 1956', in 'Byrd Speeches Drafts – Civil Rights, etc., for reference, 1956–1960', Box 1, Byrd Papers.
148. It was signed by 19 of the region's US senators, and 82 of its US congressmen. For more on the drafting process, see Bartley, *Rise of Massive Resistance*, pp. 116–17.
149. A. Philip Randolph's letter to Roy Wilkins, 16 March 1956. Randolph was so concerned by the Southern Manifesto's impact that, on 30 March, he wrote back to Wilkins calling for the organization of a counter demonstration. Both letters NAACP White Reprisals Papers, reel 7, frames 0893–4.
150. Randolph's letter to Wilkins, 16 March 1956, NAACP White Reprisals Papers, reel 7, frame 0893.
151. Radio Broadcast no. 14 'The Southern Manifesto', Defenders of State Sovereignty and Individual Liberty Radio Broadcasts, Box 21, Sarah Patton Boyle Papers, Albert H. Small Special Collections Library, University of Virginia.
152. Klarman, 'Why Massive Resistance?', p. 24.
153. For the full version of Badger's argument, see Tony Badger, 'Southerners Who Refused to Sign the Southern Manifesto', *The Historical Journal*, vol. 42, no. 2 (1999), pp. 517–34. For a briefer distillation, see Tony Badger, '*Brown* and Backlash',

in Webb (ed.), *Massive Resistance*, pp. 46–8, and also Klarman, 'Why Massive Resistance?', pp. 24–5.

154. As Badger notes, though, Cooley was driven to race-bait his opponent, and by the end of the campaign he had publicly decried *Brown*. Badger, 'Southerners Who Refused to Sign the Southern Manifesto', pp. 528–32. Public opinion quote see Badger, '*Brown* and Backlash', p. 46; also Badger, 'Southerners Who Refused to Sign the Southern Manifesto', pp. 532–3.

155. In Texas, the only signatories were Martin Dies, John Dowdy, O. C. Fisher, Wright Patman and Walter Rogers. The vestiges of New Deal liberalism, the Second World War, 'Christian principles', the cohesive pull of Senator Sam Rayburn, and Rayburn's ongoing feud with Governor Allan Shivers all contributed to the paucity of signatories in the state. Badger, 'Southerners Who Refused to Sign the Southern Manifesto', pp. 518–19 and 521–5.

156. As Badger has surmised, 'The evidence from Texas, Tennessee, and Florida suggests that there might have been more room for manoeuvre than Southern moderates were prepared to credit.' Badger, 'Southerners Who Refused to Sign the Southern Manifesto', p. 528.

Chapter 3   Resistance Rampant, 1956–1960

1. James Baldwin, 'A Negro Assays the Negro Mood', *New York Times Magazine*, 12 March 1961, reprinted as 'East River, Downtown: Postscript to a Letter from Harlem', in *Nobody Knows My Name: More Notes of a Native Son* (London: Penguin, 1991), pp. 68–75, quotations from pp. 69 and 72.

2. Mary L. Dudziak, 'Desegregation as a Cold War Imperative', *Stanford Law Review*, vol. 41, no. 1 (November 1988), pp. 61–120; Dudziak, *Cold War Civil Rights: Race and the Image of American Democracy* (Princeton and Oxford: Oxford University Press, 2000); Azza Salama Layton, *International Relations and Civil Rights Policies in the United States* (Cambridge and New York: Cambridge University Press, 2000); and Thomas Borstelmann, *The Cold War and the Color Line: American Race Relations in the Global Arena* (Cambridge: Harvard University Press, 2001).

3. For a study that focuses on southern white leaders and the Cold War, see Thomas Noer, 'Segregationists and the World: the Foreign Policy of White Resistance', in Brenda Gayle Plummer (ed.), *Window on Freedom: Race, Civil Rights, and Foreign Affairs, 1945–1988* (Chapel Hill: University of North Carolina Press, 2003), pp. 141–62. Jeff Woods, too, has sought to move the focus away from Washington DC to the southern states, although he still concentrates on southern political elites. Jeff Woods, *Black Struggle, Red Scare: Segregation and Anti-Communism in the South, 1948–1968* (Baton Rouge: Louisiana State University Press, 2004). For more of a focus on the grassroots, see George Lewis, 'White South, Red Nation: Massive Resistance and the Cold War', in Clive Webb (ed.), *Massive Resistance: Southern Opposition to the Second Reconstruction* (Oxford and New York: Oxford University Press, 2005), pp. 117–35, and George Lewis, *The White South and the Red Menace: Segregationists, Anticommunism and Massive Resistance, 1945–1965* (Gainsville: University Press of Florida, 2004).

4. Lewis, *The White South and the Red Menace*, p. 43. See also Lewis 'White South, Red Nation: Massive Resistance and the Cold War', pp. 117–35.

5. 'To segregationists', he continued, 'African independence was a clear premonition of the calamity that would follow racial equality at home.' Noer, 'Segregationists and the World', p. 142.

6. Noer has claimed that, 'Until 1964 ... allegations of direct control of the civil rights movement were rarely a major focus ... This changed dramatically in 1964 as southern whites played the anticommunist card in hopes of revitalizing and expanding the campaign to preserve segregation by enticing existing right-wing organizations to the cause.' Noer, 'Segregationists and the World', p. 149. North Carolina's Senator Samuel J. Ervin and Virginian Citizens' Council leader Wesley Critz George are two examples of devoted segregationists who refused to employ anticommunism. See Lewis, *The White South and the Red Menace*, pp. 151–4 and 156–9. By the 1950s, the term 'red-baiting' was freely used in the US to describe the process of attempting to smear or denounce opponents by insinuating that they had communist connections, were communist sympathizers, or even that they were Communist Party members.

7. Lewis, *The White South and the Red Menace*, pp. 10–12; Sarah Hart Brown, 'Congressional Anti-Communism and the Segregationist South: From New Orleans to Atlanta, 1954–1958', *Georgia Historical Quarterly*, vol. 80, no. 4 (winter 1996), pp. 785–816; Woods, *Black Struggle Red Scare*; Joseph P. Kamp, *Behind the Plot to Sovietize the South* (New York: Headlines, 1956); Grass Roots League Research Bulletin no. 2 'Truth about Supreme Court's Segregation Ruling', copy in 'Desegregation: Misc'. Box 2, Sarratt Papers.

8. Defenders of States Rights and Individual Liberties radio broadcast quoted in Lewis, 'White South, Red Nation', p. 130.

9. 'Declaration of Constitutional Principles', press release copy 'For release Monday a.m. March 12, 1956', in 'Byrd Speeches Drafts – Civil Rights, etc, For reference, 1956–1960', Box 1, Byrd Papers.

10. David L. Chappell, 'Disunity and Religious Institutions in the White South', in Webb (ed.), *Massive Resistance*, pp. 136–50; quotations from pp. 137 and 142. See also Chappell, 'Religious Ideas of the Segregationists', and a second, broader article that acts almost as an introduction to the former, 'The Divided Mind of Southern Segregationists', *Georgia Historical Quarterly*, vol. 82, no. 1 (1998), pp. 45–72.

11. Chappell, 'Disunity and Religious Institutions in the White South', pp. 138–9 and 141.

12. Dailey, 'The Theology of Massive Resistance', pp. 151–80; quotations from pp. 166, 156 and 172. See also Dailey, 'Sex, Segregation, and the Sacred After *Brown*', *Journal of American History*, vol. 91, no. 1, pp. 119–44. One of the reasons that the strength of those religious views has been consistently overlooked, argues Dailey, is that the success of the civil rights movement has led to the belief that the religious orthodoxy espoused by figures such as Martin Luther King, Jr., was the prevailing view of the time. On the contrary, she argues, it was far from all-pervasive, and there was a 'titanic struggle waged by participants on both sides of the conflict to harness the immense power of the divine to their cause'. Quote from p. 153.

13. Chappell, for example, has shown that both the Southern Baptist Convention (SBC) and the Presbyterian Church in the US (PCUS) passed resolutions in support of desegregation post-*Brown*, the SBC by 'about nine thousand votes to fifty' and the PCUS by 239 to 169. Chappell, 'Disunity and Religious Institutions in the White South', p. 137. Although showing that the odd segregationist leader such as Theodore G. Bilbo was partial to making religious-based arguments in defence of segregation, 'hundreds of Virginians' wrote to their governor, Tom Stanley, in the wake of *Brown* to urge defiance, and their 'most common argument ... was theological'. Dailey, 'The Theology of Massive Resistance', pp. 156 and 159.

14. J. Mills Thornton III, *Dividing Lines: Municipal Politics and the Struggle for Civil Rights in Montgomery, Birmingham and Selma* (Tuscaloosa: University of Alabama Press, 2002), pp. 17 and 56.

15. Martin Luther King, Jr., 'Our Struggle', *Liberation*, vol. 1, no. 2 (April 1956), p. 4.
16. For a contemporary account that reflects the far-reaching ramifications of Lucy's attempt, see 'Exclusive Interviews with Principals in "Bama Violence"', *Ohio Sentinel*, 11 February 1956, copy in NAACP White Reprisals Files, frames 0199–0205. For secondary accounts, see Michael J. Klarman, *From Jim Crow to Civil Rights: the Supreme Court and the Struggle for Racial Equality* (Oxford and New York: Oxford University Press, 2004), pp. 258–9; Numan V. Bartley, *Rise of Massive Resistance: Race and Politics in the South during the 1950's* (Baton Rouge: Louisiana State University Press, 1969), p. 146. For the most comprehensive analysis, see E. Culpepper Clark, *The Schoolhouse Door: Segregation's Last Stand at the University of Alabama* (New York: Oxford University Press, 1993).
17. Neil R. McMillen, *The Citizens' Council: Organized Resistance to the Second Reconstruction, 1954–1964* (Urbana: University of Illinois Press, 1994), p. 44; Shores and Bennett quoted in 'Exclusive Interviews with Principals in "Bama Violence"', *Ohio Sentinel*, 11 February 1956.
18. King quoted in 'Exclusive Interviews with Principals in "'Bama Violence'", *Ohio Sentinel*, 11 February 1956.
19. Lewis, 'White South, Red Nation', p. 121; *The Citizens' Council*, vol. 1, no. 2 (August 1956), p. 3; Brita Counselman's letter to Senator Sam Ervin, 18 March 1956, Folder 1124, Samuel J. Ervin Papers, Southern Historical Collection, Wilson Library, University of North Carolina, Chapel Hill.
20. Wallace Westfeldt, 'Communities in Strife', in Don Shoemaker (ed.), *With All Deliberate Speed: Segregation–Desegregation in Southern Schools* (New York: Harper & Brothers, 1957), esp. pp. 36–9, 44–9; school principal quoted p. 46, Mayor Clark quoted pp. 48–9. For brief analyses of the importance of events in these towns, see Bartley, *Massive Resistance*, pp. 146–8.
21. Westfeldt, 'Communities in Strife', p. 50.
22. Westfeldt, a native of New Orleans, was a correspondent of *Southern School News* and a staff reporter for the *Nashville Tennessean*. 'Communities in Strife', pp. 37–9.
23. Harry Ashmore, 'The Easy Chair: The Untold Story of Little Rock', *Harper's* (June 1958), p. 4, reprinted by the Southern Regional Council, copy in NAACP White Reprisals Papers, reel 6, frames 0594–8; Bartley, *Massive Resistance*, p. 251.
24. According to Kirk, this resulted in 'an ambiguous and confusing stance that pandered to racism while leaving the way open for compliance and racial progress'. John A. Kirk, *Redefining the Color Line: Black Activism in Little Rock, Arkansas, 1940–1970* (Gainesville: University Press of Florida, 2002), p. 89. About a quarter of Little Rock's 100,000 population were African American in 1956.
25. Dale Bumpers Interview, Hoxie Tapes.
26. Governor Francis Cherry quoted in Kirk, *Redefining the Color Line*, pp. 86–7.
27. Kirk, *Redefining the Color Line*, pp. 91–2.
28. Bartley argued that Little Rock represented 'the most decisive test of the decade'. Bartley, *Rise of Massive Resistance*, p. 252. As McMillen noted, 'If mere long-range planning were a valid index to peaceful desegregation, Little Rock's submission to the dictates of the *Brown* decision would have been accomplished without incident'. McMillen, *The Citizens' Council*, p. 269; Kirk, *Redefining the Color Line*, pp. 92–3.
29. McMillen, *The Citizens' Council*, pp. 270–1.
30. Kirk, 'Massive Resistance and Minimum Compliance', p. 79.
31. Bartley, *Rise of Massive Resistance*, p. 253.
32. For the most recent work documenting the role of women in southern segregationist resistance, see Karen S. Anderson, 'Massive Resistance, Violence, and Southern

Social Relations', and Elizabeth Gillespie McRae, 'White Womanhood, White Supremacy, and the Rise of Massive Resistance', both in Webb (ed.), *Massive Resistance*, pp. 203–20 and 181–202 respectively. For a case study of one such segregationist woman, see Elizabeth Gillespie McRae, '"To Save a Home": Nell Battle Lewis and the Rise of Southern Conservatism, 1941–1956', *North Carolina Historical Review*, vol. 81, no. 3, pp. 262, 265–7.

33. Anderson, 'Massive Resistance, Violence, and Southern Social relations', pp. 207 and 210.
34. As Kirk's research has recognized, the Bird Report watered down Johnson's interposition stance, recommending 'little more than a token gesture placing Arkansas on record as opposing the *Brown* decision but precluding any further action. The second provision was a Pupil Assignment Law similar to the one already approved by the Arkansas General Assembly in 1955'. Kirk, *Redefining the Color Line*, p. 103.
35. McMillen, *The Citizens' Council*, pp. 272–3.
36. Perry Morgan, 'The Case for the White Southerner', *Esquire* (January 1962), p. 45. Thomas R. Waring, 'The Southern Case against Desegregation', *Harper's* (January 1956), pp. 39–45; quotes from pp. 39–43.
37. For accounts of the stand-off, see Bartley, *Massive Resistance*, pp. 261–9; Francis M. Wilhoit, *Politics of Massive Resistance* (New York: George Brazillier, 1973), pp. 176–82; Kirk, *Redefining the Color Line*, pp. 106–38.
38. Michael S. Mayer, 'With Much Deliberation and Some Speed: Eisenhower and the *Brown* Decision', *Journal of Southern History*, vol. LII, no. 1 (February 1986), pp. 43–76.
39. As Bartley notes, 'Caldwell could only explain that the Eisenhower administration did not wish to get involved and would assume no advance responsibility for maintaining order. Even at this late date, the federal government had no plans for dealing with opposition to desegregation.' Bartley, *Rise of Massive Resistance*, p. 263; see also pp. 264–6.
40. Ashmore, 'The Easy Chair', p. 5.
41. Blossom latched on to the equivocation inherent in the Supreme Court's second *Brown* decision, and took every available opportunity to fine down the criteria by which black students were to be considered for places in previously all-white schools. By the time that Blossom's carefully constructed plan unravelled in the face of the Little Rock mob, it was a strategy for massive resistance rather than gradual compliance. Kirk, 'Massive Resistance and Minimum Compliance', pp. 76–98. As Bartley has argued, Blossom also 'did little to construct a solid foundation of support', while the city's 'civic elite watched from the sideline, accepting school segregation as an administrative question properly to be dealt with by school authorities'. Bartley, *Rise of Massive Resistance*, pp. 254–5.
42. Anderson, 'Massive Resistance, Violence, and Southern Social Relations', pp. 203–4. Reed quoted on p. 208.
43. For examples, see Lewis, *White South and the Red Menace*, pp. 12–13.
44. Ashmore, 'The Easy Chair', p. 2.
45. Faubus himself often resorted to the 'powerful rhetoric of invasions and emasculation'. Anderson, 'Massive Resistance, Violence, and Southern Social Relations', pp. 206, 208, 211 and 213.
46. Harry Ashmore, 'The Easy Chair', p. 2.
47. 'Speech by Senator George Smathers, Fruit and Vegetable Association Convention, Miami – October 10, 1957', NAACP White Reprisals Papers, reel 6, frames 0826–9.
48. *Defenders' News and Views*, vol. 3, no. 7 (June–July–August, 1958), pp. 1–8. The edition was a cobbled-together reprint of articles that had appeared in *The Standard-*

Times of New Bedford, Mass., 21–25 July 1958, which the paper's editors claimed documented and reviewed 'the Communist campaign to promote racial unrest in the South and the influence of that campaign in the origin of, and the aftermath to, the impasse at Little Rock'. Reprint in Box 82, Folder 8, Basil Lee Whitener Papers, Special Collections Library, Duke University, Durham, North Carolina.

49. Membership Card of Butler County, Alabama, Citizens' Council, NAACP White Reprisals Papers, reel 12, frame 0389.

50. C. C. Collins' letter to Thomas Stanley, 7 June 1954, 'Segregation June 1954', Box 100, Stanley Papers.

51. Ervin quoted in Citizens' Council Forum 'Discussion of Constitutional Rights and Civil Rights with Sam Ervin (16 minutes) 1959', Tape 1, Film 2; Ervin's letter to Dr Isaac M. Taylor, 2 June 1954, 'School Segregation June 23–Dec 31 1954', both in Ervin Papers.

52. S. G. Lindsay to Governor's Special Advisory Committee on Education, 3 September 1954, Folder 6, Box 1, Pearsall Papers.

53. As Klarman has recently noted, the Supreme Court justices knew full well that 'individual blacks could rarely litigate without the NAACP's assistance and that Congress was not about to authorize the Justice Department to bring desegregation suits'. Klarman, *From Jim Crow to Civil Rights*, p. 335. It was not only the justices who were aware of that fact, however, for many segregationists understood it only too well.

54. Roy Wilkins' letter to W. Lester Banks, 20 August 1957, NAACP White Reprisal Papers, reel 12, frame 0982. The belief that he was simply being bullish is supported by the fact that, in May 1957, Wilkins told the NAACP Board that the White South's assault on the Association raised 'the whole question of the future operation of the NAACP in the Southern states'. Wilkins quoted in Klarman, *From Jim Crow to Civil Rights*, p. 335.

55. Klarman, *From Jim Crow to Civil Rights*, p. 335; Walter F. Murphy 'The South Counterattacks: The Anti-NAACP Laws', *Western Political Quarterly*, vol. 12 (June 1959), p. 373.

56. SRC figures and Arkansas attorney general both quoted in 'Problems of the South – Acts of Violence and Intimidation by Rabbi Arthur Gilbert: A Paper Read at the Interracial Consultation on "Southern Churches and Race Relations"', The College of the Bible, Lexington, Kentucky, July 20, 1960', Folder 1, Box 5, Aubrey Brown Papers, Virginia Historical Society, Richmond, Virginia.

57. Robert W. Saunders, 'Report on Florida Legislative Committee No. 2', 5 February 1957, received by Roy Wilkins, Gloster B. Current, Henry Lee Moon, Thurgood Marshall and Robert L Carter, NAACP White Reprisals Papers, reel 7, frames 0293–6.

58. Byrd's 'personal and confidential' letter to Almond, 6 March 1959, 'Byrd, Harry Flood, 1887–1966', Box 2, J. Lindsay Almond, Jr., Gubernatorial Papers, Archives and Research Services, Library of Virginia, Richmond.

59. For the Louisiana law, see Murphy, 'The South Counterattacks', pp. 376–7; for the Mississippi laws, see 'The "Law" in Mississippi', NAACP White Reprisals Papers, reel 2, frame 0134.

60. As legal historian Walter F. Murphy describes them, 'Barratry is the "habitual stirring up of quarrels and suits"'. Champerty describes a situation where a person with no real interest in a particular piece of litigation assists one of the actual parties by money or service in return for a share of the expected proceeds of the case. Maintenance is the more general term which encompasses "officious intermeddling in a suit which in no way belongs to one, by maintaining or assisting either party, with money or otherwise, to prosecute or defend it"'. Murphy, 'The South Counterattacks', p. 373.

61. Attorney General Bruce Bennett's letter to Daisy Bates, 30 August 1957, NAACP White Reprisals Papers, reel 6, frames 0454–5. A second ordinance, dated 14 October 1957, demanded that all financial and membership records from the branch be handed over to the Little Rock city clerk. 'L Rock Ordinance 10,638', NAACP White Reprisals Papers, reel 6, frames 0461–2.
62. Harold V. Kelly, Temporary Counsel, Legislative Committee on Law Reform and Racial Activities, letter to Virginia State Conference of NAACP Branches, 30 January 1957, NAACP White Reprisals Papers, reel 12, frames 0887–8.
63. The bill was introduced on 21 January 1957. House Bill 32, copy in NAACP White Reprisals Papers, reel 12, frames 0266–7.
64. Arkansas NAACP Field Secretary Frank W. Smith wrote to Roy Wilkins on 11 March 1957, enclosing four segregation bills recently passed by the state legislature. While one bill created the Sovereignty Commission, another, House Bill 324, required organizations such as the NAACP to lodge information on their economic activities and the contributions that they had received with the newly formed committee. NAACP White Reprisals Papers, reel 6, frames 0427–40.
65. *Report of the Committee on Offenses against the Administration of Justice* (Richmond: Commonwealth of Virginia Division of Purchase and Printing, 1957). Copy in NAACP White Reprisals Papers, reel 12, frames 1012–48.
66. Medgar Evers' special report on 'General Legislative Investigating Committee, Miss'., 20 November 1959, NAACP White Reprisals Papers, reel 3, frames 0615–16.
67. *Tampa Morning Tribune* clippings, 1 and 13 February 1958, NAACP White Reprisals Papers, reel 7, frames 0348 and 0372–3.
68. Washington, DC, *Evening Star* clipping, 2 May 1957, NAACP White Reprisals Papers, reel 12, frame 0742.
69. Almost 250 branches were shut down, and southern membership dropped from 128,000 in 1955 to 80,000 in 1957. The sharpest drop was in the Deep South, where Louisiana lost some 11,300 members and South Carolina lost 6,000. As Klarman notes, the Supreme Court was successful in halting anti-NAACP legislation in a number of cases, but, by 1963, the justices 'began to divide over how far to stretch the Constitution to protect the association from the harassment of southern states'. Klarman, *From Jim Crow to Civil Rights*, pp. 335 and 340; figures quoted in p. 383. For Murphy, the drop in membership was clear evidence of segregationists' 'excellent tactical judgement' in the battle against the NAACP. Murphy, 'The South Counterattacks', p. 380.
70. Historian Robert A. Pratt refers to Cook as the man who 'led the campaign to cripple Georgia's NAACP. ' Robert A. Pratt, *We Shall Not Be Moved: The Desegregation of the University of Georgia* (Athens and London: University of Georgia Press, 2002), p. 50. For a discussion of the genesis of Cook's 'Ugly Truth about the NAACP', see M. J. Heale, *McCarthy's Americans: Red Scare Politics in State and Nation, 1935–1965* [American History in Depth Series, eds A. J. Badger and Howell Harris] (London: Macmillan, 1998), pp. 251–2, and Woods, *Black Struggle, Red Scare*, pp. 58–63.
71. Those groups were the Yale chapter of the NAACP, the John Dewey Society, the New Haven Civil Liberties Union, the Yale Hillel Foundation, the Yale Christian Association and the Young Democrats of Yale. William D. Workman, Jr. *The Case for the South* (New York: Devin-Adair, 1960), p. 247.
72. Eugene Cook statement on the NAACP, NAACP White Reprisals Papers, reel 8, frame 0820. Considering the contemporary ubiquity of 'The Ugly Truth about the NAACP', remarkably few copies have survived intact. For a copy reprinted by the North Carolina Defenders of States' Rights Inc., see Box 115, George Papers.

73. Mrs Marian Gattermann's letter to Governor Stanley, 29 March 1956, 'Segregation March, April, May 1956', Box 105, Stanley Papers.
74. Brita Counselman's letter to Ervin, quoted in Lewis, *The White South and the Red Menace*, p. 57.
75. The transcript was reproduced by a number of different segregationist groups, the vast majority of them Citizens' Councils. For one such version 'transcribed and distributed as an educational service by your CACC', see 'Transcription of a Speech Made by Roosevelt Williams, A Negro High in the Councils of the NAACP, at a Secret NAACP Meeting in Mississippi in December of 1954', NAACP White Reprisals Papers, reel 4, frame 0556.
76. Roy Wilkins' 'Day Letter' to Hon. Rankin Fite, Hon. George Hawkins, Lieutenant Governor Guy Hardwick and Hon Broughton Lambert, 19 January 1956, NAACP White Reprisals Papers, reel 4, frame 0558. When pushed on the issue, Cook claimed that it was distributed by one of his staff members without his personal knowledge. See NAACP press release, 'A Fraud Unmasked: The Strange Fate of Roosevelt Williams', NAACP White Reprisals Papers, reel 8, frame 0012.
77. 'A Fraud Unmasked: The Strange Fate of Roosevelt Williams', NAACP White Reprisals Papers, reel 8, frame 0012.
78. John H. Calhoun's letter to Gloster B. Current, 30 August 1956, NAACP White Reprisals Papers, reel 8, frame 0675; Engelhardt quoted in Tuskegee, *Crusade For Citizenship*, 23 June 1959, and in NAACP Press Release, 'Senators Learn NAACP Recording is "Fake"', 9 February 1956, NAACP White Reprisals Papers, reel 4, frame 0562.
79. 'Negro Professor Demands Intermarriage between the Races' version enclosed with William H. Oliver, Co-Director, Fair Practices and Anti-Discrimination Department, UAW letter to Roy Wilkins, 9 April 1956, in NAACP White Reprisals Papers, reel 7, frames 0915–17; 'The Ultimate Aim of the NAACP' version enclosed with Edwin J. Lukas's letter to John Morsell, 22 October 1956, NAACP White Reprisals Papers, reel 6, frames 0804–6.
80. 'The Ultimate Aim of the NAACP' version enclosed with Edwin J. Lukas's letter to John Morsell, 22 October 1956, NAACP White Reprisals Papers, reel 6, frames 0804–6.
81. J. Todd Moye, *Let the People Decide: Black Freedom and White Resistance Movements in Sunflower County, Mississippi, 1945–1986* (Chapel Hill: University of North Carolina Press, 2004), pp. 66 and 68.
82. James C. Cobb, *The Most Southern Place on Earth: The Mississippi Delta and the Roots of Regional Identity* (New York: Oxford University Press, 1992).
83. Moye, *Let the People Decide*, p. 66; Tony Badger, '*Brown* and Backlash', in Webb (ed.), *Massive Resistance*, p. 46.
84. Walter Scruggs, director of the Bank of Ruleville, quoted in Moyes, *Let the People Decide*, p. 85.
85. One of the reasons for the elaborate arrangement with the Tri-State Bank was that the NAACP's charter did not allow the association to make financial loans, even if it had sufficient money to allow it to do so. See Wilkins' letter to Rev. J. L. Tolbert, 21 June 1956, NAACP White Reprisals Papers, reel 1, frame 0432, and also 0669. Howard was from the all-black town of Mound Bayou, in Bolivar County, Mississippi.
86. Both women signed sworn affidavits in the presence of Aaron E. Henry, president of the Coahoma County NAACP. For the affidavits of Gussie P. Young and Lurleaner Johnson respectively, see NAACP White Reprisals Papers, reel 1, frames 0344–5 and

0346–7. See also NAACP press release, 'School Petitioners Fired at Federally-Aided Hospital', 9 February 1956, NAACP White Reprisals Papers, reel 1, frame 0344.

87. Wilkins' memorandum to Gloster B. Current, 'RE: Arrest of Dr Aaron Henry and Others', NAACP White Reprisals Papers, reel 1.

88. Medgar Evers' and Mildred Bond's letter to Gloster B. Current, 24 January 1956, NAACP White Reprisals Papers, reel 1, frames 0468–9.

89. Murphy, 'The South Counterattacks', p. 379.

90. W. E. Solomon, executive secretary, Palmetto Education Association letter to Wilkins, 27 July 1956, NAACP White Reprisals Papers, reel 2, frame 0083.

91. The group of 12 men was organized by Jack D. Brock, co-publisher of the *Alabama Labor News*, and Eugene S. Hall, a director of the Montgomery White Citizens' Council. 'Integration Opponents Hang Two Effigies in Court Square', *The Montgomery Advertiser*, 5 August 1956, pp. 1A and 2A.

92. In 1956, Atlanta had 48 times the population of Terrell County, but only three times the voting power because of Georgia's antiquated county unit primary system. Figures quoted in 'Death and Violence Terrorize Negroes of Georgia Town', *Washington Post and Times Herald*, 8 June 1958, clipping in NAACP White Reprisals Papers, reel 8, frames 0752–5.

93. NAACP Southeastern Regional Office 'Confidential Report re: Investigation of Terrell County, Ga'. NAACP White Reprisals Papers, reel 8, frames 0746–51. See in particular frame 0750.

94. An official NAACP report into what the association termed the 'atrocities' of Terrell County noted that 'There are inconsistencies surrounding the time of death, both on the death certificate ... and in what Mrs Brazier says she was told about the time James died and the time she received the telephone call [to inform her of her husband's death].' NAACP Southeastern Regional Office 'Confidential 'Report re: Investigation of Terrell County, Ga'. NAACP White Reprisals Papers, reel 8, frames 0746–51. Quote from frame 0748.

95. Countryman was alleged to have jumped out from behind trees in his backyard, and threatened the officers with a knife. Family members, however, reported to the NAACP's investigation team that the trees in the yard were not sufficiently large to have concealed Countryman, and, what is more, that directly after the shooting 'the officers turned Countryman's body over, went through his pockets and found nothing. Yet, when the body got to the undertaker, there was a knife in his hand, but the wrong hand'. NAACP Southeastern Regional Office 'Confidential Report re: Investigation of Terrell County, Ga'. NAACP White Reprisals Papers, reel 8, frames 0746–51. Quote from frame 0748. See also 'Death and Violence Terrorize Negroes of Georgia Town', *Washington Post and Times Herald*, 8 June 1958, clipping in NAACP White Reprisals Papers, reel 8, frames 0752–5.

96. Lee and Matthews quoted in 'Death and Violence Terrorize Negroes of Georgia Town', *Washington Post and Times Herald*, 8 June 1958. Robert E. Lee Baker, a staff reporter on the *Washington Post*, was sent to Dawson to bring publicity to the situation there after the Southern Regional Council's Harold Fleming brought the situation to the attention of a contact of his on the *Post*, Al Friendly. See NAACP Southeastern Regional Office 'Confidential Report re: Investigation of Terrell County, Ga'. NAACP White Reprisals Papers, reel 8, frame 0751.

97. Fleming testified that, on 30 July 1957, 'a Ku Klux Klan caravan parked in front of my house. In the sixth car from the front of the caravan, I saw Sheriff T. K. Jackson and one of his deputies in a car bearing his official insignia'. 'Statement of Billie S. Fleming, President of the Clarendon County, South Carolina, Improvement

Association, before the Senate Subcommittee on Constitutional Rights, April 16, 1959', NAACP White Reprisals Papers, reel 11, frames 0044–51, quote from frame 0049.

98. Dr John Morsell's memo to Henry Lee Moon, 10 February 1960, NAACP White Reprisals Papers, reel 10, frames 0668–70, quote from frame 0668.

99. Dr John Morsell's memo to Henry Lee Moon, 10 February 1960, NAACP White Reprisals Papers, reel 10, frames 0668–70; Roy Wilkins' memo to Robert L. Carter, 6 December 1960, NAACP White Reprisals Papers, reel 10, frames 0732–3.

100. 'Report of Intimidation of Mrs Bessie Veal and Family', 19 January 1957, NAACP White Reprisals Papers, reel 6, frames 0815–16.

101. Certified statements by Joe Sephers Wells, O. D. Maclin, Isiah [sic] Harris and Reverend June Dowdy, all made 13 May 1963, NAACP White Reprisals Papers, reel 11, frames 0555, 0545, 0546 and 0548.

102. NAACP White Reprisals Papers, reel 11, frames 0545–50, 0555.

103. 'Barnett Gives Segregation Credit for Landing Oil Refinery on Coast', clipping in NAACP White Reprisals Papers, reel 14, frame 0185; W. C. Smith, president of Standard Oil of Kentucky telegram to Aaron E. Henry and Medgar W. Evers, 21 September 1961, NAACP White Reprisals Papers, reel 14, frame 0184.

104. Mrs Lella Galvani's letter to Luther Hodges, 30 November 1957, 'Segregation G–H', Box 228, Hodges Papers.

105. See copies of The Virginian, Box 28, Earnest Sevier Cox Papers.

106. We the People (Baton Rouge: Louisiana State Sovereignty Commission, n.d.), copy in NAACP White Reprisals Papers, reel 9, frames 0313–20.

107. For a reprinted copy of Oliver Allstrom's 'The Mongrel' see reel 13, frame 0654; for a copy of his 'The Saddest Story Ever Told', see reel 9, frames 0906–7, both NAACP White Reprisals Papers.

108. The Independent American's 'Pro-Red Batting Averages of Members of the Supreme Court' chart was based upon remarks placed into the Congressional Record by Senator James O. Eastland on 10 July 1958. The IA calculated that Justices Black, Douglas, Warren and Brennan had all scored over 90 per cent. 'On Whose Side Is the Supreme Court?' Box 14, George Papers. See also Lewis, The White South and the Red Menace, p. 54.

109. Stuart Epperson letter to Wesley Critz George, 15 June 1960, 'June 1960', Box 8, George Papers.

110. 'The Result of Integration' drew heavily from George's Human Progress and the Race Problem, while his The Race Problem was also quoted from extensively in two programmes, 'The Race Problem' and 'Human Progress and the Race Problem'. Transcripts of many of the Defenders' broadcasts can be found in Sarah Patton Boyle's Papers. For more on the influence of Wesley Critz George on southern resistance, see Lewis, '"Scientific Certainty": Wesley Critz George, Racial Science and Organized White Resistance in North Carolina, 1954–1962', Journal of American Studies (2004), pp. 227–47.

111. For Lake's arguments before the Supreme Court, see Leon Friedman (ed.), Argument: The Complete Oral Argument before the Supreme Court in Brown v. Board of Education of Topeka, 1952–1955 (New York: Chelsea House Publishers, 1969), pp. 448–61. Reverend James P. 'Jimmy' Dees' letter to Board of Directors, Defenders of States' Rights, 28 February 1961, Folder 24, Erwin A. Holt Papers, Southern Historical Collection, Wilson Library, University of North Carolina, Chapel Hill. Dees noted that he, Helms and the station's owner, A. J. Fletcher, 'had a very rewarding visit. Mr Helms assured us that the station would be glad to carry TV programs for us

FREE OF CHARGE, if they were gotten up by me along with his advice and assistance. I have several such programs under consideration now, one of them being "The Prince Edward Story"'.

112. The show, entitled 'The Little Rock Crisis', was aired at 6.30pm Central Standard Time on 26 September 1957 by the Jackson, Mississippi-based WLBT-TV. See NAACP White Reprisals Papers, reel 14, p. 110.

113. Morphew's letter to William Munford Tuck, 23 June 1958, Folder 5288, William Munford Tuck Papers, Manuscript and Rare Books Department, Earl Gregg Swem Library, College of William and Mary, Williamsburg. Many of the *Citizens' Council Forum* programmes can be found on tape in the Southern Historical Collection, Wilson Library, University of North Carolina, Chapel Hill.

114. For the most comprehensive analysis of the Sovereignty Commission, see Katagiri, *The Mississippi State Sovereignty Commission*. First annual report quoted and Sillers both quoted on p. 12.

115. Of the 21 newspaper editors invited South by the Sovereignty Commission, only one, Roswell S. Bosworth, Jr., president of Rhode Island Press Association, could not attend. Bosworth replied that he could not go as the mooted trip clashed with 'a mechanical changeover which was going on in our plant'. See NAACP White Reprisals Papers, reel 2, frame 0966.

116. William B. Rotch's letter to Roy Wilkins, 19 October 1956, NAACP White Reprisals Papers, reel 2, frame 0969.

117. Richard P. Lewis's letter to Roy Wilkins, 20 October 1956, NAACP White Reprisals Papers, reel 2, frame 0974.

118. Rotch, for example, revealed that 'Some of us got away from the official party when we could, and tried to talk with Negroes, if only to find out that there was another side to the picture. Some of us would come back to the hotel feeling sick about the whole thing.' Rotch's letter to Wilkins, 19 October 1956, NAACP White Reprisals Papers, reel 2, frame 0969.

119. Richard P. Lewis's letter to Roy Wilkins, 20 October 1956, NAACP White Reprisals Papers, reel 2, frame 0974.

120. John A. Morsell's letter to William B. Rotch, 13 December 1956, NAACP White Reprisals Papers, reel 2, frame 0976.

121. The *Herald Tribune* letter, originally published on 17 February 1956, was reprinted and distributed by a number of *Citizens' Councils*. For one such copy, see NAACP White Reprisals Papers, reel 7, frame 0429. Rainach memo, 3 March 1958, in NAACP White Reprisals Papers, reel 9, frame 0240.

122. James Hermann's letter to editor, *New York Post*, 20 February 1958, NAACP White Reprisals Papers, reel 9, frame 0574.

123. James Lenoir's letter to Roy Wilkins, 6 October 1956, NAACP White Reprisals Papers, reel 8, frame 0795.

124. William D. Workman, Jr., *The Case for the South* (New York: Devin-Adair, 1960); James Jackson Kilpatrick, *The Southern Case for School Segregation* (Richmond: Crowell-Collier, 1962).

125. Kilpatrick's opening remarks quoted in transcript of 'Comment' Show, NBC, 31 August 1958, 'Speeches 1955: Misc speeches: Notes on Race Issue', Box 1, Kilpatrick Papers.

126. The debate was moderated by John McCaffery. King responded to Kilpatrick 'But I think, Mr Kilpatrick, you would have to agree that there is a great distinction between the immoral, the hateful, the violent resistance of many white segregationists and the non-violent, peaceful, loving, civil resistance of the negro students.

I think one is uncivil disobedience, the other is civil disobedience, if you will.' Transcript of NBC's *The Nation's Future,* 26 November 1960, in 'Kilpatrick, James J'., Box 2, Virginia Commission on Constitutional Government Papers, State of North Carolina Department of Cultural Resources, Division of Archives and History, Raleigh, North Carolina.

Chapter 4 Responsive Resistance, c. 1960-1965

1. For Byrd's own view of what he referred to as Almond's 'spectacular performance' see 'Statement by Sen. Harry F. Byrd (D.Va.) January 19 1962', Box 264, Byrd Papers. See also James W. Ely, Jr., *The Crisis of Conservative Virginia: the Byrd Organization and the Politics of Massive Resistance* (Knoxville: University of Tennessee Press, 1976), esp. chapter 8; J. Harvie Wilkinson III, *Harry Byrd and the Changing Face of Virginia Politics: 1945–1966* (Charlottesville: University Press of Virginia, 1968), pp. 133–50; Heinemann, *Harry Byrd of Virginia* (Charlottesville and London: University Press of Virginia, 1996), pp. 339–50.

2. Virginia's assignment plan was strongly reminiscent of that recommended by the Gray Commission five years earlier, although this time it was produced under the auspices of the Byrd Organization stalwart and state Senator Mosby G. Perrow. Ely, *The Crisis of Conservative Virginia,* pp. 130–5, 140–1; Wilkinson, *Harry Byrd and the Changing Face of Virginia Politics,* pp. 147–8; Heinemann, *Harry Byrd of Virginia,* pp. 349–51; John A. Kirk, 'Massive Resistance and Minimum Compliance', in C. Webb (ed.), *Massive Resistance,* esp. p. 93; Tony A. Freyer, 'The Little Rock Crisis Reconsidered', *Arkansas Historical Quarterly,* vol. 56 (Autumn 1997), pp. 360–70, esp. p. 367.

3. 1963 cases include *NAACP v. Button* and *Gibson v. Florida Legislative Investigation Committee.* For an analysis of the Supreme Court's role in turning back the states' anti-NAACP statutes, see Michael J. Klarman, *From Jim Crow to Civil Rights: the Supreme Court and the Struggle for Racial Equality* (Oxford and New York: Oxford University Press, 2004), pp. 334–9.

4. In the 11 former Confederate states, only 2.25 per cent of African Americans attended school with white children by the 1964–65 school year. In Alabama the figure was 0.034 per cent, in Arkansas 0.811 per cent, in Georgia 0.4 per cent, in Mississippi 0.02 per cent and in South Carolina 0.102 per cent. Figures quoted in *Southern School News,* vol. XI (June 1965), p. 11, also reproduced in Francis M. Wilhoit, *The Politics of Massive Resistance* (New York: George Braziller, 1973), Table B.

5. It is a crisis that has garnered considerable scholarly attention. See, for example, Morton Inger, *Politics and Reality in an American City: The New Orleans School Crisis of 1960* (New York: Center for Urban Education, 1969) and 'The New Orleans School Crisis of 1960', in Elizabeth Jacoway and David R. Colburn (eds), *Southern Businessmen and Desegregation* (Baton Rouge: Louisiana State University Press, 1982), pp. 82–97; Wilhoit, *The Politics of Massive Resistance,* pp. 183–91; Adam Fairclough, *Race & Democracy: the Civil Rights Struggle in Louisiana, 1915–1972* (Athens and London: University of Georgia Press, 1995), pp. 234–64; Neil R. McMillen, *The Citizens' Councils* (Urbana: University of Illinois Press, 1994), pp. 286–93; and James Graham Cook, *The Segregationists* (New York: Appleton-Century-Crofts, 1962), pp. 229–46.

6. Figures quoted in Cook, *The Segregationists,* p. 230.

7. The emergency sessions were called between 4 November 1960 and the end of February 1961. See Wilhoit, *The Politics of Massive Resistance,* esp. pp. 185–7 and 190; quotation from Fairclough, *Race & Democracy,* p. 242, see also pp. 235, 242–6.

8. Wilhoit, *The Politics of Massive Resistance*, p. 184; Fairclough, *Race & Democracy*, p. 242.

9. Wilhoit, *The Politics of Massive Resistance*, p. 187; Inger, 'The New Orleans School Crisis of 1960', pp. 88–9.

10. By August, as Fairclough has shown, 17 such cooperatives had either been chartered or planned. Fairclough, *Race & Democracy*, p. 236.

11. Davis's address quoted in Wilhoit, *The Politics of Massive Resistance*, p. 185. 'You Are My Sunshine' went on to become the official state song of Louisiana.

12. Perez quoted in Wilhoit, *The Politics of Massive Resistance*, p. 187.

13. John Steinbeck, *Travels with Charley* (London: Penguin, 1980), pp. 189–96, quotes from pp. 189 and 195; Wilhoit describes 'A crowd of jeering housewives [that] gathered daily at McDonogh No 19 and especially at Frantz, and their faces, congealed with hate, became famous to television viewers around the world.' Wilhoit, *The Politics of Massive Resistance*, p. 187.

14. Inger, 'The New Orleans School Crisis of 1960', p. 93.

15. Inger, 'The New Orleans School Crisis of 1960', pp. 93–4.

16. McMillen, *The Citizens' Councils*, pp. 287–8. Similarly, Fairclough has argued that 'the underlying obstacle' in the 'long-term success' of integration in the city was that 'white New Orleanians were overwhelmingly and deeply opposed to it'. Fairclough, *Race & Democracy*, p. 261.

17. For the role of businessmen in southern communities as a whole see, for example, Elizabeth Jacoway, 'An Introduction: Civil Rights and the Changing South', in Elizabeth Jacoway and David R. Colburn (eds), *Southern Businessmen and Desegregation* (Baton Rouge: Louisiana State University Press, 1982), pp. 1–14, esp. p. 9; for the specific situation in New Orleans, see Inger, 'The New Orleans School Crisis of 1960', *passim* and Wilhoit, *Politics of Massive Resistance*, p. 189. In what Fairclough has described as a monthly game of 'cat-and-mouse', the legislature refused to pay the teachers at Frantz and McDonogh No. 19, or Redmond and his staff. When payment was made, it was often weeks or even months late, and there was a financial shortfall in the schools' budgets. Fairclough, *Race & Democracy*, pp. 246–7.

18. Wilhoit, *The Politics of Massive Resistance*, p. 190; Fairclough, *Race & Democracy*, pp. 256–7.

19. Fairclough, *Race & Democracy*, p. 246. For the subtle changes in the Kennedys' position on civil rights, see Mark Stern, *Calculating Visions: Kennedy, Johnson and Civil Rights* (New Brunswick, NJ: Rutgers University Press, 1992), esp. pp. 9–114; for changing Democratic Party policies on civil rights more broadly, see David L. Chappell, *Inside Agitators: White Southerners in the Civil Rights Movement* (Baltimore: Johns Hopkins University Press, 1994), esp. pp. 147–211.

20. Reprints enclosed with Louis W. Hollis letter to Roxanne Kalb, 16 January 1961, copied to Kilpatrick. Copy in 'K 1961', Box 34, Kilpatrick Papers.

21. The leading proponent of such an argument is David L. Chappell. It is a theme that runs through his work on segregationists, but see in particular both 'Religious Ideas of the Segregationists', *Journal of American Studies*, vol. 32, no. 2 (1998), pp. 237–62 and 'The Divided Mind of Southern Segregationists', *Georgia Historical Quarterly*, vol. 82, no. 1 (1998), pp. 45–72.

22. J. Todd Moye, *Let the People Decide: Black Freedom and White Resistance Movements in Sunflower County, Mississippi, 1945–1986* (Chapel Hill: University of North Carolina Press, 2004), pp. 61–3, Eastland quoted p. 62; Jeff Woods, *Black Struggle Red Scare* (Baton Rouge: Louisiana State University Press, 2004), pp. 42–3, 181–93,

200–33; George Lewis, *The White South and the Red Menace: Segregationists, Anticommunism and Massive Resistance, 1945–1965* (Gainsville: University Press of Florida, 2004), esp. pp. 54, 58, 65, 92–3; Sarah Hart Brown, 'Congressional Anti-Communism and the Segregationist South', *Georgia Historical Quarterly*, vol. 80, no. 4 (1996), pp. 785–816.

23. The NAACP was warned against links with 'the Southern Regional Conference Education Fund [sic]' because it was 'the heir of the Southern Regional Conference on Human Welfare', and also with its 'Field Director' Carl T. Braden. Alabama Circuit Court Associate Judge William C. Bibb's letter to 'NAACP, Washington DC', 12 December 1961, NAACP White Reprisals Papers, reel 4, frame 0491.

24. Carleton Putnam, *Race and Reason: A Yankee View* (Washington: Public Affairs Press, 1961). For an analysis of Putnam's contribution to the segregationist cause, see I. A. Newby, *Challenge to the Court: Social Scientists and the Defense of Segregation, 1954–1966* (revised edition) (Baton Rouge: Louisiana State University Press, 1969), esp. pp. 148–66; James W. Silver, 'Mississippi: The Closed Society', *Journal of Southern History*, vol. 30, no. 1 (February 1964), p. 5. For the mechanics with which a coterie of scientific racists attempted to 'dismantle' the changes wrought by *Brown*, see John P. Jackson, Jr., *Science for Segregation: Race, Law, and the Case against Brown v. Board of Education* [Critical America Series] (New York: New York University Press, 2005), esp. pp. 93–147.

25. Wesley Critz George, *The Biology of the Race Problem* (n.p., 1962), p. 87. See also George Lewis, '"Scientific Certainty": Wesley Critz George, Racial Science and Organised White Resistance in North Carolina, 1954–1962', *Journal of American Studies*, vol. 8, no. 2 (2004), pp. 227–47; John P. Jackson, Jr., 'In Ways Unacademical: The Reception of Carleton S. Coon's *The Origin of Races*', *Journal of the History of Biology*, vol. 34 (2001), pp. 247–85.

26. 'Harry Flood Byrd Statement – Feb 5, 1959 with respect to the proposed civil rights legislation', Box 411, Byrd Papers. For the view that Byrd was ideologically opposed to anything but the rigid maintenance of his segregated way of life see in particular Benjamin Muse, *Virginia's Massive Resistance* (Bloomington: Indiana University Press, 1961), p. 25.

27. Chappell, *A Stone of Hope: Prophetic Religion and the Death of Jim Crow* (Chapel Hill: University of North Carolina Press, 2004), p. 165; Pittman quoted in McMillen, *The Citizens' Council*, p. 202, see also pp. 81–3; copies of reprints of three of Pittman's pamphlets, *All Men Are Not Created Equal*, *The Law of the Land*, and *The Supreme Court, The Broken Constitution and the Shattered Bill of Rights* can be found in NAACP White Reprisals Papers, reel 8, frames 0998–1004, 0979–90 and 0991–7.

28. 'Ever since I came to the Senate, I have joined other Southern Senators and Congressmen in fighting those who seek to rob Southern States and their officials and people of basic governmental and legal rights by Civil Rights legislation incompatible with the Constitution', Ervin's letter began. Ervin letter to A. C. Jordan, assistant professor of English, Duke University, 25 May 1961, Folder 2512, 'Racial problems May 1–31', Box 53, Ervin Papers.

29. 'The Court is in the hands of politicians rather than judges and lawyers', Ervin continued. 'Only one member of the Court ever served as a Judge before he became a member of the Court, and only two or three of them ever practiced law in a serious manner.' Ervin's letter to Dr Isaac M. Taylor, School of Medicine, UNC Chapel Hill, 2 June 1954, Folder 279 'School Segregation June 23 – Dec 31 1954', Ervin Papers; *The Citizens' Council Forum*, 'Discussion of Constitutional Rights and Civil Rights with Sam Ervin (16 minutes), 1959', Tape 1, Film 2, Ervin Papers.

30. In recent years, historians have been increasingly drawn to document the levels of racism that existed in the North, especially in its rural ghettos, and by doing so have successfully sought to break down a historiographical consensus which in its early stages had sought to confine the modern civil rights movement's activities to the southern states. For the most remarkable of the former, see Thomas J. Sugrue, *The Origins of the Urban Crisis: Race and Inequality in Postwar Detroit* (Princeton, NJ: Princeton University Press, 1996); for the most wide-ranging of the latter, see Jeanne F. Theoharis and Komozi Woodward (eds), *Freedom North: Black Freedom Struggles outside the South, 1940–1980* (New York: Palgrave Macmillan, 2003), and, equally importantly, Arnold R. Hirsch, 'Massive Resistance in the Urban North: Trumbull Park, Chicago, 1953–1966', *Journal of American History*, vol. 82, no. 2 (September 1995), pp. 522–50.

31. Hirsch, 'Massive Resistance in the Urban North', pp. 524–7 and 530. Quotation from p. 527.

32. Hirsch, 'Massive Resistance in the Urban North', p. 539.

33. More radically, Theoharis has also sought to challenge the dominant historiographical narrative that depicts a southern civil rights movement, honed in the craft of defeating open and demagogically driven white supremacy, moving North where it was able to win fewer successes. As a result, many northern blacks turned away from non-violent resistance to more radical, black nationalist sources of inspiration. She argues that existing historical accounts that do seek 'to take up Northern movements usually do so to trace how the movement moved from South to North, to show how tactics that worked in the South were less successful in the North, and to argue that blacks in the North had rejected integration by the mid-1960s in favour of nationalist strategies'. Jeanne Theoharis, '"I'd Rather Go to School in the South": How Boston's School Desegregation Complicates the Civil Rights Paradigm', in Jeanne F. Theoharis and Komozi Woodward (eds), *Freedom North: Black Freedom Struggles outside the South* (New York: Palgrave Macmillan, 2003), pp. 125–51. Quotes from pp. 128 and 127.

34. In 1950, per pupil spending was $240 for black pupils and $340 for whites. Theoharis, '"I'd Rather Go to School in the South"', p. 130.

35. All quotations from press release, 'Police Idle as NAACP Is Stoned in Boston Parade', 20 March 1964, NAACP White Reprisals Papers, reel 11, frame 0284. Atkins also quoted in Theoharis, '"I'd Rather Go to School in the South"', p. 132; Alan Lupo, *Liberty's Chosen Home* (Boston: Little, Brown & Company, 1970), pp. 146–7.

36. Perry Morgan, 'The Case of the White Southerner', *Esquire* (January 1962), pp. 41–5, 134; W. E. Debnam, *Weep No More My Lady: A Southerner Answers Mrs. Roosevelt's Report on the 'Poor and Unhappy South'* (Raleigh, NC: Graphic Press, 1955).

37. Pastor John A. Walker to Roy Wilkins, 24 April 1957, NAACP White Reprisals Papers, reel 10, frames 0251–2; Kilpatrick's letter to 'Brasfield', organizer of Vanderbilt University debate with Ralph McGill, 2 March 1964, 'Speeches 1964: Debate Ralph McGill Vanderbilt University on School Issue', Box 3, Kilpatrick Papers.

38. See, for example, J. Arthur Brown, President of Charleston, SC NAACP, to Henry Lee Moon, NAACP General Counsel, 7 February 1956, NAACP White Reprisals Papers, reel 10, frame 0644.

39. Jack Wright letter to NAACP Headquarters, 22 March 1957, NAACP White Reprisals Papers, reel 10, frames 0164–5.

40. 'Michigan City Is Completely Segregated ...' *Arkansas Faith*, vol. 1, no. 6 (April 1956), p. 5.

41. By August 1956, the Citizens' Council's own figures, which were notoriously unreli-

able, claimed that Council groups had been established in 30 states. 'Beyond Dixie's frontiers', though, 'the Council's greatest successes remained minor, its failures almost legion'. McMillen, *The Citizens' Council*, p. 152.

42. Press release, 'Columbus NAACP Posts Award for Information in Cross Burnings', 29 May 1957, Reel 12, 0736; Gloster B. Current letter to all NAACP northern branches, 7 February 1958, reel 13, frame 0816; Kenneth E. Banks's reply to Current, 11 February 1958, reel 13, frame 0817. All NAACP White Reprisals Papers.

43. Roy Wilkins to J. Edgar Hoover, 20 June 1956, NAACP White Reprisals Papers, reel 13, frame 0745. In April, Dearborn Mayor Orville Hubbard had been invited to a Citizens' Council meeting in Highland Park, and was told that chapters were being organized in Highland Park, Detroit, Lansing and Flint. For information on the formation of the Dearborn-based Citizens' Council, see NAACP White Reprisals Papers, reel 12, frames 0363 and 0370, and 'Race-Hate Group Invades State', *Detroit Free Press*, 29 June 1956, clipping in reel 13, frames 0370–2.

44. As Chafe has correctly noted in his case study of Greensboro, North Carolina, 'All through the latter part of the 1950's, the accelerating pace of black protest activities bespoke a groundswell of grass-roots involvement' in growing civil rights activism. William H. Chafe, *Civilities and Civil Rights: Greensboro, North Carolina, and the Black Struggle for Freedom* (New York: Oxford University Press, 1980), p. 79.

45. Merrill Proudfoot, *Diary of a Sit-In* (Chapel Hill: University of North Carolina Press, 1962), p. xi; David R. Goldfield, *Black, White, and Southern: Race Relations and Southern Culture 1940 to the Present* (Baton Rouge: Louisiana State University Press, 1990), p. 119; Chafe, *Civilities and Civil Rights*, pp. 98 and 99; Fairclough, *Race & Democracy*, p. 267. J. Mills Thornton believes that renewed interest in the sit-ins stemmed not from the Greensboro protest itself, but from the decision of Dr John O. Brown, head of the Miami branch of CORE, who sat-in with 45 others in a Miami 'variety store' in June 1959. J. Mills Thornton III, *Dividing Lines: Municipal Politics and the Struggle for Civil Rights in Montgomery, Birmingham and Selma* (Tuscaloosa: University of Alabama Press, 2002), p. 113.

46. Figures quotes in Goldfield, *Black, White, and Southern*, p. 120.

47. Goldfield, *Black, White, and Southern*, p. 121.

48. Proudfoot, *Diary of a Sit-In*, p. 85.

49. Proudfoot, *Diary of a Sit-In*, p. 45; Chafe, *Civilities and Civil Rights*, p. 85.

50. Franklin McCain and Kilpatrick quoted in Goldfield, *Black, White, and Southern*, pp. 119 and 120–1.

51. Fairclough, *Freedom & Democracy*, pp. 267–8.

52. The pamphlet, *Race and the Restaurant: Two Opinion Pieces* (Richmond: n.p., 1960), concentrated on the findings in two cases, *Williams v. Lewis* and *Williams v. Howard Johnson's*. It included a reprint of Judge Morris Ames Soper's opinion in *Williams v. Howard Johnson's*, a case in which the plaintiff had tried to sue the restaurant for damages arising from its refusal to serve him. The case was thrown out by the District Court, which decreed that the Fourteenth Amendment had no hold over what it described as discrimination on 'private' premises.

53. C. L. Harris, manager of Woolworth's, quoted in Chafe, *Civilities and Civil Rights*, p. 93

54. 'A short white man about sixty years of age' quoted in Proudfoot, *Diary of a Sit-in*, pp. 44–5.

55. As well as its more famous 'equal protection' provision, Section 1 of the Fourteenth Amendment also stated that no state shall 'deprive any person of life, liberty, or property, without due process of law'. In the context of the sit-ins, that phrase was

interpreted by segregationists to mean that a shopkeeper or store owner was at liberty to serve whomsoever he or she desired as long as transactions took place on private premises.

56. 'Declaration of Constitutional Principles'. Press release 'For release Monday a.m. March 12, 1956', in 'Byrd Speeches Drafts – Civil Rights, etc, For reference, 1956–1960', Box 1, Byrd Papers; press release, 'Citizens' Council Paper Now Admits Negroes of South Want Integration', 6 March 1958, NAACP White Reprisals Papers, reel 13, frame 0827.

57. McCain quoted in Howell Raines (ed.), *My Soul Is Rested: The Story of the Civil Rights Movement in the Deep South* (New York: Penguin, 1983), p. 81; see also Lewis, *The White South and the Red Menace*, pp. 141–2.

58. Proudfoot, *Diary of a Sit-In*, pp. 85–6; an untitled flyer issued in Memphis, Tennessee, for example, used the 'National Association for the Advancement of Communism' line. Untitled Flyer 'Compliments of the Greenview Community' [n.d.], unnamed folder, Box 16, Edmund Orgill Papers, Mississippi Valley Collection, University of Memphis.

59. Vandiver quoted in Jeff Roche, *Restructured Resistance: The Sibley Commission and the Politics of Desegregation in Georgia* (Athens and London: University of Georgia Press, 1998), p. 130.

60. Byrnes claimed that the sit-ins had been designed to aid the goals of international communism by coinciding with the Eisenhower–Khrushchev summit. Truman later retracted his remarks. Jeff Woods, *Black Struggle, Red Scare: Segregation and Anti-Communism in the South, 1948–1968* (Baton Rouge: Louisiana State University Press, 2004), pp. 131 and 135.

61. Roche, *Restructured Resistance*, p. 130; Fairclough, *Race & Democracy*, pp. 271–2.

62. Woods, *Black Struggle, Red Scare*, pp. 130–6; quotations from pp. 131 and 135.

63. Thornton, *Dividing Lines*, pp. 113–14; Clayborne Carson, *In Struggle: SNCC and the Black Awakening of the 1960s* (new edition) (Cambridge, MA: Harvard University Press, 1995), p. 11.

64. Thornton, *Dividing Lines*, p. 228.

65. For the moral dimensions of the sit-in protests, see Goldfield, *Black, White, and Southern*, esp. pp. 118–22; for the northern response, see Klarman, *From Jim Crow to Civil Rights*, p. 373.

66. Goldfield, *Black, White, and Southern*, p. 119; Fairclough, *Race & Democracy*, pp. 271 and 291.

67. As Thornton has shown, the Supreme Court overturned the convictions of those who had sat-in in cities and towns such as Birmingham, Alabama, Durham, North Carolina, Greenville, South Carolina and New Orleans, Louisiana, on the grounds that 'criminal trespassing ordinances were unenforceable in cities that also had restaurant segregation ordinances, because the trespassing arrests thus in effect became state action to require segregation'. Thornton, *Dividing Lines*, p. 228.

68. Franklin McCain quoted in Raines (ed.), *My Soul Is Rested*, p. 76; Farmer quoted in Goldfield, *Black, White, and Southern*, p. 124.

69. There were also arrests along the way: Joseph Perkins, a black Freedom Rider, was arrested in Charlotte, NC, on 8 May, and James Peck and Henry Thomas were both arrested in Winnsboro, SC, the next day. Thornton, *Dividing Lines*, p. 245.

70. For the definitive history of the Freedom Rides, see Raymond Arsenault, *Freedom Riders: 1961 and the Struggle for Racial Justice* [Pivotal Moments in American History] (New York: Oxford University Press, 2006). See also Glenn T. Eskew, *But for Birmingham: The Local and National Movements in the Civil Rights Struggle* (Chapel

Hill: University of North Carolina Press, 1997), pp. 155–65; Goldfield, *Black, White, and Southern*, pp. 124–30; for eyewitness accounts, see Catherine A. Barnes, *A Journey from Jim Crow: The Desegregation of Southern Transit* [Contemporary American History Series] (New York: Columbia University Press, 1983), pp. 157–75.

71. The numbers of Freedom Riders had been made up when three new recruits joined in Sumter, SC. Thornton, *Dividing Lines*, pp. 244–6; Barnes, *A Journey from Jim Crow*, pp. 157–75; Goldfield, *Black, White, and Southern*, p. 125.

72. Thornton, *Dividing Lines*, pp. 247–8; Goldfield, *Black, White, and Southern*, p. 126.

73. Thornton, *Dividing Lines*, esp. pp. 241–2.

74. The Freedom Rides, to use Arsenault's phrase, also provided 'the pivot of a pivotal era in civil rights history'. Arsenault, *Freedom Riders*, p. 7.

75. Dick Gregory, *From the Back of the Bus* (New York: E.P. Dutton & Co., 1962), p. 23.

76. Thornton, *Dividing Lines*, p. 17.

77. Thornton, *Dividing Lines*, pp. 200–3, 240–4.

78. Thornton refers to Kennedy's 'political obligation' to Patterson as a result of his early support. *Dividing Lines*, p. 121.

79. 'Because his political power rested upon the direct support of the most zealous segregationists, Sullivan could not afford to seem sympathetic to the Freedom Riders', argues Thornton. 'He knew well how easily a segregationist opponent could turn against him and any action such as extending police protection to demonstrators. He knew', Thornton concludes, 'because he had used just such an issue to defeat Clyde Sellars in 1959.' Thornton, *Dividing Lines*, p. 119; see also note 149.

80. Eskew, for example, argues that 'the paper's editorial policy shifted from tacitly condoning community-sanctioned vigilante violence in defense of segregation to actively opposing mob action while resisting race reform'. Eskew, *But for Birmingham*, p. 160; Robert Corley, 'In Search of Racial Harmony: Birmingham Business Leaders and Desegregation, 1950–1963', in Elizabeth Jacoway and David R. Colburn (eds), *Southern Businessmen and Desegregation* (Baton Rouge: Louisiana State University Press, 1982), pp. 170–90. See esp. pp. 181–90.

81. Howell Raines quoted in Raines, (ed.) *My Soul Is Rested*, p. 162.

82. Smyer 'black eye' quotation from Corley, 'In Search of Racial Harmony', in Jacoway and Colburn (eds), *Southern Businessmen and Desegregation*, p. 182; 'good business' quote from Raines (ed.), *My Soul Is Rested*, p. 165.

83. Eskew, *But for Birmingham*, pp. 163–4.

84. 'Statement – May 23, 1961 on the Situation in Alabama', Box 413, Byrd Papers.

85. Woods, *Black Struggle, Red Scare*, pp. 150–1; Lewis, *The White South and the Red Menace*, p. 81.

86. The United States Fidelity and Guaranty Company, based in Baltimore, cancelled its policy on the Williams Chapel Baptist Church in Ruleville. The director of the NAACP's Washington Bureau noted that 'At this point the information before us suggests a cancellation as a matter of economic pressure to prevent persons from registering and voting.' Clarence Mitchell to W. J. Jeffrey, 27 September 1962, NAACP White Reprisals Papers, reel 1, frame 0070; Matthew J. Perry to Morsell, 26 September 1960, NAACP White Reprisals Papers, reel 10, frame 0716; W. D. Burgess to Wilkins, 26 May 1960, NAACP White Reprisals Papers, reel 10, frame 0342; A. Leon Higginbotham's letter to Senator Joseph S. Clark, 8 September 1961, NAACP White Reprisals Papers, reel 9, frame 0114.

87. Wisdom and Mize quoted in James W. Silver, *Mississippi: The Closed Society* (New York: Harcourt, Brace & World, 1963), pp. 114 and 115. For historical analyses of the Ole Miss crisis, see Taylor Branch, *Parting the Waters: Martin Luther King and*

Notes

the *Civil Rights Movement 1954–63* (New York: Macmillan, 1988), pp. 647–72; Dittmer, *Local People: The Struggle for Civil Rights in Mississippi* (Urbana: University of Illinois Press, 1994), pp. 138–42; Yasuhiro Katagiri, *The Mississippi State Sovereignty Commission: Civil Rights and States' Rights* (Jackson: University of Mississippi Press, 2001), esp. 104–15; Wilhoit, *The Politics of Massive Resistance*, pp. 192–6; McMillen, *The Citizens' Council*, pp. 246–50, 342–6. For a colourful account of Barnett's role, see Robert Sherrill, *Gothic Politics in the Deep South* (New York: Grossman Publishers, 1968), esp. pp. 183–6. For an account based in part on eyewitness testimony, see Silver, *Mississippi: The Closed Society*. For popular historical accounts of the crisis, see William Doyle, *An American Insurrection: The Battle of Oxford, Mississippi, 1962* (New York: Doubleday, 2001) and Nadine Cohodas, *The Band Played Dixie: Race and the Liberal Conscious at Ole Miss* (New York: The Free Press, 1997). Although Meredith was widely touted as the first African American student at Ole Miss, it later emerged that, technically, Harry S. Murphy, Jr. had desegregated the university when he attended as a Navy student from 1945 to 1946. See Wilhoit, *The Politics of Massive Resistance*, p. 196 note 24.

88. Sherrill, *Gothic Politics*, pp. 185 and 86.
89. Kennedy and Meredith both quoted in Katagiri, *The Mississippi State Sovereignty Commission*, p. 104.
90. Dittmer, *Local People*, p. 139; McMillen, *The Citizens' Council*, p. 343; Katagiri, *The Mississippi State Sovereignty Commission*, p. 105.
91. Campbell and Eastland quoted in Silver, *Mississippi: The Closed Society*, p. 118.
92. McMillen, *The Citizens' Council*, pp. 246–8, 342–3, 344.
93. *The Liberty Bulletin* quoted in Silver, *Mississippi: The Closed Society*, p. 118. Emphasis my own.
94. McMillen, *The Citizens' Council*, p. 247.
95. Katagiri, *The Mississippi State Sovereignty Commission*, p. 110.
96. McMillen, *The Citizens' Council*, p. 247.
97. Dittmer, *Local People*, pp. 139–40; Sherrill, *Gothic Politics*, p. 185.
98. The full text of the song is quoted in Silver, *Mississippi: The Closed Society*, pp. 118–19.
99. Katagiri, *The Mississippi State Sovereignty Commission*, p. 106.
100. A clear and concise analysis of those conversations can be found in Katagiri, *The Mississippi State Sovereignty Commission*, pp. 106–13; Barnett speech quoted p. 113. See also Dittmer, *Local People*, pp. 140–2.
101. Silver, *Mississippi: The Closed Society*, p. 122; Dittmer, *Local People*, p. 140.
102. Silver's letter to his daughter Betty, 2 October 1962, Justice Department's letter to Silver, both reproduced in Silver, *Mississippi: The Closed Society*, pp. 162–7 and 124–5. Dittmer refers to 'heavily armed outsiders' who took over the campus, *Local People*, p. 141.
103. Doyle, *An American Insurrection*, p. 97. For the broad range of Walker's activities, see pp. 96–9.
104. Katagiri, *The Mississippi State Sovereignty Commission*, p. 127.
105. Carter quoted in Ann Waldron, *Hodding Carter: The Reconstruction of a Racist* (Chapel Hill: Algonquin Books of Chapel Hill, 1993), p. 298 and Sherrill, *Gothic Politics*, p. 186.
106. W. W. Chapman, editor of the *Indianola Enterprise-Tocsin* quoted in Moye, *Let the People Decide*, p. 104.
107. Katagiri, *The Mississippi State Sovereignty Commission*, pp. 120–1; Silver, *Mississippi: The Closed Society*, p. 133.

108. Dittmer, *Local People*, p. 142; Silver, 'Mississippi: The Closed Society', pp. 25 and 26.

109. Earl Lively, Jr., *The Invasion of Mississippi* (n.p.: American Opinion Reprint Series, n.d.), copy in '1962: University of Mississippi', Box 5, Byrd Papers. For the way in which Lively's rhetoric permeated through to the grassroots, see Lewis, *The White South and the Red Menace*, pp. 84–5.

110. 'Monthly Report, Mississippi Field Secretary', 5 October 1962, NAACP White Reprisals Files, reel 15, frames 0048–50. Dittmer has argued persuasively that the most immediate impact of Meredith's admittance to the University of Mississippi 'was to intensify white resistance to COFO activity in the Delta and throughout the state'. Dittmer, *Local People*, p. 138.

111. 'Allen's Army', clipping from *Newsweek*, 24 February 1964, in NAACP White Reprisals Papers, reel 5, frame 0853.

112. As McMillen points out, 'Councilors were appointed to numerous governmental posts, including key positions on the State Sovereignty Commission and a seat on the state Supreme Court', and the Citizens' Councils of America's headquarters were 'conveniently' situated across the road from the governor's mansion. McMillen, *The Citizens' Council*, pp. 334, 345–7.

113. See both Silver, *Mississippi: The Closed Society*, and 'Mississippi: The Closed Society'.

114. Wallace quoted in Stephan Lesher, *George Wallace: American Populist* (Reading, MA: Addison-Wesley, 1994), pp. 128–9. As Lesher notes, there are no reliable sources with which to cross-check the assertion that Wallace made his infamous statement, and it may be more likely that what he in fact said was that he would never be 'out-segged' again.

115. Wallace quoted in Klarman, *From Jim Crow to Civil Rights*, p. 406; Goldfield, *Black, White, and Southern*, p. 115; McMillen, *The Citizens' Council*, pp. 317–18.

116. McMillen, *The Citizens' Council*, p. 57.

117. E. Culpepper Clark, *The Schoolhouse Door: Segregation's Last Stand at the University of Alabama* (New York: Oxford University Press, 1993), pp. 216 and 204.

118. Bobby Kennedy, for example, tried to put a call through to Wallace on 8 June, although he was not successful. Clark, *The Schoolhouse Door*, p. 204; Jones quote p. 215.

119. Clark, *The Schoolhouse Door*, and Dan T. Carter, *The Politics of Rage: George Wallace, the Origins of the New Conservatism, and the Transformation of American Politics* (new edition) (Baton Rouge: Louisiana State University Press, 2000) are indispensable sources on Wallace and the University of Alabama denouement. See also Eskew, *But for Birmingham*, pp. 309–10; Goldfield, *Black, White, and Southern*, pp. 115–16; McMillen, *The Citizens' Council*, pp. 57–8, 317–18; and Wilhoit, *The Politics of Massive Resistance*, pp. 196–8.

120. Clark, *The Schoolhouse Door*, p. xix.

121. Eskew, *But for Birmingham*, p. 310.

122. McMillen, *The Citizens' Councils*, p. 57.

123. Harvey B. Gantt effectively desegregated Clemson on 28 January 1963, in a move that attracted much publicity but no violence. Wilhoit, *The Politics of Massive Resistance*, p. 198.

124. See especially Dittmer, *Local People*, p. 138.

125. Pritchett quoted in Goldfield, *Black, White, and Southern*, p. 131, and John Lewis with Michael D'Orso, *Walking with the Wind: A Memoir of the Movement* (San Diego: Harcourt Brace & Company, 1998), p. 185.

126. Pritchett quoted in Raines (ed.), *My Soul Is Rested*, pp. 361–2, and Lewis, *Walking with the Wind*, p. 185; Hansen's quote appears in a number of sources, including Lewis, *Walking with the Wind*, p. 185, and Carson, *In Struggle*, p. 61.

127. As one example of that violence, Marion King was clubbed so badly by a deputy sheriff in Camilla jail that she miscarried. See Lewis, *Walking with the Wind*, p. 191, and Carson, *In Struggle*, p. 61. *Time* magazine quoted in Eskew, *But for Birmingham*, p. 52.

128. The Birmingham and Selma campaigns have attracted widespread historical treatments, but for the Children's Crusade see in particular Eskew, *But for Birmingham*, chapter 8, and for the clash on Selma's Edmund Pettus Bridge, see David J. Garrow, *Protest at Selma: Martin Luther King, Jr. and the Voting Rights Act of 1965* (New Haven: Yale University Press, 1978), chapter 3.

129. Pritchett quoted in Raines (ed.), *My Soul Is Rested*, p. 366.

130. Eskew, *But for Birmingham*, pp. 118–19, 171.

131. Thornton, *Dividing Lines*, pp. 328–9.

132. Thornton, *Dividing Lines*, p. 401; Goldfield, *Black, White, and Southern*, p. 161. As Goldfield also notes, existing registration procedures were also lengthened to include a list of 68 questions about the state constitution and state government.

133. Thornton, *Dividing Lines*, pp. 478 and 473. See also his 'Municipal Change and the Course of the Movement', in Armistead L. Robinson and Patricia Sullivan (eds), *New Directions in Civil Rights Studies* [Carter G. Woodson Institute Series in Black Studies] (Charlottesville and London: University Press of Virginia, 1991).

134. Eskew, *But for Birmingham*, p. 226; *New York Times* quoted in Garrow, *Protest at Selma*, p. 43; Baker quoted in Raines (ed.), *My Soul Is Rested*, p. 200.

135. Williams quoted in Goldfield, *Black, White, and Southern*, p. 164.

136. Pritchett quoted in Raines (ed.), *My Soul Is Rested*, p. 366.

Chapter 5 The Confederate Chameleon

1. Glenn T. Eskew, *But for Birmingham: The Local and National Movements in the Civil Rights Struggle* (Chapel Hill: University of North Carolina Press, 1997), p. 299.

2. The changing shape of the Kennedys' response to the race issue is well chronicled in David L. Chappell, *Inside Agitators: White Southerners in the Civil Rights Movement* (Baltimore: Johns Hopkins University Press, 1994), pp. 189–211. As Chappell notes, the introduction of a civil rights bill ended the Administration's 'antilegislative' approach to the issue, and transferred the onus for change from the Justice Department to the White House itself.

3. For details of that Byrd organization convocation, see Ronald L. Heinemann, *Harry Byrd of Virginia* (Charlottesville and London: University Press of Virginia, 1996), p. 336.

4. The majority of the southern bloc had decided not to filibuster the proposed 1957 proposals after a deal with Johnson, then Senate majority leader: he would not push for a change in rules that would make it easier to end a filibuster if the southern delegation agreed not to filibuster the 1957 proposals. While the length of Thurmond's filibuster continues to stand as a record, there is some debate over its duration. The official Senate record marks him at 24 hours and 18 minutes, as does Thurmond's biographer Nadine Cohodas. In journalist Robert Sherrill's account, on the other hand, Thurmond lasted 24 hours and 19 minutes. In either case, he comfortably beat the existing record of 22 hours and 26 minutes set by Iowa's Wayne Morse. Nadine Cohodas, *Strom Thurmond and the Politics of Southern Change* (New York: Simon & Schuster, 1993), p. 249; Robert Sherrill, *Gothic Politics in the Deep South* (New York: Grossman Publishers, 1968), p. 238.

5. Byrd's handling of the budget and proposed tax cuts, and the resultant suggestion of political 'blackmail' by both Kennedy and Byrd, are discussed in Heinemann, *Harry Byrd of Virginia*, pp. 393–7. For LBJ's 'treatment', see p. 400.

6. Jeff Woods, *Black Struggle, Red Scare: Segregation and Anti-communism in the South, 1948–1968* (Baton Rouge: Louisiana State University Press, 2004), esp. pp. 172–4, but also chapter 6. James T. Patterson has long argued that anticommunism formed a central part of the conservative coalition that blossomed during the New Deal, to which Russell was here, presumably, trying to appeal. See, for example, Patterson, 'A Conservative Coalition Forms in Congress, 1933–1939', *Journal of American History*, vol. 52, no. 4 (March 1966), pp. 757–72.

7. Gilbert C. Fite, *Richard B. Russell, Jr.: Senator from Georgia* [Fred W. Morrison Series in Southern Studies] (Chapel Hill: University of North Carolina Press, 1991), pp. 408–15.

8. Russell was left to comment to his fellow Georgian, the lawyer and leading states' rights' proponent Charles R. Bloch, that 'we are in for a hard time'. Johnson and Russell both quoted in Mark Stern, *Calculating Visions: Kennedy, Johnson and Civil Rights* (New Brunswick: Rutgers University Press, 1992), p. 162.

9. As Stern has noted, Ervin put forward the argument that 'the proposed legislation was unconstitutional because it did not deal with an abridgement of the right to vote under the Fifteenth Amendment to the Constitution, but rather with a "Federal standard or substitute for all the State literacy tests"'. Stern, *Calculating Visions*, p. 74.

10. John Sewart quoted in Charles Whalen and Barbara Whalen, *The Longest Debate: A Legislative History of the 1964 Civil Rights Act* (Cabin John, MD: Seven Locks Press, 1985), p. 204. See also pp. 203–7.

11. Whalen and Whalen, *The Longest Debate*, pp. 115–18 and *passim*. Dirksen had previously announced publicly on 17 June 1963 that he was committed to Kennedy's civil rights package, but, crucially, was still opposed to the public accommodations section at that time. Stern, *Calculating Visions*, p. 90.

12. Chappell, *Inside Agitators*, p. 210.

13. Russell and Ellender quoted in Stern, *Calculating Visions*, pp. 184–5.

14. Allen quoted in Kevin M. Kruse, *White Flight: Atlanta and the Making of Modern Conservatism* (Princeton: Princeton University Press, 2005), p. 205; Weltner quoted in Stern, *Calculating Visions*, p. 184.

15. McMillen referred to 'the Council's flailing grip on the white community in Mississippi' in the wake of the 1964 Act. Neil R. McMillen, *The Citizens' Council: Organized Resistance to the Second Reconstruction* (Urbana: University of Illinois Press, 1994), pp. 262–5. In more general terms, McMillen concluded that, 'Having reached a zenith by 1957, resistance groups throughout the South began a steady decline, and by the end of the decade grassroots support for organized racism had either vanished or was greatly diminished in every southern state. Despite a vigorous remobilization effort by some of segregation's most accomplished spokesmen, the organization never regained the broad popular base it enjoyed within the region during the early post-*Brown* period.' McMillen, *The Citizens' Council*, p. 152.

16. Yasuhiro Katagiri, *The Mississippi State Sovereignty Commission: Civil Rights and States' Rights* (Jackson: University Press of Mississippi, 2001), p. 168.

17. Francis M. Wilhoit, *The Politics of Massive Resistance* (New York: George Braziller, 1973), p. 213.

18. Ralph Eisenberg, 'Virginia: The Emergence of Two-Party Politics', in William C. Havard (ed.), *The Changing Politics of the South* (Baton Rouge: Louisiana State

University Press, 1972), p. 53; Wilkinson, *Harry Byrd and the Changing Face of Virginia Politics*, pp. 145–6. More recently, Paul M. Gaston has referred to the 'sudden collapse' of Virginia's massive resistance programme in early 1959, although he does go on to state that the collapse was 'hardly a fair measure of its pernicious influence'. Paul M. Gaston, 'Foreword' in Matthew D. Lassiter and Andrew B. Lewis (eds), *The Moderates' Dilemma: Massive Resistance to School Desegregation in Virginia* (Charlottesville: University of Virginia Press, 1997), p. xi. In a 2001 study of the legacy of *Brown*, James T. Patterson took 'Massive Resistance' to refer to no more than Virginia's school closing plan. Patterson, *Brown v. Board of Education: A Civil Rights Milestone and Its Troubled Legacy* (Oxford and New York: Oxford University Press, 2001), p. 99.

19. Wilhoit, *The Politics of Massive Resistance*, p. 214.

20. Bartley further concludes that the election of Kennedy and the mass support that civil rights initiatives received from southern blacks 'further doomed neobourbon dreams of defeating the principle of the *Brown* decision'. Numan V. Bartley, *The Rise of Massive Resistance: Race and Politics in the South during the 1950's* (Baton Rouge: Louisiana State University Press, 1969), pp. 341 and 339.

21. J. Mills Thornton III, *Dividing Lines: Municipal Politics and the Struggle for Civil Rights in Montgomery, Birmingham and Selma* (Tuscaloosa: University of Alabama Press, 2002), pp. 333–47, esp. p. 338.

22. Eskew, *But for Birmingham*, pp. 318–19; Thornton, *Dividing Lines*, pp. 344–5; quote from p. 339.

23. Eskew, *But for Birmingham*, pp. 318 and 321.

24. Chambliss quoted in Frank Sikora, *Until Justice Rolls Down: The Birmingham Church Bombing Case* (Tuscaloosa: University of Alabama Press, 1991), p. 140. See also Stephan Lesher, *George Wallace: American Populist* (Reading, MA: Addison-Wesley, 1994), pp. 253–7. In 1977, Chambliss was convicted of leading the Ku Klux Klan group that carried out the bombing. Although he died in prison without providing evidence on any of his associates, Bobby Frank Cherry and Thomas E. Blanton, Jr. were eventually indicted in 2000, and were subsequently convicted. See Thornton, *Dividing Lines*, p. 661 note 177; for Chambliss's past history of racist violence, see, for example, pp. 161–6.

25. Morgan quoted in John Lewis, *Walking with the Wind: A Memoir of the Movement* (San Diego: Harcourt Brace, 1998), p. 234; Wallace quoted in Lesher, *George Wallace*, p. 255.

26. Thornton, *Dividing Lines*, p. 370.

27. Peter A. Carmichael, *The South and Segregation* (Washington, DC: Public Affairs Press, 1965), pp. 322–3 and 329.

28. Burke Marshall, *Federalism and Civil Rights* (New York and London: Columbia University Press, 1964), p. 24.

29. Steven F. Lawson, *In Pursuit of Power: Southern Blacks and Electoral Politics, 1965–1982* [Contemporary American History Series] (New York: Columbia University Press, 1985), p. 14, LBJ quoted p. 4; Marshall, *Federalism and Civil Rights*, p. 12.

30. Figures from Table 'Estimated Percentage of Adult Black and White Voter Registrants in Seven Southern States: 1964–1982', in Lawson, *In Pursuit of Power*, p. 297, and see also p. 311 note 80; 'Table D: Voter Registration in the Southern States' in Wilhoit, *The Politics of Massive Resistance*, p. 291.

31. In a situation where the vote was split between a number of white candidates and one non-white candidate on a first ballot, for example, many implementations of the 'at large' system would see the non-white candidate facing off against the best-

performing white candidate in a run-off election. Once the run-off was narrowed down to one non-white against one white candidate, the situation allowed the previously split white vote to coalesce behind a single candidate.

32. A proposal by Representative Kenneth Williams to gerrymander the Delta area with its high proportion of black enclaves into five districts all with a white majority, for example, was justified on the exclusively non-racial grounds of equalizing the population, providing more compact districts, preserving socio-economic and historical associations, and protecting incumbents. Representatives voted for an alternative plan, though, in which the Delta was split into three districts, leaving one with a slight black majority, by 25 votes to 21. Williams' plan was quite simply too obvious a racial gerrymander, and would have fallen foul of Section 5 of the Voting Rights Act. Frank R. Parker, *Black Votes Count: Political Empowerment in Mississippi after 1965* (Chapel Hill: University of North Carolina Press, 1990), p. 51.

33. Pittman quoted in Peyton McCrary, Jerome A. Gray, Edward Still and Huey L. Perry, 'Alabama', in Chandler Davidson and Bernard Grofman (eds), *Quiet Revolution in the South: The Impact of the Voting Rights Act, 1965–1990* (Princeton, NJ: Princeton University Press, 1994), p. 51.

34. The case is discussed in Lawson, *In Pursuit of Power*, pp. 276–81; Stewart quoted on p. 277.

35. David L. Chappell, *A Stone of Hope: Prophetic Religion and the Death of Jim Crow* (Chapel Hill: University of North Carolina Press, 1994), p. 141.

36. Dan T. Carter, *The Politics of Rage: George Wallace, the Origins of the New Conservatism, and the Transformation of American Politics* (Baton Rouge: Louisiana State University Press, 2000), p. 11; Wallace quoted in Lawson, *In Pursuit of Power*, p. 6.

37. Lesher, *George Wallace*, p. 270.

38. Sherrill, *Gothic Politics*, p. 258.

39. Carter, *Politics of Rage*, p. 12; Dolores Herbstreith quoted in Lesher, *George Wallace*, p. 275.

40. Carter, *Politics of Rage*, p. 12; Lesher, *George Wallace*, p. 280.

41. Wallace was still making overtly racist remarks in his speeches to northern audiences as late as November 1963. See, for example, reports of his speech before students at Harvard in Lesher, *George Wallace*, pp. 262–3.

42. The Mississippi Committee and Virginia Commission have received little historical analysis. For the founding ideas and principles of the Coordinating Committee for Fundamental American Freedoms, see Katagiri, *The Mississippi State Sovereignty Commission*, pp. 122–4, 150–2; for the Virginia Commission on Constitutional Government, see Lewis, *The White South and the Red Menace*, pp. 149–51 and 154, and 'Virginia's Northern Strategy: Southern Segregationists and the Route to National Conservatism', *Journal of Southern History*, vol. LXXII, no. 1 (February 2006), pp. 111–46.

43. 12 August 1959, Mays Diaries.

44. Kilpatrick undated letter to Verbon E. Kemp, Virginia State Chamber of Commerce, 'Correspondence K 1961', Box 34, Kilpatrick Papers.

45. As Katagiri's meticulous research has noted, those attending the conferences included 'William B. Barton, general counsel, Chamber of Commerce of the United States; Harvey M. Crow, associate general counsel, National Association of Manufacturers; Harding D. Williams, assistant director, Department of Governmental Relations, National Association of Real Estate Boards; Henry M. Shine Jr., legislative director, National Association of Home Builders; and Page L. Ingraham, director of research,

Notes

Council of State Government'. Katagiri, *The Mississippi State Sovereignty Commission*, p. 122. See also pp. 123–4.

46. Lesher noted that Wallace used the same percentage argument to attack the civil rights bill while campaigning in Berkeley, California, and that in doing so he was quoting Los Angeles attorney and former president of the American Bar Association, Lloyd Wright. Lesher, *George Wallace*, p. 272; *Civil Rights and Federal Powers* (Richmond, Virginia: Virginia Commission on Constitutional Government, n.d.), p. 4.

47. Satterfield quoted in Katagiri, *The Mississippi State Sovereignty Commission*, p. 123 (italics in original) and p. 151.

48. *'State Action' and the Fourteenth Amendment* (Richmond, Virginia: Virginia Commission on Constitutional Government, n.d.); *Voting Rights and Legal Wrongs* (Richmond, Virginia: Virginia Commission on Constitutional Government, n.d.); *One Man One Vote* (Richmond, Virginia: Virginia Commission on Constitutional Government, 1965). 1,647 of the 2,473 requests for, or comments on, *'Civil Rights' and Legal Wrongs* came from outside the South. See '"Civil Rights" and Legal Wrongs' in 'Report to General Assembly 12/1/61 12/1/63', Box 1, Virginia Commission on Constitutional Government Papers.

49. 'Amending the Constitution to Strengthen the States in the Federal System', *State Government*, vol. XXXVI, no. 1 (Winter 1963), pp. 10–15.

50. All CCG publications are listed in *Final Report: Virginia Commission on Constitutional Government*, 25 January 1969; see also *Report of the Virginia Commission on Constitutional Government: A Summary of Activities from August, 1958 through December, 1961* both in Box 1, Virginia Commission on Constitutional Government Papers.

51. *Every Man His Own Law* (Richmond, VA, 1967). Its first print run was for 60,000 copies.

52. See, for example, Lesher, *George Wallace*; Carter, *Politics of Rage*, and Carter, *From George Wallace to Newt Gingrich: Race in the Conservative Counterrevolution, 1963–1994* (Baton Rouge: Louisiana University Press, 1996); Thomas Byrne and Mary D. Edsall, *Chain Reaction: The Impact of Race, Rights, and Taxes on American Politics* (New York: Norton, 1992).

53. For examples of what might be termed the 'Sun Belt strategy' rather than 'southern strategy' view, see Kruse, *White Flight*, Matthew D. Lassiter, 'The Suburban Origins of "Color-Blind" Conservatism: Middle-Class Consciousness in the Charlotte Busing Crisis', *Journal of Urban History*, vol. 30, no. 4 (May 2004), pp. 549–82; Lassiter, *The Silent Majority: Suburban Politics in the Sunbelt South* [Politics and Society in Twentieth Century America] (Princeton and Oxford: Princeton University Press, 2005); and Joseph Crespino, *In Search of Another Country: Mississippi and the Conservative Counterrevolution*, (Princeton University Press, forthcoming).

54. Kruse, *White Flight*, pp. 69 and 77.

55. William Melkild quoted in Kruse, *White Flight*, p. 161.

56. In a movement that started as early as the late 1940s, but continued into the early 1960s and beyond, Kruse has identified a strand of segregationist resistance that replaced the increasingly tired, traditional ideology of the white South with what was, effectively, 'a new, middle-class rhetoric of rights and responsibilities'. Kruse, *White Flight*, p. 245. Equally, Crespino has argued that 'Sunbelt southerners rearticulated the racially-explicit appeals of massive resistance politics into a "colorblind" conservative language of rights and responsibilities that protected race and class privilege in the suburbs and contributed to the rights-based language of modern conservatism.' See 'Introduction' in Crespino, *In Search of Another Country*.

57. Atlanta figures quoted in Kruse, *White Flight*, p. 165; Mississippi figures quoted in Crespino, *In Search of Another Country*, Chapter 8.
58. Lassiter, 'The Suburban Origins of "Color-Blind" Conservatism', p. 578.
59. McMillan quoted in Lassiter, 'The Suburban Origins of "Color-Blind" Conservatism', p. 555.
60. Wilhoit, *The Politics of Massive Resistance*, p. 156. For an in-depth analysis of *Swann*, its impact and its attempted implementation, see Davison M. Douglas, *Reading, Writing & Race: The Desegregation of the Charlotte Schools* (Chapel Hill and London: University of North Carolina Press, 1995), esp. pp. 107–29.
61. In Richmond, for example, Rubin argues that the liberal school board's decision to delay implementation until the majority had been won over did nothing other than 'sanction more unconscionable delays in redressing the legitimate grievances of black parents and their children'. Lillian B. Rubin, *Busing and Backlash: White against White in a California School District* (Berkeley, LA: University of California Press, 1972), p. 207. See also pp. 195–208.
62. Protestor quoted in Douglas, *Reading, Writing & Race*, p. 162.
63. For a nuanced analysis of the Stennis Amendment, see Joseph Crespino, 'The Best Defense is a Good Offense: The Stennis Amendment and the Fracturing of Liberal School Desegregation Policy, 1964–1972', *Journal of Policy History* (forthcoming).
64. Carter, *The Politics of Rage*, pp. 447–8 and 426.
65. Carter, *The Politics of Rage*, p. 426; Carter, *From George Wallace to Newt Gingrich*, p. 45.
66. In October 1969, for example, *Newsweek* ran an article titled, 'The Troubled American: A Special Report on the White Majority', which showed overwhelming resistance among white Americans to both busing and integration, but, whereas 90 per cent of respondents were hostile to the integration of their neighbourhoods, 98 per cent were hostile to busing. Figures quoted in Carter, *The Politics of Rage*, p. 375. McKeithen quoted in Wilhoit, *The Politics of Massive Resistance*, p. 155.
67. Kilpatrick to Mrs Gibbs, 9 August 1962, '1950–1962 Personal Correspondence G (1 of 2)', Box 3, Kilpatrick Papers.
68. Marshall, *Federalism and Civil Rights*, pp. 34–5.

SELECT BIBLIOGRAPHY

Anderson, Karen S. (2005) 'Massive Resistance, Violence, and Southern Social Relations: The Little Rock, Arkansas, School Integration Crisis, 1954–1960', in Clive Webb (ed.), *Massive Resistance: Southern Opposition to the Second Reconstruction*, Oxford and New York: Oxford University Press, pp. 203–20.

Arsenault, Raymond (2006) *Freedom Riders: 1961 and the Struggle for Racial Justice* [Pivotal Moments in American History Series], New York: Oxford University Press.

Badger, Tony (1999) 'Southerners Who Refused to Sign the Southern Manifesto', *The Historical Journal*, vol. 42, no. 2, pp. 517–34.

Badger, Tony (2005) '*Brown* and Backlash', in Clive Webb (ed.), *Massive Resistance: Southern Opposition to the Second Reconstruction*, Oxford and New York: Oxford University Press, pp. 39–55.

Baldwin, James (1991) 'East River, Downtown: Postscript to a Letter from Harlem', in *Nobody Knows My Name: More Notes of a Native Son*, London: Penguin, pp. 68–75.

Barnes, Catherine A. (1983) *A Journey from Jim Crow: The Desegregation of Southern Transit* [Contemporary American History Series], New York: Columbia University Press.

Bartley, Numan V. (1969) *The Rise of Massive Resistance: Race and Politics in the South during the 1950's*, Baton Rouge: Louisiana State University Press.

Bass, Jack and De Vries, Walter (1976) *The Transformation of Southern Politics: Social Change and Political Consequence Since 1945*, New York: Meridian.

Bolton, Charles C. (2000) 'Mississippi's School Equalization Program, 1945–1954: "A Last Gasp to Try to Maintain a Segregated Educational System"', *Journal of Southern History*, vol. 66, pp. 781–812.

Borstelmann, Thomas (2001) *The Cold War and the Color Line: American Race Relations in the Global Arena*, Cambridge, MA: Harvard University Press.

Brady, Tom P. (1955) *Black Monday*, Winona: Association of Citizens' Councils of Mississippi.

Branch, Taylor (1988) *Parting the Waters: Martin Luther King and the Civil Rights Movement 1954–63*, New York: Macmillan.

Brown, Sarah Hart (1996) 'Congressional Anti-Communism and the Segregationist South: From New Orleans to Atlanta, 1954–1958', *Georgia Historical Quarterly*, vol. 80, no. 4, pp. 785–816.

Butler, J. Michael (2002) 'The Mississippi State Sovereignty Commission and Beach Integration, 1959–1963: a Cotton-patch Gestapo?', *Journal of Southern History*, vol. 68, no. 1 (February), pp. 107–48.

Byrne, Thomas and Edsall, Mary D. (1992) *Chain Reaction: The Impact of Race, Rights, and Taxes on American Politics*, New York: Norton.

Carmichael, Peter A. (1965) *The South and Segregation*, Washington, DC: Public Affairs Press.

Carson, Clyaborne (1995) *In Struggle: SNCC and the Black Awakening of the 1960s* (new edn), Cambridge, MA: Harvard University Press.

Carter, Dan T. (1996) *From George Wallace to Newt Gingrich: Race in the Conservative Counterrevolution, 1963–1994*, Baton Rouge: Louisiana University Press.

Carter, Dan T. (2000) *The Politics of Rage: George Wallace, the Origins of the New Conservatism, and the Transformation of American Politics* (new edn), Baton Rouge: Louisiana State University Press.

Carter III, Hodding (1959) *The South Strikes Back*, Garden City, NY: Doubleday.

Cecelski, David (1994) *Along Freedom Road: Hyde County, North Carolina, and the Fate of Black Schools in the South*, Chapel Hill: University of North Carolina Press.

Chafe, William H. (1980) *Civilities and Civil Rights: Greensboro, North Carolina, and the Black Struggle for Freedom*, New York: Oxford University Press.

Chappell, David L. (1994) *Inside Agitators: White Southerners in the Civil Rights Movement*, Baltimore: Johns Hopkins University Press.

Chappell, David L. (1998) 'The Divided Mind of Southern Segregationists', *Georgia Historical Quarterly*, vol. 82, no. 1, pp. 45–72.

Chappell, David L. (1998) 'Religious Ideas of the Segregationists', *Journal of American Studies*, vol. 32, no. 2, pp. 237–62.

Chappell, David L. (2004) *A Stone of Hope: Prophetic Religion and the Death of Jim Crow*, Chapel Hill: University of North Carolina Press.

Chappell, David L. (2005) 'Disunity and Religious Institutions in the White South', in Clive Webb (ed.), *Massive Resistance: Southern Opposition to the Second Reconstruction*, Oxford and New York: Oxford University Press, pp. 136–50.

Clark, E. Culpepper (1993) *The Schoolhouse Door: Segregation's Last Stand at the University of Alabama*, New York: Oxford University Press.

Cobb, James C. (1992) *The Most Southern Place on Earth: The Mississippi Delta and the Roots of Regional Identity*, New York: Oxford University Press.

Cohodas, Nadine (1993) *Strom Thurmond and the Politics of Southern Change*, New York: Simon & Schuster.

Cohodas, Nadine (1997) *The Band Played Dixie: Race and the Liberal Conscious at Ole Miss*, New York: The Free Press.

Cook, James Graham (1962) *The Segregationists*, New York: Appleton-Century-Crofts.

Corley, Robert (1982) 'In Search of Racial Harmony: Birmingham Business Leaders and Desegregation, 1950–1963', in Elizabeth Jacoway and David R. Colburn (eds), *Southern Businessmen and Desegregation*, Baton Rouge: Louisiana State University Press, pp. 170–90.

Crowther, Edward R. (1990) 'Alabama's Fight to Maintain Segregated Schools, 1953–56', *Alabama Review*, vol. XLIII, no. 3 (July), pp. 206–25.

Dailey, Jane (2004) 'Sex, Segregation, and the Sacred after *Brown*', *Journal of American History*, vol. 91, no. 1, pp. 119–44.

Dailey, Jane (2005) 'The Theology of Massive Resistance: Sex, Segregation, and the Sacred after *Brown*', in Clive Webb (ed.), *Massive Resistance: Southern Opposition to the Second Reconstruction*, Oxford and New York: Oxford University Press, pp. 151–80.

Davidson, Chandler and Grofman, Bernard (eds) (1994) *Quiet Revolution in the South: The Impact of the Voting Rights Act, 1965–1990*, Princeton, NJ: Princeton University Press.

Debnam, W. E. (1955) *Weep No More My Lady: A Southerner Answers Mrs. Roosevelt's Report on the 'Poor and Unhappy South'*, Raleigh, NC: Graphic Press.

Dittmer, John (1994) *Local People: The Struggle for Civil Rights in Mississippi*, Urbana: University of Illinois Press.

Douglas, Davison M. (1995) *Reading, Writing & Race: The Desegregation of the Charlotte Schools*, Chapel Hill and London: University of North Carolina Press.

Doyle, William (2001) *An American Insurrection: The Battle of Oxford, Mississippi, 1962*, New York: Doubleday.

Dudziak, Mary L. (1988) 'Desegregation as a Cold War Imperative', *Stanford Law Review*, vol. 41, no. 1 (November), pp. 61–120.

Dudziak, Mary L. (2000) *Cold War Civil Rights: Race and the Image of American Democracy*, Princeton and Oxford: Oxford University Press.

Dunbar, Anthony P. (1981) *Against the Grain: Southern Radicals and Prophets, 1929–1959*, Charlottesville: University Press of Virginia.

Dunford, Earl (1995) *Richmond Times-Dispatch: The Story of a Newspaper*, Richmond: Cadmus Publishing.

Eagles, Charles W. (2000) 'Toward New Histories of the Civil Rights Era', *Journal of Southern History*, vol. 66, no. 4 (November), pp. 815–48.

Eisenberg, Ralph (1972) 'Virginia: The Emergence of Two-Party Politics', in William C. Havard (ed.), *The Changing Politics of the South*, Baton Rouge: Louisiana State University Press.

Ely, James W., Jr. (1976) *The Crisis of Conservative Virginia: The Byrd Organization and the Politics of Massive Resistance*, Knoxville: University of Tennessee Press.

Eskew, Glenn T. (1997) *But for Birmingham: The Local and National Movements in the Civil Rights Struggle*, Chapel Hill: University of North Carolina Press.

Fairclough, Adam (1995) *Race & Democracy: The Civil Rights Struggle in Louisiana, 1915–1972*, Athens and London: University of Georgia Press.

Fairclough, Adam (2005) 'A Political *Coup d'Etat*?: How the Enemies of Earl Long Overwhelmed Racial Moderation in Louisiana', in Clive Webb (ed.), *Massive Resistance: Southern Opposition to the Second Reconstruction*, Oxford and New York: Oxford University Press, pp. 56–75.

Fite, Gilbert C. (1991) *Richard B. Russell, Jr.: Senator from Georgia* [Fred W. Morrison Series in Southern Studies], Chapel Hill: University of North Carolina Press.

Frederickson, Kari (2001) *The Dixiecrat Revolt and the End of the Solid South, 1932–1968*, Chapel Hill: University of North Carolina Press.

Freyer, Tony A. (1997) 'The Little Rock Crisis Reconsidered', *Arkansas Historical Quarterly*, vol. 56 (Autumn), pp. 360–70.

Friedman, Leon (ed.) (1969) *Argument: The Complete Oral Argument before the Supreme Court in Brown v. Board of Education of Topeka, 1952–1955*, New York: Chelsea House Publishers.

Garrow, David J. (1978) *Protest at Selma: Martin Luther King, Jr. and the Voting Rights Act of 1965*, New Haven: Yale University Press.

Gates, Robbins L. (1962) *The Making of Massive Resistance: Virginia's Politics of Public School Desegregation, 1954–1956*, Chapel Hill: University of North Carolina Press.

George, Wesley Critz (1962) *The Biology of the Race Problem*, n.p.

Gilmore, Glenda Elizabeth (1996) *Gender & Jim Crow: Women and the Politics of White Supremacy in North Carolina, 1896–1920*, Chapel Hill: University of North Carolina Press.

Goldfield, David R. (1990) *Black, White, and Southern: Race Relations and Southern Culture 1940 to the Present*, Baton Rouge: Louisiana State University Press.

Grantham, Dewey W. (1988) *The Life and Death of the Solid South: A Political History* [New Perspectives on the South], Lexington: University Press of Kentucky.

Gregory, Dick (1962) *From the Back of the Bus*, New York: E.P. Dutton & Co.

Halberstam, David (1956) 'The White Citizens' Councils: Respectable Means for Unrespectable Ends', *Commentary*, vol. 22, no. 4 (October).

Hale, Grace Elizabeth (1998) *Making Whiteness: The Culture of Segregation in the South, 1890–1940*, New York: Vintage Books.

Havard, William C. (ed.) (1972) *The Changing Politics of the South*, Baton Rouge: Louisiana State University Press.

Heale, M. J. (1998) *McCarthy's Americans: Red Scare Politics in State and Nation, 1935–1965* [American History in Depth Series, ed. A. J. Badger and Howell Harris], London: Macmillan.

Heinemann, Ronald L. (1996) *Harry Byrd of Virginia*, Charlottesville and London: University Press of Virginia.

Hershman, James H., Jr. (1998) 'Massive Resistance Meets Its Match: The Emergence of a Pro-Public School Majority', in Matthew D. Lassiter and Andrew B. Lewis (eds), *The Moderates' Dilemma: Massive Resistance to School Desegregation in Virginia*, Charlottesville and London: University Press of Virginia, pp. 105–33.

Hirsch, Arnold R. (1995) 'Massive Resistance in the Urban North: Trumbull Park, Chicago, 1953–1966', *Journal of American History*, vol. 82, no. 2 (September), pp. 522–50.

Houghton, Jonathan T. Y. (1993) 'The North Carolina Republican Party: From Reconstruction to the Radical Right', Dissertation, Chapel Hill.

Huie, William Bradford (1956) 'The Shocking Story of Approved Killing in Mississippi', *Look*, 24 January.

Inger, Morton (1969) *Politics and Reality in an American City: The New Orleans School Crisis of 1960*, New York: Center for Urban Education.

Inger, Morton (1982) 'The New Orleans School Crisis of 1960', in Elizabeth Jacoway and David R. Colburn (eds), *Southern Businessmen and School Desegregation*, Baton Rouge: Louisiana State University Press, pp. 82–97.

Jackson, John P., Jr. (2001) 'In Ways Unacademical: The Reception of Carleton S. Coon's *The Origin of Races*', *Journal of the History of Biology*, vol. 34, pp. 247–85.

Jackson, John P., Jr. (2005) *Science for Segregation: Race, Law, and the Case against Brown v. Board of Education* [Critical America Series], New York: New York University Press.

Jacoway, Elizabeth (1982) 'An Introduction: Civil Rights and the Changing South', in Elizabeth Jacoway and David R. Colburn (eds) *Southern Businessmen and School Desegregation*, Baton Rouge: Louisiana State University Press, pp. 1–14.

Jacoway, Elizabeth (2002) 'Jim Johnson of Arkansas: Segregationist Prototype', in Ted Ownby (ed.), *The Role of Ideas in the Civil Rights South*, Jackson: University Press of Mississippi, pp. 137–56.

Jacoway, Elizabeth and Colburn, David R. (eds) (1982) *Southern Businessmen and Desegregation*, Baton Rouge: Louisiana State University Press.

Jeansonne, Glen (1977) *Leander Perez: Boss of the Delta*, Baton Rouge: Louisiana State University Press.

Kamp, Joseph P. (1956) *Behind the Plot to Sovietize the South*, New York: Headlines.

Katagiri, Yasuhiro (2001) *The Mississippi State Sovereignty Commission: Civil Rights and States' Rights*, Jackson: University Press of Mississippi.

Key, V. O., Jr. (1984) *Southern Politics in State and Nation* (new edn), Knoxville: University of Tennessee Press.

Kilpatrick, James Jackson (1962) *The Southern Case for School Segregation*, Richmond: Crowell-Collier.

Kirk, John A. (2002) *Redefining the Color Line: Black Activism in Little Rock, Arkansas, 1940–1970*, Gainesville: University Press of Florida.

Kirk, John A. (2005) 'Massive Resistance and Minimum Compliance: The Origins of the 1957 Little Rock School Crisis and the Failure of School Desegregation in the South', in C. Webb (ed.) *Massive Resistance: Southern Opposition to the Second Reconstruction*, Oxford and New York: Oxford University Press, pp. 76–98.

Klarman, Michael J. (1994) 'How *Brown* Changed Race Relations: The Backlash Thesis', *Journal of American History*, vol. 81 (June), pp. 81–118.

Klarman, Michael J. (2004) *From Jim Crow to Civil Rights: The Supreme Court and the Struggle for Racial Equality*, Oxford and New York: Oxford University Press.

Klarman, Michael J. (2005) 'Why Massive Resistance?' in Clive Webb (ed.), *Massive Resistance: Southern Opposition to the Second Reconstruction*, Oxford and New York: Oxford University Press, pp. 21–38.

Klibaner, Irwin (1983) 'The Travail of Southern Radicals: The Southern Conference Educational Fund, 1946–1976', *Journal of Southern History*, vol. XLIX, no. 2 (May), pp. 179–202.

Kluger, Richard (1977) *Simple Justice: The History of Brown v. Board of Education and Black America's Struggle for Equality*, New York: Vintage.

Kruse, Kevin M. (2005) *White Flight: Atlanta and the Making of Modern Conservatism*, Princeton and Oxford: Princeton University Press.

Lassiter, Matthew D. (2004) 'The Suburban Origins of "Color-Blind" Conservatism: Middle-Class Consciousness in the Charlotte Busing Crisis', *Journal of Urban History*, vol. 30, no. 4 (May), pp. 549–82.

Lassiter, Matthew D. (2005) *The Silent Majority: Suburban Politics in the Sunbelt South* [Politics and Society in Twentieth Century America], Princeton and Oxford: Princeton University Press.

Lassiter, Matthew D. and Lewis, Andrew B. (eds) (1998) *The Moderates' Dilemma: Massive Resistance to School Desegregation in Virginia*, Charlottesville: University of Virginia Press.

Lassiter, Matthew D. and Lewis, Andrew B. (1998) 'Massive Resistance Revisited: Virginia's White Moderates and the Byrd Organization', in Lassiter and Lewis (eds), *The Moderates' Dilemma*, pp. 1–21.

Latimer, James (1996) 'The Rise and Fall of Massive Resistance', *Richmond Times-Dispatch*, 22 September, pp. A1, A9–A12.

Lawson, Steven F. (1985) *In Pursuit of Power: Southern Blacks and Electoral Politics, 1965–1982* [Contemporary American History Series], New York: Columbia University Press.

Layton, Azza Salama (2000) *International Relations and Civil Rights Policies in the United States*, Cambridge and New York: Cambridge University Press.

Lechner, Ira M. (1998) 'Massive Resistance: Virginia's Great Leap Backward', *Virginia Quarterly Review*, vol. 74, no. 4, pp. 631–40.

Leidholt, Alexander S. (1997) *Standing before the Shouting Mob: Lenoir Chambers and Virginia's Massive Resistance to Public-School Integration*, Tuscaloosa and London: University of Alabama Press.

Lemmon, Sarah McCulloh (1951) 'The Ideology of the Dixiecrat Movement', *Social Forces*, vol. 30 (December), pp. 162–71.

Lesher, Stephan (1994) *George Wallace: American Populist*, Reading, MA: Addison-Wesley.

Lewis, George (2004) *The White South and the Red Menace: Segregationists, Anti-communism, and Massive Resistance, 1945–1965*, Gainesville: University Press of Florida.

Lewis, George (2004) '"Scientific Certainty": Wesley Critz George, Racial Science and Organised White Resistance in North Carolina, 1954–1962', *Journal of American Studies*, vol. 8, no. 2, pp. 227–47.

Lewis, George (2005) 'White South, Red Nation: Massive Resistance and the Cold War', in Webb (ed.) *Massive Resistance: Southern Opposition to the Second Reconstruction*, Oxford and New York: Oxford University Press, pp. 117–35.

Lewis, George (2006) 'Virginia's Northern Strategy: Southern Segregationists and the Route to National Conservatism', *Journal of Southern History*, vol. 72, no. 1 (February), pp. 111–46.

Lewis, John with D'Orso, Michael (1998) *Walking with the Wind: A Memoir of the Movement*, San Diego: Harcourt Brace & Company.

Lively, Earl, Jr. (n.d.) *The Invasion of Mississippi*, n.p.: American Opinion Reprint Series.

Lupo, Alan (1970) *Liberty's Chosen Home*, Boston: Little, Brown & Company.

Marshall, Burke (1964) *Federalism and Civil Rights*, New York and London: Columbia University Press.

Martin, John Bartlow (1957) 'The Deep South Says "Never!" Part III', *Saturday Evening Post*, 29 June.

Martin, Waldo E., Jr. (1998) *Brown v. Board of Education: A Brief History with Documents* [Bedford Series in History and Culture], Boston: Bedford / St Martin's.

Mason, Gilbert R. with Smith, James Patterson (2000) *Beaches, Blood, and Ballots: A Black Doctor's Civil Rights Struggle*, Jackson: University Press of Mississippi.

Mayer, Michael S. (1986) 'With Much Deliberation and Some Speed: Eisenhower and the *Brown* Decision', *Journal of Southern History*, vol. LII, no. 1 (February), pp. 43–76.

McCrary, Peyton, Gray, Jerome A., Still, Edward and Perry, Huey L. (1994) 'Alabama', in Chandler Davidson and Bernard Grofman (eds), *Quiet Revolution in the South: The Impact of the Voting Rights Act, 1965–1990*, Princeton, NJ: Princeton University Press, pp. 38–66.

McMillen, Neil R. (1994) *The Citizens' Council: Organized Resistance to the Second Reconstruction, 1954–1964* [Illini Book Edition], Urbana: University of Illinois Press.

McRae, Elizabeth Gillespie (2004) '"To Save a Home": Nell Battle Lewis and the Rise of Southern Conservatism, 1941–1956', *North Carolina Historical Review*, vol. 81, no. 3, pp. 262, 265–7.

McRae, Elizabeth Gillespie (2005) 'White Womanhood, White Supremacy, and the Rise of Massive Resistance', in Clive Webb (ed.), *Massive Resistance: Southern Opposition to the Second Reconstruction*, Oxford and New York: Oxford University Press, pp. 181–202.

Morgan, Perry (1962) 'The Case for the White Southerner', *Esquire* (January).

Moye, J. Todd (2004) *Let the People Decide: Black Freedom and White Resistance Movements in Sunflower County, Mississippi, 1945–1986*, Chapel Hill: University of North Carolina Press.

Murphy, Walter F. (1959) 'The South Counterattacks: The Anti-NAACP Laws', *Western Political Quarterly*, vol. 12 (June), pp. 371–90.

Muse, Benjamin (1961) *Virginia's Massive Resistance*, Bloomington: Indiana University Press.

Newby, I. A. (1969) *Challenge to the Court: Social Scientists and the Defense of Segregation, 1954–1966* (rev. edn), Baton Rouge: Louisiana State University Press.

Newman, Roger K. (1994) *Hugo Black: A Biography*, New York: Pantheon.

Noer, Thomas (2003) 'Segregationists and the World: the Foreign Policy of White Resistance', in Brenda Gayle Plummer (ed.), *Window on Freedom: Race, Civil Rights, and Foreign Affairs, 1945–1988*, Chapel Hill: University of North Carolina Press, pp. 141–62.

Norrell, Robert J. (1985) *Reaping the Whirlwind: The Civil Rights Movement in Tuskegee*, New York: Alfred A. Knopf.

Opotowsky, Stan (n.d.) *Dixie Dynamite: The Inside Story of the White Citizens Councils*, New York: National Association for the Advancement of Colored People.

Ownby, Ted (ed.) (2002) *The Role of Ideas in the Civil Rights South*, Jackson: University Press of Mississippi.

Parker, Frank R. (1990) *Black Votes Count: Political Empowerment in Mississippi After 1965*, Chapel Hill: University of North Carolina Press.

Patterson, James T. (1966) 'A Conservative Coalition Forms in Congress, 1933–1939', *Journal of American History*, vol. 52, no. 4 (March), pp. 757–72.

Patterson, James T. (2001) *Brown v. Board of Education: A Civil Rights Milestone and Its Troubled Legacy* [Pivotal Moments in American History], Oxford and New York: Oxford University Press.

Plummer, Brenda Gayle (ed.) (2003) *Window on Freedom: Race, Civil Rights, and Foreign Affairs, 1945–1988*, Chapel Hill: University of North Carolina Press.

Pratt, Robert A. (2002) *We Shall Not Be Moved: The Desegregation of the University of Georgia*, Athens and London: University of Georgia Press.

Proudfoot, Merrill (1962) *Diary of a Sit-in*, Chapel Hill: University of North Carolina Press.

Putnam, Carleton (1961) *Race and Reason: A Yankee View*, Washington: Public Affairs Press.

Quint, Howard H. (1958) *Profile in Black and White: A Frank Portrait of South Carolina*, Westport, CT: Greenwood Press.

Raines, Howell (ed.) (1983) *My Soul Is Rested: The Story of the Civil Rights Movement in the Deep South*, New York: Penguin.

Robinson, Armistead L. and Sullivan, Patricia (eds) (1991) *New Directions in Civil Rights Studies* [Carter G. Woodson Institute Series in Black Studies], Charlottesville and London: University Press of Virginia.

Roche, Jeff (1998) *Restructured Resistance: The Sibley Commission and the Politics of Desegregation in Georgia*, Athens and London: University of Georgia Press.

Rubin, Lillian B. (1972) *Busing and Backlash: White Against White in a California School District*, Berkeley: University of California Press.

Sherman, Richard B. (1988) '"The Last Stand": The Fight for Racial Integrity in Virginia in the 1920s', *Journal of Southern History*, vol. LIV, no. 1 (February), pp. 69–92.

Sherrill, Robert (1968) *Gothic Politics in the Deep South*, New York: Grossman Publishers.

Shoemaker, Don (ed.) *With All Deliberate Speed: Segregation–Desegregation in Southern Schools*, New York: Harper & Brothers.

Sikora, Frank (1991) *Until Justice Rolls Down: The Birmingham Church Bombing Case*, Tuscaloosa: University of Alabama Press.

Silver, James W. (1963) *Mississippi: The Closed Society*, New York: Harcourt, Brace and World.

Silver, James W. (1964) 'Mississippi: The Closed Society', *Journal of Southern History*, vol. 30, no. 1 (February), pp. 3–34.

Smith, J. Douglas (2002) *Managing White Supremacy: Race, Politics, and Citizenship in Jim Crow Virginia*, Chapel Hill: University of North Carolina Press.

Steinbeck, John (1980) *Travels with Charley*, London: Penguin.

Stern, Mark (1992) *Calculating Visions: Kennedy, Johnson and Civil Rights*, New Brunswick, NJ: Rutgers University Press.

Sugrue, Thomas J. (1996) *The Origins of the Urban Crisis: Race and Inequality in Postwar Detroit*, Princeton, NJ: Princeton University Press.

Talmadge, Herman E. (1955) *You and Segregation*, Birmingham, AL: Vulcan Press.

Theoharis, Jeanne (2003) '"I'd Rather Go to School in the South": How Boston's School Desegregation Complicates the Civil Rights Paradigm', in Theoharis and Woodward (eds), *Freedom North: Black Freedom Struggles outside the South, 1940–1980*, New York: Palgrave Macmillan, pp. 125–51.

Theoharis, Jeanne F. and Woodward, Komozi (eds) (2003) *Freedom North: Black Freedom Struggles outside the South, 1940–1980*, New York: Palgrave Macmillan.

Thornton III, J. Mills (1991) 'Municipal Change and the Course of the Movement', in

Robinson and Sullivan (eds), *New Directions in Civil Rights Studies* [Carter G. Woodson Institute Series in Black Studies], Charlottesville and London: University Press of Virginia, pp. 38–64.

Thornton III, J. Mills (2002) *Dividing Lines: Municipal Politics and the Struggle for Civil Rights in Montgomery, Birmingham and Selma*, Tuscaloosa: University of Alabama Press.

Tindall, George Brown (1967) *The Emergence of the New South, 1913–1945*, Baton Rouge: Louisiana State University Press.

Waldron, Ann (1993) *Hodding Carter: The Reconstruction of a Racist*, Chapel Hill: Algonquin Books of Chapel Hill.

Wallenstein, Peter (2004) *Blue Laws and Black Codes: Conflicts, Courts, and Change in Twentieth Century Virginia*, Charlottesville: University of Virginia Press.

Ward, Brian (1998) *Just My Soul Responding: Rhythm and Blues, Black Consciousness and Race Relations*, Berkeley: University of California Press.

Waring, Thomas R. (1956) 'The Southern Case Against Desegregation', *Harper's*, (January), pp. 39–45.

Warren, Robert Penn (1957) *Segregation: The Inner Conflict in the South*, London: Eyre & Spottiswoode.

Webb, Clive (ed.) (2005) *Massive Resistance: Southern Opposition to the Second Reconstruction*, Oxford and New York: Oxford University Press.

Westfeldt, Wallace (1957) 'Communities in Strife', in Don Shoemaker (ed.) *With All Deliberate Speed: Segregation–Desegregation in Southern Schools*. New York: Harper & Brothers, pp. 36–55.

Whalen, Charles and Whalen, Barbara (1985) *The Longest Debate: A Legislative History of the 1964 Civil Rights Act*, Cabin John, MD: Seven Locks Press.

Whitfield, Stephen J. (1988) *A Death in the Delta: The Story of Emmett Till*, Baltimore: Johns Hopkins University Press.

Wilhoit, Francis M. (1973) *The Politics of Massive Resistance*, New York: George Braziller.

Wilkinson III, J. Harvie (1968) *Harry Byrd and the Changing Face of Virginia Politics 1945–1966*, Charlottesville: University Press of Virginia.

Woods, Jeff (2004) *Black Struggle, Red Scare: Segregation and Anti-Communism in the South, 1948–1968*, Baton Rouge: Louisiana State University Press.

Woodward, Bob and Armstrong, Scott (1979) *The Brethren: Inside the Supreme Court*, New York: Simon & Schuster.

Workman, William D., Jr. (1957) 'The Deep South', in Don Shoemaker (ed.), *With All Deliberate Speed: Segregation–Desegregation in Southern Schools*, New York: Harper & Brothers, pp. 88–109.

Workman, William D., Jr. (1960) *The Case for the South*, New York: Devin-Adair.

INDEX

Index

Index